Washburn-Crosby Co.'s

new

Gold Medal Cook Book

IMPORTANT NOTICE.

EACH owner of a GOLD MEDAL Cook Book is entitled to four additional copies without any cost whatever. These copies may be obtained in the following manner:

Please turn to Page 71 where you will find four coupons. As fast as you desire to use your privilege for four additional copies cut out the coupon, fill in your friend's address and mail to us. No postage is required for these extra copies.

We trust you will avail yourself of this privilege immediately.

Address all communications to Washburn-Crosby Co., Minneapolis, Minn.

Be Sure and Read the Article on White Bread Appearing on Page 70

Ottenheimer
PUBLISHERS

© 1998 Ottenheimer Publishers, Inc.

This commemorative edition is published by Ottenheimer Publishers, Inc.
which is not associated with Washburn-Crosby Co., the original publisher, or its successors.
Printed in Italy.
ISBN 0-8241-0294-0
BC103MLKJIHGFEDCBA

....TABLES ....

TABLE OF MEASURE.

A speck makes one-quarter saltspoon.

Four saltspoons make one teaspoon.

Three teaspoons make one tablespoon.

Eight tablespoons of dry and solid material make one cup.

Sixteen tablespoons of liquid material make one cup.

Two gills make one cup.

One wine glass makes one-half gill.

One cup contains eight ounces of liquid.

Ten eggs, average size, make one pound.

One-half ounce bottle extract makes twelve teaspoons.

One tablespoon butter makes one ounce.

One tablespoon granulated sugar makes one ounce.

One heaped teaspoon powdered sugar makes one ounce.

One tablespoon flour makes one-half ounce.

Two tablespoons ground spice make one ounce.

Five nutmegs make one ounce.

One quart sifted pastry flour makes one pound.

One quart less one gill, sifted patent flour makes one pound.

One scant pint granulated sugar makes one pound.

One pint butter makes one pound.

One pint chopped meat, packed, makes one pound.

One cup rice makes one-half pound.

One cup cornmeal makes six ounces.

One cup stemmed raisins makes six ounces.

One cup cleaned currants makes six ounces.

One cup stale bread crumbs makes two ounces.

TABLE OF PROPORTIONS.

One quart of flour requires one pint of butter, or butter and lard mixed for pastry.

One quart of flour requires one heaping tablespoon of butter for biscuit.

One quart of flour requires two tablespoons of butter for shortcakes.

One quart of flour requires one cup of butter for cup cakes.

One quart of flour requires one-half level teaspoon of salt.

One quart of flour requires four teaspoons of baking powder.

One quart of flour requires one pint of milk for muffins, gems, etc.

One quart of flour requires one scant quart of milk for batters of all kinds.

One measure of liquid to three measures flour for bread.

One teaspoon of soda to one pint of sour milk.

One teaspoon of soda to one cup of molasses.

One teaspoon of salt to one pound of meat.

A spoon means that the material should lie as much above the edge of the spoon as the bowl sinks below it. A heaping teaspoon means that the material should be twice as high above the edge of the spoon as the bowl sinks below it. A level teaspoon should hold sixty drops of water. All dry materials are measured after sifting.

A spoon of salt, pepper, soda, spice is a level spoon.

One-half of a spoon is measured by dividing through the middle lengthwise.

A speck is what can be placed within a quarter inch square surface.

TIME FOR BAKING

Loaf Bread	40 to 60 minutes.
Rolls and Biscuit	10 to 20 "
Graham Gems	30 "
Gingerbread	20 to 30 "
Sponge Cake	45 to 60 "
Plain Cake	30 to 40 "
Fruit Cake	2 to 3 hours.
Cookies	10 to 15 minutes.

Bread Pudding	1 hour.
Rice and Tapioca	1 hour.
Indian Pudding	2 to 3 hours.
Steamed Pudding	1 to 3 "
Steamed Brown Bread	3 hours.
Custards	15 to 20 minutes.
Pie Crust	about 30 "
Plum Pudding	2 to 3 hours.

TIME FOR SUMMER VEGETABLES

Greens—Dandelions	1½ hours.
Spinach	1 hour.
String Beans	2 hours.
Green Peas	20 minutes.
Beets	1 to 3 hours.
Turnips	1 to 3 hours.
Squash	1 hour.
Potatoes	⅓ hour.
Corn	⅓ hour.
Asparagus	⅓ hour.

This applies to young and fresh vegetables.

TIME FOR WINTER VEGETABLES

Squash	1 hour.
Potatoes,	½ hour.
Potatoes, baked	1 hour.
Sweet Potatoes	¾ hour.
Baked Sweet	1 hour.
Turnips	2 hours.
Beets	3½ hours.
Parsnips	1 hour.
Carrots	1½ hours.
Cabbage	3 hours.

TIME FOR BROILING

Steak, one inch thick	4 to 6 minutes.
Steak, two inches thick	8 to 15 minutes.
Fish, small and thin	5 to 8 minutes.
Fish, thick	15 to 25 minutes.
Chickens	20 to 30 minutes.

TIME FOR MEATS

Beef, underdone, per pound	9 to 10 minutes.
Beef, fillet of	20 to 40 minutes.
Mutton, leg, per pound	10 to 12 minutes.
Mutton, stuffed shoulder, per pound	18 minutes.
Veal, loin of, plain, per pound	15 to 18 minutes.
Veal, stuffed	20 minutes.
Pork, spare rib, per pound	15 to 20 minutes.
Pork, loin or shoulder, per pound	20 to 30 minutes.
Liver, baked or braised	1 to 1½ hours.
Corned Beef, per pound	25 to 30 minutes.
Boiled (simmered) Beef, per pound	20 to 30 minutes.
Ham, after water or cider begins to boil	15 to 20 minutes.
Bacon, per pound	15 minutes.
Chickens, baked, three to four pounds	1 to 2 hours.
Turkey, ten pounds	3 hours.
Goose, eight pounds	3 hours.
Duck, tame	40 to 60 minutes.
Duck, wild	30 to 40 minutes.
Grouse, Pigeons and other large birds	30 minutes.
Small birds	10 to 15 minutes.
Venison, per pound	15 minutes.
Fish, long and thin, six to eight pounds	1 hour.
Fish, thick, six to eight pounds	1½ to 2 hours.
Fish, small	25 to 30 minutes.

SOUPS

THE making of stock calls for no more than the ordinary amount of skill and attention and it should not be thought either a mystery or a trouble. A crock of well made stock is indispensable for the soups and sauces required in every well ordered household. It is well worth planning for.

In the first place then the material is to be considered. Meat and bones for soup should be perfectly fresh, and about equal in proportion, hock or shin of beef, ends of rib roasts, and portions of the neck or shoulder are all suitable, although coarse and cheap. The first mentioned furnish chiefly gelatine, the latter give flavor. A knuckle of veal and the bit of bone trimmed from a leg of mutton with a few ounces of lean ham or smoked beef may be added. Examine carefully and cut out any bits that are at all stale or discolored by the hanging hook. Sponge the outside skinny portion with a cloth wrung out of warm water, but do not wet the freshly cut surfaces of meat. Scrape with a dull knife and wipe again with a clean cloth. Cut the meat from the bones and put them in the soup kettle, having first inverted in it a perforated pie plate to keep the bones from resting on the bottom of the kettle. This, by the way, should always be of aluminum or agate ware, never of iron. It should have a closely fitting cover, and if larger than three gallons there should be two handles.

The meat should be cut into half inch slices, across the grain, and laid upon the bones, cold water put in and the kettle placed where it will be at least one hour in coming to a boil. By this time the juice will be well drawn from the meat and the bones heated through. It may be allowed to boil gently for five minutes and then the kettle must be pushed back where it will simmer steadily for not less than eight hours. After cooking two hours seasoning should be added; a level teaspoon of salt and four peppercorns to each quart of water. After it has been strained, the meat and bones simmered another two hours with two quarts of water will yield a stock of lighter quality but of much value, which can be used in making bean porridge, tomato or pea soup. This stock should be cooled as quickly as may be—in warm weather set in a pan of cold water. Do not break the cake of fat on the surface until the stock is needed for use. When cold set in the ice box.

To Prepare Stock for Use.

If the cover of the soup pot fitted closely and the soup was not allowed to boil, there should be about five quarts of soup in the first crock. Contrary to the usual custom, this has been seasoned only with pepper and salt and is really a plain beef broth. It needs more color and flavor. Take off the fat and dip out carefully one quart of the broth, boil over a quick fire until it is reduced to one-fourth, then simmer carefully until it has a thick, syrupy consistence and has changed to a reddish brown color. The rest of the stock may now be added. A bay leaf, two or three sprays of parsley, half a blade of mace, any or all may be added or a few sprigs of thyme, summer savory, or marjoram. Vegetables may be added in proportion of one-half tablespoon each of onion, carrot and turnip to each quart of soup. These should be cut rather fine and thoroughly scalded before putting into the soup. After simmering an hour it can be strained again and put away, it may be drawn off the fire and allowed to settle, two and a half or even three quarts of the clear stock dipped off for future use and the remainder served as a vegetable soup.

To Clear Soup-Stock.

Remove the fat, and allow the white and shell of one egg for every quart of stock. If you wish to flavor the stock more highly, add half a saltspoon of celery-seed and the thinnest possible shavings from the rind of half a lemon. Add also the lemon-juice, and more salt and pepper if needed. Mix celery-seed, lemon, egg, etc., with the *cold* stock, and beat it well. If the stock is hot when the egg is added, the egg will harden before it has done its work. This is the point where many fail. Set it over the fire and stir it all the time until it is hot, to keep the egg from settling. Then leave it and let it boil ten minutes. By this time a thick scum will have formed, and as it breaks the liquid will be clear and sparkling, like wine, and darker than before. Draw it back on the stove, and add half a cup of cold water. Let it stand ten minutes, while you get your jar, colander, and fine napkin ready for straining. Wring the napkin out of hot water, and lay it over the colander. Put the finest wire strainer on the napkin, and then pour it all through. The strainer will catch the scum and shells which would otherwise clog the napkin. Let it take its own time to drain, but if you must hasten it, raise the napkin first at one corner and then at another, and let the liquid run down to a clean place. This is better than squeezing. This is all ready to serve as a clear soup by simply heating to the boiling-point. Serve with it, in the tureen, thin slices of lemon, a glass of sherry, yolks of hard-boiled eggs, or delicate flavored force meat balls; or put on each plate a poached egg, or a spoonful of grated Parmesan cheese.

Thickening for Soups.

Soups are thickened with flour, corn-starch, or rice-flour; one tablespoon for a quart of soup—heaping, if flour; scant, if rice-flour or corn-starch. Flour is the cheapest, but corn-starch gives a smoother consistency. Mix the flour with a very little cold water or milk until it is a smooth paste, then add more liquid until it can be poured easily into the boiling soup. Remember to boil the soup fifteen or twenty minutes after the thickening is added, that there may be no raw taste of the flour. Where butter and flour are used, put the butter in a small saucepan, and when melted and bubbling stir in the flour quickly until smooth (be careful not to brown the butter for any white soup); then add gradually about a cup of the hot soup, letting it boil and thicken as you add the soup. It should be thin enough to pour. In vegetable soups, or purees, as soon as the hot butter and flour are blended, they may be stirred at once into the soup. This is what is meant in many of the recipes by thickening with butter and flour which have been cooked together. The hot butter cooks the flour more thoroughly than it can be cooked in any other way. When a brown thickening is desired, melt the butter and let it become as brown as it will without burning, then add all the flour at once and stir quickly, that every particle of it may be moistened in the hot butter; add the water or soup gradually. Flour that is browned while dry, either in the oven or over the fire, colors, but does not thicken. A certain amount of moisture, of either fat or water, is necessary with the heat to thoroughly swell the grains of starch in the flour. Thickened soups should be about the consistency of good cream. Purees are thicker.

Soup may be thickened with bread instead of plain flour, corn-starch or arrow-root. When this is done, force meat, egg or spinach balls may be served in it instead of vegetables. The French and German rules for Garbures say that the bread should be saturated with broth and fat from the top of the pot, and baked until the broth has evaporated and the crusts are slightly browned. This is not recommended. The bread should be dried and browned slightly and added to a small amount of stock, simmered until soft and crushed to a panada with a wooden spoon or potato masher, then diluted with more stock. An ounce of dried bread or two tablespoonfuls dried bread crumbs for a quart finished soup will be quite as thick as most people like; strain again if wanted perfectly smooth.

The German rye bread is excellent for this purpose. It may be used with stock, or simply boiled in water and enriched with eggs. The true German seasoning is caraway seed and caramel. The sugar should not be browned enough to destroy its sweetness.

Glaze is simply clear stock boiled down to one-fourth of its original amount. Put two quarts of rich, strong stock into a sauce-pan, and boil it uncovered until reduced to one pint. It should have a gluey consistency, and will keep a month if put in a closely covered jar in a cool place. It is useful in browning meats which have not been colored by cooking, but which we wish to have the appearance of having been roasted or browned.

For enriching a weak stock or gravy, or adding flavor and consistency to sauces, there is nothing that can take its place.

Plain Brown Soup Stock.

Six pounds shin of beef in the proportion of four pounds lean meat to two pounds bone, gristle, etc., six quarts cold water, one-half a chili (red pepper), one large onion, one tablespoonful salt. Wipe the meat with a wet cloth, cut it from the bone and into thin slices across the grain. Reserve several of the largest slices with all the marrow, put remainder of meat and bones into six quarts of cold water with the spices and herbs. Set one side of the fire, where it will be at least an hour in coming to the boil. If convenient broil the reserved slices till very brown before adding; if not, fry them in the marrow, being very careful not to let the fat scorch. Simmer eight to ten hours and strain. The next day remove the fat and use the stock plain for a beef broth or with macaroni or vermicelli, rice, vegetables, etc., according to taste.

Clear Soup Stock, for Consommé.

Add four pounds knuckle of veal or a small fowl to the above rule, with two ounces lean ham or a bone of bacon, brown only the onion, in order to have the soup light colored. After removing the fat add the beaten white and shell of one egg to each quart of jelly, with one saltspoonful celery seed, a few bits of lemon rind, one teaspoonful lemon juice. Mix well together, bring to a boil as quickly as possible, stirring very often. Simmer ten minutes more, strain through a thick napkin and heat to the boiling point before serving. It should be sparkling clear and of a light brown or straw color.

Foundation for Soups make with Milk.

One quart milk, one tablespoon butter, one teaspoon chopped onion, one-half tablespoon flour, one stalk celery, one teaspoon salt, cne-half saltspoon white pepper, speck of cayenne, one-half teaspoonful celery salt. Cook milk, onion and celery twenty minutes in double boiler; cook the flour and butter together five minutes, being careful not to brown it, then pour it into the soup; add the seasoning and it is ready to finish in any way.

Beef Purée.

One pint good beef broth, boil in it one tablespoon scalded sago until soft and partially dissolved, add the yolk of an egg mixed with a little broth, heat for three minutes, stirring in also two ounces of tender raw beef, perfectly free from fat and reduced to a pulp.

Bouillon.

For receptions or other large parties, is simply beef tea on a large scale and should be prepared like a plain soup stock, allowing one pound of meat and bone to each pint of broth, season with pepper, salt, celery and onion if liked, but other vegetable flavors are too suggestive of a dinner soup. It is best made the day before it is to be served. Set on ice over night and remove every atom of grease while cold. Re-heat to the boiling point before serving, adding more seasoning if needed and strain through a thick napkin to remove sediment.

Summer Julienne.

One quart consomme, one half cup cooked onion cut in rings, one-half cup of cooked peas, one-half cup asparagus tips, one-half cup cooked string beans, salt and pepper if needed. Heat the vegetables and put them into the tureen; pour boiling soup over them.

Winter Julienne.

One quart of brown stock, one-half teaspoonful of salt, one pint mixed vegetables, one-half saltspoonful pepper. Cut the celery and turnip into dice, carrot into match-shaped pieces. Use only the very smallest onions, which should be cut in halves, so that the layers will separate in cups. Cabbage should be coarsely chopped. Cook the vegetables in boiling salted water till tender, but not broken. Drain them and add to the soup a few minutes before serving. Macaroni, vermicelli, rice, tapioca, sago and barley should all be cooked till tender in boiling salted water before adding to the soup, and then allowed to simmer a few minutes to season through.

Oxtail Soup.

Wash and cut up two oxtails, separating them at the joints. Select about half of the largest and nicest joints to brown in hot fat before cooking. Simmer in enough water to cover well until perfectly tender. Take out the browned joints and boil the rest to rags; strain, cool and remove fat. Re-heat this stock, adding one quart strong brown stock, more salt and pepper if needed, and the reserved joints. It should be served boiling hot.

Jugged Soup.

This is a delicious soup, a little after the order of a Brunswick stew. Boil any carcasses of cold fowl, bones of roast meat or steak, with the trimmings, in three quarts of water, till reduced to two. Strain, cool and take off the fat. Slice six potatoes very thin and lay in a gallon stone jar with lid. Lay on these a sliced onion, three sliced tomatoes or a cup of canned, a sliced turnip, a cup of canned peas, a grated carrot, another cup of tomato, and quarter of a cup of raw rice. On each layer should have been sprinkled seasoning made by mixing one tablespoonful each of salt and sugar, half a teaspoonful of pepper, and a pinch of allspice. Pour the broth over all, put on the lid, and cover the edges with a thick paste to keep in the steam. Set the jar in a pan of hot water, put all in the oven and cook from four to six hours. Pour all into tureen and serve with crisped crackers.

Left-Over Soup.

Bones and trimmings from a roast of beef, beefsteak bones and trimmings, mutton chop bones, any cold vegetables except squash, cold cooked eggs in any shape, crusts of bread. There should be about six pounds of meat altogether; add whatever gravy was left over and four quarts of cold water; add one-half teaspoonful celery seed, one tablespoonful salt, one clove, four peppercorns, and simmer eight or ten hours till the meat is in rags and the water reduced one-half. Strain and set away for stock.

Calf's Head or Mock Turtle.

One calf's head cleaned with the skin on, cut in halves, and well washed in salt water. Remove the brains and tie them in coarse muslin to be cooked separately; boil in four quarts of water till the meat is tender and ready to slip from the bones. Lay the meat flat on a platter, return bones to the pot and boil till the water is reduced to two quarts, then strain and cool. Remove fat and return to the fire with two quarts rich brown stock, two whole cloves, a blade of mace, six allspice berries, one chili, more salt if needed. While this is simmering cut the meat and tongue into dice; there should be a generous pint; chop the trimmings to a paste; cook the brains twenty minutes and pound with the chopped meat, season with salt, pepper and thyme, add a little beaten egg to bind it well together and shape in balls size of a large hickory nut and fry them brown in a little butter. Brown four tablespoonfuls flour in two tablespoonfuls butter or bacon fat and add hot soup to it slowly, stirring well till smooth; add it to the stock. Put meat balls and diced meat into a hot tureen and strain the boiling stock over them. As one head is enough for a gallon of soup it will pay to put a part of it into glass jars exactly as you would fruit. This soup is usually served with very thin slices of lemon, and sometimes a teaspoon of catsup in it.

Veal-Stock.

6 pound knuckle of veal.	Cellery root, or
4 quarts cold water.	½ teaspoon celery seed.
1 tablespoon salt.	1 onion.
6 peppercorns.	

Wipe the veal, cut the meat fine and break the bones. Put it into the kettle with the cold water. Skim as it boils, and when clear add the seasoning. Simmer until the bones are clean and the liquor reduced one-half. Strain, and when cool remove the fat. Use it for white or delicate soups.

Velvet Soup.

One quart of any kind of good stock, one cup cream, seasoned to taste, pour it boiling hot on the beaten yolks of four eggs, diluted with one-half cup cream. Re-heat and serve at once in bouillon cups.

Thick Vegetable Soup.

One quart of sediment left from clear soup, one quart of water, quarter cup of pearl barley, one cup each of diced turnip, carrot, celery, onion, cabbage and potatoes, salt and pepper.

Wash the barley and let it come to the boil, pour off the first water and add the quart; let simmer gently for two hours. Then add all the vegetables (except the potatoes and celery) scalding them first in boiling water. Boil gently till nearly tender; then add potatoes and celery with salt and pepper. Cook 30 minutes longer or till all are tender.

Tomato Soup, with Stock.

Take the bones and trimmings from a roast-beef dinner and any other scraps of meat or bone you may chance to have. Put them in a kettle and cover with cold water, twice as much water as meat. Add two onions, two whole cloves, six peppercorns, a bit of celery root if you have it, and a tablespoon of salt. When it has cooked four hours, skim off all the fat, and add six tomatoes sliced, or one quart of canned tomatoes. Cook another hour, then skim out the bones and meat, and strain the liquor through a puree-strainer, rubbing all the tomato-pulp through. Heat again and thicken with flour, one tablespoon each of butter and flour for every quart of broth.

Okra Soup.

One quart okra, two quarts tomatoes, five lbs. shin of beef, cayenne pepper and salt. Cut the okra in short bits, skin and slice the tomato. Cut the meat in thin slices across the grain, and put all together with five quarts cold water. Bring to a boil and simmer steadily for six or seven hours. Skim well at first, add the salt and pepper at the end of the first hour. Remove all bones and unsightly pieces and skim off the grease before serving.

Purée of Chestnuts.

1 pint chestnuts.	1 tablespoon butter.
1 pint milk.	Salt and pepper.
1 cup cream.	1 egg.

Shell and blanch the chestnuts. Cook in boiling salted water to cover, till very soft. Mash them in the water left in the pan, and rub them through a fine strainer into the milk. Heat again, add the cream, salt and pepper to taste, and when ready to serve, stir the beaten egg in quickly and serve at once with croutons. Add more milk if too thick.—Mrs. D. A. Lincoln.

Black Bean Soup.

Soak over night one-half pint black beans. Put them on to boil in three pints of water, adding one-half saltspoon soda if the water is hard. When the beans begin to soften pour the water away and renew, adding some bits of fat meat; ham is good but not more than an ounce of any kind should be used. Add one small onion sliced and one clove. It may boil fast and the beans may be mashed with a potato masher; do not try to strain until perfectly soft or the soup will have a granular feeling on the tongue, and it should be as smooth as cream. Strain through a fine sieve. Add more water or stock

if it is thicker than liked. Season to taste and serve over hard boiled eggs cut in quarters, and the thinnest possible slices of lemon.

Oyster Soup.

Prepare foundation as for soups made with milk, omitting onion and celery, and using two tablespoons flour. Put one quart oysters in a large bowl and pour over them one cup water, take out each oyster with the fingers to make sure no shell adheres to it and drain in the colander. Strain the oyster liquor through the finest strainer, put it on to boil and skim well, add the oysters and simmer till they grow plump, and begin to curl on the edges. Add oysters to foundation with as much of the broth as will make it of the right consistency. Add more salt and pepper if needed and all the butter it will bear without floating on the top. Crackers browned in the oven are good with this soup.

White Soup (from Chicken.)

3 or 4 pounds fowl.	1 pint cream.
3 quarts cold water.	1 tablespoon butter.
1 tablespoon salt.	1 tablespoon corn-starch.
6 peppercorns.	1 teaspoon salt.
1 tablespoon chopped onion.	1 saltspoon white pepper.
2 tablespoons chopped celery.	2 eggs.

Singe, clean and wipe the fowl. Cut off the legs and wings, and disjoint the body. Put it on to boil in cold water. Let it come to a boil quickly, because we wish to use the meat as well as the water, and skim thoroughly. The meat may be removed when tender, and the bones put on to boil again. (Use the meat for croquettes or other made dishes.) Add the salt and vegetables. Simmer until reduced one-half. Strain and when cool remove the fat. For one quart of stock allow one pint of cream or milk. If cream, use a little less flour for thickening. Boil the stock, add the butter and flour, cooked together, and the seasoning. Strain it over the eggs, stirring as you pour, or the eggs will curdle. The liquor in which a fowl or chicken has been boiled, when not wanted for any other purpose, should be saved for white soup. If the vegetables and spices are not boiled with the fowl, fry them five minutes without burning, add them to the stock, and simmer fifteen minutes.—From Mrs. Lincoln's "Boston Cook Book."

Easy Soupe à la Reine.

Take a small, cold, roast chicken and cut all the meat from the bones, chopping it fine as possible. In the meantime put all the bones in two quarts of cold water, and boil slowly for two hours. Add a cup of boiled rice to the meat and pound all together to a pulp. Strain the broth on it; stir well and rub through a puree sieve. When wanted bring only to boiling point, add a gill of good cream, and season with a teaspoon of salt and a pinch of white pepper.

Mutton Soup with Barley.

Put all the trimmings from a fore-quarter of mutton (neck, bones of the shoulder, breast, trimmings of the chops, etc.) in a saucepan with two pounds soup-beef, one tablespoon salt, eight peppercorns, a bunch of sweet herbs, a quartered carrot, an onion stuck with three cloves, a small turnip, two leeks and a stalk of celery; add six quarts cold water and simmer three or four hours. Meanwhile wash well and boil separately four ounces of barley in one quart salted water two hours. Cut meat from the shoulder in dice and cook it also separately in broth for an hour. Drain the meat over the mutton-broth, drain also the barley, skim the fat from the broth and strain three quarts of the broth over the meat and barley. Boil ten minutes, adding more seasoning if needed, color with a little caramel and serve hot.

Oyster Stew.

Boil one cup of strained oyster-liquor and half a cup of water. Skim, add half a teaspoon of salt, half a saltspoon of pepper, one tablespoon of butter, and one tablespoon rolled cracker. When it begins to boil add one quart of oysters. Boil one minute. Put half a cup of cream or cold milk into the tureen, and pour the boiling stew over it.

Schrimp Soup.

Parboil one quart of oysters, strain the liquor and put it on to boil with one pint of water or veal stock. Thicken with one tablespoon of flour cooked in one tablespoon of hot butter, and add salt, pepper and cayenne to taste. Prepare one pint canned shrimps, remove the black vein and cut them fine. Add them to the soup. Simmer five minutes, then put in the oysters and half a cup of rich cream, and when hot serve.

Corn Chowder, No. 2.

1 quart raw sweet corn.	2 tablespoons flour.
1 pint potato dice.	1 pint milk.
1 teaspoon salt.	1 pint croutons.
1 saltspoon pepper.	2 hard-boiled eggs.
¼ cup butter.	

Cut each row of kernels, and scrape the raw corn from the cob. Boil the cobs twenty minutes in water to cover. Pare and cut the potatoes into small dice. Pour boiling water over them, drain and let them stand while the corncobs are boiling. Remove the cobs, add the potatoes, salt and pepper. When the potatoes are nearly done, add the corn and milk and cook five minutes. Cook the flour in the hot butter, add one cup of the corn liquor, and when thick stir it into the chowder. Add the eggs, whites chopped fine, and yolk rubbed through a strainer. Serve with croutons.—Mrs. D. A. Lincoln.

Mock Bisque.

Simmer one-half quart can of tomatoes till very soft, strain it and pour into the foundation after the latter has been strained into the tureen. Most palates prefer the addition of one-half teaspoonful sugar to the tomatoes.

Potato Soup.

Add three boiled potatoes, mashed very fine, to the foundation; rub through a sieve into hot tureen.

Celery Soup.

Add one pint stewed and sifted celery to the foundation and strain over one egg beaten to a cream, stirring well.

Cream of Celery Soup, No. 2.

Two pounds of veal; a small slice of ham or a ham bone, one large bunch of celery, one pint of milk, two tablespoons of butter; one onion, one teaspoon of sugar, two tablespoons of cornstarch dissolved in a little cold water, three quarts of water, salt and pepper. Chop the meat; fry the onion after mincing it, in the butter, till a light brown. Chop the celery and put all over with the water and seasoning; a teaspoon of salt to the quart, and a saltspoon of pepper. As soon as the celery is soft, it is to be rubbed through a sieve, and may stand till the meat is boiled to rags which will require at least four hours. Then strain, add the sugar and the celery with the milk, and when at boiling point, the cornstarch and the butter. Boil up once and serve.

Duchess Soup.

One quart of milk, two onions, three eggs, two tablespoons of butter, two of flour, salt, pepper, two tablespoons of grated cheese. Put milk on to boil. Fry the butter and onions together for eight minutes; then add dry flour, and cook two minutes longer, being careful not to burn. Blend with the milk, and cook ten minutes. Rub through a strainer, and return to the fire. Now add the cheese. Season to taste with salt and pepper. Beat the eggs, dilute with two tablespoons of soup, strain, and pour slowly into the soup, stirring it briskly. It must not boil again but should stand hot for three minutes.—Miss Parloa's "New Cook-Book."

Purée of Cucumbers.

Pare three or four cucumbers, according to size; cut in slices and boil five minutes; drain and cook in a sautoir with four ounces of butter, salt, white pepper and nutmeg; set to boil, cover and let simmer gently for one hour. Sprinkle four ounces of flour over, mix well and dilute with two quarts boiling milk and a quart veal broth; stir steadily and boil ten minutes. Press through a puree sieve, return it to the sautoir and heat till near boiling. Add two ounces butter, cut in small bits, one-half teaspoon sugar, one-half pint cream. Serve with croutons in the tureen.

Cream of Asparagus Soup.

For this delicious soup will be needed one small can of asparagus and two quarts of white stock. Melt in a large saucepan two tablespoons of butter, and when it boils stir in three of flour. Stir perfectly smooth, gradually adding the broth. Cut off the tips of the asparagus and set aside, adding the rest to the broth with six pepper-corns and a teaspoon of salt. Boil for half an hour; strain through a sieve, add the asparagus tips and half a cup of cream; bring to boiling-point and serve very hot. Often this soup is served with croutons souffles, which are simply puff-paste rolled thin, cut in bits no bigger than a small bean, and fried in boiling lard. Drain them on brown paper and put into the soup at the last moment. They can also, if preferred, be baked in a quick oven, and will be done in two minutes.

Soupe aux Choux.

The foundation of this soup is a rich bouillon blanc, or white broth made as follows: A large knuckle of choice veal thoroughly cracked and covered with three quarts of cold water, adding a tablespoon of salt. As it boils skim off every particle of scum. Add one well-scraped carrot, one white turnip, three leeks, one well-cleaned parsley root, and two stalks of firm celery. Boil very slowly for six hours, then strain through a wet cloth into a stone jar, and when cold remove all the fat. Choose a very small, firm, white cabbage, shred it fine and put in a frying-pan in which a tablespoon of butter is boiling, covering close for a few moments. Then add a pint of water and stew half an hour, with a teaspoon of salt and half a one of white pepper. Run then through a puree sieve. Bring the white broth to boiling point, in the meantime making a thickening of one tablespoonful of butter to which is added two of flour, stirring it till smooth, but not browned. Add boiling soup slowly, stirring it constantly till all is smooth and creamy; then pour into the soup and add the puree of cabbage. Half a cup of cream is often added.

Cream of Cauliflower Soup.

Heat one pint of chicken or veal stock, one pint of milk and half a cup of sweet cream. When boiling, thicken with one tablespoon of fine whole wheat flour, add salt and white pepper to taste. Cook half a cauliflower in boiling salted water about twenty minutes. Cut off the little flowerets, using none of the stalk, put in enough to thicken the broth.

Southern Chicken Soup.

Cut all the meat from a fowl weighing three pounds, reserve the breast whole, cut the rest in small bits, break the bones and put on with two quarts of water, putting the breast on top of the other meat. Cook four hours, skimming often at first. Take out the breast as soon as tender, strain and add three tablespoons cooked rice, (there should be about three pints of broth), the breast cut in dice and one teaspoon minced parsley, salt and pepper as desired.

Soupe à la Reine.

Boil a large fowl in three quarts of water until tender (the water should never more than bubble). Skim off the fat, and add a teacup of rice, and also a slice of carrot, one of turnip, a small piece of celery, and an onion, which have been cooked slowly for fifteen minutes in two large tablespoons of butter. Skim this butter carefully from the vegetables, and into the pan in which it is, stir a tablespoon of flour. Cook until smooth, but not brown, add this with a small piece of mace. Cook all together slowly for two hours. Chop and pound the breast of the fowl very fine. Rub the soup through a fine sieve; add the pounded breast and again rub the whole through a coarse sieve. Put back on the fire and add one and a half tablespoons of salt, a fourth of a teaspoon of pepper, and a pint of cream, which has come just to a boil. Boil up once and serve.

Tortue Verte Claire, or Clear Green Turtle Soup.

For this soup the turtle should be killed and allowed to bleed for twelve hours before using. The sides are to be opened, the meat removed and cut in small pieces, which are to be blanched five minutes in boiling water. If the turtle is medium sized, lift off the top shell, lay it in the soup kettle and cover it with white broth, made as in the previous rule.

Add a spoonful of whole peppers, one dozen cloves, half a bunch of thyme, and six bay leaves, all to be tied in a cloth. Add two tablespoons of salt, and boil for one hour. Strain the broth, remove the bones, and cut the meat in squares the size of dice. Boil the broth till reduced three quarters in quantity, then add the meat, and boil ten minutes. This is the manner of preparing the whole turtle, given by Delmonico. It is then put in small stone jars, and, when cool, hot lard is poured over the top. It will keep a long time, and simply requires heating when wanted. But for a small quantity one can buy a pint of green-turtle meat in market, and prepare it with a quart of white broth, and the same treatment as for the whole turtle. A glassful of Madeira wine is a great improvement. It can be served with or without the meat, the latter making it clear green turtle.

Purée of Lentils.

Pick over three pints of lentils and soak over night in cold water. In the morning drain and wash them well. Put to boil and cook hard and fast till they go to pieces. As the water evaporates fill the kettle with good broth until two quarts have been used. Shred in a leaf of parsley, four stalks celery, two leeks and one onion, four ounces salt pork. Cover and simmer till all are soft enough to rub through a puree sieve. Return to the stew-pan and add more broth if needed. Skim and finish with three ounces butter, one ounce flour, one teaspoon sugar. Serve with slices of lemon in the tureen, and small squares of brown bread fried in butter, served separately on a plate.

Bisque of Crabs, No. 2.

Wash and boil four large crabs. Open them and take out all the meat. Cut fine and then pound in a mortar. To three pints of white stock highly seasoned, put a teacup of washed rice and the crab, and boil for half an hour. Rub through a sieve, boil up once, add a cup of cream, and serve with very small croutons.

Fish Chowder.

For this, cod, bass or haddock may be used, but the fish must always be a firm, thick one, with few bones, and these carefully removed, as well as the skin. Take four pounds of fish, seven good-sized potatoes, quarter of a pound of salt pork, two onions, one tablespoon of salt, half a teaspoon of white pepper, one tablespoon of butter, one quart milk, eight butter crackers. Cut the fish in two-inch pieces and set aside, putting over the bones and head to boil in a pint of cold water. Pare and slice the potatoes about an eighth of an inch thick and parboil them for ten minutes; pour off all the water. Cut the pork in dice and fry in an omelet pan; then mince the onions and fry in the fat. As soon as a light brown, put all in a kettle, lay in the potatoes, strain on the water in which the bones have boiled with the seasoning, and when all boils, add the fish, and simmer for fifteen minutes. Then add butter and the hot milk, boil up once more; split the crackers, put them in the tureen and pour the hot chowder over them.

A cup of fine cracker crumbs may be added, if a thicker broth is desired, or two eggs may be beaten light and mixed with the hot milk before it is added to the chowder.

A teaspoonful of Worcestershire sauce is liked by many.

Purée of Lima Beans.

One pint of Lima beans; if dry, soak over night in cold water; boil in water or stock, or a mixture of water and stock, or the thin part of a can of tomatoes (using the thick part for escalloped tomatoes), until they are soft. If the water reduces very much, add a little milk, or more stock or water. Sift very closely and add salt, pepper and cayenne to taste; if you like add a little onion juice, mace or any other seasoning. To keep the thick part from separating, add one scant tablespoon of flour cooked in one tablespoon of butter. Let the butter stand in a warm place until it is melted, then rub the butter and flour together until it is perfectly smooth, pour in one cup of boiling soup and stir hard; then stir into the remainder of the soup. Slice three small tomatoes very thin, put them into the soup, and it will be ready to serve as soon as it boils. Use just enough water when first boiling the beans to keep them from sticking to the bottom of the kettle.

A Swedish Fish Soup.

Take one dozen small panfish, skin and bone them. Boil the heads and bones in two quarts of water with a tablespoonful of salt and a handful of dried mushrooms. Egg and crumb the pieces of fish, and fry in boiling lard, letting them drain on brown paper. Pare and chop fine a red beet, two onions and half a dozen leeks, and a parsley root. Cut fine, also half a small white cabbage. Cook these separately in salted water for half an hour. Strain the fish broth upon them, put the fried fish in the tureen and pour broth and vegetables upon them. Small dumplings are often added, and sometimes part of the fish is minced fine and mixed with them.

Farina Soup.

One pint boiling water, four tablespoons farina wet with cold water, one-half teaspoon salt. Stir the farina into the boiling water gradually, cover it and let it boil gently thirty minutes, adding milk to thin it until one pint has been used. Beat the yolk of three eggs with three tablespoons cream and add at the last moment with more salt if needed. This soup should be of a creamy smoothness.

Soup Pastes

A great variety of pastes cut in ornamental forms are used in consomme and other soups by the French cook. These pastes serve as a garnish and are often very delicious. They add a finishing touch to the plate of clear, golden consomme or to a rich puree, which is the triumph of the master-cook.

The foundation of most soup pastes and the forcemeats used in soups is egg. In the case of the "royal" paste, used by all chefs from time immemorial, a simple mixture of eggs and milk or cream is used. For this paste, break into a bowl four egg yolks and one white; add a scant half saltspoon of cayenne, a scant half teaspoon of salt and a little nutmeg. Beat the egg and seasoning well together; add a gill of cream or the same quantity of milk, and strain the whole through a fine gravy strainer into little buttered timbal moulds, tiny tin cups, that cost about ten cents. These moulds should be set in a saucepan with boiling water reaching to half their height, and then put in the oven, still in the saucepan, till the paste is firm in the centre. As soon as the royal paste is cool enough, cut it in slices or in ornamental shapes with a tin star or any other fancy cutter and add it to a quart of clear consomme.

For another paste, beat the yolks of three eggs together and add to them three tablespoons of white broth through which a chestnut, boiled soft and pounded to a paste, has been mixed. Use the large French chestnuts which are sold at large fruit stores for culinary purposes, not the small American nuts. Mix the eggs and chestnut puree together, season the mixture with salt and a little pepper, and cook it like royal paste in moulds.

An excellent paste is made like royal, with consomme substituted for cream; and still another by adding a half teaspoon of onion juice to the royal paste before it is cooked.

Noodles are comparatively unknown in American kitchens, though all good German housewives make noodle soup, and the French use noodles, or nouilles, extensively in soup and served as a vegetable, like macaroni, and in desserts. Noodles are simply made, but require care. Take half a pound of flour and sift it on a board. Stir into it three eggs, two tablespoons of lukewarm water and an even teaspoon of butter; mix these ingredients together for several minutes and gradually add the flour. Knead the paste for at least ten minutes, folding it over and over like bread dough, and set it away for about quarter of an hour. Then roll it out—to the thickness of a "fifty-cent piece," says a famous French chef— and cut it into strips two inches wide, shredding each one of these strips into narrow match-like pieces. Let the noodles lie on the board for thirty minutes to dry, and they are ready for use. This is the French method of cutting noodles. The German housewife rolls out the noodle paste to the same thinness and then forms it into rolls which she slices off at the end in quarter-inch pieces. These little whorls of paste are dried about half an hour longer than are French noodles, and when dropped into the soup or boiling water or stock unroll in ribbons of paste. Add a cup of French noodles to a quart of clear boiling consomme and cook the noodles rapidly for ten minutes; or parboil the noodles for five minutes in plenty of boiling water and add them drained to the boiling consomme and cook five minutes longer. This last method insures a clear consomme.

Noodles should be stirred with a fork once or twice while cooking, to prevent their boiling together, as they sometimes do, especially if there is not abundance of liquid around them. Served as a vegetable, French noodles are boiled ten minutes, and German twenty, in a large kettle of stock or in water

GOLD MEDAL FLOUR—It's a Biscuit Flour—It's a Bread Flour.

The stock is by no means injured by cooking the noodles, and gives them a richer flavor than water. When drained, each piece of paste should be distinct. Put them on a vegetable platter, and fry in butter half a cup of coarse bread crumbs till very brown and crisp. Mix the fried crumbs with the noodles, saving part to sprinkle over the top. This is an excellent dish to serve with fried chicken, or wherever macaroni is served. Noodles are also often dressed like macaroni, with Parmesan cheese or with tomato sauce.

Boiled paste or pate-a-choux, used in making cream cakes, eclairs and other dishes, is often formed in little balls the size of peas, which are fried and all added to the tureen at the time the soup is served. Or they are served separately to each individual dish. A simple rule for this paste is a scant half cup of butter, a cup of warm water, a liberal cup of flour, a teaspoon of sugar and four eggs. Put the butter and water to boil over the fire, and as soon as it boils, stir in the flour and sugar and set the paste aside for a few moments, then stir in the eggs one by one. Let the paste rest for half an hour. For soup balls roll out a cupful of the dough in bits the size of peas and fry them in hot lard.

"Spun eggs" are simply beaten eggs seasoned and passed through a colander into clear boiling consomme, where they form vermicelli-like pieces. Square croutons for soup should be cut in pieces about half an inch square, dried thoroughly and fried in butter a golden brown, not in lard. American housewives frequently add dumplings or little biscuits to their boiling soups, with the inevitable result of heavy leaden little pieces of dough. This is a certain result if the dumplings are dropped into the liquid, which must permeate them before they have time to rise. If the bits of dough are laid on a buttered steamer, covered and cooked in the steam over the soup for ten minutes, they will be ready to serve, light and delicious, but must be served as soon as ready.

Marrow Balls.

One tablespoon finely cut marrow, three tablespoons fine stale crumbs, one teaspoon chopped parsley, salt and pepper to taste. Work to a smooth paste with the fingers, adding a little raw egg if needed to make it smooth. Form in balls the size of a filbert. Drop into the boiling soup and simmer about fifteen minutes.

Spinach Balls.

Equal bulk of finely chopped spinach that has been well seasoned, and very fine dry bread crumbs. Season highly with pepper, salt and cayenne. Add enough white of egg to moisten well, then stand aside to stiffen. Shape in balls size of a hickory nut; poach in the hot soup for five minutes and serve three or four to each plate of clear soup. They are especially pretty in cream of Spinach Soup.

Sponge Balls.

Put the whites of two eggs in a teacup, fill the cup with milk and pour the contents into a stewpan; add one teacupful of flour and one ounce of butter (or size of an egg); stir well over the fire until the batter is thick and smooth; set it to cool, after which stir into it the two yolks, a few pinches of salt, a little mace (if liked), and drop into the boiling hot soup, a teaspoonful at a time. Cook from eight to ten minutes.—Mrs. Bayard Taylor's letters to Young Housekeepers.

Forcemeat Balls.

Scrape fine enough raw lean veal (or chicken) to make one-half pound. Soak two ounces of bread (free of crust) in milk, when soft pour it in a clean towel and squeeze dry; add two ounces butter, the scraped meat, and the yolk of two eggs, pound the whole smooth, and force through a rather coarse sieve. Season with salt, pepper and nutmeg. Form into almond shaped balls between two teaspoons. Cook about ten minutes in stock that must only simmer.

Ham Dumplings.

Proceed as above, using lean ham with parsley or a few drops of onion juice; leave out salt and nutmeg. Chop fine and pound to a paste, but it need not be sifted. Shape in larger balls, about the size of a pullet's egg, and cook in stock. They should be as light as sponge and may be served in consomme.

IN the many standard books on cookery clear explanations about the composition and value of flesh foods are to be found with full instruction about marketing, the best cuts, etc. The reader is referred to these for a careful study of the subject.

In a book of recipes there is room for only general principles, but the following table compiled from the "Diaetetisches Kochbuch" of Dr. Wiel furnishes material for profitable study and frequent reference.

	Water.	Albuminoids.	Fats.	Mineral Matter.
Lean beef.........	76.5	21.0	1.5	1.0
Medium fat beef...	72.5	21.0	5.5	1.0
Very fat beef......	55.5	17.0	26.5	1.0
Medium fat mutton	76.0	17.0	6.0	1.0
Fat mutton........	48.0	15.0	36.0	1.0
Lean pork........	72.0	20.0	7.0	1.0
Fat pork..........	47.0	14.5	37.5	1.0

The excessive amount of water found in underfed meat is largely lost in cooking, and being so much waste shows clearly the great economy in buying only well fattened meats.

There are a few simple principles to be considered in cooking meats and one of the most important points is that much of its value depends upon the albumen and fibrine contained in it; since both of these become hard and indigestible when exposed to a high temperature, it follows that while we expose the surface of meat to a fierce heat, until the outside is seared sufficiently to keep in the juices, the bulk of the meat should be cooked at a temperature much below boiling point, from 160° to 200° allowing sufficient time to thoroughly soften the connective tissues.

Roasting.

All meats should be raised at least an inch from the bottom of the baking-pan, using a trivet or rack made for the purpose. Rub the joint well with salt and pepper and dredge with as little flour as will insure a dry surface. Very lean meat is improved by having thin slices of fat meat, either bacon, pork or its own fat laid over the surface at first until there is sufficient dripping to baste with.

Do not add water to the pan until within an hour of taking up; it is better not to use any, but after the meat has been lifted to the platter, drain off all the grease, add enough thin broth to dissolve the glaze left in the pan, and use this for gravy, either "au jus" or thickened slightly with brown roux.

Braising.

Braising is particularly adapted for meats that are lacking in flavor or are tough. A deep pan with a close fitting cover is necessary; granite ware is the most satisfactory for small ones, while larger ones should be made of Russia iron with folded seams, as both pan and cover must be without solder.

A true braising kettle should have an iron lid with a depression for holding hot coals and ashes—but satisfactory results can be obtained from an ordinary pan with tightly fitting cover.

The covered pans sold as "roasters" are really braising pans and owe their excellence to the fact that the two parts fit together so tightly as to confine the steam, thus this meat is cooked in its own vapor. The most stubborn pieces will yield to the persuasion of a braising pan and become tender, especially if a few drops of lemon juice or other acid be added to the gravy in the pan. This affords an opportunity to render coarse pieces savory by laying them upon a bed of vegetables or sweet herbs; while dry meats can be enriched by the process known as daubing. (See page 12).

Broiling.

The fire for broiling must be clear, and for meats it should be hotter and brighter than for fish. Coals from hard wood or charcoal are best, but in all large towns and cities hard coal is nearly always used, except in hotels and restaurants, where there is usually a special place for broiling with charcoal. The double broiler is the very best thing in the market for broiling meats and fish. When the meat is placed in it, and the slide is slipped over the handles, all there is to do is to hold the broiler over the fire, or, if you have an open range, before the fire. A fork or knife need not go near the meat until it is on the dish. A great amount of the juice is saved. If the old fashioned broiler is used, let the meat be turned with two long handled forks having blunted points that will not make holes for the juice to run. Meats broiled over a fire should be turned as often as every fifteen seconds, but when under a gas flame, it need be turned only once to secure a good brown on both sides.

Pan-broiling.

Heat a cast-iron or steel frying-pan to a blue heat. Rub it with a bit of fat meat till well oiled, but do not leave any fat in the pan. Season the meat and lay in the pan just long enough to sear thoroughly, then turn and sear the other side and continue turning often enough to keep the juice from escaping. Cook about four minutes for a slice one inch thick. If the pan is hot enough and the fat drained away as fast as it cooks out, this is not frying but broiling on a hot surface instead of over coals.

Frying.

To fry is to cook in deep hot fat; the fat must be deep enough to float whatever is placed in it, or to entirely cover such articles as do not float, and while its temperature is far below the boiling point of fat (565° to 600°) it should be much hotter than the boiling point of water. About 400° is best for most kinds of meat or fish, while preparations of flour and egg will cook at a much lower degree, 360° being hot enough for any batter or dough. If one has no thermometer test the fat with a small bit of the dough, and for croquettes draw a match over the surface; it should light at once.

An equally important condition is that the article should either contain albumen, or be coated with beaten egg to insure a fat-proof crust. Mixtures containing egg will generally form such a crust at once, but meat, fish, etc., should be wiped as dry as possible, and then rolled in fine bread-crumbs to dry them thoroughly, coated with beaten egg and rolled in bread-crumbs again. The safest way is to put in all articles a few at a time, adding fresh pieces as fast as the fat reheats.

A Scotch bowl is the best utensil for frying; a woven wire egg-beater is needed to move and lift the food, and a broad, flat wire basket for draining when first lifted from the fat, laying it afterwards on soft paper. The best fat for frying is undoubtedly olive oil, but it is too expensive for general use in this country, the next best thing is cottolene. There is no longer any excuse for using the penetrating grease known as drippings, or almost equally objectionable lard. Have read slices of raw potato to put into the fat the instant the last piece of food is removed, as it loses its heat so slowly that it will go on browning even if removed from the fire. If cooled quickly and carefully strained each time the same fat can be used repeatedly.

Boiling.

In boiling as in roasting the general principle is to subject the meat to a high degree of heat at first and until a layer of albumen hardens over the entire surface. The temperature should then be dropped much below boiling point, some authorities say as low as 160°, and kept there until the gelatine and connective tissues are softened to almost the point of dissolving. Let the meat partly cool in the liquor, and if the slices are served on very hot plates, they will be juicy, tender and well-flavored, an utter contrast to the tasteless, stringy abomination usually offered under the name of boiled meat.

The same treatment applies to all kinds of stews.

Those who like to kill two birds with one stone may take a lesson from the French fashion of serving bouillon. It may be varied to advantage as follows: When ordering the standard amount of meat for soup, six pounds, ask for two more and see that there is one solid piece of three pounds or more, neck or low down on the round will do, trim this to shape, brown well on every side over coals and tie compactly with eight or ten turns of cord. Cut the rest of the meat fine and crack bones as usual, add the cold water and four drops of muriatic acid for each pound of meat, that is, if eight pounds were ordered and four were reserved to brown, there will be left four in the kettle for soup and these will take sixteen drops of acid, stir well and set in a cool place for two hours. During this time the juice of the meat will have been extracted thoroughly and will require less cooking than usual. Heat gradually and when it really boils put in the browned meat. Cook gently until the meat is tender, adding such vegetables as you wish in time to have them done together, they should be parboiled first for five minutes, and, if they are wanted to serve with the meat for the day's dinner, should not be cut up as usual for soup. If boiled meat is not liked for dinner it may be kept for lunch or breakfast; it is good sliced cold or it can be used in a hash, a stew or croquettes.

Daubing.

Cut pieces of fat salt pork about one-third inch square and as long as the meat is thick. Cut a slit through the meat with a narrow boning-knife, force the strips of pork quite through till they show on the opposite side; this takes much less time than to lard and answers very well except when the appearance of the finished dish is to be considered.

Larding.

Is usually applied to the tenderloin of beef when roasted whole, to the thick part of the leg of veal, the breast of turkey or grouse and to liver; it is also nice for a large fish.

Select a piece of clear, fat salt pork, having fine, close grain and pinkish color, shave off the rind as closely as possible, cut the meat in slices parallel with it, from one-eighth to one-fourth of an inch thick, cut these again into strips of the same width and lay on ice till used. With a larding-needle draw these strips into the meat in hand, taking pains to have the stitches evenly distributed (they are usually set in alternate rows) until the whole upper surface is covered.

A short, deep stitch will make the ends of the lardon stand up, and is more ornamental than a shallow one. Directions for boning will be given in full with the recipe for boned turkey.

Roast Beef.

One of the best pieces for roasting is the tip of the sirloin. Have the backbone trimmed very close, cut the ribs close to the solid part of the meat and remove them from the flank part. Roll the flank end toward the backbone and with a large needle and twine secure it by two or three stitches through the tough skin. Do not wash, but sponge with a wet cloth, rub lightly with pepper and salt and dredge on flour enough to dry the surface. Put plenty of flour in the bottom of the pan if a thickened brown gravy is wished. Lay on the rack with the serving-side down at first. If the oven is hot enough it will need to be turned in about an hour. Watch carefully, basting every fifteen minutes, and as soon as well browned on all sides pour in enough water to cover the bottom of the pan. Let the water cook away toward the last, so that the fat can

be poured away. After the meat is done set it into a hot closet, but do not cover while making the gravy. Add one pint hot water to the sediment left in pan after the fat has been poured off. Place on the stove and scrape all the glaze from bottom and side of the pan. When it boils add a thickening made of two teaspoons of flour, rubbed smooth with four tablespoons of cold water, pouring it in slowly, as it is not possible to know just how much the browned flour already in the pan will help to thicken it. Boil well, add salt and pepper to taste and strain into a hot sauce-bowl.

Yorkshire Pudding.

Beat two eggs very light, add one scant teaspoon of salt and two-thirds pint of milk, pour half a cup of this mixture on one-half cup of flour, and stir to a smooth paste, add the remainder of the mixture and beat well. Bake in hot gem-pans forty-five minutes. Baste with the drippings from the beef. This is a more convenient way than to bake in the pan under the beef, and gives more crust. Serve as a garnish for roast beef.

French Roast.

If the piece of meat be lean or of second quality it will be improved by rubbing it well with a preparation of four tablespoons salad oil, two tablespoons chopped parsley, one sliced onion, two bay-leaves, juice of one-half lemon. Rub meat well all over and let it lie from eighteen hours to two days, turning in the dressing once or twice. Baste the meat with the same dressing, adding salt and pepper to taste. Serve "au jus" as in plain roast.

Fillet of Beef, Larded.

The true fillet is the tenderloin, although sometimes one will see a rib roast, boned and rolled, called a fillet. A short fillet, weighing from two and a half to three pounds (the average weight from a very large rump), will suffice for ten persons at a dinner where this is served as one course, and if a larger quantity is wanted a great saving will still be made if two short fillets are used. They cost about two dollars, while a large one, weighing the same amount, will cost five dollars. First, remove from the fillet with a sharp knife every shred of muscle, ligament and thin, tough skin. If it is not then of a good round shape, skewer it into shape. Draw a line through the center and lard with two rows of pork, having them meet at this line. Dredge well with salt, pepper and flour, and put, without water, in a very small pan. Place in a hot oven for thirty minutes. Let it be in the lower part of the oven the first ten minutes, then place on the upper grate. Serve with mushroom or tomato sauce, or with potato balls. If with sauce; this should be poured around the fillet. The time given cooks a fillet of any size, the shape being such that it will take half an hour for either two or six pounds. Save the fat trimmed from the fillet for frying, and the lean part for soup stock.—Miss Parloa.

Rolled Rib Roast.

Either have the butcher remove the bones or do it yourself by slipping a sharp knife between the flesh and bones—a simple matter with almost any kind of meat. Roll up the piece and tie with strong twine. Treat the same as plain roast beef, giving the same time as if it were a piece of rump (one hour and a half for eight pounds), as the form it is now in does not readily admit the heat to all parts. This piece of beef can be larded before roasting or it can be larded and braised. Serve with tomato or horseradish sauce.

Pot Roast.

Four to six pounds from the middle or face of the rump, the vein or the round. Wipe with a clean wet cloth. Sear all over by placing in a hot frying-pan and turning till all the surface is browned. Put in a kettle with one cup of water and place it where it will keep just below the boiling point. Do not let the water boil entirely away, but add only enough to keep the meat from burning. Have the cover fitting closely to keep in the steam. Cook until very tender, but do not let it break. Serve hot or cold. The meat when cold is delicious, cut in quarter-inch slices and sautéd in hot butter.

Braised Beef.

Trim a piece weighing about four pounds into a smooth shape, lard it on each side with three or four pieces of salt pork, let it marinate for twelve hours in the juice of one lemon, one tablespoon salad oil, one tablespoon salt, one tablespoon peppercorns, a sprig each of thyme and parsley. Brown the meat well on all sides in a frying-pan, then lay it in the braising-pan on a bed of chopped onion, carrot and parsley, pour in boiling water to half cover and cook in a moderate oven two hours or more until very tender, turn once in the time, lift the meat onto a hot platter, skim the fat from the gravy and skim out the vegetables to serve with the meat if liked. Thicken the gravy with one heaping tablespoon of flour and strain it over the meat. This dish is often served with a garnishing of several different kinds of vegetables cooked separately in clear water and arranged around it. It is then called a la jardiniere.

Beef Steak.

Have it cut thick. It will never be good, rich and juicy if only from one-fourth to one-half an inch thick. It ought to be at least three-quarters of an inch thick. Trim off any suet that may be left on it, and dredge with salt, pepper, and flour. Cook in the double broiler, over or before clear coals, for ten minutes, if it be rare; twelve, if to be rather well done. Turn the meat constantly. Serve on a hot dish with butter and salt, or with mushroom sauce, maitre d'Hotel butter, or tomato sauce. Do not stick a knife or fork into the meat to try it. This is the way many people spoil it. Pounding is another bad habit; much of the juice of the meat is lost.- -Miss Parloa.

Pan Broiled Steak.

Wipe and trim as above. Heat an iron frying pan smoking hot. Sprinkle salt and pepper on the steak and lay in the pan. Sear each side quickly, then draw back to cook more slowly about four minutes, turning often. When done lift to a hot platter, and spread with soft butter, or better dissolve glaze in frying pan in two or three tablespoon hot water and pour over the steak.

Broiled Meat Cakes or Hamburg Steak.

Chop raw lean beef quite fine, season with salt, pepper and a little chopped onion or onion juice. Make it into small flat cakes and broil on a well greased gridiron, or in a hot frying pan. Serve very hot with butter or Maitre d'Hotel sauce. The flank end of the sirloin is better when cooked in this manner than when broiled with the other part of the steak. Make the proportion about one-fourth fat to about three-fourths lean meat. The seasoning for this is in the proportion of one teaspoon of salt, one saltspoon pepper and a few drops of onion juice for one pint of meat after it is chopped.

Mark Twain's Beef Steak.

"They have the beefsteak in Europe, but they don't know how to cook it. Neither will they cut it right. It comes on the table in a small, round pewter platter; it is the size, shape, and thickness of a man's hand with the thumb and fingers cut off. It is a little overdone, it is rather dry, it tastes perfectly insipid, it arouses no enthusiasm." This is painfully true if one has in mind such a porterhouse steak as may be found on many American tables; "a mighty one an inch and a half thick, hot and spluttering from the gridiron; dusted with fragrant pepper, enriched with little melting bits of butter of the most unimpeachable freshness and genuineness; the precious juices of the meat trickling out and joining the gravy; archipelagoed with mushrooms; a township or two of tender yellow fat gracing an outlying district of this ample county of beefsteak, the long white bone which divides the sirloin from the tenderloin still in its place."

What to do with Cold Beefsteak.

Chop the best and most tender portions, add hot water enough to moisten slightly, heat quickly, and serve as soon as hot. Add butter, salt and pepper. The tough parts of steak or of roast-beef are much more palatable if boiled first in water to cover until tender. Then use them in any of the ways given for cold meat, as croquettes, hash, mince on toast, stew, ragout, meat and potato pie, braised meat, etc.

Beefsteak Pâté.

Chop one pound of best round steak till it is a soft pulp. Season highly with salt and pepper. Add a little of the tender fat also chopped fine. Mix two beaten eggs with one pint of milk. Pour this slowly into one cup of flour mixed with one teaspoon of baking-powder. When well mixed, stir it thoroughly into the meat. Bake in a moderate oven about an hour.

Stewed Steak.

For this, a cut from the round is good enough. First pan broil till well browned, add water to nearly cover. Cover closely and simmer till very tender. Lift the meat to a deep platter, skim the gravy if it shows much fat, add to it one tablespoon flour wet in cold water, more salt and pepper if needed, and a few drops of catsup or horse radish.

Corned Beef.

Select a piece of lean beef well streaked with fat that has been corned only three days. When it is possible, choose the meat before corning, and request the marketman to send it in three days. Wash it carefully and put it into boiling water. Simmer (not boil) until very tender. Cool in the stock. Then press between two plates and serve in thin slices.

Scotch Roll.

Remove the tough skin from about five pounds of the flank of beef. A portion of the meat will be found thicker than the rest. With a sharp knife cut a thin layer from the thick part, and lay it upon the thin. Mix together three tablespoons of salt, one of sugar, half a teaspoon of pepper, one-eighth of a teaspoon of clove, and one teaspoon of summer savory. Sprinkle this over the meat, and then sprinkle with three tablespoons of vinegar. Roll up, and tie with twine. Put away in a cold place for twelve hours. When it has stood this time. place in a stewpan, with boiling water to cover, and simmer gently for three hours and a half. Mix four heaping tablespoons of flour with half a cupful of cold water and stir into the gravy. Season to taste with salt and pepper. Simmer half an hour longer. The dish is good hot or cold.

Beef a la Mode.

Four to six pounds of beef from the under side of the round, cut thick. Wipe and trim off the rough edges. Put in a deep dish and pour over it spiced vinegar made by boiling five minutes one cup vinegar, one onion chopped fine, three teaspoons salt and one-half teaspoon each whole mustard, pepper, clove and allspice. Let the meat stand several hours, turning it often. Then daub it with several strips of salt pork one-third of an inch wide and as long as the meat is thick. Tie it into good shape with a narrow strip of cotton Dredge it with flour and brown all over in hot drippings. Cut two onions, one-half carrot and one-half a turnip fine and fry them in the same fat. Lay the vegetables in a deep braising-pan (of granite ware if possible), the meat on top, with some bits of parsley and thyme, pour over the spiced vinegar adding enough beef broth or water to half cover. Cover closely and simmer four hours, turning once meantime. Take up carefully, remove the strings and lay on a large platter. Remove fat from the gravy, add more seasoning if needed, thicken with brown roux and strain it over the meat.—Adopted from "Boston Cook Book."

Beef Stew.

Two pounds of beef, the round, flank or any cheap part, (if there is bone in it, two and a half pounds will be required), one onion, two slices of carrot, two of turnip, two potatoes, three tablespoons of flour, salt and pepper to taste and a generous quart of water. Cut all the fat from the meat and put it in a stewpan, fry gently for ten or fifteen minutes. In the meantime cut the meat in small pieces and season well with salt and pepper, and then sprinkle over it two tablespoons of flour. Cut the vegetables in very small pieces and put in the pot with the fat. Fry them five minutes, stirring well to prevent burning. Now put in the meat and move it about in the pot until it begins to brown, then add the quart of boiling water. Cover, let it boil up once, skim, and set back where it will just bubble for two and a half hours. Add the potatoes, cut in thin slices, and one tablespoon of flour mixed smooth with half a cupful of cold water, pouring about one-third of the water on the flour at first and adding the rest when perfectly smooth. Taste to see if the stew is seasoned enough, and if it is not, add more salt and pepper. Let the stew come to a boil again and cook ten minutes, then add dumplings. Cover tightly and boil rapidly ten minutes longer.

Mutton, lamb or veal can be cooked in this manner. When veal is used, fry out two slices of pork, as there will not be much fat on the meat. Lamb and mutton should have some of the fat put aside, as there is so much on these meats that it makes them too rich.

GOLD MEDAL FLOUR—It's a Pastry Flour—It's a Cake Flour.

Beef Stew with Peas.

3 pounds soup meat.	1 slice carrot.
3 quarts cold water.	½ slice turnip.
1 large onion.	2 potatoes.
1 tablespoon salt.	1 pint split peas.
1 saltspoon pepper.	

Choose the meat from the under part of the round, face of the rump, aitch-bone or the remainder of roast beef. Remove all the slivers of bone. Cook it four hours. When it begins to boil, remove the scum and fat. Cook the peas in another kettle in water to cover, and as the water boils away replenish with water from the meat. Keep the meat covered with water and when half done add the vegetables, all cut fine, and the seasoning. When ready, serve the meat by itself. Rub the peas through a puree-strainer, and, after removing the fat, add the peas to the meat-liquor. Season to taste and serve very hot. Cut the meat in small pieces and serve it in the stew.—Mrs. Lincoln.

Braised Tongue.

Wash a fresh beef tongue of three pounds and fasten the tip to the roots with a stout string. Cover with boiling water and cook gently two hours. Peel, trim, and cool slightly; rub with flour and brown all over in a deep pan or kettle. There should be six ounces of fat, half butter and half drippings, in which have been cooked for five minutes one tablespoon each, carrot, turnip and onion. Cover the tongue half way with the stock in which it was boiled; a bit of cinnamon, a clove, a bouquet of sweet herbs may be added to the necessary salt and pepper. Cook slowly two hours. At the last half hour the juice of half a lemon is put in. When perfectly tender take up, melt two tablespoons of glaze and pour over it, set in a warm place while the gravy is made. Add one tablespoon corn starch dissolved in water and stir into the gravy, which should be reduced to a pint. Boil five minutes and pour around the tongue on a hot platter.

Baked Tongue.

Wash a fresh ox tongue, put it   a saucepan with some carrots, turnips, a celery root, pepper, salt and plenty of water; boil it, removing the scum as it rises. When soft, take it out of the pan and skim it, cut up an onion and a little lemon-peel very finely; brown them in bacon fat, make holes in the tongue and fill them with the mixture, return it to the saucepan with part of the liquor in which it was boiled, and steam it for a few minutes, then place it in a baking-dish, mix half a pint of cream with some of the liquor, baste the tongue with it and bake it a nice brown. Cut it in slices, lay them in the center of a dish, pour the sauce over and serve with baked potatoes round them.

Escalloped Tongue.

Chop some cold tongue, not too fine, and have for each pint one tablespoon of onion juice, one teaspoon of chopped parsley, one heaping teaspoon of salt, one teaspoon of capers, one cup of bread crumbs, half a cup of stock and three tablespoons of butter. Butter the escalop dish, and cover the bottom with bread crumbs. Put in the tongue, which has been mixed with the parsley, salt, pepper and capers, and add the stock, in which has been mixed the onion juice. Put part of the butter on the dish with the remainder of the bread crumbs, and then bits of butter here and there. Bake twenty minutes and serve hot.

Tongue in Jelly.

Boil and skin either a fresh or salt tongue. When cold, trim off the roots. Have one and a fourth quarts of aspic jelly in the liquid state. Cover the bottom of a two quart mould about an inch deep with it and let it harden. With a fancy vegetable cutter, cut out leaves from cooked beets and garnish the bottom of the mould with them. Gently pour in three tablespoons of jelly, to set the vegetables. When this is hard add jelly enough to cover the vegetables, and let the whole get very hard. Then put in the tongue, and about half a cup of jelly, which should be allowed to harden, and so keep the meat in place when the remainder is added. Pour in the remainder of the jelly and set away to harden. To serve: Dip the mould for a few moments in a pan of warm water and then gently turn on to a dish. Garnish with pickles and parsley. Pickled beet is especially nice.

Fillets of Tongue.

Cut cold boiled tongue in pieces about four inches long, two wide, and half an inch thick. Dip in melted butter and in flour. For eight fillets put two tablespoons of butter in the frying-pan, and when hot put in the tongue. Brown on both sides, being careful not to burn. Take up, and put one more spoon of butter in the pan, and then one heaping teaspoon of flour. Stir until dark brown, then add one cup of stock, half a teaspoon of parsley and one tablespoon of lemon juice or one teaspoon of vinegar. Let this boil up once and then pour it around the tongue, which has been dished on thin strips of toast. Garnish with parsley and serve. For a change, a tablespoon of chopped pickles or of capers, can be stirred into the sauce the last moment.—Miss Parloa.

Beef Olives.

One and one-half pounds of beef, cut very thin. Trim off the edges and fat; then cut in strips three inches wide and four long; season well with salt and pepper. Chop fine the trimmings and the fat. Add three tablespoons of powdered cracker, one teaspoon of sage and savory mixed, one-fourth of a teaspoon of pepper, and two teaspoons of salt. Mix very thoroughly and spread on the strips of beef. Roll them up and tie with twine. When all are done, roll in flour. Fry brown a quarter of a pound of pork. Take it out of the pan, and put the olives in. Fry brown, and put in a small stewpan that can be tightly covered. In the fat remaining in the pan put one tablespoon of flour, and stir until perfectly smooth and brown; then pour in gradually nearly a pint and a half of boiling water. Stir for two or three minutes, season to taste with salt and pepper, and pour over the olives. Cover the stewpan, and let simmer two hours. Take up at the end of this time and cut the strings with a sharp knife. Place the olives in a row on a dish, and pour the gravy over them.

Sautéing.

What is often called frying, that is, cooking the article in a shallow pan with a little fat, browning first one side and then the other; is not really frying, and there is no word in English for it. The French call it "saute" and it will answer very well for omelets, pancakes, and many other things that are just browned in butter, but is only adapted for dishes that are to be lightly cooked.

MUTTON AND LAMB.

Roast Lamb.

Choose a rather large shoulder, have it lifted from the ribs and with a sharp knife remove the shoulder blade and bone of the leg. Sponge carefully and rub inside and out with pepper, salt and fine mint, rub soft butter on the outside and dust with flour. Place in very hot oven for ten minutes or till flour is brown, then reduce the heat and baste with drippings from the pan or any sweet beef dripping. Turn at the end of forty-five minutes and roast one and one-third hours for a six pound shoulder.

Gravy.

Drain off fat from dripping-pan, dredge in two tablespoons flour and brown well. Add one pint water in which the bones have been boiled and rub smooth. Add more salt and pepper if needed and one tablespoon lemon juice. Strain and send to the table in a hot sauce bowl.

Spring Lamb, Mint Sauce.

Rub the saddle of lamb with salt and butter, and while roasting baste frequently with the gravy and salted water. Cook ten minutes to a pound. The sauce is made from young leaves of mint chopped fine, adding two tablespoons of powdered sugar to three tablespoons of mint; after mixing add six tablespoons of white wine vinegar or cider, pouring it slowly over the mint. In order to extract all the flavor of the mint the sauce should be made in advance of dinner-time.

Roast Mutton.

Roast mutton is cooked in the same way, but the piece chosen is usually the leg or loin. The leg is greatly improved by having the bone removed and filling its place with a stuff-

GOLD MEDAL FLOUR—It's a Pastry Flour—It's a Cake Flour.

ing made of one coffee cup coarse cracker crumbs, one teaspoon salt, one saltspoon pepper, one teaspoon mint, dried and powdered, moisten with melted butter.

Roast Shoulder of Mutton.

Remove the bone and fill the space with a moist stuffing made with grated stale bread crumbs, highly seasoned with butter, salt, pepper and thyme. Add the yolk of one or two eggs and enough warm water to soften the bread thoroughly. Put the bones and scraps of meat in a kettle with barely water enough to cover, lay the stuffed shoulder on them and let the whole simmer gently for an hour or more to make it tender. Lift onto the rack in a roasting-pan, dredge with salt, pepper and flour and bake an hour or till tender. Use the water in the kettle for basting and for gravy, with a little butter and flour at the last to froth the surface. Garnish with forcemeat balls made from its own trimmings.

Imitation Barbecue of Mutton.

Roast the mutton as usual, but about one hour before it is ready to serve, prepare the following mixture:

One-third cup each of Worcestershire sauce, tomato catsup, and vinegar, saltspoon pepper, one rounded teaspoon mustard. Stick the meat all over with a sharp pointed knife, pulling the gash open and filling with the mixture just prepared. If any is left pour it over the roast when it comes to the table. This is excellent.

Leg of Lamb à la Française.

Put a leg of lamb, weighing about eight pounds, in as small a kettle as will hold it. Put in a muslin bag one onion, one small white turnip, a few green celery leaves, three sprigs each of sweet marjoram and summer savory, four cloves and twelve allspice. Tie the bag and place it in the kettle with the lamb, then pour on two quarts of boiling water. Let this come to a boil and then skim carefully. Now add four heaping tablespoons of flour, which has been mixed with one cup of cold water, two tablespoons of salt, and a speck of cayenne. Cover tight and set back where it will just simmer for four hours. In the meantime make a pint and a half of veal or mutton force-meat, shape into little balls and fry brown. Boil six eggs hard. At the end of four hours take up the lamb. Skim all the fat off the gravy, and take out the bag of seasoning. Now put the kettle where the contents will boil rapidly for ten minutes. Put three tablespoons of butter in the frying-pan, and when hot stir in two of flour, cook until a dark brown, but not burned, and stir into the gravy. Taste to see if seasoned enough. Have the whites and yolks of the hard-boiled eggs chopped separately. Pour the gravy over the lamb, then garnish with the chopped eggs, making a hill of the whites, and capping it with part of the yolks. Sprinkle the remainder of the yolks over the lamb. Place the meat balls in groups around the dish. Garnish with parsley and serve.—Miss Parloa.

Braised Breast of Lamb.

With a sharp knife remove the bones from a breast of lamb, then season it well with salt and pepper, roll up and tie firmly with twine. Put two tablespoons of butter in the braising-pan, and when melted add one onion, one slice of carrot and one of turnip, all cut fine. Stir for five minutes and then put in the lamb, with a thick dredging of flour. Cover, and set back where it will not cook rapidly, for half an hour, then add one quart of stock or boiling water and place in the oven, where it will cook slowly for an hour. Baste often. Take up the meat skim all the fat off the gravy and then put it where it will boil rapidly for five minutes. Take the string from the meat. Strain the gravy and pour over the dish. Serve very hot, or serve with tomato or Bechamel sauce. The bones should be put in the pan with the meat, to improve the gravy.

Broiled Mutton.

Select lean mutton from the leg or any other lean part. Remove the fat and membranes. Put on a board and chop or pound with an iron meat-hammer until broken to a pulp. Fold over and press into a mass half an inch thick, take it up carefully and broil in a fine wire gridiron well greased. Turn it often and cook it quite rare. Serve very hot with butter and salt.

Ballotin of Lamb.

Bone a shoulder of lamb, leaving the end for a handle. Sew it up with a needle, tie it firmly and boil for five minutes. take out and cool, then lard it as for a fricandeau. Put a slice of bacon in a saucepan with one tablespoon minced onion and one of carrot, brown the lamb with these for five minutes, add a pint of white broth and cook for one hour. The sauce should reduce one-half, thicken slightly, pour it over one pint boiled green peas and lay the lamb upon them.

Haricot.

Fry an onion, then cut all the fat from eight mutton chops, flour them well and brown them with the onion. Cover with water and stew slowly two hours. Then add tomato or any other vegetable. Or cover at first with a quart of sliced tomato instead of water. Pepper and salt.

Sanders.

Mince cold mutton with seasoning and enough gravy to moisten. Put into patty-pans, cover with mashed potatoes and brown.

Boiled Leg of Mutton.

Leg of mutton when boiled to a turn is a very acceptable joint and also a very profitable one for small families, as many excellent dishes may be prepared from that not used at the first meal. Many suppose that mutton should be well done, but this is an error. It should be cooked about the same as "medium" roast beef, and red juice should follow the knife when carving. Rare mutton is indigestible. Put the leg in an oval boiler, cover it with plenty of fast boiling water, slightly salted, skim off the rising scum, as it will discolor the joint if it comes in contact with it. A medium sized leg of mutton requires only two hours and a half to boil. A puree of young spring turnips, with a sauce made of melted butter, with small capers added to it, is the proper accompaniment.

Lamb Tongues a la Soubise.

Parboil, scrape and pare as many tongues as you wish to serve persons, put in saucepan with salt, parsley, celery, pepper-corns and water enough to cover. Cook slowly till very tender, drain and keep warm while the liquid is strained, freed from fat and reduced to a demi-glaze, pour a little soubise sauce in a dish, cut tongues in two and arrange in rosette, pour more sauce in the center and the demi-glaze over the meat and serve.

Leg of Mutton or Lamb Rechauffé.

Slice the tender part into nice pieces for serving. Cut up the trimmings and bones and stew with an onion in water to cover until tender. Strain, remove the fat, heat again, and thicken the liquid with flour cooked in hot butter. Add one teaspoon of mixed mustard and salt and pepper to taste. Simmer ten minutes, then add the sliced meat and two tablespoons of capers, and serve as soon as the meat is hot. There should be about one cup of sauce to a pint or more of meat.

❋ VEAL. ❋

Gouffe, the great authority on French cookery, says that a veal cutlet when well trimmed weighs seven or eight ounces, and that it is cut from the neck of the veal. This is plainly not the veal cutlet of our market. The thick portion of the neck of veal which the French make into the most delicious little cutlets is utilized here chiefly for potpies and stews.

By purchasing the entire fore-quarter of veal we may secure it at a very low price, because of the breast, which, though it is a most delicious cut when properly stuffed and braised, is little known and generally despised. This fore-quarter contains the ribs, which correspond to the favorite rib-roast of beef. From these are cut the best chops, which become less choice in quality the nearer we come to the neck. The rack of veal, as the chops are known to the marketmen. cut entire, makes an excellent roasting piece, equalled only by the loin and the fillet. It is probably to be preferred for this purpose in a well-grown calf. Sometimes the breast of veal is left on and turned over on the ribs to allow for a stuffing roast, but this is not a good plan. The ribs require

GOLD MEDAL FLOUR—It's a Biscuit Flour—It's a Bread Flour.

quite a different treatment from the breast. The neck of the veal, after the scrag end, is passed, which is only fit for broth and stews, may be cut into excellent little breakfast cutlets or chops, as they would probably be called in our markets, though the true chop is always taken from the ribs. The fleshy portions of the foreleg or shin of veal, make excellent potpies or stews, and the leg itself may be used for soup or stock.

A roast-rack of veal is most properly served by itself without stuffing. Season the meat thoroughly with salt and pepper, rub it with butter and dredge it with flour and lay it on a rack in the dripping-pan. The oven should be heated very hot at the beginning, and the roast should be turned twice in the first fifteen minutes to thoroughly glaze the surface of the meat and seal up its juices. After this a cup of boiling water should be poured in the bottom of the pan, and the meat should be basted with a little broth or stock and roasted steadily for an hour and a quarter longer, basting once in every fifteen minutes. After the first basting, the liquor in the bottom of the pan may be used for this purpose. If the liquor in the bottom of the pan seems exhausted after the basting, add a little more water to it to prevent its burning. Eight potatoes peeled and laid in the pan during the last three-quarters of an hour that the meat is roasting are an excellent garnish and accompaniment. Sweet potatoes are especially good cooked in this way. The potatoes should always be basted when the meat is basted to insure their being well flavored with the juices of the meat and nicely browned.

Shoulder of Veal.

Veal at its best and well cooked is wholesome, but underdone veal is a thing to be shunned. Chop the ends of the ribs into neat square pieces and use them next day as an entree. Take out the shoulder blade without cutting the meat more than is absolutely necessary. If the butcher does not remove the blade it may be accomplished as follows: Lay the joint on the table, outer or skin part downwards, make incisions on both sides of the knuckle until the smallest end is free from the meat; now keep the knife close to the bone, using care not to cut through the outer skin. Pull on the bones firmly with the left hand while cutting. When the bone is quite free disjoint it at the socket and remove it. Then stuff the meat with well seasoned bread or rice stuffing, turn it over and put it in the pan, add a very little water and a sliced onion. Salt and pepper the joint. Add also a little sweet butter to prevent the outside from drying too much, baste frequently and cook an hour and three-quarters.

Fillet of Veal, Roasted.

About eight or ten pounds of the fillet, ham force-meat (see rule for force-meat), half a cup of butter, half a teaspoon of pepper, two tablespoons of salt, two lemons, half a pound of salt pork. Rub the salt and pepper into the veal, then fill the cavity from which the bone was taken, with the force-meat. Skewer and tie the fillet into a round shape. Cut the pork into thin slices and put half of these on a tin sheet that will fit into the dripping pan; place this in the pan, and the fillet on it. Cover the veal with the remainder of the pork. Put hot water enough in the pan to just cover the bottom, and place in the oven. Bake slowly for four hours, basting frequently with the gravy in the pan and with salt, pepper and flour. As the water in the pan cooks away it must be renewed, remembering to have only enough to keep the meat and pan from burning. After it has been cooking for three hours, take the pork from the top of the fillet, spread the top thickly with butter and dredge with flour. Repeat this after thirty minutes, and then brown handsomely. Put the remainder of the butter, which should be about three tablespoons, in a saucepan, and, when hot, add two heaping tablespoons of flour, and stir until dark brown. Add to it half a pint of stock or water; stir a minute and set back where it will keep warm, but not cook. Now take up the fillet and skim all the fat off of the gravy, add water enough to make half a pint of gravy, also the sauce just made. Let this boil up and add the juice of half a lemon and more salt and pepper if needed. Strain and pour around the fillet. Garnish the dish with potato puffs and slices of lemon.

Roast Veal, No. 2.

Six pounds of breast of veal, boned, sponged and pounded to uniform thickness; rub both sides with salt and pepper and lay flat on board. Spread evenly with stuffing to within an inch of the edges, roll loosely and sew or tie in shape. Dredge well with flour, lay on a rack in the dripping-pan, laying thin, narrow strips of fat salt pork over the upper side. Set on a grate in a very hot oven till the surface is well browned, then bake more slowly, covering the meat with a buttered paper if it browns too fast. Allow a full half hour for each pound, with an extra half hour if the roast is large. Baste once in twenty minutes with two tablespoons butter melted in one cup hot water, or add water to the drippings in the pan and use.

Stuffing: One pint fine bread or cracker crumbs, one level teaspoon salt, one tablespoon thyme or summer savory, one scant teaspoon white pepper, one-half teaspoon onion juice. Moisten with one egg well beaten, two heaping tablespoons butter melted in one cup hot water, or use one inch salt pork chopped fine in place of butter.

Fricandeau of Veal.

Cut a block weighing about three pounds from the leg, remove the sinews and lard the top with rather small strips of salt pork. Brown it lightly in a frying-pan and lay on a bed of one sliced carrot, one sliced onion and a bouquet. Season with one scant tablespoon salt, a dust of pepper; cover the bottom of the pan with white broth and cook in a braising pan for one and one-half hours, basting occasionally. Serve with one-half pint puree of spinach on the dish, placing the veal on top.

Galantine of Veal, No. 1.

Take a piece of breast of veal, about twelve to fourteen inches long; bone and trim it carefully, removing all gristle and superfluous fat, as well as some of the meat (about one pound). Take the meat and one-half pound of fat bacon; pound together in a mortar, season with powdered spice and sweet herbs, pepper and salt to taste, then pass the mixture through a wire seive. Cut one-half pound of boiled tongue in pieces about an inch square; cut half a dozen truffles, each into three or four pieces. Lay the prepared breast of veal, skin downwards on the table, sprinkle it with pepper, salt and powdered spices; lay the pounded meat, the truffles, and the tongue on it, then roll it up neatly as a roly poly pudding, and tie it up tightly in a cloth. Put all the trimmings and bones of the breast into a saucepan large enough to hold the galantine, add a calf's foot cut in pieces, the trimmings of the bacon (they must be perfectly sweet), two or three onions and two carrots cut in pieces, a clove of garlic, a bunch of sweet herbs (thyme, marjoram, parsley and bay leaf), cloves, whole pepper, mace and salt in proportions, according to taste. Fill up with such quantity of cold water as will leave room for the galantine to be put in. Set the saucepan on the fire, when the contents begin to boil put in the galantine. Let it boil gently without interruption from two to two and a half hours. Then lift it out, put it on a plate, and when it has cooled a little take off the cloth, tie it up afresh, and lay it between two dishes with a moderate weight upon it, to remain till cold. Care must be taken in this last operation that the "seam" of the galantine be made to come undermost. When quite cold undo the cloth, glaze the galantine, and garnish it with savory jelly made from the liquor in which it was boiled.

Veal Loaf.

Three and one-half pounds of minced veal (the leg is best for this purpose), three eggs well beaten, one tablespoon of pepper and one of salt, one grated nutmeg, four rolled crackers, one tablespoon of cream, butter the size of an egg. Mix these together and make into a loaf, roast and baste like other meats. Beef may be used in place of veal by adding one-fourth pound of salt pork, minced fine.

Veal Pot-Pie.

One quart pieces of cold cooked veal, either roast or braised. Season with one scant teaspoon salt, one-half saltspoon pepper, one teaspoon shredded onion, pile loosely in a three pint or two quart pan, fill to almost cover the meat with gravy, stock or water. Cover and set on top of stove to heat while making.

Crust: One quart flour, one even teaspoon salt, two heaping teaspoons baking powder, one heaping tablespoon butter, well rubbed together. Mix as quickly as possible with enough cold milk to make a soft dough. Shape on the board into a flat cake to fit the pan. Cut holes to let the steam escape, lay quickly over the boiling meat and bake about forty minutes in a rather hot oven. While baking make

Gravy: Put all bones and scraps into one pint cold water, cover and set where it will simmer as long as possible. When wanted for use brown one tablespoon flour in one tablespoon butter, strain the hot stock over it, stirring well. Boil three minutes, adding more seasoning if needed, and serve with the pie. If the pie is to be eaten cold, pour this gravy through the crust to bed the pieces of meat in a jelly.

Calf's Head, Tortue Sauce.

Take out the brains and lay them in ice-cold salted water. Wash the head thoroughly and cover with cold water, boil until the flesh will drop from the bones; lift from the kettle and take out every bone; put the kettle, with the water in which the head was boiled, back on the range, and add to it a knuckle of ham or a half pound of lean ham. When this soup has boiled three hours gently, strain it into a stone jar, and leave it until the next day for mock turtle soup.

Cut the thick skin and flesh of the calf's head into two-inch strips and keep it warm. Make the Tortue Sauce thus: One and one-half pints of brown consomme, one bay leaf, the liquor from half a can of mushrooms, half a can of tomatoes; boil about fifteen minutes and strain. Put it back into a sauce-pan with a dozen mushrooms cut into halves, one truffle chopped finely, and one large wineglass of sherry. Let it boil for five minutes, stirring in at the last one teaspoon of blended flour; boil up once and pour over the calf's head. Garnish with new beets sliced, water cresses or parsley.

Veal Tongues.

Lay fresh veal tongues in brine for twenty-four hours, then wash and drop into boiling water enough to cover well. Bring to boil again as quickly as possible and boil fast five minutes; then set back where it will only simmer, and skim well. As it boils away fill up with cold water. Allow one hour to each pound of a large tongue, in cooking small ones remove as soon as tender. Peel carefully, reheat and serve with Sauce Piquante.

Veal Tongue, a la Tartare.

Have ready six veal tongues which have been boiled till tender, the skins removed, and rolled neatly, pressed between two plates until cold. Dip each in egg and bread crumbs, brown well on each side in hot butter. Dish them upon cold Tartare sauce, garnish with pickles and serve. These are delicious when cut in small bits and heated in a Hollandaise, Bechamel or any good sauce that can be made in a chafing-dish.

Calf's Liver.

Calf's liver is braised in the same way as the fricandeau of veal, except that sweet herbs are added to the broth, and just before serving one-half pint of Spanish sauce is poured over it. It will cook in forty-five minutes. Strain the thickened gravy over the garnish with small boiled onions.

Souffles of Poultry or Veal

To two cupfuls of chopped cooked meat, add two tablespoons of butter, three beaten eggs, two cups milk, two tablespoons flour and one tablespoon chopped parsley. Melt the butter without scorching and add the flour, stirring until smooth, pour in the milk and stir until it thickens. Add the meat, and when it is heated through, put in the eggs. Pour in a buttered dish and bake twenty minutes.

❋ **SWEETBREADS.** ❋

Sweetbreads.

Sweetbreads are found in calves and lambs. The demand for calves' sweetbreads has grown wonderfully within the past ten years In all our large cities they sell at all times of the year for a high price, but in winter and early spring they cost more than twice as much as they do late in the spring and during the summer. The throat and heart sweetbreads are often sold as one, but in winter when they bring a very high price, the former is sold for the same price as the latter. The throat sweetbread is found immediately below the throat. It has an elongated form, is not so firm and fat, and has not the fine flavor of the heart sweetbread. The heart sweetbread is attached to the last rib and lies near the heart. The form is somewhat rounded, and it is smooth and firm.

To Clean Sweetbreads.

Carefully pull off all the tough and fibrous skin. Place them in a dish of cold water for ten minutes or more, and they are then ready to be boiled. They must always be boiled in slightly salted water with a litle lemon juice twenty minutes, no matter what the mode of cooking is to be.

Sweetbread Patties.

To two pair of sweetbreads use one can of mushrooms. Cut mushrooms in four pieces. To this amount take a cupful of cream and one-half cup of milk, one teaspoon of butter and one teaspoon of flour. Rub butter and flour together, have the milk scalding hot, stir in slowly. Season to taste. Put mushrooms and sweetbreads in oven to get hot. Mix all together and season to taste. Add wine-glass of sherry wine. One can of mushrooms and two pair sweetbreads will fill eighteen shells if not too large.

Sweetbreads Larded and Baked.

When the sweetbreads have been cleaned, draw through each one four very thin pieces of pork (about the size of a match). Drop them into cold water for five or ten minutes, then into hot water, and boil twenty minutes. Take out, spread with butter, dredge with salt, pepper and flour, and bake twenty minutes in a quick oven. Serve with green peas, well drained, seasoned with salt and butter, and heaped in the center of the dish. Lay the sweetbreads around them and pour a cream sauce around the edge of the dish. Garnish with parsley. One pint of cream sauce is sufficient for eight or ten sweetbreads.

Fried Sweetbreads.

Soak sweetbreads in salt and water an hour or more to draw out the blood, prepare according to directions given—roll in salted corn meal—fry in hot, sweet lard, using enough to cover bottom of frying pan—cook thoroughly, do not parboil.

Sweetbreads in Cases.

Cut the sweetbreads, after being boiled, in very small pieces. Season with salt and pepper and moisten well with cream sauce. Fill the paper cases, and cover with bread crumbs. Brown and serve.

❋ **PORK.** ❋

The main points in buying pork are to purchase from a dealer who has all his meat tested by a microscopist, and then to choose young meat, not over-loaded with fat. In whatever manner pork is cooked it should be thoroughly done, twenty minutes to the pound is none too much.

Pork Chops and Steaks.

Chops are cut from the loin and ribs; cuts from the leg and shoulder being known as steaks. Either piece is best cooked by laying them in a frying-pan until well seared on each side, then drain off all the fat and set into a hot oven for five or ten minutes, according to the thickness of the piece. Season with pepper and salt just before laying in the pan, and serve with fried apples or a pickle gravy.

Pork steaks, chops and even roasting pieces may be cooked ready to serve then cover with lard. They will keep perfectly for weeks, and when wanted the lard can be melted, the meat reheated, and any sauce desired served with them.

Roast Pork.

The chine, loin and the spare-ribs, are the best pieces for roasting. Rub well with pepper or sage, salt and flour, and bake twenty minutes for each pound. Baste often and do not have the oven as hot as for other meat. Roast pork is more wholesome when eaten cold. Serve Pomona rice.

GOLD MEDAL FLOUR—It's a Pastry Flour—It's a Cake Flour.

Roast Leg of Pork.

If used with the skin on score it in inch squares, taking care to cut only through the skin. Make a cut just below the knuckle with a boning knife, slide the knife up along the bone and turn it outward, making a half-dozen cuts two-thirds of the way to the skin and fill them with this:

Stuffing: One cup grated bread crumbs. one medium sized sour apple and one small onion chopped fine (chop the onion to a paste before the apple is put in), six powdered sage leaves, two tablespoons butter, pepper and salt; melt the butter, add the crumbs, rubbing them hard to distribute the butter evenly, add the seasonings and two beaten egg yolks. Half an hour before serving sprinkle with one tablespoon cracker crumbs seasoned with pepper, salt and sage; do not baste again. Serve with this apple sauce. Wipe, quarter and core twelve tart cooking apples; steam till tender and sprinkle with four tablespoons sugar and a little salt. Do not make it too sweet; if the apples are not much sour add the juice of a half lemon.

Roast Pork.

The choicest piece is the loin, but the spare-ribs are good. The meat is usually cut quite close from these and used for steaks, but if a nice roast is wanted order the meat left on. Follow the general directions for roasting and allow thirty minutes for each pound. Serve with apples roasted in the same pan or fried, or with canned barberries. Save all the drippings from the baking pan and see that the glaze is all dissolved. If the oven has not been too hot this fat will serve for frying and the gravy can be made to serve with the cold roast when it is really nicer.

The loin does not require so long cooking, twenty minutes to the pound, with a quarter hour's grace, will do.

The chine or rump is liked by many, but the meat is dry; it may be daubed with salt pork or stuffed in a half dozen places with the following:

Stuffing: Three tablespoons grated crumbs, one tablespoon finely chopped salt pork, ten drops of onion juice, one-half teaspoon sage, one-half saltspoon pepper. Gash the meat with a boning knife and press the stuffing in. Baste often.

Pork Tenderloin No. 1.

Split open and broil. Brown well and thoroughly, but do not burn. Season with pepper, salt and one freshly powdered sage leaf for each one. If very dry rub with soft butter.

No. 2.

Split, but do not cut quite in two, put in a layer of oysters that have been dipped in soft butter and then in seasoned bread crumbs. Wind with coarse thread a dozen turns, but not too tight, brown on each side quickly and then lift from the fire for ten minutes more cooking. Tartar sauce.

No. 3.

Split and fry in pan with butter. Allow one tablespoon chopped pickles with mustard to each one, heat in butter and pour over.

No. 4.

Split them nearly through, so that they will lie flat. Make a dressing with bread, butter, salt, pepper, onion and a little sage. Spread the dressing on one-half the tenderloin, turn the other half over it and sew all around. Bake.

Fricatelli.

Chop one pound raw fresh pork very fine, add one teaspoon salt, one saltspoon pepper, one-half teaspoon onion juice (half as much stale bread crumbs), two eggs beaten together, mix well, taste, add more seasoning if needed. Shape in cakes the size and thickness of a large oyster. Pan-broil them on as hot a pan as possible. If there is any fear that they are not thoroughly cooked, transfer to a tin plate and set in oven but they should not be kept on the pan more than two minutes for each side. Good for breakfast with baked or fried potato. For supper serve with parsley and lemon or cold slaw.

Pork Pie.

English style. Take two pounds of fresh raw pork—neck or trimmings will do—cut it in pieces the size of an English walnut, season with salt and pepper and two glasses sherry or diluted vinegar; let it steep an hour and turn it once in ten minutes; have one pound of good and fine sausage meat.

Take one measure of pie paste and line the bottom and sides of a well buttered pie mould, put a thin layer of sausage on the bottom, then half the pork, another layer of sausage, the rest of the pork, and finish with sausage meat. Wet the edge of the pie, roll the cover to fit, pinch the two edges lightly, egg the surface, ornament with pretty shapes of the paste, cut a two inch hole in the center and fill with a roll of paper to keep it open; brush again with egg and bake in a moderate oven for about three hours; the oven should be quick enough to set the paste for the first half hour, and as soon as the meat steams up reduce the heat. When done, fill with meat jelly; allow it to cool thoroughly in the mold, then take it off and serve on a folded napkin. It is quite as good, though not so ornamental, if baked in an ordinary two-quart pan. Do not cover the bottom with crust; make a rim two inches wide and half an inch thick; fill and cover as before. Cut the rest of the paste in leaf shapes, bake in a quick oven and arrange on the jellied meat when the pie is turned out. Set the broad ends in the center and put rounds or stars of paste on the outer edge between their tips.

Breakfast Bacon.

Remove the rind, slice as thin as paper with the same machine that is used to slice dried beef. Lay the slices in a cold pan and set over a moderate fire. Watch and turn them often and as soon as they look opaque, tilt the pan, draw the slices up from the grease to dry, and transfer to a thick brown paper to drain before laying them on the platter. They should hardly grease the fingers, and should be perfectly crisp.

Breakfast Bacon, No. 2.

Slice the bacon very thin, cut off the rind and hard part before slicing. Fill a shallow pan with cold sweet potatoes sliced. Cover the potatoes with the bacon and bake until the pork is crisp.

Fried Salt Pork.

Cut in quarter inch slices, take off the rind, freshen if very salt, fry slowly and evenly till dry. It is a good garnish for fish, fish balls, tripe, etc., and is quite good enough to serve by itself with baked potatoes and a white gravy made like a white sauce, only the fat from the pork is used instead of butter. If there is much salt in the pan see that it is mostly removed before beginning the gravy.

Roast Ham.

Wash and scrape carefully and soak in cold water twenty-four hours. Scrape again and dry thoroughly. Make a dough with two quarts of flour and water enough for a stiff paste. Roll this into a sheet large enough to wrap the ham; fold the ham in it and place on a meat rack in the dripping pan. Bake in a moderate oven six hours. On taking from the oven remove the paste and skin, sprinkle with fine crumbs and return to the oven for half an hour. Dust very carefully with cayenne and baste every five minutes with wine, using one cup claret and two tablespoons sherry. It will be delicious either hot or cold, and is especially nice if served hot with champagne sauce.

Stuffed Ham.

Soak a ten or twelve pound ham in cold water over night. In the morning remove the bone and fill with stuffing. Sew up the slit where the bone was taken out and bind the ham firmly in a strong piece of cotton. Boil slowly for two or three hours and cool in the bandage. When cold, remove the rind and brown fat. Sprinkle with sugar and fine crumbs. Bake about one hour in a very moderate oven and serve either hot or cold.

Stuffing: One pound of pecans or chestnuts, one can mushrooms, six truffles, one slice raw ham, one ounce mustard seed, two cucumber pickles. Boil the nuts till they are tender enough to chop fine. Cut the truffles into strips and chop all the other ingredients. Season to taste with one-half saltspoon red pepper, one saltspoon allspice, one saltspoon cloves, two tablespoons parsley, one tablespoon onion and salt and add enough raw egg to make the whole into a soft paste.

Boiled Ham.

Soak in cold water until the outside can be scraped and brushed clean; cut away every bit that seems rusty. Put it in a boiler where it will have plenty of room and can be covered an inch deep. It should be two hours in coming to a boil, then simmer fifteen minutes for every pound. It should cool in the pot, but if this cannot be, let it stand two hours at least. To finish in the oven peel the skin carefully in two inch strips, brush with beaten egg and dust thickly with fine bread crumbs. Set in an oven quick enough to brown in fifteen minutes.

Make rings or figures with cloves stuck in the crust before browning, add a paper ruffle to the shank bone before sending to table; if served hot, send in cauliflower, cabbage, saurkraut, asparagus, spinach or some sort of greens. It is also very handsome bedded in sapic and ornamented with vegetables cut in fancy shapes and cooked separately in stock. To glaze a ham after cooking and peeling, brush with beaten egg and coat with a paste made of one cup cracker crumbs made into a smooth paste with one cup milk and tablespoon melted butter; brown in a moderate oven. French cooks add a teaspoon powdered sugar to the bread crumbs, and there is no objection if they are sure to be browned enough to change all the sugar to caramel. There are many modifications of this rule; Mrs. Rorer adds a bay leaf, a blade of mace and six cloves to the water when first put on. Another famous cook adds one pint sour wine for every five pounds, another uses all cider with a good handful clean hay; still another boils half the alloted time and finishes in a moderate oven, basting every fifteen minutes with vinegar. In any method the main point is to heat gradually, cook slowly and cool in liquor. Of course, if vinegar or sour wine is used the cook will not put it in an iron pot; agate, aluminum or porcelain lined will do.

Broiled Ham.

Cut in very thin slices, remove all the fat and if very salt lay the lean part in hot water for a few minutes. Lay the fat in a frying pan and cook as directed for breakfast bacon, but let come to a delicate brown. Dry the lean part on a soft towel and broil quickly. It will take about two minutes for each side if the fire is as hot as it should be.

Potted Ham.

When a ham is boiled there is often much waste of the harder portions and of pieces that do not make presentable slices. Take them while fresh and mince until a smooth paste so that the fat cannot be distinguished from the lean; there should be one-third fat. Allow one pepperspoon cayenne to each pound of meat and salt to taste. Heat thoroughly and pack firmly in small pots.

Ham Puffs.

Ham puffs are a change that will be relished by many. Stir a pint of flour into a pint of boiling water; beat it well. Take it from the fire and beat in four eggs, one at a time; add the ham, about three ounces of it, finely chopped, two-thirds of a teaspoon of curry powder, a pinch of cayenne pepper and a little salt, unless the ham is salt enough without it. Into a pan of deep lard drop this batter, a small dessert-spoon at a time, fry a golden brown and decorate with parsley.

Roast Pig.

It should be from three to six weeks old. Choose it like a chicken, plump, with small bones. They are always scalded and scraped by the butcher, but this is not half the business of cleaning. If there is a strong animal odor wash thoroughly in warm water, then in soda and water for five minutes; during this time cleanse all the passages of the head and throat with a wooden skewer wrapped in a small piece of soft cloth, changing it often; wash again with clear water and wipe inside. If it is not time to cook wrap in a wet cloth to keep the skin soft and white and keep cool. It may be filled with mashed potato, veal force meat or a stuffing made as follows: One cup of bread crumbs, one heaping tablespoon chopped suet, one teaspoon each of minced parsley, sage, salt and onion, one-half teaspoon pepper, a dust of nutmeg and one of thyme, one tablespoon lemon juice and two of melted butter, a cup of oyster liquor (plain stock will do), and two well beaten eggs. Stuff the pig into its natural size and shape, sew and truss. Bend the ore foot backward from the knee and the hind legs forward. Set in a moderate oven at first and increase the heat gradually. In half an hour begin basting; use melted butter until there is enough fat from the pig; brush thoroughly once in ten minutes, cover the ears and tail with caps of oil paper, serve in a bed of parsley, with a lemon in the mouth (this should be propped open from the first with a potato of the same size). It is quite as agreeable also to serve surrounded with heaps of cauliflower and to put a handful in its mouth; the sprigs hide the shrivelled skin better than the lemon does.

Braised Liver (Veal.)

Scald slightly by pouring boiling water over, remove the thin skin that covers it and pull out as many of the large veins as can be removed without breaking it too much. Lard the upper side and dredge with pepper, salt and flour and brown all over in hot drippings. Lay on a bed of vegetables and parsley in a pan not much larger than will hold it easily. Half cover with some good beef broth, cover closely and set into a hot oven for about one hour. Baste every fifteen minutes and leave it open to brown the top at the last. Thicken the liquor in the pan with a tablespoon of cornstarch, add more seasoning and caramel—or, one teaspoonful beef extract to color—if necessary.

Heart.

The heart is often stuffed with a tablespoon of bread-crumbs well seasoned with thyme, onion juice, salt and pepper and moistened with melted butter. Lard the sides with three rows of fine lardoons, brown it well and lay by the side of the liver. It will need to be turned once or twice.

Stewed Liver.

Parboil for twenty minutes, then cut into inch dice, freeing from skin and strings. Have ready a pint of good brown sauce, add one gill of cooking wine, a pint and a half of diced liver; let simmer till the liver is soft, add more seasoning if needed and serve with a garnish of broiled potatoes.

Chicken Livers en Brochette.

Clean and parboil as usual, roll in seasoned flour and string them on a skewer alternately with small squares of bacon. Broil over a clear fire until the bacon is crisp. Serve on toast. If one has a gas stove, by all means lay the pieces of toast under the skewer to catch the dripping gravy. Send quartered lemon to the table with it.

Liver with Chestnuts.

Boil the livers from two fowls or a turkey. When tender mash them fine. Boil one pint of shelled chestnuts until soft. Blanch and mash them to a smooth paste. Rub the chestnuts and liver through a puree-strainer. Season to taste with salt, pepper and lemon juice and moisten with melted butter. Spread the paste on bread like sandwiches, or add enough hot chicken stock to make a puree. Heat again and season with salt, pepper and lemon juice.—Mrs. D. A. Lincoln.

Liver and Bacon.

Prepare the bacon as directed for breakfast bacon. Cut the liver in slices one-third inch thick, parboil for five minutes, dry well and roll in seasoned flour. Lay the slices in smoking hot bacon fat and when they are brown on each side they will be sufficiently cooked.

Chicken Livers in Sandwich Paste.

Wash and soak well in salt and water. Put on to cook in cold water and let simmer fifteen minutes after it begins to boil. Free from all the skin and strings and rub to a smooth paste, adding highly seasoned strong stock to soften the dry bits. Press through a puree-sieve and to a cup of the sifted liver add three tablespoons soft butter and work smooth with a wooden spoon. The juice from fresh mushrooms is a great improvement and if you have bits of truffle to put in it will seem much more like the imported pate-de-foie-gras. Add more salt and pepper if needed and set away to cool. If too stiff when cold reheat and add a little oil from the fat of chicken.

Liver à la Bordelaise.

Cut eight medium-sized slices, parboil, trim, pare nicely, season with salt and pepper, baste with sweet oil and roll in fresh bread crumbs. Broil over a moderate fire till thoroughly well done, dish in a circle, alternating with fillet-shaped slices of Boston brown bread fried in butter; pour a Bordelaise sauce in the center.

Kidneys, (stewed.)

Take two pair lamb's kidneys when perfectly fresh, split in two and trim with scissors the fat and sinews from the inside. Cut them in small pieces, put them in a stewpan, cover with cold water and bring nearly to the boiling point; do this three times, each time being sure that the water does not boil or the kidneys will be hard. Put one tablespoon butter in a frying pan and stir until a nice brown; add one tablespoon flour, cook three minutes, add a half pint of stock or boiling water, stir constantly with a wooden spoon until it boils; add one tablespoon Worcestershire, one of mushroom catsup, salt and pepper and the kidneys; let them heat through, take up add four tablespoons sherry and serve.—Mrs. Rorer.

Tripe.

In whatever way it is to be served, tripe is usually better to be simmered gently until perfectly tender in clear water. If it has a strong smell, add a little vinegar to the water and change it several times. Dry carefully on a cloth before broiling or frying.

Fried Tripe.

Cut in bits for serving. Roll them in seasoned flour then in egg, and last in very fine dry bread crumbs. Fry a good brown in deep fat and serve with a leaf of fried parsley on top.

Tripe in Batter.

Cut in bits and roll in flour as before. Dip in batter and saute in hot butter.

Stewed Tripe.

One pound of tripe that has not been pickled, wash carefully and cut into inch squares. Put it into a stewpan with a saltspoon each of salt, sugar and made mustard, with milk enough to cover, about one pint. Boil up and skim carefully, then set back to simmer for three hours, watching closely lest it stick on the bottom of the pan, and skimming again if needed. Mix a dessertspoon of gluten flour with a gill of cold milk, and stir it in, simmer half an hour longer and serve with more seasoning if liked.

Tripe Fricasseed with Onions.

Simmer as above, but one hour before serving cook six medium sized onions half an hour. Drain and slice them and put them into a dry frying pan with two ounces of butter. Sprinkle over them one teaspoon each of salt, sugar, dry mustard, a saltspoon of white pepper and a speck of nutmeg. Let them cook till there are delicately browned pieces in the hottest parts, then pour them over the tripe which has been previously thickened with two dessertspoons of baked or gluten flour. This should be served at once and very hot.

 # POULTRY.

This meat is not as nutritious as beef and mutton, but its tenderness and flavor renders it most agreeable as a change in the usual bill of fare; neither has it as much fat, except in the case of geese and old fowls, but this can be supplied in the way of butter or cream. Game with dark meat should be cooked rare, as venison, canvas-back duck and almost all birds, while the white-fleshed animals, turkeys, chicken, etc., should be well done.

HOW TO KNOW GOOD FOWLS.

Choose those that are heavy in proportion to their size; this is a general rule in buying oranges, lobsters or fowls; a bird ten inches from tip to tail has a larger proportion of bone than one eight inches, and is consequently less profitable. Avoid also a prominent breast bone, although if the bird is desirable in other respects this may be reduced for a roast fowl by running the point of a sharp knife through the points of the ribs and pressing the whole breast into position; for a broiler it should always be taken out. The best chickens have clean, smooth, yellow feet, moist and delicate skin, and plump breasts; the end of the breast bone yields readily to pressure and the hairs are neither long nor coarse. An old fowl has coarser skin and hairs, roughened scales on legs and feet and the hens usually have too much fat. The combs and spurs show a cock before it is dressed, afterwards judge by the distance from the end of breastbone to the rump. The egg producing hen has an abdomen of much greater capacity than a cock; the meat is softer fibred and less highly flavored, it is good to roast, boil or fricassee, and most of the dark meat can be used for salad; while a cock of more than a year old is better used for croquettes and highly seasoned entrees, though if in good condition they are nice boiled or for soup. The foregoing is true of turkeys as well. Geese and ducks should not be more than a year old; the breasts will be plump and firm, the fat white and soft, the wings tender, the feet yellow and the webbing tender. If the windpipe is too tough to crack when pinched the flesh is probably tough also. Young pigeons have tender pink legs and light red flesh on the breast; in old ones it is very dark. Squabs are young tame pigeons; they are as large as old birds, but soft and plump and covered with pin feathers. Grouse, partridge and quail should have full breasts, dark legs and yellowish bills.

HOW TO CLEAN POULTRY.

All poultry should be dressed as soon as killed; the feathers come out much easier while the bird is warm and there is no excuse for scalding; pull them, one or two at a time, toward the head, with a quick motion; a sharp-pointed knife or a darning-needle is a help in getting out pin feathers. Draw out the ash pan, drop into it a roll of lighted paper and singe the bird thoroughly; hold it up against the light to see if all have been removed; stray hairs or tufts of down are not a pleasing garnish, nor creditable to the cook; do not smoke or scorch the skin. Now the skin should be carefully wiped with a cloth wet with warm water. Do not put the bird in water unless it must be done, though geese and ducks are so greasily dirty that nothing but soap-suds and a brush will clean them. Dry on a soft towel, take off the head and legs, cut open the skin on the back of the neck, disjoint the neck (it can be easily held in a towel) and cut it off close to the body; separate the crop carefully from the skin of the neck and cut off that and the windpipe; insert one finger into the opening at the breast and loosen the organs from the breastbone. It is best to take one's first lesson on a broiler, which, at this stage may be split down the back with a sharp vegetable knife, taking care that the point goes no deeper than is necessary. Now open the chicken like a book and learn the arrangement of the viscera; see the heart and lungs in the chest and find how they are fastened; note the position of the gizzard on the left side capped by the two lobes of the liver and connected with the coil of intestines or entrails below; take out the kidneys from their bony sockets near the base of the backbone and the last bit of the lungs from the spaces between the ribs; these organs are often eaten and in a young healthy bird are not unwholesome; but they, as well as the liver, are particularly liable to disease, and should never be used from an old fowl. All this can be done in a little time and the lesson learned can be applied by drawing a fowl for roasting—a process too often both tedious and disgusting.

If the fowl is to be dressed for fricassee, it should be jointed first, that is, legs and wings cut smoothly off; find the joint in the back, make a cut to it with the point of the knife on each side from the end of the breast-bone; bend the body backward and empty it of viscera in the same way as before; cut out the oil bag in the tail, wipe with a damp cloth and the fowl is ready to cook, with not a tissue broken but what is necessary to get rid of inedible portions.

It is a little more difficult to prepare for roasting; remove crop as before; cut around the vent with scissors, lengthen the slit enough to admit two or three fingers, slide them cautiously around the mass inside until the heart is reached and held, and the whole bulk detached from breast and backbone; it can then be drawn down and out, care must be taken to keep them all together; if dragged apart there is danger either that the entrails or the gall bladder may be broken; this last is an almost fatal accident, for if the fowl is washed and soaked enough to get rid of that bitter taste it will have lost much of its own flavor.

Roast Turkey or Chicken.

For a roast turkey or chicken cut through the skin of the leg an inch or two below the joint; break the bone by a light blow with the back of the cleaver and draw out the tendons, picking them up one by one with a stout fork or a wooden skewer, leave the bits of leg bone on till the fowl is roasted; it is much easier to fasten them in position and they can easily be taken off before serving.

To Stuff a Fowl.

The easiest way is to set it in a deep bowl; fill the breast till it is rather plump, but do not put in as much as it will hold; the stuffing swells in cooking; it might crack the skin and would surely be heavy. Fold the skin of the neck neatly but loosely back and fasten with a bird skewer, turn the bird and fill the body, but do not crowd; if the opening is more than three or four inches it should be closed by half a dozen deep stitches; use a larger darner and soft cotton, do not draw the thread tight nor try to tie it; leave a long end for convenience in pulling out.

To Truss a Fowl.

Push the legs up until the knees are well above the point of the breast-bone, cross them at the tail and tie firmly. Run a skewer through the body at the wings and thighs, press them close to the body and tie across the back.

To Prepare Giblets.

It is well to repeat the caution: Do not use any from old fowls nor from a young one unless thoroughly sound; a healthy liver has a light color and uniform texture; cut away any portion that has been discolored by the gall bladder; remove that without allowing a drop of its contents to fall on the meat, trim off superfluous tissue from liver and heart, cut through the thick muscle of the gizzard and peel it off without breaking into the little gristmill inside; wash and let them lie in salted water from five minutes to five hours. The strong smell of an old fowl does not make the meat unwholesome, it may be removed by this soaking in salt or soda water, but if the fowl has been tainted by lying undressed or, worse yet, by careless dressing, it is recommended to throw away these parts. Simmer till tender in water or stock. Cook the neck with the giblets, but save the wing tips and legs for the long slow cooking of the stock pot. Use only the smooth legs of a fowl less than a year old. Scald lightly and the skin and claw cases will peel off like a glove; three pairs of chicken feet will make a pint of jelly as fine and just as nutritious as the noted calves feet jelly.

Gravy for Roast Poultry.

See Brown Sauce. Only in this case use the stock in which giblets were cooked; mash the liver, chop heart, gizzard and neck meat fine and mix with only half the sauce sending in one-half plain for those who prefer it.

Broiled Chicken.

Chickens allowed the range of a large yard will run all the fat off them. It is better to pen them into a small space for at least a week before killing. It is hardly worth while to try to broil them when over three months old, though by steaming them first they can be broiled up to five months old. Split down the back, and spread open as flat as possible, crush down the breastbone and pin the wings and thighs closely to the body, fastening the giblets under the wings. Wipe as dry as possible, sprinkle with salt and pepper and rub well with soft butter before laying on the broiler. Cook the inside next the coals first for as long as possible without scorching, then turn and cook on the skin side till a handsome brown. After each side is brown, turn often till well done, it will take from twenty to thirty minutes. Covering the broiler with a pan keeps in both heat and steam and finishes the work in less time. Serve on a hot platter and butter very well. Garnish with watercress, and serve thin, well-browned baking powder biscuit with them.

Roast Chicken.

For general directions see roast turkey; for time see table page 2. If the breast stands high and there is danger of scorching it, cover with a buttered paper. For stuffings see page 22.

Boiled Chicken.

Dress and clean according to general directions. Place in a kettle of boiling water deep enough to cover, and with a fowl weighing four pounds boil a pound of fat bacon. Skim carefully when it begins to cook and after the scums cease to rise set it back to simmer gently for three hours or more, until ready to fall apart. Add a handful of rice and a cup of milk to make it look white, and keep it under water with an inverted deep plate. Add more salt, if needed, about half an hour before taking it up. Lay on a hot dish while the liquor is reduced to rather more than a pint, skim off all the fat, add chopped parsley, celery and thyme and hard boiled eggs, chopped fine, if liked, and send to table in a sauce bowl.

Steamed Chicken.

Wipe very dry after cleaning. Rub salt, pepper and plenty of butter in the cavity of the body; fill it with large oysters well seasoned with salt, pepper and celery salt. Tie the legs and wings close to the body and lay in as small a dish as will hold it, and set in a steamer to cook four hours. Meantime cook a pint of chopped celery till it will rub through a puree sieve. Make a pint of white sauce with the liquor of the oysters, add the celery to it and pour it over the fowl on the platter. Garnish with curly parsley and serve with baked sweet potatoes and boiled rice. This is a delightful way to cook a turkey.

Chicken Pot-Pie.

Cut the chicken into nice pieces for serving, drop them into just enough boiling water to cover and skim carefully at first. Set back to simmer closely covered until tender, taking care that it does not boil dry. While it is cooking cut off one pound of light bread dough, work into it a large tablespoon of butter, shape it into small dumplings and set them to rise; wash and pare potatoes, cutting to about half the size of an egg. Parboil for ten minutes in salted water and add them to the chicken when nearly done. It is well to taste and add more seasoning at the same time if it is needed. When the potatoes begin to boil, lay on the dumplings, first adding a cup of cold water or milk, to check the boiling and give the dumplings a chance to rise. Cover very close and do not open the lid till they are done, which will be in from twenty to thirty minutes. Test them by taking out one and breaking open to see if it is cooked through. If one likes the dumplings dry and very light they may be cooked in a steamer quite separate from the meat and potatoes. Make gravy for chicken-pie, adding more water or milk as may be needed. A baking powder dumpling can be used instead of the raised dough and the sponge-balls given to go with soup on page 10 are excellent with pot-pie. Some recipes call for onion, carrot and turnip, but such strong flavors are too much for the chicken and are better suited to beef or mutton stews. A tablespoon of rice or a half cup of tomatoes are the only vegetables recommended.

To make a Poloe.

Take a pint of Rice, boil it in as much Water as will cover it; when your Rice is half boiled, put in your Fowl, with a small Onion, blade or two of Mace, some whole Pepper, and some Salt; when 'tis enough, put the Fowl in the Dish and pour the Rice over it.—From the Complete Housewife, published in London in 1734.

Chicken Pie.

Divide the chicken into pieces at the joints, boil until part done, or about twenty minutes, then take it out, fry two or three slices of fat salt pork and put in the bottom, then place the chicken on with one cup of water, two ounces of butter, one teaspoon of salt, pepper to taste and cover the top with a light crust, the same as for biscuit. Bake in an oven that is hotter at the top than at the bottom, and when well risen and brown cover with a paper or the crust will burn before the pie is baked through. Remove fat from the water in which the chicken was boiled, thicken with a little flour, season to taste, add one cup good cream and when the pie is done pour this gravy through the holes of the crust.

Chicken Turnovers.

Chicken turnovers are a pleasing variety of chicken pies. Roll out trimmings of puff paste or any good pastry, and cut in rather large rounds. Have ready some cooked chicken, chopped fine and highly seasoned; a little finely minced ham is an improvement. Moisten with its own gravy if you have it, if not, cream will answer. Lay a tablespoon of the mixture on one-half the paste, fold the other half over it, press the wetted edges closely together and bake in a quick oven or fry in hot fat, according to convenience. When fried these are called Rissoles.

Chicken and Oyster Pie.

Cold boiled chicken and fifty good-sized oysters with a small slice of ham are required for this. Make one quart of good white sauce, using the strained oyster juice as part of the liquid. Line a deep pie dish with pastry, building up the edges with two layers. Cut the chicken in even pieces and lay in the dish alternately with oysters and ham cut in dice. Pour the sauce over all and make a cover half an inch thick of the pastry, making a hole in the middle for steam to escape and pinching the edges well together. Bake a leaf or any fancy shape, to cover the hole with when done. Bake the pie half an hour and serve hot. Very good.—From "The Epicure."

GOLD MEDAL FLOUR—It's a Pastry Flour—It's a Cake Flour.

Chicken Fricassee.

White. Prepare the chicken by general directions, brown in butter; it should be done over a quick fire, but not allowed to take much color; cover with boiling water and simmer till tender; a year-old chicken should not need more than forty minutes; reduce the stock to one pint and use it to make a sauce with one tablespoon of butter and two of flour. Season with one-half teaspoon celery salt, one teaspoon lemon juice, salt and pepper as needed. Add one cup hot cream and pour the sauce slowly over one well-beaten egg; stir well and put on a hot platter; arrange the pieces of chicken in something like the order in which they grow, garnish with toast points and two sprays of parsley laid in the center of the dish.

Egyptian Chicken.

Select a well-fattened hen a year old or even more. Clean and truss as usual, tying the legs and wings very close to the body. Rub all over inside and out with salt, pepper and soft butter. Pick over and wash one and one-fourth cups rice, season it with one teaspoon salt, one-half saltspoon pepper, one teaspoon curry powder. Put three tablespoons rice inside the fowl and the remainder around it in a dish just large enough to hold all nicely. Set it all into a steamer with a close-fitting cover and cook for at least four hours. The giblets may be scalded and cooked separately for an hour and then laid inside the fowl with the rice. If the broth in which they are cooked is not too strong, pour it over the rice in the dish. Serve with summer squash and cucumbers.—Mrs. F. A. Crosby, Milwaukee, Wis.

Fried Chicken.

Chickens will do for frying up to six months old if they are plump and in good condition. Clean, singe and wipe with a wet cloth. Cut them in quarters, and season with salt and pepper, roll them in flour and fry in hot fat from salt pork until brown on both sides. Cover closely and set back to cook slowly till done, about twenty minutes more; dissolve the glaze with two or three tablespoons water and pour over the chicken. Serve with corn pone if you can get sweet, soft corn meal and have an open fire; if not, with some other form of corn-bread.

Chicken à La Marengo.

Cut a large chicken in small joints, dry it carefully and fry to a good brown in olive oil. Place in a clean sautoir with six mushrooms peeled a d sliced, one gill of stewed tomato, one small onion or six chives, and a few truffles if you have them, one gill of brown sauce. Cover closely and simmer half an hour, adding more water if it boils away too much. Taste to see if more seasoning is needed. Serve on a chafing dish, garnishing with croutons of puff paste and poached eggs.— Manual of South Kensington Cooking School.

Chicken and Corn Pudding.

Clean and cut one chicken in small pieces, simmer in a closely covered kettle till it begins to grow tender. Then take out and lay in a baking dish, seasoning well with salt and pepper. Have ready one quart green corn cut fine, three eggs well beaten and one pint sweet milk, salt and pepper to taste. About one teaspoon of salt, one-half saltspoon pepper and a dust of cayenne. Pour this mixture over the chicken, dredge thickly with flour (or very fine dry breadcrumbs), lay on bits of butter and bake in a moderately hot oven until set and a delicate brown. Make a good gravy with the water in which the chicken was cooked, and serve with the pudding.

Chicken Pudding, No. 2.

Make a batter with a pound of flour, one teaspoon salt, one quart milk and six eggs beaten light. Pour over chicken as above. This should be baked in a very gentle heat, and served as soon as done, with a gravy as before.

Deviled Fowl.

Cut the thighs and wings from two underdone fowls, either roast or boiled. Score them closely about one-quarter inch deep, and rub in a paste made with two teaspoons mixed mustard, one teaspoon good salad oil, one teaspoon salt, one-half saltspoon cayenne, lay them aside to season while the rest of the meat is chopped fine and stirred into a pint of Bechamel or any good sauce.

Put a good tablespoon of butter in the sautoir and when it browns add one teaspoon each vinegar, Worcestershire sauce and mustard. Broil the legs and wings till a handsome brown, and roll each one in the butter mixture as it is taken from the gridiron. Put the mince in the center of a hot platter, arrange the grilled bones around it and serve piping hot.

Poultry Stuffing

No. 1. For an eight-pound turkey take one quart stale bread crumbs; they should be of uniform size, but need not be sifted; moisten with three-quarters of a cup of butter, melt d; season well with pepper and salt. use fine herbs if desired. but the flavor of chicken and turkey is too delicate to be covered with much seasoning.

If the fowl is very large and a good deal of stuffing is liked, the body may be filled with thin slices of bread well buttered, sprinkled with seasoning and dipped lightly in stock. Do not crowd either crop or body or the stuffing will be heavy.

No. 2. Soak four ounces dried bread in cold water until soft, press out all the water, add four ounces fine sausage meat, one tablespoon each of parsley and of onion chopped and parboiled, two ounces of butter, one teaspoon salt, one-half tea spoon pepper, a dash of nutmeg and two well-beaten eggs. If the sausage meat is quite fat the butter may be omitted, or chopped salt pork may be substituted with rather more seasoning. If one objects to pork in any form, use a full cup of butter and an extra cup of coarse crumbs.

A good and rich variation is as follows: Chop the liver with one small onion and brown lightly in a very little butter; mix them with one pound of sausage meat and three dozen chestnuts boiled and blanched.

No. 3 stuffing with chestnuts. Remove the sinews from one-half pound raw lean veal and the strings from the same weight of leaf lard; chop them separately till very fine, then pound vigorously till well blended; moisten with one-half pint broth, add one teaspoon salt, one saltspoon pepper, four dozen chestnuts, blanched and boiled; fill the turkey, breast and body. One cup of the cooked chestnut crumbs may be reserved, mashed, sifted and used to thicken the gravy; this should be lightly browned, not to cover the chestnut flavor.

No. 4. For roast chicken of three or four pounds take one cup coarse cracker crumbs, moisten with butter, the amount varies with the kind of cracker, from one-fourth to one-third cup, season well with salt, pepper and thyme.

Stuffing for Ducks.

One-half pound onions, minced, blanched and drained, add three tablespoons grated bread crumbs, one teaspoon powdered sage, the liver of the duck parboiled and minced, pepper, salt and cayenne to taste. This quantity is sufficient for one medium size duck.

No. 2 for duckling. Two ounces bread crumbs, two ounces butter, a little chopped parsley, two leaves sage, a dust of grated lemon peel, three shallots chopped, with salt and pepper to taste.

No. 3 celery stuffing. One cup coarsely chopped celery, one-half cup onion, one heaping cup dried bread. Remove all crust from the bread and fry them in enough butter to crisp them well, mix all together and add salt, pepper and cayenne to taste.

Roast Turkey.

Get one which is plump and young. Clean as usual (see page 20); do not omit drawing the tendons in the leg and removing the lungs and kidneys; clean and truss as usual (see page 21). Place on a rack in the dripping pan; brush well with soft butter and dredge with flour. Set in a hot oven and when well browned reduce the heat; lay it on the side, turn and brown the other and finally lay it on the back to brown the breast; this ensures an even color. Baste with butter till nicely browned, then add a pint of water and renew it as needed. Dredge with flour at every alternate basting. If the cook cannot be trusted to baste often, a hen turkey should be chosen, but the cock has higher flavor and is better for boning, boiling and braising. Allow two hours for an eight pound turkey; this is a good size for a family of six. It gives good cuts for the first day, allows remnants for some made dish and still enough trimmings for a soup. Test by running a long pin through the second joint between the leg and body. If the giblets are not liked in gravy, use them for forcemeat balls, or cook, chop and mix them for the stuffing—either No. 1 or No. 2.

Many like the flavor of both turkey and chicken better if roasted without stuffing; in this case season the inside of the bird with salt and pepper, baste freely and allow less time for roasting, from one-half to one hour, according to the size. It can be tested by running a long pin through the thigh between the leg and the body. An older fowl takes longer and is much better braised.

Braised Poultry.

Make ready as for roasting; brown lightly in a frying pan or quick oven, put in braising pan with onions and sweet herbs or vegetables, or rice, hominy or macaroni, as preferred. (Macaroni must be first parboiled for ten minutes.)

Boned Turkey.

Choose a young hen that has been dry picked, with skin unbroken; if killed the day before it should have been washed clean, wrapped in a damp cloth and hung in a cool place. The work can be done more easily if the bird is not drawn and there can be no objection if it has had no food for twenty-four hours before it is killed. Separate legs and wings at the first joint and cut off neck inside the skin, close to the body. Make a clean cut to the bone down the back from neck to the rump; then, holding the edge of the knife to the bone, scrape away all the meat on both sides, making a cut across the "pope's" nose, taking it off whole. Great care must be used not to break through the skin on the breast bone. The thigh and wing bones may be disjointed and taken off separately, though a professional cook takes pride in removing the carcass entire; turn the flesh back from the bone while working, like pulling off a glove wrong side out; take the wing and leg on one side before touching the other; when the ridge of the breastbone is reached it is better to cut off a thin layer of cartilage with the skin than to run any risk of breaking through. When the boning is finished lay the bird open on the damp cloth and bring each part to proper position, take off the minion fillets and some small slices from the breast where the meat is thick and lay them where it is thinner so that the meat will be nearly of uniform thickness. Put one or two small fillets from the thighs in the breast and replace them with breast meat; do the same with the wings. Make a layer of force meat not more than one inch thick; place on this a layer of tongue, pork and veal or pork tenderloin; dot it with truffles cut in matches, cover with another layer of force meat, put a layer of very thin slices of fat pork on top, bring up the sides carefully, so as not to disarrange the stuffing, and sew the back from end to end, roll firmly in cloth and fasten both ends tightly; put in a braising-pan, as near the size of the bird as may be, two sliced onions and carrots, the veal and pork trimmings, then the turkey, parsley, a dozen pepper-corns, three stalks of celery, a blade of mace and a clove; pack the crushed bones of the turkey around and cover with thin white stock. Bring to a boil quickly, then simmer three to four hours; test with a long steel pin, cool in the liquor; take off the cloth and roll it again closely, tieing securely and put to press under a heavy weight. Reduce the stock to three pints, strain, cool, remove the fat and reheat; add two-thirds package gelatine which has been soaked in cold water until soft. Taste for seasoning and strain one-half pint into a mold and the remainder into two pans, color one with one teaspoon and the other with two of caramel. Use the jelly when stiff to garnish the turkey, with peas, canned mushrooms and fancy cut vegetables. Garnish the turkey with celery tips and groups of force meat balls. If the giblets are not liked in the gravy those may be used for the balls, make very fine, mix with an equal bulk of bread crumbs, allow one teaspoon of butter to each cup of the mixture, season highly, moisten with egg yolk, make in balls the size of a hickory nut and brown in hot butter.

Jelly for Boned Turkey.

Strain the broth in which it was cooked and skim off every speck of grease. Let boil for five minutes, then pour it over one ounce of well soaked gelatine. Crack into another bowl the whites and shells of two eggs, juice of one-half lemon, one gill of Maderia wine and whisk them all well together. Add the soup very slowly, stirring fast with a wire whip. Place over a moderate fire and let come gently to a boil. Simmer a few minutes until there is a thick scum like leather. Hold this back with a skimming spoon while the clear soup is poured into a flannel bag to filter. Set to cool over night and it will be fit for use.

Roast Goose.

Clean and wash thoroughly, (see page 20), rinse well in clear water, wipe dry inside and out. Chop an onion fine, blanch and drain, fry with a little butter, mix it with well seasoned mashed potatoes, adding sage if liked, truss and roast two hours for a medium size, covering breast with a buttered paper for the first hour. Soak the giblets in salted water, scald, cook gently until tender in a little water, chop and add to the gravy. For this the fat should all be poured from the dripping pan and fresh fat added, butter, pork fat or dripping, according to taste; brown two level tablespoons flour in it, blend with one pint strong stock. Pour this upon a hot platter, lay on the goose and garnish with apples cooked as follows: Take small, round, sour apples, pare smoothly and brown in butter and sugar, one tablespoon of each will do for six apples. Stew in broth enough to barely cover and take out as soon as tender, boil the broth to a glaze and roll the apples in it.

Forcemeat for Boned Turkey.

Chop fine separately two pounds of white lean veal and the same amount of fresh fat pork, pound vigorously in a mortar, add seasoning to taste and four egg yolks one at a time, beating and pounding continually. Take a half pound of fat pork, red beef tongue or ham and lean of veal or pork tenderloin; cut each into slips as long as may be and one-quarter inch square. Use as directed.

Roast Duck.

To really enjoy domestic duck they should be kept in a small pen for a day or two and fed on barley meal or cracked wheat, with plenty of clean fresh water to cleanse them before they are dressed. As a general rule two small young ducks make a better dish than a large drake, the flesh of which is hard and dry and best adapted for a stew, salmi or braise. Clean and truss according to general directions, except that the feet are generally scalded, skinned and twisted across the back, while the pinions and long neck are entirely removed. Stuff and skewer the wings close to the side to make the breast as plump as possible. Roast from thirty to forty-five minutes, basting often and dredging with flour if it is wished to have a frothy appearance. Serve with a good brown gravy and with apple sauce in a side dish.

Stewed Duck, (Irish.)

Singe, draw and cut into eight pieces each, two spring ducks. Season with pepper and salt and fry to a light brown on both sides in butter. Add a sliced onion and four ounces raw, lean ham cut in dice. As soon as these have browned a little dredge with one and one-half ounces of flour and fry again till the flour is brown, then add one and one-half pints beef broth, a gill of port wine, a bunch of parsley and sweet herbs to taste, cover closely and cook three-quarters of an hour. Remove the herbs, skim off all the fat and serve in a potato border.

Salmi of Ducks, (English.)

Stew the giblets of one or more ducks in veal gravy till they are tender, seasoning them highly with cayenne, shallots, pepper and salt. Cut the roast duck into large dice and lay in the stewpan with the gravy, simmer till hot through, then squeeze a bitter orange into the gravy, strain it over the pieces of duck neatly arranged on bread croutons and send to table smoking hot.

Braised Duck.

See braised fowl, page 23, using green peas instead of other vegetables. Season with salt and pepper and serve with the peas under the duck and the gravy poured over.

Stuffed or Boned Duck.

Bone according to general directions, being careful not to break the skin. Fill with a forcemeat made from one-half pound veal, one-fourth pound suet, parsley, chives and plenty of mushrooms. Add salt and pepper to taste and make into a paste with two well-beaten eggs and sufficient water. Fill the inside of the duck, cook in a braising-pan and serve with stewed chestnuts prepared with the gravy from the bones.

Broiled Squab.

The birds should be full-grown but not yet out of the nest, or not more than a day or two. Singe, draw, split down the back. Crack the large bones, flatten with a heavy cleaver. Season with salt and pepper and broil slowly. Serve on dry toast with hot maitre d' hotel butter poured over. Garnish with water cress.

GOLD MEDAL FLOUR—It's a Biscuit Flour—It's a Bread Flour.

Salmi of Duck, (America.)

Three small wild ducks (teal, widgeon or wood-duck) roasted and cut in even pieces, free from bones, skin and gristle. Break all the bones and put them with other trimmings in a stewpan with two glasses sherry, one quart Spanish sauce, one pint beef stock, a sprig of thyme, a bay leaf, two cloves, six peppercorns, parsley and one onion sliced. Cover closely and boil gently for one hour; strain and reduce to a smooth consistency. Dish the duck on a large thick slice of fried bread, add the juice of a lemon and two ounces butter to the gravy and pour it over.

Roast Pigeons.

Prepare exactly according to the directions for roast chicken, but unless they are surely young and fat they are much better to be steamed for thirty to forty minutes before putting them into the oven. Use a generous measure of butter as the meat is rather dry.

 GAME.

Under this head is included all wild animals and wild fowl used for food. In cooking either apply the same general rules already given for meats and poultry, remembering that all white meated game should be cooked well done; dark meated game rare, and both must be sent to the table very hot, with hot plates. Wild meat contains a much greater percentage of phosphates, and much more lean than fat, while the lean is of much greater density than the flesh of domesticated animals. It follows that they are a strong food and if well digested, very nutritious.

When game is to be kept many days it should be drawn, the inside rubbed with salt and pepper, and it does no harm to put some lumps of charcoal in the cavity. If there is any objection to washing, it must be very carefully drawn and then wiped with a damp cloth until perfectly clean. Neither salt nor pepper should touch the outside of the meat until it is cooked.

Simplicity is the highest perfection of cooking, especially of game, and all seasoning, sauces and accompaniments should be subordinate to the flavor of the meat.

Antelope.

Antelope meat is prepared like venison and is hardly to be distinguished from it except by its stronger flavor.

Bear.

The haunch and saddle of a young bear is very good roasted, tasting almost like pork, but old bear meat is extremely hard and tough and is only palatable in a highly seasoned ragout.

Rabbits or Hares.

Rabbits and hares are only fit to use when young, and their age may be known by the ears and paws, which should be soft, the edges of the ears smooth and the paws not worn. They are best in the fall and early winter when fat from an abundance of their favorite food. They should be drawn as soon as possible after killing, but should not be skinned until ready to use. Wash and soak them for a little while in salted water.

Roast Hare.

Parboil the heart and liver, chop them fine with an equal bulk of fat salt pork; make a moist stuffing as for chicken, using the water in which giblets were boiled and working in the minced meat. Stuff the body with this and sew it up. The English fashion is to leave the head on, but American taste generally prefers it removed. Truss the forelegs back and the hind legs forward. Fasten thin slices of fat bacon over the shoulders and back and put it to roast in a very hot oven at first. Baste faithfully with butter and water until the fat flows freely from the bacon. When half done dredge with flour and baste with butter once more. When done enough dress on a hot dish with a little gravy poured over and garnish with slices of lemon. Serve fried bacon with it on a separate dish.

If the rabbit is very plump and young, it is nice to roast it without stuffing, serving force meat balls on the platter with it. It is also good with a chestnut stuffing made as for turkey.

Broiled Rabbit.

Skin and lay in salt and water for a time to sweeten. Prepare for the broil like chicken and cook over charcoal embers till done. Season with salt and pepper just before it is finished and pour over melted butter mixed with two tablespoons vinegar and one of made mustard before sending to the table. Serve with a ravigote sauce.

Rabbit Stew or Fricassee.

See directions for fricasseed chicken, adding rather more seasoning and a glass of any good red wine if liked.

Squirrels.

The large grey and fox squirrels are the best for eating, and may be cooked in any way suitable for rabbits, but they are in greatest request for

Squirrel Pot-Pie.

Four squirrels, skinned and cleaned and cut in neat pieces. Flour them and fry brown in a little good dripping. Add one quart of boiling water, one large onion minced, quarter of a lemon sliced very thin, a teaspoon of salt, half a one of pepper, a small glass of sherry. Fry the minced onion brown in a spoon of butter and add to the water, etc. Cover all closely and stew for one hour. Make a delicate biscuit crust, and cut in rounds, laying them on top of the squirrel. Let them boil, covered closely, for fifteen minutes. Pile the squirrel in the center of a platter, arrange the dumplings around it, thicken the gravy with a spoonful of browned flour and pour over it, and serve hot.

Roast Venison.

Roast venison is best to be thoroughly larded, using half a pound of pork to a leg or saddle weighing eight to ten pounds. Cut the flanks from a saddle, and trim the haunch to good shape. Roast according to general directions, basting at the end of the first five minutes and every fifteen minutes after It is very nice to use claret instead of the dripping of the pan. An hour and a quarter will cook it very rare; for most people an hour and three-quarters will be none too much. Make a good gravy from the drippings in the pan, adding stock made from the bits trimmed away before roasting. Currant jelly is usually served with it, but those who have once tried barberry or wild plum jelly will never be contented with anything else.

Venison Steaks.

Venison steaks are prepared and served like beef steak, cutting them only about three-quarters of an inch thick, however, instead of an inch and one-half.

Slices of cold rare roast venison are extremely nice when reheated in a brown or curry sauce.

Deviled Venison.

Cut thick slices from rare-roasted venison, make slanting incisions and fill them with mixed mustard and salad oil. Brush the slices with melted butter and dredge them with flour. Broil over clear coals till a good brown and serve with butter.

Venison Cutlets.

Treat like cutlets of mutton and serve with only salt, pepper and butter, or they may be served with an olive sauce.

Venison Hash.

This is particularly nice for lunch. Chop the meat from a cold roast quite coarsely. Season with salt, pepper and cayenne and set aside till the gravy is hot. If there is not enough gravy left make a brown sauce for it, using stock from the bones and trimmings of the roast. Add the meat only one minute before serving. Arrange on hot buttered toast, garnish with quarters of lemon and serve with green grape marmalade (Verjus.)

Fillets of Venison.

Have as many small steaks as there are to be covers. Trim and flatten into good shape. Lard one side of each steak with tiny strips of pork and lay them in an earthen dish with salt, pepper, an onion, a minced carrot, two bay leaves, two sprigs thyme, one-half gill of salad oil, a gill of vinegar. Let them

GOLD MEDAL FLOUR—It's a Biscuit Flour—It's a Bread Flour.

steep in this mixture for six hours, turning often. Twenty minutes before serving drain and wipe them. Fry them to a handsome brown in a little very hot salt pork fat. It must be done quickly or they will become hard and tough. Arrange in a circle on a hot dish, the larded side uppermost alternately with heart-shaped croutons of puff paste. Serve with a brown gravy made from the marinate.

Venison Collops.

Have a venison steak cut one inch thick; divide it into portions about two inches square. Season with salt. Lay it in a chafing-dish in which two tablespoons of butter are boiling. Brown each side as quickly as possible; then add a dust of cayenne, two tablespoons Port wine, one tablespoon currant jelly. Epicures would say "Serve at once." Most people prefer to let it simmer till the inside shows only pink when cut.

Venison Pasty.

Use for this the neck, breast, flank and other portions that are not suitable for roasting. Wash with vinegar, rub with sugar and hang in a cool airy place as long as possible. Examine every day and wipe night and morning with a dry cloth. When it is to be used sponge with lukewarm water and dry with a cloth. Bone it and cut the meat free from skin into pieces two inches square. Parboil till the meat begins to be tender, then season well and lay in a baking dish of which the sides have been lined with good pastry. Arrange the pieces of fat and lean together, adding more seasoning if needed and dot well with bits of butter and enough stock to cover the bottom or the dish well. Cover with a thick crust and bake till the crust is thoroughly done.

While it is being baked put all the bones and trimmings in a covered stewpan with a strip of mace, pepper, salt and cold water to cover the pieces. Simmer till all the goodness is out of the bones and the water reduced one-half. Strain, cool and remove the fat. When the pie is done heat up the gravy with lemon juice and enough port wine to flavor well. Put a funnel through the hole in the crust and pour the gravy in. Good either hot or cold.

Pigeon or Game Pasties.

Lincolnshire and Oxfordshire. Bake these pasties in meat-pie moulds which open and allow the form to be taken out. Make a crust of one pound of flour, half a pound of butter, half a pint of water, the yolks of two eggs and a teaspoon of salt. Work all this into a firm paste and line the buttered mold, reserving part for the cover. For a two quart pie remove the large bones from four pigeons, season the inside of each one well with a mixture made of one large teaspoon of salt, half a one each of pepper, clove and mace. Spread on each a layer of good force meat and lay in the mould, filling in with more force meat and bits of veal and ham. Wet the edges and pinch together, ornamenting the top with a cluster of pastry leaves placed over the hole made in the center of the crust. Put in a moderate oven, after brushing it over with yolk of egg and bake four hours. In the meantime boil the bones and trimmings in one quart of water till reduced to half a pint, season it highly and pour it into the pie through the hole in the top. These pies are eaten cold, and often truffles or mushrooms are added. Small ones are made with one pigeon and forcemeat. Game of any sort can be used, enormous pies being often served.

Wild Turkey.

Wild turkey is without doubt the most delicious of all the large game birds and should be treated almost exactly like the domestic turkey; stuffing with chestnuts or a veal force meat, and roasting till tender.

Wild Goose.

Wild goose is selected and cooked like wild duck, remembering that it will bear much higher seasoning in both meat and sauce.

Ducks.

The list is almost endless, but they will all bear substantially the same treatment. A few epicures may like (or think they like) their canvas-back kept until upon the point of falling to pieces and served barely warmed through. But the majority of those who enjoy game like it hung and cooked upon the same principles that govern poultry and other meats. Dark meat of any kind should always be cooked rare, and red

juice, not blood, should follow every cut with the knife. The best authorities agree that game birds should be roasted plain, that is, without stuffing, but there is no reason why any of the force meats given for poultry should not be used for wild duck, grouse, prairie chickens, etc., if one prefers them so cooked. The following directions, however, will suppose that no stuffing is to be used except when specified.

Canvas-back Red-head and Mallard.

Should be carefully picked, singed, drawn and wiped with a wet cloth, trussed with the neck twisted around to close the opening in the breast, and the rump turned down to close the opening through which it was drawn. Season with salt and roast rare from eighteen to twenty-five minutes. Place them on a hot dish and put a tablespoon of cold water inside to prevent the coagulation of the juice. Send a glass of currant jelly or wild plum jelly to table with it, or serve with essence of celery.

Red-head, Teal or Widgeon Broiled.

After cleaning, split down the back and flatten a little with a heavy cleaver. Pare off the neck, pinions and ends of the legs, baste well with salad oil and broil rare over a quick fire. Dish on dry toast. Melt two tablespoons of maitre d'hotel butter with a little brown gravy, pour it over the ducks and serve with any sharply acid jelly, or orange, or olive sauce.

Teal.

Teal when roasted sometimes has a plain, dry stuffing as for chicken. Sometimes it is filled with a chopped onion and celery stuffing. Serve with slices of fried hominy and watercress or with green grape jelly.

Fillets of Widgeon.

Roast quick and rare four widgeons; slip off the fillets with a sharp knife, lay them on pieces of buttered toast and place in a dish sprinkled with parmesan cheese; place two fillets of anchovy on each fillet of duck, sprinkled with more cheese, grated bread crumbs, chopped parsley and melted butter. Bake in a very hot oven about two minutes. Squeeze the juice of two lemons over and serve hot.

Salmi of Wild Duck or Grouse.

See page 24, adding sherry or Burgundy to finish.

Grouse.

Pluck with care not to tear the skin. Draw and wipe, but do not wash. Cut off the head and truss like fowls. They are much improved by larding, but if that is not convenient fasten thin slices of salt pork all over the breast and thighs. Baste every five minutes. About ten minutes before taking up lay a thick slice of toast under each and serve on this. Fry coarse bread crumbs to a handsome brown in butter and strew them on the platter or over the bird. Send either bread sauce or brown gravy to table with them. The Scotch fashion is to put three tablespoons of butter into each bird instead of larding it. Parboil the liver and pound it to a paste with butter, salt and cayenne and use this to spread on the toast on which the birds are to be served.

Potted Grouse.

Prepare as if for roasting; season rather highly and put plenty of butter inside, pack them in a deep pie dish and dot butter on top. Pour over a small glass of claret for each pair of birds and tie two or three folds of buttered paper over. Bake in a moderate oven one hour. Pack them by twos in small pots, cover with clarified butter and set away to keep till wanted. They will keep for three or four weeks and are excellent for breakfast or lunch.

Fillets of Grouse.

If the birds are badly shot to pieces or much disfigured in dressing, it is sometimes better to serve them filleted. After they have been removed separate the large from the small fillet. Season them with salt and pepper and dip them in a mixture of one tablespoon chopped parsley, one tablespoon lemon juice and one-half cup melted butter. Let the butter cool on them, then dip in a beaten egg, then in bread crumbs and fry in deep hot fat. Six minutes is enough for the large,

GOLD MEDAL FLOUR—It's a Pastry Flour—It's a Cake Flour.

four minutes for the small fillets. Drain on brown paper while arranging a mound of vegetables a la jardinere in the center of a hot dish. Rest the fillets against the mound and serve with Bechamel sauce poured around.

Smothered Grouse.

Pick, singe, void and sponge as usual. Split in halves as for broiling; rub well with salt and chili and baste with Salad oil; brown delicately on a hot spider, then cover steam tight and set back to let it cook for half an hour or more in its own steam. Add one cup brown stock to the pan in which they were browned; let it simmer to a demi-glaze and pour over the birds. Serve with green peas.

Other Game Birds.

Partridge, pheasant, quail and prairie chicken may all be prepared according to the several directions for grouse.

Quail à la Cendre.

Dress as many quail as there are to be covers. Dry them and put the livers inside again with a little salt and butter. Wrap each in a thin bairde of salt pork, tucking a leaf of sage under each wing. Wrap again in well-buttered thick white paper and roast half an hour in hot wood ashes as you would potatoes. Remove the paper and serve with a sauce-bowl of gravy, reduced with sauterne.

Ptarmigan.

Ptarmigan are roasted, broiled, etc., like teal duck.

Snipe.

The best season for snipe is from August till the frosts come in the latter part of October or November. After cleaning as usual, remove the skin and eyes from the head, draw it down to the legs and skewer the bill through the lower part of the thighs. Pin a thin slice of larding pork around each bird and string them on a long skewer. Season with salt, pepper and a dust of cayenne, roll the uncovered ends in salad oil or melted butter and broil for four or five minutes on each side. Serve on hot toast that has been moistened with maitre d'hotel butter and send to table with watercress.

Roast Snipe.

Roasted snipe are prepared as above and roasted for ten minutes in a very hot oven. The hearts and livers are minced very fine with a teaspoon each of chives and butter. Salt and pepper to taste. Spread pieces of stale bread with this dusting, a few fresh crumbs on top and set in fierce oven for two minutes. Dress the snipe on these, garnish with watercress and serve the gravy that drips from the roasting birds in a small bowl.

Woodcock, reed birds, rice birds, doe birds, plover, rail, etc., are cooked in the same way.

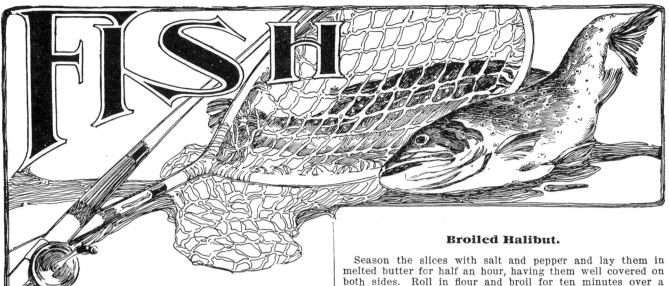

FISH

THIS is an important part of our food supply. It furnishes nitrogen, chiefly in the form of albumen and gelatine, not in so large proportion as meat, but sufficient to make a nourishing food. It is, for most people, easily digested, and it makes an agreeable change in the usual routine of roast, broil, fry and boil. Indeed most people in this land of plenty eat far too much meat; its cheapness brings it within the reach of all, and the stimulus which it yields is so agreeable that we easily fall into the habit of taking it morning, noon and night, while fish is forgotten or neglected. A notable advantage, especially in hot weather, is the short time required to cook fish; another is the great variety of kinds, through the long list of fresh and salt water, red or white fleshed, dry, salt or fresh. It is cheap too as compared with meat, and ought to be still more so, for very little time or expense is required to produce, only to bring it to the market. Those who do not live on the seaboard or near the great lakes may still get fish reasonably fresh with the refrigerator car service, while the remotest dweller on mountain or plain may have them dried, pickled, smoked or tinned.

Very large fish are as a rule better when boiled or steamed, medium sized ones should be baked or split and broiled and small ones fried. Fish with dark meat being richer in fat and higher flavored should not be fried.

A fish is in good condition when its gills are a bright clear red, its eyes full and the body firm and stiff. Before cooking they should be well washed in cold water, and kept in salt water for a short time, but they should not be allowed to stand in water for any length of time, and should be kept up on ice until wanted.

Scrape with a dull knife from the tail toward the head. If the fish is to be cooked at once, it will be much easier to remove the scales if the fish is rinsed in boiling water. Small fish to be served whole, have the entrails removed by opening under the gills and pressing out their contents with the thumb and finger. Larger fish are split half way down the belly and the inside scraped and washed with salt and water after it is empty. For broiling it is best to remove the back bone entirely. Lay the fish flat on a board and with a sharp knife lift the flesh from the bones on one side, then turn and repeat on the other side, being careful not to hack the meat. Split the head with the body and leave on both head and tail unless too large for your broiler.

Broiled Fish.

Large fish should be split through the back to broil and for most stoves the head and tail must be removed. Use a double wire broiler and grease it well before laying in the fish. Dust the fish with salt and pepper and broil the flesh side first till almost done, then cook on the skin side just long enough to brown it well. Small fish require from five to ten minutes. Thick ones from fifteen to twenty minutes. Turn a dripping-pan over the broiler and it will cook more evenly. There is no excuse for scorching the fish, as one can always scatter a few ashes over a hot fire. Spread generously with butter and set in the warming oven a minute to let it penetrate the fish. Garnish with parsley or water-cress after taking from the oven.

Broiled Halibut.

Season the slices with salt and pepper and lay them in melted butter for half an hour, having them well covered on both sides. Roll in flour and broil for ten minutes over a clear fire. Serve on a hot dish, garnishing with parsley and slices of lemon. The slices of halibut should be about an inch thick, and for every pound there should be three tablespoons of butter.—Miss Parloa.

Broiled Halibut with Maitre d'Hotel Butter.

Butter both sides of the broiler. Season the slices of halibut with salt and pepper, place them in the broiler and cook over clear coals for twelve minutes, turning frequently. Place on a hot dish and spread on them the sauce, using one spoonful to each pound. Garnish with parsley.—Miss Parloa.

Broiled Scrod.

Scrod is one of two famous Boston importations, the other is broiled lobster. Scrod is young cod, and one may weigh from two and a half to five pounds; the best weigh four or five pounds. When thoroughly broiled it should be rich, flaky and delicious. Rub the gridiron with fat pork and broil the inside of the fish first. Twenty minutes is usually sufficient to broil a fish of ordinary size. Serve with warmed butter, pepper and salt.

Brook Trout.

Wash well in salted water; score a little across the back, oil it thoroughly with Lucca oil and broil slowly. Dish on a very hot platter with Maitre d'Hotel sauce, or better still, with only fresh butter.

Spanish Mackerel.

Draw by the gills; wash, rubbing with coarse salt and trim off all the fins closely. Split down the back, remove the bone, wipe, dry and season with salt and pepper; brush over thoroughly with oil and broil slowly till well cooked. Slide on a hot dish and pour over melted butter or any suitable sauce.

Salmon Bone Broiled.

In filleting a fish to be broiled, leave a half inch or more of meat on the backbone. Rub well with salt and cayenne pepper and broil over a clear fire till well browned. This is delicious for breakfast.

Baked Fish.

The best fish to bake are white fish, bass, pickerel, pike, red-snapper, shad, etc., all having white flesh. They should be basted often and a stuffing also serves to keep the fish moist as well as to season it.

Clean, wipe and dry the fish. If the fish is slimy, like a muskalonge, scald with hot water before attempting to clean. Rub with salt inside and out, stuff and sew with soft darning cotton, leaving a large knot at one end that you can find after the fish is baked; cut gashes two inches apart on each side so they will alternate—not opposite each other—and skewer into the shape of an S or an O; put the fish on a sheet, rub all over with soft butter, salt and pepper and place narrow strips of salt pork in the gashes; dredge with flour (or not, just as you please), and put into a hot oven without water; baste with hot water and butter as soon as it begins to brown and repeat every ten minutes afterwards. Remove it carefully from the fish sheet and place it on a hot platter draw out the string, wipe off all the water or fat which runs from the fish and remove the pieces of pork. Pour Hollandaise sauce around (not over) the fish, or serve a drawn butter sauce flavored with lemon, and pile Saratoga chips lightly around the fish. Garnish the head of the fish with parsley or water-cresses. Fish that have been frozen are almost sure to break; if they do, fill the broken places with parsley.

Stuffing for Baked Fish.

For a fish weighing four to six pounds take one cup of cracker crumbs, one saltspoon of salt, one saltspoon of pepper, one teaspoon of chopped onions, one teaspoon of chopped parsley, one teaspoon of capers, one teaspoon of chopped pickles.

Bread Stuffing.

Soak half a pint of bread crumbs in cold water; when soft press out all the water. Fry one tablespoon minced onion in two of butter, add the bread, a teaspoon chopped parsley, pepper and salt. Let cook till nearly dry, cool for a few minutes and beat in one egg.

Meat Stuffing.

One-quarter pound tender lean veal, one-eighth pound fat bacon chopped fine. Add one-fourth the measure of white bread crumbs, soaked and pressed, season to taste with chopped onion, parsley or mushroom and plenty of salt and pepper.

Small Fish Baked.

Lay in a baking dish with chopped onion, mushrooms and parsley, rub the fish with salt, pepper, a bit of nutmeg and dot with butter. Pour in enough thin broth to cover bottom of dish, add the juice of one-half lemon and bake till the flesh parts easily from the bone.

Whitefish, Point Shirley Style.

Split the fish and lay open with the meat side up. Season with salt and pepper and place in a baking-pan on a bed of pork chips. Bake in a very quick oven, brushing it over once or twice with beaten egg while it is cooking.

Boiling.

Boiling, unless done au Court Bouillon is a most unsatisfactory way of preparing fish, as it renders the meat insipid and imparts a peculiar wooly texture not pleasant to the sensitive tongue. Steaming is better in every way and much easier for the unskilled cook. An hour before the fish is to be cooked cover it thickly inside and out with salt, let it stand till five minutes before time to put it over the fire. Wash off the salt, pin in a piece of coarse muslin and drop into fresh boiling water, or lay in a steamer over boiling water.

Allow about six minutes to the pound, and test by lifting the flesh from the bones in the thickest part. If it separates easily it is cooked enough and should be taken up at once, and well drained before serving. Lay on a folded napkin on the platter, as the juice will run. Underdone fish are dangerously unwholesome.

Steamed Fish.

Clean carefully, but without removing head or fins. Rub inside and out with salt, pepper and lemon juice, laying slices of onion inside, if liked. Lay on a buttered paper and steam till the flesh parts easily from the bones. Lay on a folded napkin, dress with lemon and parsley and send to the table with Poulette Sauce.

Salmon, Boiled Plain.

Have ready a fish-kettle with enough boiling soft water to cover the fish; wash off the water from the fish and let it come rather slowly to the boil again. Simmer very gently till done, allowing about fifteen minutes to each pound. Throw in one tablespoon salt just before it is done. Serve with plain drawn butter sauce.

Darne of Salmon.

Is the middle cut; there are but two or sometimes three from a large fish. Lay in a stew-pan on a bed of sliced carrots and onions, (two tablespoons each) parsley and pepper-corns; dredge lightly with salt and pour over one pint claret, one pint thin broth, dot with three tablespoons butter and cover with a buttered paper. Bring quickly to a boil and simmer very gently one hour. Drain and remove the skin, mask with a Remoulade sauce. The liquor in which the fish is cooked can be strained and used several times.

Pike à la Soyer.

Cleanse as usual, leaving head and tail on. Place on the drainer in a fish-kettle with (four pounds fish) one level tablespoon salt, six pepper-corns, two leaves parsley, one tablespoon butter, one carrot, one onion sliced fine, one cup white wine, one pint water. Cover with a thickly buttered paper, set to boil and simmer forty minutes. Meantime prepare a sauce; one ounce butter and one tablespoon flour worked together, add enough fish gravy to make a white sauce, thicken with one egg yolk beaten with an equal bulk of water and strain, finish with lemon-juice, one tablespoon Soyer's sauce and all the butter it will absorb. Slide the fish on a folded napkin; garnish with parsley and potato chips. Send sauce to table in a bowl.

Boiled Cod with Oysters.

(The only thing that can be urged against this most excellent fish is its homely name. Were it not so cheap, its good qualities would rapidly find favor at all gastronomic entertainments.) Put the fish into boiling water, slightly salted; add a few white cloves and peppers and a bit of lemon-peel; pull gently on the fins, and when they come out easily the fish is done. Arrange neatly on a folded napkin, garnish, and serve with oyster sauce. Take six oysters to every pound of fish and scald (blanch) them in a half-pint of hot oyster liquor; take out the oysters and add to the liquor salt, pepper, a bit of mace and an ounce of butter; whip into it a gill of milk containing a quarter of a tablespoon of flour. Simmer a moment, add the oysters, and send to table in a sauce-boat.

Stewed Fish with Oysters.

Cut the fish in pieces for serving, remove the skin and bone. Spread a thick coating of butter over the bottom of a stew-pan, lay in the fish, season each layer with salt and pepper, pour on boiling water to more than cover, add a tablespoon of lemon-juice or vinegar and simmer fifteen or twenty minutes, or till the fish is cooked but not broken. Add a tablespoon of flour cooked in a tablespoon of hot butter; mix it well with the boiling liquid without breaking the fish. Add a quart of oysters, or enough to equal the amount of fish. Simmer until the oysters are plump. Add more seasoning if needed and serve very hot.

Smelts as a Garnish.

Smelts are often fried plain or, rolled in meal or flour and then fried, they are used to garnish other kinds of fish. With baked fish they are arranged around the dish in any form that the taste of the cook may dictate; but in garnishing fish or any other dish, the arrangement should always be simple, so as not to make the matter of serving any harder than if the dish were not garnished. Smelts are also seasoned well with salt and pepper, dipped in butter and afterwards in flour and placed in a very hot oven for eight or ten minutes to get a handsome brown. They are then served as a garnish, or on slices of buttered toast. When smelts are used as a garnish, serve one on each plate with the other fish. If you wish to have the smelts in rings for a garnish, fasten the tails in the opening at the gills with little wooden toothpicks; then dip them in the beaten egg and in the crumbs, place in the frying-basket and plunge in the boiling fat. When they are cooked take out the skewers and they will retain their shape.

Panned Fish.

This is suitable for any small fish or such as can be cut in slices. Have the fish well cleaned, seasoned with pepper and salt and dried with a little flour, or better still, very fine bread crumbs. Have a large frying-pan smoking hot with as little grease in it as will keep the fish from sticking. Dripping from good, sweet salt pork is the best, but any sweet dripping will do. When the fat begins to smoke blue lay in the fish and brown quickly on both sides, then cover closely and set back to cook more slowly, from ten to twenty minutes, according to the size of the fish. Bass in all its varieties, black, green, striped, calico, Oswego and grass are suitable to cook in this way, so are butter-fish, cisco, perch, herring, trout, bream, etc.

Fried Fish.

Fish for frying should be thoroughly dried after cleaning, seasoned with salt and pepper rolled in fine bread crumbs, dipped in beaten egg, rolled in crumbs again, fried in deep fat like doughnuts; put in only a few pieces at a time to avoid chilling the fat and let it reheat before frying any more. The temperature should not fall below 375 degrees. From two to five minutes is sufficient for any but extra large pieces. The fish is done when it rises to the top of the fat. Drain perfectly dry on paper and arrange on a folded napkin. Fry the parsley that is to garnish the dish, taking care to have it crisp, without changing its color.

Fried Cod or Haddock.

Remove the skin (ask the fish-dealer to remove it for you), cut in square pieces and remove the backbone. Scrape all the fish from the bones, and press it with a knife into the larger pieces. Season with salt and pepper and roll in fine white corn meal. Fry several slices of salt pork, enough to have a cup of fat. Lay the fish in the hot fat, cook brown on each side. Drain on soft paper and serve hot. Spread with butter, and garnish with slices of lemon.

Any fish having firm white flesh can be prepared in this manner and it is a vast improvement on the old method of sending all the bones to the table.

Fried Halibut.

Let the slices lie in cold salted water, to which has been added one cup of vinegar, for ten or fifteen minutes. Dry them afterwards thoroughly by wiping with a towel, and dusting cracker meal on both sides. Lay them in smoking hot salad oil, and they will be well cooked and of a pale brown in three or five minutes, according to the thickness of the slices.

Halibut, Maitre d'Hôtel.

Cut three pounds of halibut into pieces three inches square. Dip each in beaten egg, then in sifted bread crumbs. Fry in boiling lard to a rich brown. Rub a heaping teaspoon of butter to a cream, add the juice of a lemon, a tablespoon of chopped parsley, salt and pepper, mix and spread on the hot squares of halibut, set in the oven just long enough to melt, then serve. Not difficult, and delicious for summer breakfasts.

Fried Roe.

Wash and wipe, fry twenty minutes in hot fat in a frying-pan, turning at the end of fifteen minutes. Season, dish on a hot platter and garnish with fried oysters or fried potatoes. Garnish with a great bunch of parsley at each end and a half lemon set in the parsely .

Fish au Gratin.

Six pounds of any fish with white meat, steamed, freed from skin and bone and broken into flakes. One pint of cream sauce No. 1 and one cup cracker crumbs moistened with melted butter; put a layer of fish in a gratin dish, season well with salt, pepper, cayenne and celery salt, and sprinkle with chopped parsley, pour over a part of the cream sauce, repeat till the fish is all used, reserving most of the sauce to pour over the top; sprinkle buttered crumbs over the top and bake in a rather quick oven until it boils up in the middle and the crumbs are brown.

A Norwegian Fish-Pudding.

Take a five or six pound haddock, clean, skin, fillet and scrape to a pulp with a knife. Pound in a mortar until it is smooth; add one teaspoon salt and one tablespoon butter, and continue working for ten minutes. Transfer to a large bowl and work in with a potato masher two egg yolks blended with one cup of cream, putting it in by spoonfuls; add another cup cream and one-half pepperspoon allspice. Beat furiously and when it is frothy put in a buttered mold and steam for three hours. If desired the top may be browned before serving, but it should be quickly done. Serve with cream and caper sauce. It should be fine, smooth and firm as blanc mange. Fresh cod may be used instead of haddock. Instead of making a pudding the paste may be formed into balls the size of an egg, steamed in a close mold or box and afterwards fried brown in butter and served either with or without sauce, or they may be poached in a curry sauce or made very small and dropped into a thick fish soup. In frying fish Norwegian cooks often dust the pieces with grated cheese and add a little to the sauce served with the fish.—Adopted from "The Epicure."

Dropped Fish Balls.

One-half pint of raw fish, one heaping pint of pared potatoes (let the potatoes be under medium size), two eggs, butter the size of an egg and a little pepper. Cut the fish in half-inch slices across the grain, and measure it lightly. Put the potatoes into the boiler and the fish on top of them; then cover with boiling water and boil half an hour, or until tender. Drain off all the water and mash fish and potatoes together until fine and light. Then add the butter and pepper and the egg, well beaten. Have a deep kettle of boiling fat. Dip a tablespoon in it and then take up a spoonful of the mixture, having care to get it into as good shape as possible. Drop into the boiling fat and cook until brown, which should be in two minutes. Be careful not to crowd the balls and also that the fat is hot enough. The spoon should be dipped in the fat every time you take a spoon of the mixture. These balls are delicious.

To Cook Salt Codfish.

The fish should be thoroughly washed and soaked in cold water twelve hours. Change the water and put on to cook. As soon as the water comes to a boiling point set back where it will keep hot, but will not boil. From four to six hours will cook a very dry, hard fish, and there are kinds which will cook in half an hour. If it has hung in a furnace heated cellar till hard it will never come tender. It is best not to buy more than will be used in a week or two. Like ham, bacon and meat in general, it should be hung, not laid on a shelf.

Fish Cutlets.

Cut the fish in squares or in slices across the back, removing all the bones. Dry, dip in batter and fry in deep boiling lard. It is quite necessary that the lard should boil. When a gold color, drain till dry on brown paper and serve on a folded napkin with a quantity of parsley or cresses and a thin slice of lemon. A tomato, mayonnaise or tartare sauce may be served with the cutlets.

Frog Legs.

The green marsh frogs furnish the best hams, as they are more tender and have less of the strong muddy flavor. They are generally liked fried. Pare off the feet and truss them by inserting the stump along the shin of the other leg. Put them with salt, pepper and lemon juice to steep for an hour, then drain and roll in flour, then in beaten egg and in fine bread crumbs. Fry to a light brown in hot fat. Serve with fried parsley.

Stewed Frogs à la Poulette.

Trim, truss and marinate as for frying. Cook in a sautoir with two tablespoons butter, salt, pepper and a speck of nutmeg. Cook briskly and long enough to evaporate the water without allowing them to burn. Add two glasses white wine, a pint of velvet sauce; cover and boil till quite tender. Skim, add a liaison of four egg yolks, one tablespoon chopped parsley, the juice of a lemon and two ounces of butter. Mix well and serve with fried croutons.

Frog Legs à la Marinière.

Saute three dozen legs with two ounces of butter, one-half pint chopped mushrooms, four shallots. As soon as well colored add a tablespoon flour, a little salt, pepper and cayenne, and moisten with a half pint of white wine and enough consomme to nearly cover. Boil ten minutes. Mix the yolks of four eggs with two tablespoons cream and stir it into the boiling mixture. Remove at once from the fire and serve.

❋ SHELL FISH. ❋

Oysters on the Half Shell.

Keep on ice till serving time. Have small soup-plates half full of fine ice and lay the oysters in the deep half of the shell on the plates as fast as opened. Salt, pepper and a cut lemon should be served at the side, and a true oyster lover will use no other sauce. Small oysters are preferred, and four to six are enough for each plate.

On a Block of Ice.

Have the dealer chip in a ten pound block of perfectly clear ice, a cavity large enough to hold as many oysters as are to be served. Clean and drain them as usual, but do not season, as

GOLD MEDAL FLOUR—It's a Biscuit Flour—It's a Bread Flour.

it causes the juice to flow. Fold a large towel and cover it with a napkin to lay in the platter; prop the block of ice carefully with wads of cloth, lest it should tilt in melting. Fill the platter full of parsley, so that the ice should seem to be resting on green leaves only, and garnish the edge of the oysters with fine small sprigs of parsley and celery tips.

To Prepare Oysters for Cooking.

Pour half a cup of cold water over one quart of oysters; take out each oyster separately with the fingers and free from any bits of shell. The oyster liquor may be strained and used in soup, stew or escallop if desired. Fried and broiled oysters are much better and cook easier if parboiled slightly before crumbing. Place one pint of cleaned oysters in a frying basket and dip it for one-half minute in a kettle of boiling water deep enough to cover them. Drain, dry on a soft towel and proceed as usual.

Broiled Oysters.

Take the largest oysters, scald, drain, dry on a towel and dip one by one into softened butter till well coated and then in seasoned flour. Lay them on a buttered broiler. Cook over clear coals until a light brown. Serve on slices of buttered thin toast. If done by a gas stove lay the toast under the broiler to catch the drip. Fine cracker crumbs may be used instead of flour. Oysters that have been breaded for frying are good broiled.

Broiled Oysters, No. 2.

Take two dozen large oysters, cleaned, drained and dried in a soft cloth. Sprinkle with salt and pepper. Melt two ounces butter in a large frying pan, lay in one dozen, as soon as the last one is in, turn the first one and when all have been turned begin taking out, laying them closely on a large buttered oyster broiler; cook to a light brown over moderate fire. While these are browning the other dozen may "set" in the butter. Have six rounds of toast on a hot platter; put four oysters on each, sprinkle on the butter in which they were stiffened and serve with lemon cut in eighths.

Deviled Oysters.

One heaping saltspoon dry mustard, one-half saltspoon each pepper and salt and the yolk of one egg. Mix to a smooth paste and coat six large oysters with it. Roll them in fine crumbs and broil over a clear fire. Arrange and serve.

Spindled Oysters.

For six persons take two dozen large oysters, two ounces bacon and six small slices of thin toast. Six slender steel skewers will be needed. Cut two dozen wafers of bacon. Fill the skewers with bacon and oyster alternately, running the skewer cross-grain through the muscle of the oyster and stringing the bits of bacon by one corner so that each slice may overlie an oyster; do not crowd them. Lay the skewers across a baking-pan and cook under gas or in a quick oven for five minutes. Do not take the oysters from the spindle but lay each one on a slice of toast, pour over them the drip from the pan and serve at once.

Griddled Oysters, No. 2.

Clean, scald and drain two dozen large oysters. Have a large griddle evenly heated; drop on it a bit of sweet butter as large as a pea and put an oyster on it; lay on one dozen and give them plenty of room; put on another bit of butter and turn the first oyster on to that; proceed in this way for all. Do not let them burn, but they must brown quickly. If too much butter is put on it will spread over the griddle and scorch and the smoke will ruin the oysters. Serve four to each person on a two-inch square of rye short cake.

Oysters Roasted in the Shell.

Wash the shells clean and wipe dry. Place in a baking-pan and put in a hot oven for about twenty minutes. Serve on hot dishes the moment they are taken from the oven. Though this is not an elegant dish, many people enjoy it, as the first and best flavor of the oysters is retained in this manner of cooking. The oysters can, instead, be opened into a hot dish and seasoned with butter, salt, pepper, and lemon juice. They should be served immediately.

Roasted Oysters on Toast.

Eighteen large oysters, or thirty small ones, one teaspoon of flour, one tablespoon of butter, salt, pepper, three slices of toast. Have the toast buttered and on a hot dish. Put the butter in a small sauce-pan, and when hot add the dry flour. Stir until smooth, but not brown; then add the cream, and let it boil up once. Put the oysters (in their own liquor) into a hot oven for three minutes; then add them to the cream. Season and pour over the toast. Garnish the dish with thin slices of lemon, and serve very hot. It is nice for lunch or tea.

For oyster soup see chapter on soup.—Miss Parloa.

Oyster Stew.

Boil one cup of strained oyster-liquor and half a cup of water. Skim, add half a teaspoon of salt, half a saltspoon of pepper, one tablespoon of butter, and one tablespoon rolled cracker. When it begins to boil add one quart of oysters. Boil one minute. Put half a cup of cream or cold milk into the tureen, and pour the boiling stew over it.

Fried Oysters.

Pick over, scald and drain dry two dozen oysters, sprinkle lightly with red pepper, roll in cracker dust, dip in egg mixed with an equal quantity of thick cream; drain and roll in fresh fine bread crumbs; press gently with a palette knife, fry half a dozen at a time in clear fat, hot enough to brown them in one minute. As soon as the first basket is lifted drop in a half dozen slices of raw potato to keep the fat from burning while the oysters are changed for another half dozen; proceed in this way until all are done. Put in a whole potato in slices and take from the fire at once; with a little care the same fat may be used repeatedly, when otherwise it would be blackened the first time. Drain the oysters on soft, brown paper. Have a tuft of parsley on a hot folded napkin; range the oysters quickly and serve instantly. It is better not to begin frying until they are wanted than to delay serving. Nothing can be less inviting than a cold fried oyster or one that has been kept hot for five minutes.

Philadelphia Fry.

Proceed as before, but after they are rolled in crumbs the first time, dip them in very cold, thick mayonnaise, then into egg, and roll in crumbs again before frying. This is difficult, but delicious.

Sautéed.

To one pint prepared oysters put one pint stale bread crumbs, season and add two eggs beaten lightly. Let them stand one hour, then lay by spoons in a frying-pan and brown quickly on both sides in hot butter. Serve at once.

Creamed Oysters.

Prepare cream sauce No. 1, taking one-half the quantity of butter, scald the oysters until the edges begin to curl, drain and drop them into the cream sauce; let all stand in bain marie for five minutes to season thorough. Serve in Swedish timbales or in pate shells. It is very nice used as a filling for short cake, croustade, or on toast.

Oyster Short-cake.

Boil one quart oysters in their own liquor. As soon as scum is set, remove it and drain and return one-half pint of liquor to sauce-pan. Mix scant tablespoon of flour with two heaping tablespoons of butter. When the mixture is light and creamy, gradually turn upon it the boiling liquor and season with salt and pepper. After boiling up once, stir in three tablespoons of cream, also the oysters. Stir over the fire one-half minute. Serve immediately. Have short-cake No. 1 ready to fill.

White Fricassee of Oysters.

Put one tablespoon of butter into a frying-pan, and, when hot put in one pint of oysters washed and drained. Cook till plump and drain again. Pour the oyster liquor into a cup and fill with cream. Cook one tablespoon flour with one of butter and blend with the cream and oyster liquor; add one-half saltspoon pepper and about one-half teaspoon salt. (Oysters vary in freshness.) Beat one egg very light and pour the oyster sauce upon it; add the oysters and return to the pan to be well heated, but it must not boil. Stir gently that it may cook evenly. Serve in crust or pastry shells if for lunch or dinner; for breakfast or tea, on toast.—Miss Amy Barnes.

GOLD MEDAL FLOUR—It's a Biscuit Flour—It's a Bread Flour.

Brown Fricassee of Oysters.

One quart oysters, two large tablespoons butter, one scant tablespoon flour, a dust of cayenne, salt according to the oysters, and one-half teaspoon chopped parsley, brown the butter and flour, add the oysters prepared as directed, stir carefully not to break them, and as soon as they curl serve on a hot platter with eight triangles of toast, one for each portion.

Panned Oysters.

Put one tablespoon butter in a covered saucepan with one-half saltspoon of white pepper, one teaspoon salt, and a few grains of cayenne, when hot add one pint of washed and drained oysters, cover closely and shake the pan to keep them from sticking; cook about three minutes or until plump. Serve on toasted bread or crackers.

Oysters Panned in the Shell.

Wash the shells and wipe dry. Place them in a pan with the round shell down. Set in a hot oven for three minutes; then take out and remove the upper shell. Put two or three oysters into one of the round shells, season with pepper and salt, add butter, the size of two peas, and cover with cracker or bread crumbs. Return to the oven and brown.

Scalloped Oysters.

One quart solid oysters, cleaned and drained, one-half cup butter, one cup grated bread crumbs, one cup coarse cracker crumbs. Rub the pudding-pan thickly with cold butter and sprinkle a layer of bread crumbs, moisten the rest of the bread with part of the butter melted and stir the rest of the butter into the cracker. Arrange oysters and bread in alternate layers, using cracker for the top. Season each with pepper and salt, allowing one and one-half teaspoon of salt, one saltspoon of pepper and about one tablespoon of lemon juice for the whole. Pour over one-quarter cup of the oyster liquor and set aside for an hour. If it looks very dry add another one-quarter cup of oyster juice before baking. Cook about twenty-five minutes in a quick oven. Wine, milk or Worcestershire sauce are sometimes used, but are no improvement. One suspects that the oysters are not fresh when disguised by such high seasoning.

To Pickle Oysters.

Two hundred large oysters, half a pint of vinegar, half a pint of white wine, four spoons of salt, six spoons of whole black pepper and a little mace. Strain the liquor, and add the above-named ingredients. Let boil up once, and pour, while boiling hot, over the oysters. After these have stood ten minutes, pour off the liquor, which, as well as the oysters, should then be allowed to get cold. Put into a jar and cover tight. The oysters will keep some time.—Miss Parloa.

Clams.

There is really no special season for these most nutritious fish, but custom decrees that they shall be served only during the season when oysters are forbidden. Most of the methods of serving oysters can be applied with slight modifications to the cooking of clams—but the following directions for cooking in a chafing dish are worth noting:

Select one dozen large Guilford clams, wash thoroughly and plunge them into boiling water for a moment. Drain and open them and use the round plump part only. Put in the chafing-dish a pat of butter and when quite hot add a dust of flour and cayenne to suit the taste; simmer the clams till they are slightly cooked, about four minutes and pour in one gill light sherry. Cover and simmer five minutes. Serve on hot toast.

Clam Broth.

Twenty-five clams washed and drained, steam till the shells open easily; save every drop of juice that comes with opening and add enough water to make one quart. With a pair of scissors trim off the soft part of the clam and reserve to serve with the broth. Chop the tough portion a little and simmer fifteen minutes in the broth. Strain and add pepper and salt if needed and serve in very small bouillon cups. Send the reserved portion to the table with melted butter and lemon juice poured over them.

Scallops.

The only edible part of the scallop is the central muscle by which the mollusk opens and closes its shell. Shippers sometimes add saleratus to the scallops to improve their appearance, but this is a detriment to the fish. In buying, avoid the large ones that are very white, choosing instead those of medium size and the natural creamy white color. They are most appetizing when fried. Rinse them in salt water, dry in a napkin and dredge with flour. Fry in very hot pork fat. Egg and crumbs are not needed.

Scallop Broth.

Wash and cut in small pieces one-half pint, add one-half pint each of milk and water, a dot of butter and salt to taste. Simmer twenty minutes, strain and serve.

Scallops in Shell.

Drain a pint of them and toss them with a tablespoon of butter in a sauce-pan letting them brown lightly for about ten minutes. Then take them out and chop them fine. Melt a spoonful of butter in a sauce-pan, add a small onion minced fine and brown it lightly. Then add a heaping teaspoon of flour and stir in slowly a cupful of the liquor drained from the scallops. Season with a teaspoon of salt, a pinch of cayenne, and a little white pepper. Mix with the chopped scallops four tablespoons of bread crumbs and the yolks of three eggs, and cook all together for three minutes. Then fill the shells, sprinkle fine bread crumbs over the top, and dot with bits of butter, and set them in a hot oven to brown for ten minutes. Serve them on a platter with a garnish of green.

Lobster.

Lobster, to be eatable, should be perfectly fresh. One of the tests of freshness is to draw back the tail, for if it springs into position again, it is safe to think the fish good. The time of boiling varies with the size of the lobster and in different localities. In Boston, Rockport, and other places on the Massachusetts coast the time is fifteen or twenty minutes for large lobsters and ten for small. The usual way is to plunge them into boiling water enough to cover, and to continue boiling them until they are done. Some people advocate putting the lobsters into cold water and letting this come to a boil gradually. They claim that the lobsters do not suffer so much. This may be so, but it seems as if death must instantly follow the plunge into boiling water. Cooking a lobster too long makes it tough and dry. When, on opening a lobster, you find the meat clinging to the shell and very much shrunken, you may be sure the time of boiling was too long. There are very few modes of cooking lobster in which it should be more than thoroughly heated, as much cooking toughens it and destroys the fine, delicate flavor of the meat.

Lobster Newburg.

Cut the meat of two small lobsters into small thin slices and cook them slowly in four tablespoons of butter for five minutes. Then add one teaspoon of salt, one saltspoon pepper, a speck of cayenne, two tablespoons each of brandy and sherry, a dash of mace and simmer five minutes longer. Beat well the yolks of four eggs, mix with them one cup cream and pour it over the cooking mixture. Stir constantly for one and one-half minutes, then serve quickly in a warm dish. Garnish with triangles of puff-paste.

Lobster Soufflé.

Dice a two-pound lobster, showing the red side as much as possible. Put bands of writing paper, about two inches high, around as many individual ramequin cases as you wish to serve. Beat three tablespoons of stiff mayonnaise, one cup aspic jelly, one-half cup tomato sauce together until they begin to look white, then stir in the pieces of lobster, adding a very little tarragon vinegar, or better still, one teaspoon chopped tarragon and put away to stiffen in a very cold place. When set take off the papers carefully, garnish with pounded coral or browned crumbs.

Stewed Lobster.

Take the meat of two medium lobsters cut in dice, season with salt as needed, one-half saltspoon cayenne, and one-half lemon. Make a white sauce, add another tablespoon butter and the seasoned lobster; let it simmer ten minutes and serve hot.

Soft Shell Crabs.

Lift each point of the back shell and remove the spongy substance found beneath it, taking care to scrape and cut away every bit. Turn the crab on its back and remove the semi-circular piece of dark, soft shell called the "apron" or "flap" and more of the same spongy substance lying under it. Wash in cold water and dry carefully on a towel. Season with salt and pepper, dip in egg and roll in crumbs. Fry about three minutes in very hot fat, putting in only two at a time, as they should be ice-cold when prepared. Serve with tartar sauce.

Thomas J. Murrey in his little book on "Oysters and Fish" says they should be only seasoned with flour, but most people enjoy the crisp and savory crumbs.

Broiled Crabs.

Prepare as above, but cook in a double broiler over clear, hot coals for eight to ten minutes. Serve with melted butter and lemon juice poured over.

Deviled Crabs.

One dozen fresh crabs boiled and pickled; quarter of a pound of fresh butter, one small teaspoon of mustard powder, cayenne pepper and salt to taste. Put the meat into a bowl and mix carefully with it an equal quantity of fine bread crumbs. Work the butter to a light cream, mix the mustard well with it, then stir in very carefully, a handful at a time, the mixed crabs and crumbs. Season to taste with cayenne pepper and salt, fill the crab shells with the mixture, sprinkle bread crumbs over the tops, put three small pieces of butter upon the top of each and brown them quickly in a hot oven. They will puff in baking and will be found very nice.

Shrimp.

Shrimps are caught in immense quantities along the seashore from early spring till late autumn, but are chiefly used for bait and for lunches for the parties of children who have unlimited time to pick them from their paper-like shells. If one can take the trouble to pick them out, they are really more delicate in fibre and finer flavored than their larger cousins from the Gulf. The dainty pink morsels make an appropriate and appetizing garnish for boiled fish of all kinds, and added to any sauce for fish they are more satisfactory than lobster, whose coarser flavor often dominates the fish it is intended to complement. As a curry, or deviled, or salad, or in a bisque, they are always good. They may be prepared by any of the formulas already given for lobsters or crabs, remembering that the seasoning should be less heavy as the flavor of shrimp is more delicate. Tinned shrimps should always be rinsed in lightly salted water and well drained and aired before they are used.

Crawfish.

Crawfish are inhabitants of fresh water streams. They have a striking resemblance to lobster in every respect, and are largely used by caterers for garnishes, sauces, salads, etc. Those that come from Milwaukee have a high reputation in New York and other markets.

Crawfish Bordelaise.

For this dish either crawfish or fresh boiled lobster may be used. Cut half a small carrot into bits and mince a small onion fine, cooking both for a few minutes in a spoon of butter. Add a glass of red wine and then a pound and a half of crawfish or lobster meat, and half a pint of cream sauce, with a very little nutmeg, a half teaspoon of salt and pinch of cayenne pepper. Boil up once and serve very hot.—"The Epicure."

Green Turtle.

These sea monsters vary in weight from 25 to 500 pounds and in price from 30 to 50 cents per pound. They are so immense that they can rarely be served in a private house unless, as sometimes happens, a fish-monger can secure a few pounds from some of his customers among the larger hotels. In that case simmer the meat for twenty minutes in a strong beef stock, well flavored with vegetables and herbs, allowing a pound of meat to each quart of stock. Put shells and fins into another quart of stock and simmer closely covered for an hour or till the bones will slip easily. Remove the bones and cut all the meat in small squares. Mix the whole and add more seasoning if needed. Thicken three quarts of soup with four ounces of flour browned in butter; boil half and skim well; add half a pint of sherry wine, a gill of port wine, let it boil up once and serve with slices of pared lemon on a plate.

Turtle Steaks.

Cut slices about one-half inch thick from what is known as the "veal," the thick, fleshy portion of green turtle. Rub them well with oil, lemon juice, pepper and a little salt, and let them stand for at least an hour before cooking. Broil like steak, cooking very thoroughly.

❋ ENTRÉES. ❋

"A maxim, too, that must not be forgot,
Whatever be your dinner, 'serve it hot,'
Your fine ragouts, like epigrams, require
A little salt—but to be full of fire."
—The Banquet.

Fillet of Beef.

When larded and roasted is frequently served as an entree with a mushroom, Spanish, financiere or Chateaubriand sauce poured around it.

Fillet of Beef à la Béarnaise.

Cut little steaks from the tenderloin, trim to uniform shape and size, season rather more than for a plain steak and serve with Bearnaise sauce. With a touch of onion flavor added and Chateaubriand sauce, they are called Fillet Steaks a la Chateaubriand.

Grenadins of Fillet of Beef.

Cut slices as above, lard each on one side with strips of pork not bigger than a match. Season with pepper, salt and soft butter and lay on a rack in a dripping pan. Roast in a fiercely hot oven about eight minutes, basting once with two tablespoons of madeira and three of glaze heated together. Range on a hot dish and serve with musroom sauce.

Little Fillets with Marrow.

Trim six small slices as before and saute for three minutes on each side. Range on a hot dish, pour a pint of hot madeira sauce over with six drops of tarragon vinegar and eighteen round slices of marrow. Let boil once only, then pour the sauce around the dish, dressing the marrow on top of the fillets and serve.

Tenderloin Pique a la Sevigne.

Trim, lard and season a small fillet (four pounds is enough) and roast in a very hot oven about ten minutes; then set it aside to cool and afterwards mask it with a chicken forcemeat; sprinkle with fresh bread crumbs, baste with three tablespoons of fresh butter and roast thirty-five minutes. Pour over one-half pint madeira sauce and garnish with tiny patties filled with puree of spinach highly seasoned with butter and meat glaze.

Fillet of Beef à la Chipolata.

No. 1. Take three pounds of fillet; the roll cut from a small rib roast will do; rub with flour and brown all over on a brisk fire in two ounces of butter; drain off the fat, add one pint beef broth, one-half pint white wine, one ladle tomato sauce, one tablespoon each carrot and onion, some parsley and one clove of garlic. Cover and simmer for two hours or until tender; drain and trim the beef, strain the gravy, take off the fat and reduce with one-half pint Spanish sauce. Serve with Chipolata garnish.

No. 2. Take the same amount of beef, trim and tie into shape and steep it for two days in the following marinade: One and a half cups claret, one-half cup water, one tablespoon each chopped carrot and onion, twenty peppercorns and a bit of bay leaf with one teaspoon salt. Boil for five minutes, cool and pour over the beef. Drain dry, brown lightly and braise as usual, forty-five minutes if it is the true fillet, two hours or more if the rib roll is used. The braising stock may be used to make a brown sauce for it. Serve with Chipolata garnish.

Beef Steak, Bohemian Sauce.

Trim, season and broil rather rare two porterhouse steaks; put on hot platter with a little butter and serve Bohemian sauce in a sauce bowl.

GOLD MEDAL FLOUR—It's a Pastry Flour—It's a Cake Flour.

Beef steak seasoned, buttered, sprinkled with bread crumbs, mixed with chopped olives and parsley, then broiled rare and dressed with a maitre d'hotel sauce, mingled with two tablespoons beef extract is called a la Soyer.

Peel two cucumbers, cut in four lengthwise; if overgrown trim off the seeds, cut in slices; there should be one pint of this and one pint sliced onion; blanch, drain and simmer till tender, salt and cayenne to taste; drain and simmer till tender in one pint good gravy and pour over broiled steak when ready to serve; or pour the raw vegetables over a pan broiled steak as soon as browned and simmered. This is an excellent dish for every day use. If the vegetables, after being drained, are fried a light brown in butter (a dust of sugar will help) then simmered till tender in one pint poivrade sauce and served around two good porterhouse steaks it will be an elegant entree known as Steak a la Rosny.

South Carolina Rice Pie.

Take one quart cooked meat, if beef or veal allow one-fourth fat, if mutton trim away all fat and substitute two ounces butter; the meat should be cut in shavings and lightly measured. Chop fine one medium sized onion, one large Irish potato, one ounce fat salt pork, blanch, drain and fry gently to a light yellow, put in the meat, with salt and pepper and sweet herbs or spice to taste, let it heat through, stirring carefully, If the meat was tough in the first case, add one pint stock and simmer till tender. Meanwhile cook one cup good rice, season it with one cup stewed and strained tomato, one ounce of butter and two hard boiled eggs sliced; turn the hashed meat into a buttered baking dish, place the rice over; handle carefully so as not to crush the rice or break up the egg; cut two more eggs in four slices each and press them into the rice on top; put a bean of butter on each and set in a moderate oven for one-half hour. Fold a napkin around the dish if not a regular baker. Do not let the meat get two dry; if it did not need the simmering add cold gravy, freed from all fat, and water enough to moisten well. "A thorough southern dish, and a great favorite in our rice country." Make chicken and rice pie in the same way, but leave out the potato; one cup rich milk may be substituted for the tomato.—Mrs. W. P. Ferguson, Columbia, S. C.

Baltimore Meat Pie.

Pare three pints of potatoes, cover them with hot water and let them simmer till done. Mash them and add a little cream and salt. Spread in the style of a paste in a dish. Place on thin slices of underdone meat, either beef, mutton, veal or chicken. Lay them in thickly, pour over them some gravy and a wineglass of catsup. Then cover thick with mashed potatoes and bake moderately about fifty minutes.

Hash.

"A good hash has merits unknown to the meat in its first cooking. Mind you, I say a good one. It must be scientifically constructed. There must be a spark of genius, but no recklessness, which is counted to go with genius. On the contrary, true genius is half patience, and that counts in hash or anything else." The best meat for a hash is from a stew or the sides of a la mode beef, though corned beef is excellent and any scraps of cold meat can be used if care be taken to first simmer till tender all tough bits. Mince evenly, but not too fine, allowing about one-quarter fat meat; add an equal bulk of chopped potatoes, freshly cooked are best, but cold ones will do, if more convenient. Mix well together and season with salt and pepper. Put into a sautoir one cup of stock or beef or veal gravy, adding enough hot water to make one cup for each pint of meat and potato, one teaspoon butter and the meat as soon as the stock boils. Stir only enough to mix well, then let stand on a moderately hot fire till a brown crust has formed on the bottom. Fold over and turn out like on omelet and serve hot. A tepid hash is an abomination.

Baked Hash.

Prepare like either of the proceeding, adding more seasoning, onion, catsup, Worcestershire sauce, etc., and one raw egg. Pack into a well-buttered baking dish and bake till hot through and well browned. Serve in the dish in which it was baked.

Hash, (English Style.)

Chop the meat rather coarsely, season with onion and catsup, salt and pepper, and simmer a few minutes in a good gravy. Serve on toast or in a deep platter garnishing with toast.

Mutton and Veal Hashes.

Mutton and veal hashes are much improved by the addition of curry, a few oysters or even a half cup of oyster liquor left from some other dish.

Beef Rolls or Olives.

One and a half pounds of round steak cut in quarter inch slices, trim into six pieces about three by four inches; pound carefully not to make holes in them. Cover with the following stuffing: Chop two ounces beef suet very fine and then the trimmings of the beef; there should be about eight ounces or one cup when done; mix well with one cup or four ounces stale bread grated, season with one teaspoon salt, one saltspoon pepper, a speck of nutmeg and two or three grates of lemon peel; moisten with one beaten egg; it may need a spoonful or so of stock. Divide this into six portions, form them into rolls and wrap each one in a piece of the beef; make a half dozen turns of soft twine or cotton yarn about the rolls, but do not draw it tight enough to mark them; do not trouble to tie, just twist the ends of the string with wet fingers. Place these rolls in a stewpan with one pint brown sauce and stew gently for three quarters of an hour. Serve with potato baked or fried in rather thick slices.

Westphalia Loaves.

Mix a quarter of a pound of grated ham with one pound of mashed potatoes well beaten until quite light and add a little butter, cream and two eggs, but do not get too moist. Make into small ball and fry with a little lard to a light brown. Serve with a brown, thick gravy. Garnish with fried parsley. Use more ham if liked or add chopped parsley.

Ragout of Mutton.

Slice thinly two small turnips and two onions, brown them with two ounces butter or dripping, dredging in a tablespoon of flour, a teaspoon of sugar, and stirring to get an even brown. Cut six small, but rather thick chops from a cooked loin or neck or cut square pieces from a breast of mutton that has been boiled, and pressed till cold; roll them in seasoned flour, skim out the vegetables and brown the meat in the same fat. Return the vegetables to the pan, add one-half pint stock, season to taste, cover closely and simmer till tender. This ragout may be made with green peas in season; and they should always be used for a Lamb Ragout.

Veal Cutlets Broiled.

Cut six even cutlets from a loin, flatten lightly, season with pepper, salt and one tablespoon salad oil, turning them several times. Broil over a rather slow fire eight minutes for each side, place on a hot dish, spread with one ounce maitre d'hotel butter and serve at once.

Veal cutlets pan broiled and served with some kind of sauce or garnish are known in French cookery as escallops. Small even slices should be cut not more than one-half inch thick; they may be treated according to taste and the other parts of the bill of fare; lightly seasoned and served with a plain sauce or some bland puree like spinach, chicory or cucumber, or highly seasoned with onion, shallot, garlic, (not all at once) or mushrooms. Finish with Spanish or some high flavored brown sauce and garnish with stuffed peppers or something piquant.

Veal Cutlets.

Take two pounds veal; the small pieces cut from the rump bone are good where slices cannot be had. Chop several times in a machine; add two ounces of raw, finely chopped veal suet; season with one tablespoon salt, one-half teaspoon pepper and one-fourth teaspoon nutmeg; mix well with one-half cup good cream, one chopped shallot and two raw eggs. Shape in six pieces like chops. Sprinkle with bread crumbs and saute in two ounces butter, four minutes on each side; the fire should be quick enough to brown well, but not scorch. Serve with a gill of any kind of sauce.

Veal Cutlets à la Milanaise.

Trim six veal cutlets, season with salt and pepper, dip in egg diluted with one tablespoon salad oil, drain, dip in grated Parmesan and then in fresh bread crumbs; flatten them and saute in six ounces of clarified butter; giving them five minutes on each side. Serve with one cup garnishing Milanaise.

GOLD MEDAL FLOUR—It's a Biscuit Flour—It's a Bread Flour.

Veal Cutlets with Tomato Sauce.

Prepare six cutlets as in the preceding, but leave out the cheese; cook as described and serve with a half pint tomato sauce.

Calf's Brain Breaded.

Separate the two lobes of the brain with a knife, soak them in cold water with a little salt for one hour; then pour away water and cover with hot water, clean and skin them; then dip in egg and milk, roll in bread crumbs and fry slowly in deep hot fat, serve tomato sauce with it.

Brains au Beurre Noir.

Prepare as for frying. Lay them on a hot platter and pour over them black butter sauce.

Ragout of Mutton.

Cut into dice one pint of cold roasted or boiled mutton. If boiled, dredge it with flour and brown in butter. Add one small onion cut fine, half a cup of diced turnip, and one-fourth cup of grated carrot. Salt and pepper to taste. Cover with boiling water and simmer till tender. Put the bones and trimming into another stew-pan, cover with cold water, and let them simmer until the liquor is reduced one-half. Then strain it and add the liquor to the ragout. When the meat is tender remove the fat, add a tablespoon of brown roux and a teaspoon of Worcestershire sauce or two tablespoons of wine or half a cup of currant jelly.

Cutlets Served in Paper.

Fold and cut half-sheets of thick white paper, about the size of commercial note, so that when opened they will be heart-shaped. Dip them in melted butter, and set aside. After trimming all the fat from lamb or mutton chops, season them with pepper and salt. Put three tablespoons of butter in the frying pan, and when melted, lay in the chops, and cook slowly for fifteen minutes. Add one teaspoon of finely chopped parsley, one teaspoon of lemon juice, and one tablespoon of Halford sauce. Dredge with one heaping tablespoon of flour, and cook quickly five minutes longer. Take up the cutlets, and add to the sauce in the pan four tablespoons of glaze and four of water. Stir until the glaze is melted and set away to cool. When the sauce is cold, spread it on the cutlets. Now place these, one by one, on one side of the papers, having the bones turned toward the center. Fold the papers and carefully turn in the edges. When all are done, place them in a pan, and put into a moderate oven for ten minutes; then place them in a circle, and fill the center of the dish with thin fried, or French fried potatoes. Serve very hot. The quantities given above are for six cutlets.

Chicken à la Hollandaise.

Take out the breast bone of a large young fowl, and fill up the space with a force meat of pate de foie gras. Make a batter as for fritters, and when the fowl has roasted half its time pour the batter over, and, when dry, pour more, until it is thickly coated and of a nice brown color. Cut up into neat pieces as for fricasee, and serve with melted butter and lemon quarters.

Chicken Shortcake.

Make one-half the rule for biscuit, but add one large teaspoon butter or mix with creamy milk, roll to fit an eight-inch cake tin and bake in a quick oven. When done pull, not cut, it apart, and fill with one pint of creamed chicken.

Stuffed Chicken Legs, (Cantons de Rouen.)

After removing the fillets from chickens, the legs may be removed, leaving on them as much of the skin as is convenient. Bone them carefully and fill them with any good stuffing or force meat that is convenient. Wrap the extra breadth of skin about them and, after trimming into compact shape, sew the edges with a few deep stitches. Lay them on a bed of vegetables in a small braising pan to cook for one hour. Meantime simmer the bones and trimmings of the carcasses to make one and one-half pints stock. Finish the chickens with the cover removed to brown them well, and send to the table with a white Bechamel sauce.

Chaud-Froid of Chicken.

Cut a cold boiled chicken carefully into smooth joints, removing the skin. Mask each piece with Bechamel sauce, and arrange in a ring on a bed of lettuce. Mix sliced cucumber, diced beets and chopped tarragon with the heart-leaves of the lettuce and heap them in the center. Served either with or without mayonnaise.

Chicken Terrapin.

Put in the chafing dish the dark meat of cold chicken, turkey or grouse, cut in small slices with half a pint of cream or stock; and when it comes to a boil stir in the following mixture: Two tablespoons of butter rubbed into a smooth paste with a tablespoon of flour and the yolk of three eggs, a teaspoon of dry mustard, a little cayenne pepper and salt, all mixed with a little cream or stock. Let it simmer a few minutes (not boil) and when ready to serve stir in a large wine glass of Madeira.

Chicken Souffle.

One pint of cold chicken chopped very fine. Melt one tablespoon of butter in a saucepan, and add one of flour and gradually a pint of hot milk or stock, stirring to smooth cream. Add to this a teaspoon of chopped parsley, half a cup of bread crumbs, a pinch of pepper, a teaspoon of salt, and the chicken, with the yolks of four eggs. Last, add the whites beaten to a stiff froth and turn into a buttered dish. Bake in a quick oven half an hour and serve at once, English Fashion.

Coquilles of Chicken, English Fashion.

Fill six table-shells with a thick salpicon of chicken, mushrooms and truffles. Sprinkle the tops with grated bread crumbs well buttered. Bake a handsome brown in a very hot oven. Serve on a folded napkin.

Chicken Curry.

Prepare a three or four pound chicken as for fricasee. Brown lightly in butter and move to a stewpan. Fry a thinly-sliced onion in the same pan and make a roux with one large tablespoon flour, one teaspoon sugar and one teaspoon curry powder (more if it is liked very hot) and one pint water. Add one-half cup chopped sour apple, salt and pepper; pour this sauce over the chicken and simmer till tender. Add one cup of hot cream. Serve with boiled rice.

Indian Curry.

Proceed as before and when the chicken is browned mix dry one teaspoon sugar and one of curry powder, one tablespoon flour and sift over the meat. Stir till the meat is thoroughly coated with the powder; add two or three sour apples cut in eighths but neither cored nor peeled, the juice of one-half lemon and two ounces of raisins; add one pint hot water, cover closely and simmer one hour. More curry and lemon may be used if liked, salt to taste.—Mrs. James Farish, Yarmouth, N. S.

White Curry.

One fowl, one onion, two tablespoons butter, two tablespoons curry powder, two ounces sweet almonds, one-half teaspoon salt, one-half tablespoon lemon juice, one-half pint water. Cook the sliced onion in the butter till soft, but do not brown. Then add the fowl cut in very small pieces ready for serving. Sprinkle over the curry powder (most people would prefer half the quantity) and stir over the fire for five minutes. Blanch the almonds and pound them with a little water. When they are quite fine, put the remainder of the water to them and grind them well. Strain this through a strong strainer cloth, pressing hard. It should come through looking like milk. Add this with salt to the fowl and simmer till tender; put in lemon juice just before serving. This is excellent made with veal. Grated cocoanut may take the place of almonds. Serve with rice. An "Ida" grater is better than pounding for almonds, cocoanut, etc.

Kebob Curry.

Two pounds of tender beef, mutton or veal cut in slices one-half inch thick and again one and a half inches square. Peel and slice thickly two or three onions and three pieces of green ginger; arrange them on skewers, putting two bits of meat, one of ginger, one of onion, and repeat until all are used; brown in two ounces of butter, sprinkle over two tablespoons curry powder (one is enough for most people), cook gently and stir for five minutes, add one-half pint stock, salt if needed. Simmer, closely covered, until tender, from forty-five minutes to an hour and a half; just before serving add the juice of one-half lemon. This is quite enough for ten people.

GOLD MEDAL FLOUR—It's a Biscuit Flour—It's a Bread Flour.

Dry Curry.

Proceed as before, leaving out the skewers, the ginger and half the lemon; brown the meat in the butter and sprinkle the curry; stir over the fire five minutes, add two tablespoons chopped gherkins, one dessert spoon Chutney; cover closely and cook on a very slow fire; add lemon just before serving. Serve with soft boiled rice; one cup rice to three of water, with one teaspoon salt; boil fast for fifteen minutes, then set back and watch it; lift often with fork to make sure it does not stick. Pile high in the middle of platter and serve the curry as a border. Fish may be treated in the same way, but needs less cooking—fifteen to thirty minutes, according to the kind of fish.

Rissoles.

Any kind of delicate meat or fish may be used for them with puff paste. Careme recommends Brioche paste. It may well be used, if at hand, or a little might be laid aside for this purpose when it is baked, but it takes so long to prepare that it is hardly worth while unless one requires a great number of Rissoles. When oysters are used they must first be treated as directed. With care in preparation and skill in flavoring a great variety of appetizing dainties may be made from remnants of pastry and game. For an illustration take Chicken Rissoles.

One cup cold chicken (roast is best) cut in small dice, two tablespoons minced fresh mushrooms; make a white sauce with one-half cup milk, one tablespoon flour and two of butter; season with a scant teaspoon of salt and one pepperspoon pepper, add the meat and mushroom, let it cook one minute and set away to cool. Take one-fourth the rule for puff paste, roll one-eighth inch thick and cut twelve four-inch rounds; divide the chicken paste into twelve parts and put one on each round of paste a little to one side of the center, flatten it slightly, wet the rim of paste a little way from the edge with white of egg, fold the paste over and press together along the line of egg; add another egg to the one from which you used and beat well with one tablespoon of milk. Dip the rissoles in this, taking care not to handle the edges nor to separate the cover. Drain them and cook in hot fat till a golden brown. The fat should be hotter than for doughnuts, but not so hot as for croquettes. Dry on paper and serve at once. This gives two for each of the six persons at lunch, but in a course dinner one is quite enough for each person.

Aspic Jelly, No. 1.

To three pints of clear, strong consomme, add two ounces gelatine previously soaked in cold water, and the whites and shells of two eggs; whisk well together, adding more seasoning if needed, one gill of light wine, or enough lemon juice or tarragon vinegar to make a pleasant flavor. Clear according to directions for clear soup. It is then ready for use in any way required.

Aspic Jelly, No. 2, (without Meat.)

1½ pints of water.	1 each carrot, turnip, onion.
1 gill sherry.	1 stalk celery.
2 tablespoons each malt, tarragon and chilli vinegar.	½ teaspoon salt.
The rind of ½ a lemon.	Chervil and parsley if at hand.
The white and shell of 2 eggs.	2 ounces gelatine.
	10 peppercorns or 1 inch chilli.

Put all the ingredients except the gelatine and egg into a stew pan and set over the fire till it boils, then pour it on the gelatine previously soaked in cold water, whisk in the egg and let come to the boil again; draw to one side of the fire to stand a few minutes and filter through a thick napkin. It is ready for use as soon as set.

Aspic of Chicken.

Once the rule for Aspic Jelly:

1 hard boiled egg.	1½ pints very tender cold chicken.
3 slices cooked beet.	
3 slices cooked carrot.	½ pint cooked vegetables.
½ pint mayonnaise.	½ bunch celery.

Rinse a three pint border mold in cold water and pour in semi-congealed aspic to cover the bottom, set in ice water to become firm, and as soon as they can be laid on without sinking garnish with the prepared vegetables, bits of parsley and egg. Pour on more of the jelly and harden again. Sprinkle the bits of meat well with salt, pepper and celery salt and mix with them some of the cool aspic. As soon as the vegetables are firmly bedded in their layer fill the mold nearly to the top with the chicken, pour over more liquid aspic to make sure

that every crevice is filled, and set to cool again. Lastly fill brim full with aspic and set on ice for ten or twelve hours. At serving time turn on a flat dish, fill the center with the celery finely shaved and dressed with the mayonnaise. Garnish with delicate celery leaves, laying a star of red beet on each.

Slice of Salmon Baked.

Take two slices about three-quarters of a pound each. Rub both sides with this seasoning: Two tablespoons oil, one tablespoon chopped gherkin, one shallot chopped, one anchovy chopped and rubbed smooth, one teaspoon chopped parsley, half a teaspoon of chilli vinegar. Wrap the salmon in a buttered paper and bake about half an hour. Serve in the paper.

Whitebait.

Is in season during the early months of summer, and is so exceedingly delicate that it must be eaten as soon as possible after catching. Drain them carefully on a soft cloth and shake.

Patty Cases.

Make either of the rules for puff paste; it will be sufficient for twelve large cases or twenty small ones. To shape the paste for patties, roll to about one-third inch in thickness and stamp out with two and one-quarter inch cutter twice as many pieces as you wish shells. Cut centers from one-half of them, leaving the rim about one-half inch wide. Lay these rings on the whole rounds pressing them down that they may stick together. In very cold weather it may be needful to wet the top of the large rounds near the edge to make sure that the rings shall not slip. To make very deep shells roll the paste about one-eighth inch thick and lay on two rings, or even three, but they are troublesome to make as they are apt to slip to one side.

Patty shells should rise in ten minutes and then take about twenty minutes longer to bake through and brown. There will usually be a little soft dough in the center that should be picked out with a fork, taking great care not to break through the side or bottom crust. Large Vol au Vent cases should be rolled to the thickness of an inch and one-half, and they may be round or oval in shape. Mark out an inner line about two and one-half inches from the edge, and with a thin, sharp knife-blade (dipped first in hot water) cut from two-thirds to three-quarters of the way through the paste. These are much more difficult to bake than the smaller shells and there is always much uncooked paste to be removed from the center. The filling gives the name to the dish, and their names are legion. Any kind of delicate meat, game, fish or shell-fish may be used in connection with velvet, poulette, Bechamel, or supreme sauce, or for game and other dark meats a brown mushroom, Bordelaise or Spanish sauce at pleasure.

	FORCEMEAT.	

Is used so extensively in the making of garnishes and entrees that a cook should understand the principles of its preparation thoroughly. The finest kinds of forcemeat consist of raw meat or fish, a panada, either butter, suet or veal udder, eggs and seasoning. To prepare the meat or fish, take only clear muscle, chop it fine and pound it to a paste. Then force it through a wire puree sieve with a wooden vegetable masher. Panada is bread and cream or milk or stock, in the proportions of half as much bread as liquid, cooked until a smooth paste is formed. If beef suet is used it must be freed from strings, chopped fine, and pounded with the bread. It is often rubbed through the puree sieve. This is not as delicate as butter or calf's udder and is not so often used, but is somewhat cheaper. Forcemeat made in this way is called "godiveau." To prepare calf's udder, tie it in a piece of netting and boil it in the stock pot for one hour; cool, chop and pound, and rub through a puree sieve; then pound again in a mortar with the other ingredients to make sure that it is perfectly blended. Always try the mixture after it is finished. To do this drop a small ball of it into a saucepan of boiling water and set back where it will not boil, and cook for about ten minutes. If it cuts smooth and fine all through and is tender, it is all right; if it should be tough add two tablespoons cream, or better still, of veloute sauce, to each half-pint of forcemeat. If, on the contrary, the forcemeat ball is too soft and shrinks when cut add one well-beaten egg to every pint of the forcemeat. The greatest care must be used in cooking. If the water with which the article is surrounded is kept at the boiling point or a little below it, the forcemeat will be smooth, fine-grained and delicate. Whenever it is spongy and tough, be sure that the water has been allowed to get too hot.

Forcemeats are used for quenelles, boudins, border-molds, balls to serve in soup, raised pies, timbales, etc.

Condensed from "Kitchen Companion," by Miss Parloa.

Chicken Forcemeat, (White.)

One-half pint meat.	3 tablespoons butter.
One-half pint cream.	One-half tablespoon salt.
1 gill fine stale bread crumbs.	One-half blade of mace.
Three egg whites.	One-eighth teaspoon pepper.

Prepare the meat according to general directions, by chopping, pounding and rubbing through a sieve. It will probably take all the (raw) white meat from two large fowls. Boil the bread, mace and cream together until they are cooked to a smooth paste, about ten minutes; then take from the fire, add the butter, then the meat and seasoning. Beat whites of eggs well and add the last thing. Test to make the texture right and set away to keep cool until wanted.

Chicken Forcemeat, (Dark.)

Make as above, using only dark meat and yolks of eggs instead of whites.

Game Forcemeat.

Game forcemeat is most savory and is prepared like veal forcemeat. It is used to make balls to serve with game soups, to garnish salmis, etc.

Oyster Forcemeat.

One generous pint of stale bread crumbs, one dozen large oysters, three tablespoons butter, one teaspoon salt, one-eighth teaspoon of cayenne, one teaspoon minced parsley, a grate of nutmeg, one tablespoon lemon juice, three tablespoons oyster juice and yolks of two raw eggs. Chop the oysters very fine, add the rolled ingredients, pound to a smooth paste and rub through a sieve. Taste to verify seasoning.

Liver Forcemeat.

Large livers from very fat geese are the best for this. They can be obtained in the winter weighing from one and one-half to three pounds each. The small size will yield enough for one and one-half pints forcemeat. Cook the livers in enough boiling salted water to cover, letting them simmer very gently for about twenty-five minutes. If they do not break apart easily at the end of that time cook until they do. Then pound and rub through a sieve. Cook one-half pint bread crumbs in one pint rich chicken stock, season to taste with salt, pepper and mace. Use 8 ounces butter and three eggs well beaten. Otherwise proceed as in chicken forcemeat. Chicken, turkey or veal liver can be substituted.

Fish Forcemeat.

Any kind of white-meated fish may be used. Use only the solid meat and scrape, pound and sift as in other forcemeats. Prepare a large half-pint and proceed as for chicken, adding a little cayenne and a suspicion of onion or garlic.

Veal Forcemeat.

Make like chicken, using one-half pint veal pulp, instead of chicken.

Chicken Quenelles.

The breast of one chicken, half a calf's brains, half a gill of cream, one heaping tablespoon stale bread crumbs, one ounce butter, one egg, one teaspoon salt, one-half teaspoon lemon juice, a grate of nutmeg, a dust of pepper. Clean the brains, tie in a piece of cheese cloth to boil for half an hour in well seasoned stock. Cool and pound smooth and add to the chicken meat also chopped and pounded and rub both through a sieve. Cook the bread and cream together until a smooth panada, add the meat and seasoning and lastly the egg and set away to cool. When ready to use dip two teaspoons in hot water, fill one spoon with the mixture and slip from one to the other until it is smooth and shaped like the bowl of the spoon. Slide on a butter pan. When all are formed cover with boiling stock and let stand where it will just not boil for ten minutes, keeping the dish covered with buttered paper.

Quenelles of Grouse.

Quenelles of grouse or other game prepared by taking equal weight of meat and stale bread crumbs are good served as a ragout. To one-half pound of meat allow a saltspoon each of chopped parsley and lemon rind, half an anchovy, boned, salt, pepper, nutmeg and half a clove of garlic. Beat and pound all thoroughly together, mix in one ounce clarified butter and enough beaten egg to make the consistency of soft paste. Cool and shape in balls the size of a small egg. These may be poached and served with a Bechamel sauce or fried and served with any good brown or mushroom sauce.

Lobster Quenelles.

Pound to a paste the meat, tom-alley and coral of a hen lobster; mix with it two tablespoons fine bread crumbs and three ounces of butter. Season with salt, pepper, a speck of nutmeg and cayenne and moisten with yolks of two eggs and white of one. If it proves too soft when tested add the other white; if too stiff work in a little water. These may be cooled after poaching and then fried in butter and served as a garnish for steamed fish or in soup. They are delicious poached and served cold with sauce Tartare. If served hot the sauce should be Poulette or some other bland sauce.

Timbale of Macaroni.

Cook one-half pound of macaroni in salted water until it is soft enough to divide easily. Rinse in cold water and cut into short lengths. If time is no consideration it is very pretty to cut in pieces one-third of an inch long and line the mold, setting the open ends against the bottom and sides which have been thickly spread with cold butter. Spread over the macaroni a good forcemeat suitable to whatever is to constitute the filling of the timbale, and afterwards fill up the mold with a highly seasoned mince of game, poultry, fish, oysters or sweetbreads. Moisten with a good sauce, cover with more of the forcemeat, pinching the edges well together lest the gravy should break through in cooking. Set the mold into a pan of hot water or into a steamer, and cook gently until hot through, but the water must not boil.

Chicken Timbales.

The quantity given will fill one quart mold or twelve small ones.

Forcemeat. Cook half a pint of fine stale bread crumbs in pint of cream with a blade of mace for twenty minutes. Remove the mace and with a wooden spoon mash to a smooth firm paste. Add six tablespoons butter, one tablespoon salt, one-eighth teaspoon white pepper, one pint of raw, lean veal scraped to a pulp and pounded smooth. Beat all well together and lastly add the whites of four eggs beaten stiff. Set away to cool.

Filling. Make a white sauce with one and one-half cups cream, one level teaspoon butter, one round tablespoon flour, one teaspoon salt, one-half saltspoon pepper. Mix with it three cups diced chicken, adding mushrooms truffles, etc., to your taste.

Butter the molds with cold butter, dot the bottom and ides with tiny dice of truffle and line them with the forcemeat (take care to have the lining thin at the bottom of the mold and thick around the top, or it will break when turned out) Fill the molds to within three-quarters inch of the top with the creamed preparation, and cover with the forcemeat. Place the molds in a deep pan and pour in hot water to fill almost to the top of the molds. Cover with a buttered paper and cook in a slow oven for twenty-five minutes. The water must not boil. Serve with Bechamel yellow sauce.

Swedish Timbales.

For the shells, use one cup of flour, one cup of milk, one egg, half a teaspoon of salt. Put all the ingredients together in a mixing bowl and with a Dover beater beat to a smooth batter. Put the timbale iron in a kettle of hot fat for about twenty minutes. Take the bowl of batter in the left hand and hold it near the kettle of hot fat; with the right hand lift the iron from the fat, wipe it on soft paper, dip it into the batter, coating the iron to within three-quarters of an inch from the top, allow the batter to dry and then dip it in the hot fat, holding the iron a little sidewise until it is in the fat, then turn perpendicularly and cook until the batter is a delicate brown, or about one minute. Take the iron out the same way it is put in, being very careful not to drop the timbale into the fat, drain the grease off and lay it on a paper to drain. Wipe the drops of grease from the iron with a soft paper every

GOLD MEDAL FLOUR—It's a Pastry Flour—It's a Cake Flour.

time it is used. These may be filled with creamed oysters, creamed fish, green peas, macaroni, oranges, bananas, apricots, strawberries, etc., or mixed fruits, with whipped cream over the top. They may be made at any time and put in a dry warm place, where they will keep indefinitely.

Croquettes.

Care and practice are required for successfully making croquettes. The meat must be chopped fine, all the ingredients be thoroughly mixed, and the whole mixture be as moist as possible without spoiling the shape. Croquettes are formed in pear, round and cylindrical shapes. The last is the best, as the croquettes can be moister in this form than in the two others.

They are well adapted for using any remnants of meat, fish, or game; for making a savory dish from the more insipid vegetables, and a sweet croquette is often accepted as an entrement or for a lunch dish.

To shape: Take about a tablespoon of the mixture, and with both hands shape in the form of a cylinder. Handle as gently and carefully as if a tender bird. Pressure forces the particles apart, and thus breaks the form. Have a board sprinkled lightly with bread or cracker crumbs, and roll the croquettes very gently on this. Remember that the slightest pressure will break them. Let them lie on the board until all are finished, when, if any have become flattened, roll them into shape again. Cover a board thickly with crumbs. Have beaten eggs, slightly salted, in a deep plate. Hold a croquette in the left hand, and with a brush, or the right hand, cover it with the egg; then roll in the crumbs. Continue this until they are all crumbed. Place a few at a time in boiling fat. Cook till a rich brown. It will take about a minute and a half. Take up and lay on brown paper in a warm pan.—Miss Parloa.

Chicken Croquettes, No. 1.   (with Brains.)

2 chickens boiled.
1 pair veal brains boiled.
1 cup suet chopped.
1 lemon, juice and one-half
   the rind grated.
¼ nutmeg grated.
Salt to taste.
2 sprigs parsley.
1 teaspoon onion juice.
Cayenne and white pepper.
1 pint cream sauce, No. 1.

Chop or grind the meat as fine as possible, (use Enterprise Chopper), mix meat and seasoning well together and add as much thick cream sauce as you dare; it should be very soft as it stiffens in cooling. Set on the ice until thoroughly cold and firm enough to shape easily. Roll in cork shape about one by two and one-half inches. Roll in sifted bread crumbs, then in beaten egg diluted with two tablespoons milk, then in crumbs again, and set away till needed. Fry as in the preceding recipes.

N. B. The croquettes should be as soft as thick cream in the inside when served, with a delicate gold-colored covering outside.—Condensed from "Good Living" by Madame S. V. B. Brugiere.

Chicken Croquettes, No. 2.

Cook and chop the chicken as in No. 1. Weigh the meat after chopping and to each pound allow one teaspoon each salt and celery salt, one saltspoon white pepper, one-fourth salt-spoon cayenne. Make a sauce with one quart of the stock in which the chicken was cooked (reduced till very rich and strong) four ounces of butter, four ounces of flour. Cook a long time, beating long and hard till perfectly smooth, add the meat and stir only enough to mix thoroughly. Taste for seasoning and put away till ice cold. Shape, egg and crumb, and fry as in No. 1.

Chicken Croquettes, No. 3.

The meat of one-half a chicken, one-half a can of mushrooms or six large oysters chopped together very fine. Cook a tablespoon of flour in a heaping tablespoon of butter and moisten with a gill of chicken stock, one-half gill of cream and one-half gill of mushroom or oyster liquor. Stir vigorously till the sauce is thick, smooth and glossy. Add the chopped chicken and mushroom with one saltspoon salt, one-half salts-spoon pepper and one teaspoon lemon juice. Stir well and if it seems too thick add carefully a very little more stock. It

should be a sort of thick mush and very creamy. Cool, shape and fry as before.—Condensed from Catherine Owen.

Royal Croquettes.

Half a boiled chicken, one large sweetbread, cleaned and kept in hot water for five minutes; a calf's brains, washed and boiled five minutes; one teaspoon of chopped parsley, salt, pepper, half a pint of cream, one egg, quarter of a cup of butter, one tablespoon of corn starch. Chop the chicken, brains and sweetbread very fine, and add the egg well beaten. Mix the corn starch with a little of the cream. Have the remainder of the cream boiling, and stir in the mixed corn starch; then add the butter and the chopped mixture and stir over the fire until it bubbles. Set aside to cool. Shape and roll twice in egg and in cracker crumbs. Put in the frying-basket and plunge into boiling fat. They should brown in less than a minute.—Mrs. Furness, of Philadelphia.

Croquettes of Calf's Brain.

For these croquettes boil the brains in well salted water, with a small sweetbread also, and when cold mince together. Add half a can of mushrooms, chopped fine, half a cup of warm boiled rice, and one cup of thick, highly seasoned cream sauce. Cool, and then shape in small rolls. Roll in fine crumbs; egg and crumb again and fry in boiling lard or oil. Drain and serve.

Sweetbread Croquettes.

1 pint cooked and chopped
   sweetbreads.
4 tablespoons chopped mushrooms.
2 tablespoons butter.
1 tablespoon flour.
1 tablespoon scant salt.
½ pint cream.
One-third teaspoon white pepper.
A dust of nutmeg.
½ teaspoon chopped parsley.
2 eggs.
1 tablespoon lemon juice.

Mix the salt, pepper, nutmeg, parsley and lemon juice with the mushrooms and sweetbreads, and set aside to season while making a white sauce according to direction with the butter, flour and cream. Add the meat to the sauce and lastly the beaten egg. Set away to cool or stiffen for two or three hours, then shape, crumb and fry according to directions above. Serve with mushroom, white sauce or Bechamel yellow sauce.—Miss Parloa, "Kitchen Companion."

Veal and Sweetbreads.

Veal and sweetbreads could be prepared like chicken.

Game.

Game like chicken croquettes No. 3.

Beef Croquettes.

Prepare by any of the recipes for chicken or veal croquettes if liked soft, but the following is recommended: Mince fine, but not to make it pasty; add an equal bulk of hot, boiled rice, cooked much softer than it is usually served for a vegetable; season highly with salt, pepper, cayenne and onion juice, and set to cool. If it is too stiff, work in a little stock or gravy.

Fish Croquettes.

One pint cold boiled fish, free from skin and bone and minced fine, one pint hot mashed potato, one tablespoon butter, one-half cup hot milk, one egg well beaten; pepper and salt and a little chopped parsley. Mix thoroughly and let cool. When cold make into balls, dip into a beaten egg, roll in bread crumbs and fry in hot lard. Very nice made of shad roes. For salmon croquettes use (if made of canned salmon) bread crumbs instead of potatoes, and an extra egg, omiting the milk.

Shad Roe Croquettes.

One pint of cream, four tablespoons of corn-starch, four shad roe, four tablespoons of butter, one teaspoon of salt, the juice of two lemons, a slight grating of nutmeg, and a speck of cayenne. Boil the roe fifteen minutes in salted water; then drain and mash. Put the cream on to boil. Mix the but-

GOLD MEDAL FLOUR—It's a Biscuit Flour—It's a Bread Flour.

ter and corn-starch together, and stir into the boiling cream. Add the seasoning and roe. Boil up once, and set away to cool. Shape and fry as directed.—Miss Lizzie Devereaux.

Lobster Croquettes.

Two cups of finely chopped lobster, one saltspoon salt, one of mustard, a trifle cayenne. Mix with one cup cream sauce. Make into croquettes, roll in beaten egg and bread crumbs and fry in hot lard.

Oyster Croquettes.

Half pint raw oysters, half a pint of cooked veal, one heaping tablespoon of butter melted, three tablespoons of cracker crumbs, the yolks of two eggs, one tablespoon of onion juice. Chop the oysters and veal very fine. Soak the crackers in oyster liquor, and then mix all the ingredients, and shape. Dip in egg and roll in bread crumbs, and fry as usual.

Croquettes of Macaroni.

Boil one-quarter pound macaroni in salted water until very tender. Drain and toss in a sauce-pan with one heaped tablespoon butter, one-half ounce Parmesan cheese, one-quarter ounce cooked tongue cut in fine dice. Spread on a well-buttered platter, about one inch thick, cover with a buttered paper, press it well down and set away to cool. Divide with a back of a knife into six parts, roll each one in grated cheese, then in beaten egg and in crumbs. Fry in very hot fat till well browned. Drain and serve on a folded napkin.

Rice Croquettes.

Take a teacup of hot well-boiled rice and a teaspoon each of sugar and butter, with half that quantity of salt, and to them add one beaten egg and sufficient milk to bring all to the consistency of a firm paste after thoroughly beating and mixing. Shape into oval balls and dip in beaten egg, followed by a dipping in bread crumbs. Fry in sweet, hot lard, turning with care, and when done to a nice brown put into a heated colander. These are very nice to have a well-plumped raisin or candied cherry pushed into the center before frying and served with maple sauce.

Savory Rice Croquettes.

Prepare the rice as for pilaff and then add two eggs well beaten to each pint. Shape in oval balls, egg and crumb and fry as usual.

Potato Croquettes.

Season hot mashed potatoes with salt and pepper, a little nutmeg; beat to a cream, with a tablespoon of melted butter and ten drops of onion juice to every pint of potatoes; add one beaten egg yolk and some chopped parsley. Roll into small balls, dip in egg and milk, coat them with bread crumbs and fry in hot cottolene.

 FRITTERS.

Fritter Batter, No. 1.

For Swedish Timbales and wherever an article is to receive a very thin coating.
One egg, one cup milk, one cup flour, one teaspoon salt. Put all together in a deep, narrow bowl and beat with Dover egg-beater until smooth, but not frothed. When used for a sweet dish add a teaspoon of sugar.

Fritter Batter, No. 2.

Two eggs beaten smooth, one cup flour, one-half teaspoon baking powder, one-half cup milk, one teaspoon salt, one tablespoon salad oil. Beat with Dover beater till smooth and glossy.

Bell Fritters.

One pint water—put on stove to boil. Butter the size of an egg. Salt. While boiling stir in one pint flour. When flour is well mixed, take it off to prevent burning; then add four eggs, stirring in one at a time. When well stirred, drop by tablespoonfuls into boiling fat.

Chicken Fritters.

One cup chicken stock, one heaping tablespoon flour, one tablespoon butter, one-half teaspoon salt, one-half teaspoon celery salt, one cup cold chicken. Mix the flour smoothly in the hot butter, add the boiling stock gradually and when smooth, the seasoning, let simmer till quite thick. Pour half the sauce onto a small platter, and spread the chopped chicken evenly over the top. Then cover with the remainder of the sauce. Place on ice and when cold and hard cut into inch by two inch pieces. Dip them quickly into fritter batter No. 2 and fry in deep, hot fat.—Mrs. D. A. Lincoln.

Oyster Fritters.

Pick over and parboil the oysters; drain them well and use their liquor in place of milk to mix the batter No. 2, adding more salt and pepper, if needed.

Fish Fritters.

Boil one pound of the fish and mince it very fine, boil and mash two Irish potatoes; chop half a small onion; mix with two raw eggs, a little salt and pepper and two tablespoons of Worcestershire sauce. Make into balls, roll in cracker dust and fry in boiling fat.

Vegetable Fritters.

Vegetables of any kind should be thoroughly cooked, drained and either chopped fine or cut in pieces convenient for serving before being added to the batter, using No. 1 or No. 2.

Banana Fritters,

Mash fine three bananas. Mix one cup flour, one teaspoon baking powder, two tablespoons sugar and one-half saltspoon of salt. Beat one egg light, add one third cup milk; add to dry ingredients. Add the bananas and one teaspoon lemon juice. Drop by spoonfuls into deep fat and fry. Drain on paper and sprinkle with powdered sugar.

Pineapple Fritters.

Cut the fruit in thin, small sections, sprinkle with sugar and let lie for an hour or two, then drain as dry as possible. Roll each piece in sifted bread crumbs before dipping in batter No. 1. Drain on soft paper, sift powdered sugar over and serve with pineapple sauce.

Pineapple Sauce.

Make a heavy syrup with one cup sugar and one-half cup water, boiling it till it will spin. Then strain and add whatever juice has drained from the cut pineapple (syrup, if canned pine is used) and enough white wine to make one pint in all. Do not boil after adding the wine. Finish with a teaspoon of Santa Cruz, or Old Jamaica, or Curacoa.

Apple Fritters.

Take soft tart apples, peel and remove the pips; cut in round, thin slices; plunge them in a mixture of brandy, lemon juice and sugar until they have acquired the taste; drain and dust them with flour. Pour in the chafing dish three tablespoons of butter; when very hot fry the slices on both sides, sprinkle powdered sugar and cinnamon, and serve very hot.

Preserved Plums.

Plums or other preserves should be cut in small pieces and masked with batter. A spoonful of marmalade, or any firm jelly makes a delicious mouthful treated in the same way.

 MEAT AND FISH SAUCES.

The foundation for almost all our common sauces is what the French call a "roux," made as follows:
Melt one ounce (one rounded tablespoon) butter in a sauce-pan and let it boil till it begins to show a pale straw color. Add two tablespoons flour and stir briskly. Add one pint hot milk, or milk and water, or water, pouring slowly and beating hard, add one-half teaspoon salt, one-half saltspoon white pepper and a speck of cayenne and you have a plain white sauce or drawn butter to which a good tablespoon of butter should be added just long enough to melt before going to the table.
When the butter and flour are allowed to become brown it

GOLD MEDAL FLOUR—It's a Biscuit Flour—It's a Bread Flour.

is called a brown roux and is used for soups, stews, gravies, etc.

Cream Sauce, No. 1.

One pint cream, one-half teaspoon salt, one tablespoon butter, one-half saltspoon pepper, two tablespoons flour, a speck cayenne. Make as above.

Cream Sauce, No. 2.

Make as in No. 1, using only one scant tablespoon flour and thickening with a liaison of two egg yolks beaten with an equal bulk of cold water, return to the sauce pan until the sauce thickens like soft custard.

Cream Sauce, No. 3, for Croquettes, Etc.

Allow two tablespoons butter and four heaping tablespoons flour to a pint of cream, seasoning as before. This sauce is much improved by using half or more rich chicken stock in place of all cream.

Velvet.

Melt one ounce butter, add two tablespoons flour and stir well. Moisten with one quart good veal or chicken stock, add a bouquet, one-half cup of mushroom liquor, six whole peppers, one saltspoon salt, a suspicion of nutmeg. Boil for 20 minutes, stirring continuously, then remove to side of fire, skim well, and simmer very slowly one hour. Strain and add more salt and pepper if needed.

Béchamel.

One pint white stock, two tablespoons butter, four tablespoons flour, six mushrooms or the liquor from a half can, one cup cream, one and a half tablespoons lemon juice. Cook the butter and flour well together with salt and pepper if the stock is not already well seasoned. Add the stock as in plain white sauce, then the mushrooms, washed, peeled and cut small; let the sauce simmer twenty minutes with the lid half on. Skim off the butter as it rises. Strain through a fine sieve, pressing hard: add the cream and lemon juice and let boil about three minutes. Pour out and stir often while cooling. If this is to be used to mask a chaud-froid it will need one tablespoon gelatine.

Yellow Béchamel.

Add a blade of mace and one tablespoon minced carrot to the seasoning of the above, and finish with liaison of four egg yolks and one-half cup cream.

Hollandaise.

Cook one tablespoon flour in one teaspoon butter, add slowly one cup strong veal or chicken stock; when it boils remove from the fire and whisk in the yolks of four eggs beaten smooth with one tablespoon lemon juice and a few drops of onion juice, if liked; return to the fire and stir constantly till it begins to stiffen, then drop in one tablespoon butter and beat with whisk till dissolved and smooth. It sounds like more trouble than it is, and it is the best sauce made for boiled fish, cauliflower, asparagus, etc.

Russian.

To three-quarters pint of good Bechamel, add one teaspoon powdered sugar, a scant saltspoon red pepper, three tablespoons grated horse-radish and two of thick cream, (or a liaison of four egg yolks and one-half pint of light wine).

Oyster.

One-half pint Bechamel, one-half teaspoon essence anchovy, ten drops simla sauce. Pour boiling hot over one-half pint oysters that have been parboiled and drained.

Aurora.

To one pint Bechamel, add four ounces butter, a little cream, a pinch of red pepper, one tablespoon taragon vinegar, and enough lobster butter to make a fine reddish tint. Mix well without boiling.

Lobster, for Boiled Fish.

One small lobster, four tablespoons of butter, two of flour one-fifth of a teaspoon of cayenne, two tablespoons of lemon juice, one pint of boiling water. Cut the meat into dice. Pound the "coral" with one tablespoon of the butter. Rub the flour and the remainder of the butter to a smooth paste. Add the water, pounded "coral," and butter, and the seasoning. Simmer five minutes, and then strain on the lobster. Boil up once and serve.

Asparagus.

Make a white roux as usual, taking one pint of the water in which the asparagus was boiled; when smooth, add one tablespoon lemon juice and a half teaspoon sugar.

Soubise.

Peel, slice and parboil four Spanish onions. Drain and put them into a stew pan with two ounces butter, salt, pepper and a dust of nutmeg, if liked. Simmer gently till they can be rubbed through a fine puree sieve. Add one pint Bechamel or velvet sauce and simmer for fifteen minutes.

Meat Glaze.

Is excellent for giving color and flavor to soups and adds the finishing touch to many of the best sauces. Place eight quarts of well flavored consomme over a brisk fire and reduce it to one-half pint. Put it in a stone jar, cool and cover it, and it will keep in the ice-box for a long time.

Bouquet.

Four stalks parsley, one stalk celery, one bay leaf, two cloves, one-half blade mace, one sprig thyme. Wrap all in the parsley and tie closely at each end. Dry for winter use.

Mirepoix.

Cook two ounces of fat, butter, dripping or chicken oil, two small carrots, one onion, one sprig of thyme, one bay leaf, six peppercorns, three cloves and an ounce of lean ham; bits of the outside of roast meat may be added. Chop the vegetables and cook gently for fifteen minutes, add two stalks of celery and one-half parsley root; simmer covered for ten minutes more, add pepper and spice if desired and store for use.

Tomato.

One quart tomatoes, two tablespoons mirepoix, one teaspoon sugar. Simmer till reduced one-half; sift, add either white or brown roux and let simmer five minutes longer, add more seasoning if needed.

Spanish.

Two carrots, one onion, cut fine and cooked in two ounces bacon or sausage dripping, add one sprig thyme, one bay leaf, six peppers, one clove, two sprigs parsley, four stalks celery (or one-quarter teaspoon celery seed). Two quarts weak white broth of any kind and simmer gently for one-half hour; then add strong brown stock enough to make four quarts. Boil slowly three hours, adding any bones of roast veal or ham at hand. Cook four ounces of flour in two ounces dripping till a light brown; moisten with the boiling stock and skim well before straining. Strain and put away for constant use. It will keep a month in cold weather and is the foundation for numberless fancy sauces.

Madeira.

Add one gill mushroom liquor to one pint of Spanish sauce, also one gill Madeira wine and one-half teaspoon pepper. Cook gently for thirty minutes, taking off the fat; the sauce will be left rather thin. Strain and use as needed.

Colbert.

Heat one-half pint Madeira sauce, add to it gradually one ounce fresh butter and two tablespoons meat-glaze. Mix well together without boiling; then squeeze in the juice of one-half a large lemon (about two tablespoons) and add one teaspoon chopped parsley when serving.

Poivrade.

Fry in one-half ounce butter one-half an onion and one-half carrot. Cut small a sprig of thyme, one bay leaf, six peppercorns, three cloves, four parsley leaves and one-half ounce raw ham. Cook for five minutes, then moisten with two tablespoons tarragon vinegar and one pint Spanish sauce. Boil twenty minutes then remove grease and strain.

GOLD MEDAL FLOUR—It's a Biscuit Flour—It's a Bread Flour.

Olive Brown.

Stone two dozen olives. Cook for one-half hour in water enough to cover. Drain and put into a stew-pan with one pint plain brown sauce. Set over steam for five minutes. This is especially nice for roast duck.

Orange, for Duck or other Game.

Reduce the glaze in the pan with a pint of broth; strain and remove the fat, reduce to one-half with one-half pint of thick brown gravy and the juice of two oranges. Strain, add the rind of one orange very finely shred.

Bordelaise.

One-half pint sauterne, one tablespoon chopped shallots, three-fourths pint Spanish sauce, scant saltspoon red pepper, about two inches cooked marrow. Boil the shallots in the wine until reduced one-half, add the Spanish sauce and cook fifteen minutes, then add the red pepper and the marrow cut in eighteen round slices; they should be less than one-eighth inch thick. Boil up once and serve.

Robert.

Slice one-half an onion and fry with one-half ounce butter and one teaspoon sugar until a golden color; moisten with one-half pint Spanish sauce and simmer ten minutes; then add one teaspoon mustard flour, rubbed smooth with four tablespoons white wine vinegar (diluted). Stir till it comes to the boil, strain and serve.

Perigueux.

Put into a sauce-pan three ladles of browned and thickened stock, two glasses of chablis (any white wine will do), and half a saltspoon of pepper; reduce one-quarter by boiling, and add half a pint of truffles chopped finely.

Indian.

One sliced onion, one ounce raw, lean ham, one sprig thyme, twelve whole peppercorns, one ounce butter, one teaspoon curry, one-half cup cream, two egg yolks, two tablespoons lemon juice, one pint velvet sauce. Cook the onion, ham, thyme and peppers with the butter until well reduced, but do not brown. Rub the curry into the velvet sauce, add to the cooked onion and boil ten minutes, then strain into the beaten egg yolks which have been diluted with the cream. Stir over ot water until it begins to thicken, then add the lemon and serve at once.

Piquante.

Put into a sauce-pan an ounce of butter, a chopped onion and carrot and simmer till brown. Add one gill vinegar, a bay leaf, one clove, six peppercorns, six allspice berries, one-half blade of mace, one and one-half pints Spanish sauce; simmer twenty minutes. Finish with two tablespoons each chopped gherkins, capers, olives and parsley.

Champagne.

Cream together one tablespoon of butter and one of flour; stir into it slowly a half pint of hard-boiling brown soup stock; let it boil up once or twice to cook the flour, remove it from the fire, and stir in half a pint of champagne.

Cucumber.

Grate two good-sized cucumbers and allow all the water to drain away. Add one-half teaspoon salt, a dash of cayenne, a tablespoon of vinegar and serve at once.—S. T. Rorer.

Horse-Radish.

One cup of freshly grated horse-radish, one teaspoon salt, one-half saltspoon pepper, one teaspoon made mustard, one teaspoon sugar, two tablespoons vinegar, well mixed together. Add one cup cream whipped very stiff.

Mint.

Pick the leaves from the stems, wash them thoroughly and wring them dry in a cloth. Chop as fine as sawdust, sprinkle powdered sugar over thickly, and barely cover with vinegar. If any vinegar rests in the bottom of the sauce-boat, it should be thrown away. Make this sauce half an hour before using, and set it on the ice.

Mustard.

Two teaspoons of dry mustard, one teaspoon of flour, one teaspoon of salt, one teaspoon of soft butter, one teaspoon of sugar, two tablespoons of vinegar.

Mix in the order given, in a granite sauce-pan; add one-half cup of boiling water and stir on the fire till it thickens and is smooth. Add two tablespoons finely chopped pickles and serve it cold.

Mayonnaise.

Three raw egg yolks in a cold bowl with one level teaspoon dry mustard, one teaspoon salt, one-half saltspoon cayenne, one half saltspoon sugar. Beat with a Dover beater till smooth, then add drop by drop one pint of salad oil, beating constantly. If it thickens too much to stir well, put in lemon juice alternately with oil until two tablespoons have been used, then add vinegar until as sour as wished, but avoid thinning too much.

Oil should be kept in the dark and at a moderate temperature, sixty-five degrees to seventy-five degrees, to secure the best results.

The sauce should have a jelly like, not pasty consistency and should keep its shape when drawn up to a point; the harder it is beaten the sooner this result is attained. If a thick, smooth sauce is required for masking, a part of the sauce can be taken out before all the lemon juice or vinegar is added, and the remainder finished to suit the taste or the dish being made. If the sauce is to be served separately and a spongy texture is desired, all the acid dilution may be put in when half the oil has been used; beat furiously until foamy and finish with the rest of the oil. The size of the eggs and the sharpness of the vinegar are so variable that the sauce made with a pint of oil may vary at different times. If the vinegar is too strong, substitute one tablespoon of water. The sugar in this recipe is a concession to the present popular taste, a true mayonnaise has none; palatable sauces may be made at one's pleasure with wine, cream, bacon fat—even flour or cornstarch may be used—but they should not be called mayonnaise.

If the oil is added too fast the sauce may curdle or break; in this case take a fresh, cold egg yolk in another bowl, beat till thick, add the curdled sauce by the half teaspoon at first, then more freely until all has been taken in, then go on as usual.

When making half the quantity use a small bowl to begin with and take one large or two small egg yolks; when it begins to spatter, as it should before it is half done, turn into a larger one.

Green Mayonnaise.

Green mayonnaise is made by the addition of three tablespoons ravigote herbs to this recipe.

Red Mayonnaise.

Red mayonnaise, by adding one tablespoon lobster coral, dried and pounded to powder.

Sauce Tartare.

Sauce tartare is made by adding to the green mayonnaise fifteen drops onion juice, one teaspoon capers, one teaspoon gherkins, one teaspoon parsley, each chopped exceedingly fine, one teaspoon chervil, if you have it.

Remoulade.

Rub well together the yolks of two hard-boiled eggs with one raw, one teaspoon mustard, one-half teaspoon salt, one-half saltspoon white pepper, one teaspoon chopped parsley. Add two tablespoons vinegar and beat in by degrees one-half pint oil alternating with more vinegar until three tablespoons of tarragon vinegar have been used, beat with Dover beater till very light and thick.

Bearnaise.

Chop very fine two medium sized shallots, place them on the fire with two tablespoons of chervil vinegar and five crushed peppers. Reduce until nearly dry, then put away to cool. Rub into it six raw egg yolks, beating sharply, then work in gradually one and one-half ounces of fresh butter (or lightly salted creamery), season with one teaspoon salt, a dust of grated nutmeg and twelve finely chopped tarragon leaves. Set the sauce-pan into boiling water and cook until the sauce is firm, beating briskly with a whisk, add one teaspoon melted meat glaze, beat till well mixed, strain and send at once to the table, arranging over it any article required to be served. —Adapted from Filipini.

Ravigote Sauce. (Cold.)

Add one tablespoon each of finely minced parsley, chives, chervil, tarragon and shallot to one pint of mayonnaise, and add a little spinach green if not colored enough with the herbs.

Ravigote Sauce. (Hot.)

Put into a sauce-pan one-half pint of consomme stock, one-half teaspoon of vinegar, a very little green garlic and the same of tarragon leaves and chervil. Boil ten minutes, drain the herbs, press all moisture from them with a cloth and chop very fine. Cook one-half ounce flour in one-half ounce butter, moisten with the consomme and vinegar and when it comes to a smooth mixture add the chopped herbs and serve.

Ravigote Butter.

To the above herbs add one-half teaspoon of essence of anchovy, an ounce of fresh butter and a few drops of spinach green. Rub through a fine sieve and keep in a cold place for general use.

Horseradish Butter.

Pound in a mortar one teaspoon of grated horseradish with one tablespoon of butter. Season with one-third saltspoon of red pepper. Rub through a fine sieve and keep in a cool place. When this butter is added to other sauces it should not boil again.

Shrimp Butter.

Pick the meat from twelve cooked shrimp; dry the shells and pound all together in a mortar, adding one tablespoon of good butter; place in a sauce-pan on a moderate fire, stirring until it clarifies, it will take about five minutes. Strain through a napkin pressing hard, and letting it drop into cold water. When it is hard take it out and place it in a warm bowl, stirring till it takes the desired color. Lobster butter is made in the same way.

Bread.

Crumble one and one-half ounces of stale bread and place it in a sauce-pan with a scant half cup of cold milk and six whole peppers. Let simmer for five minutes; then pour in one-half cup cream, one-half teaspoon onion juice, simmer five minutes longer and serve in a sauce-bowl, removing the peppers. Do not stir.

Bohemian.

Put in a sauce-pan one cup fresh bread crumbs, one-half cup good beef broth, season with salt, stir occasionally and boil for ten minutes; rub through a puree sieve; add four tablespoons fresh grated horseradish and two ounces butter; mix well, but do not boil. Serve with beefsteak or cold boiled beef or roast veal.

Black Butter.

Cook one ounce of butter in the frying pan until it becomes brown; add six parsley leaves, heat again for one minute, then throw in five drops of vinegar. Pour it into a sauce bowl and serve.

Tartar.

Mix one tablespoon vinegar, one teaspoon lemon juice, one saltspoon salt and one tablespoon Worcestershire and heat over hot water. Brown one-third cup butter, strain it in the other mixture and pour over the dish.

Vinaigrette.

Chop together very fine one shallot, two branches parsley, the same of chives and chervil. Place them in a sauce bowl with one tablespoon of salt, a teaspoon of pepper, and three teaspoons of vinegar. Stir all well together, then add four tablespoons good oil; mix well again and serve.

Garnishing Chipolata.

Make ready equal quantities of carrots, turnips, chestnuts, mushrooms, pieces of bacon and small sausages, as many as are required to garnish the dish. Roast or boil and peel the chestnuts, fry the pieces or bacon, boil separately all the other ingredients in seasoned broth. When they are ready, drain them and put into a sauce-pan with sufficient Spanish sauce to cover, add a glass of sherry and it is ready for use. It is better prepared the day before.

Garnishing Provençale, No. 1.

Put a chopped onion and one bruised clove of garlic in the sautoir; fry a little, add one pint finely sliced mushrooms and fry a little longer; wet with a pint of Spanish sauce and a gill of tomato sauce and boil five minutes. Finish with a pinch of red pepper, chopped parsley and lemon juice.

Garnishing à la Provençale, No. 2.

Peel two solid white onions, mince them and parboil for five minutes; drain well and toss them in an omelet pan with one tablespoon fresh butter for five minutes. Rub the spoon with a freshly cut clove of garlic, add a dash of lemon juice or white wine, one-half tablespoon grated Parmesan cheese and one-half cup good white sauce. Season with salt and pepper. Stir all well until it comes to the boil, then set away to cool.

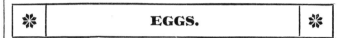

EGGS.

Breakfast Eggs.

Should never be boiled. A thin shell of the white is made hard and indigestible, while the bulk of the egg is barely warmed through. The following is a better way: Put six into a vessel that will hold two quarts. Fill with boiling water, cover closely and set on the stove shelf for seven minutes to cook very soft; ten minutes for medium, twelve to fifteen minutes for very firm. Crumple a napkin in a hot dish and serve ranged in its folds.

Scrambled Eggs.

For six persons allow six eggs and one tablespoon milk, one saltspoon salt, a speck of pepper and one-half teaspoon of butter to each egg. Break the egg into a bowl, add the seasoning, but do not beat. When the milk begins to boil pour in the eggs and seasoning. Do not stir, but as the egg cooks, scrape gently from bottom of the dish, drawing the cooked mass to one side. Remove from the fire before it is quite firm through, turn into a hot dish and serve quickly. This dish may be varied by using, instead of the milk, strained tomato, soup stock or gravy.

Poached Eggs.

For this the eggs should be new laid and cold. Put a quart of water, one teaspoon salt and one teaspoon vinegar in a shallow pan, arrange in it as many muffin rings as there are eggs to be cooked, and set the pan where the water will bubble at one side only. Break the eggs one at a time and slide them into the rings. If the water does not cover them, gently pour on a little more boiling water till it does. Cook till the white is set over the yolks; then pour off most of the water; with a cake-turner, lift each egg and lay on a slice of buttered toast, removing the ring after it is in place. Poached eggs may be done in milk, stock or in gravy which can be poured over the toast on which they are served. They may be used with various arrangements of hashed meat or cold fish reheated in white sauce or any other. They are a favorite accompaniment to ham and bacon, and are used as garnish in clear soup, and with Spanish rice, etc.

Griddled Eggs.

Heat the griddle almost as much as for baking cakes, butter it lightly and range small muffin rings on it. Drop an egg in each and turn as soon as lightly browned. They resemble fried eggs, but are far more delicate.

Steamed Eggs.

Cook in an ordinary steamer for five minutes, more or less, to suit the taste; they may also be broken into buttered cups and steamed with any of the variations in seasoning found under poached eggs, as they really are. When different members of the family come to breakfast at different times, it is a great convenience to be able to prepare all the portions at once, and cook and serve when needed. For an invalid, beat light, season and steam only till well warmed through.

Baked Eggs.

Beat the whites of six eggs to a stiff froth, leaving each yolk in a half shell; season with pepper and salt, put them in a buttered baking dish, make little hollows with the end of a shell and slip a yolk into each one. Bake in an oven quick enough to brown slightly in five minutes. This is pretty, but rather tasteless. Try it with thin rounds of buttered brown bread covered with cheese, either grated or cut; set in the oven long enough to heat the bread and melt the cheese, then add the beaten whites and yolks as before.

For an invalid, make a nest of the beaten white of one egg on a square of toasted white or graham bread, put a tablespoon of rich cream over the yolk and set for three minutes in a quick oven.

Golden Balls.

Have a Scotch bowl of hot fat. Stir carefully round and round until the fat hollows in the center, drop a very fresh egg into this hollow from a cup and keep up the circular motion of the fat for two minutes or less if the fat is quite hot; lay the egg on a paper and set where it will keep warm but will not harden. Only one can be done at a time and a little practice is required to get them smooth, but they make a most effective garnish for hash at breakfast, or for spinach at dinner.

Egg Timbales.

Six eggs, one and a half cups of milk, one teaspoon of salt, one-eighth teaspoon of pepper, one teaspoon of chopped parsley and one-fourth teaspoon of onion juice. Break the eggs into a bowl and beat well, add the seasoning and beat one minute longer; add the milk and stir well. Butter eight timbale molds of medium size and pour the mixture into them. Set them into a deep pan and pour in enough hot water to come almost to the top of the molds; place in a moderate oven and cook until firm in the center, from twelve to fifteen minutes; turn out on a warm dish and pour a cream or tomato sauce around them and garnish with small sprays of parsley stuck into each timbale.

Plain Omelet.

Put four eggs into a bowl with half a teaspoon salt, one scant saltspoon pepper, give them twelve vigorous beats with a fork and add four tablespoons milk or cream; put one teaspoon butter in an omelet pan, shake it over the fire till frothy, turn in the eggs and shake over a quick fire until they are set; roll and turn on to a dish. To make jelly, parsley, ham, cheese or chicken omelet spread the seasoning over the egg just before rolling it.

Omelet, No. 2.

For each egg allow one saltspoon salt, a dust of pepper, one tablespoon of liquid (milk, cream, stock, tomato, etc.). Break whites and yolks separately, beating each until very light; add seasoning and fold the yolks into the whites, stirring as little as possible. Have the omelet pan hot, melt in it one teaspoon of butter and cook over a quick fire until well browned on the bottom, then set in the oven until the top is set. Fold carefully not to break the crust, and turn onto a hot dish. Serve at once. This omelet is delicious made with ham, green peas, one cup grated or chopped sweet corn or asparagus tips. The latter should be well cooked, drained, seasoned and spread on just before folding the omelet; the ham may be folded in or mixed through the whole egg. Oysters should be parboiled and drained; the liquor from them may be strained and used instead of milk to give a richer flavor to the omelet. Other additions may be used as follows:

Three tablespoons of fresh mushrooms, peeled, chopped and fried lightly in just enough butter to keep from sticking.

One cup stewed kidney. Serve with tomato sauce, adding to it the extra gravy from the kidneys.

Three sardines, skinned and boned, broken into bits and seasoned lightly with cayenne and lemon juice.

One-half cup Lyonnaise potato.

For sweet omelets use fruit pulp, sweetened and cooked or not; garnish with whole fruit (strawberries, raspberries, etc.) or pieces of cooked fruit (apple, peach, pear).

Chicken Liver Omelet.

Take four sound livers, soak them in salted water one hour, drain and brown in one ounce butter in a rather small pan, then cook slowly til' tender; cut in small bits, add a teaspoon of minced onion, cook three minutes, then one gill of Spanish sauce or good brown gravy, one tablespoon mild vinegar and one tablespoon chopped mushrooms; season as needed with salt and cayenne; set back while preparing omelet No. 2. When set, put in the livers, fold and serve as usual.—Adapted from T. J. Murrey.

Fried Eggs.

Fried eggs may be done in butter, oil or any sweet animal fat; the pan should hold fat enough to almost cover the eggs, the eggs should be slipped into the fat singly from a cup; dip the hot fat over them; do not let the fat grow hot enough to "frizzle" the whites, it will be too hard for any but an ostrich to digest; browned butter with chopped parsley and a few drops of vinegar may be served poured over them on the platter, also with poached eggs on toast.

An Amulet of Eggs the Savoury Way.

Take a dozen of eggs, beat them very well and season them with salt and a little pepper; then have your frying-pan ready with a good deal of fresh butter in it and let it be thoroughly hot; then put in your eggs with four spoons strong gravy; have ready parsley and a few chives cut and throw them over it, and when it is enough turn it; and when done, dish it and squeeze orange or lemon over it.—From the Compleat Housewife.

Sweet Omelet.

Allow one teaspoon powdered sugar to each egg; omit the pepper and proceed as for No. 2. When ready to fold, lay in any kind of jelly, marmalade or fresh fruit, allowing one tablespoon to each egg. Fold and dust with sugar. The juice or pulp of fruit may be used, instead of milk or cream. The surface may be thickly covered with sugar and scored with a hot poker.

Omelet Celestine.

Allow one macaroon and one teaspoon apple or quince jelly for every two eggs. Roll the macaroons and braid with the jelly, moisten with a little cream if too stiff to spread easily on the omelet. Cook, fill and fold as usual, garnish with whipped cream fenced in with split lady fingers. The whipped cream may also be "piped" on in figures, but not much time can be spent on the ornamentation.

Spanish Omelet.

Cut four ounces of bacon in very thin slices and then into half inch squares; fry gently till crisp and add one small onion, a medium sized tomato and five mushrooms, all chopped rather fine; rub a freshly cut clove of garlic on the spoon used to stir, while cooking fifteen minutes. Meanwhile break six eggs in a bowl, season with one saltspoon salt, one-quarter saltspoon white pepper. Give them a dozen or so strong strokes and turn into a perfectly smooth frying-pan, in which a teaspoon of butter has been melted and spread over the bottom and side. Shake as usual, until nearly set. Spread the bacon and vegetables quickly over, fold, set it in the oven for one minute, turn it upon a heated platter and serve at once.—Mrs. Rorer.

Rice Omelet.

Warm a cup of cold boiled rice in one cup of milk with one tablespoon butter; stir and beat till well blended; add three well beaten eggs and salt as needed; melt another tablespoon butter in frying-pan; when boiling hot turn in the rice and egg, let it brown one minute, put in the oven to set, fold and serve as usual.—Miss Corson.

There are many dishes in which rice, crumbs, macaroni, flour, meat or vegetables chopped fine are mixed with the raw eggs instead of being laid thinly over the cooked egg just before folding. These are not true omelets, but may be made nourishing and attractive, and are recommended especially when eggs are dear.

Hard Boiled Eggs.

Hard boiled eggs may be served in numberless ways. Cook one-half hour as directed for breakfast, cover at once with cold water and renew it till they can be handled well; roll on the table gently till the shell is well crushed and it can be peeled off without marring the egg.

Scalloped Eggs.

Slice six eggs, season with salt, pepper and one teaspoon chopped parsley, or cheese, or onion, and cover with one pint white sauce made with stock. Sprinkle with one-half cup cracker crumbs lightly browned in butter and set in moderate oven ten minutes.

No. 2. Use one cup of scalded oysters to alternate with the eggs and cover with a plain cream sauce.

Eggs Curried.

Cut some hard-boiled eggs in halves; cut off the white end sufficiently to make them stand upright; pour some curry sauce around them.

Lyonnaise.

Cook a chopped onion in butter till yellow, not brown at all, add the whites of six eggs chopped fine, season highly with cayenne and salt, add a few drops of lemon, heap on a hot platter and garnish with the whole yolks, or rub them through a sieve, add one tablespoon of butter, two tablespoons potted ham, one raw egg yolk, shape in balls again and poach or fry in butter.

Beauregard.

Cook four eggs twenty minutes, make a white sauce with one cup milk, one tablespoon butter, one tablespoon corn-starch; lay six small squares of buttered toast on a dish, cover it with white sauce, then sprinkle with the whites chopped fine and the yolks pressed through a ricer.

Ox Eyes.

Take slices an inch thick from good light bread and cut rounds with a three inch cutter, cut a small ring one and a half inch and scoop out enough to take in an egg; brush with butter and crisp in a quick oven. Break a fresh egg in each, season with salt and pepper, moisten with one tablespoon cream and put in oven till set.

Pickled Eggs.

Six hard-boiled eggs, with four whole cloves stuck in each; rub together one-half teaspoon salt, one-half teaspoon pepper, one-half teaspoon mustard with a little cold vinegar; let one pint vinegar come to the boil, add the spice and cook one minute, pour boiling hot over the eggs, in a glass jar, cover closely. They will be ready to use in about two weeks. A few pieces of boiled beet in the vinegar will turn them a pretty pink. These are nice for picnics and lunches, or to accompany broiled beef-steak.

❋ SALADS. ❋

French Dressing.

Put into a tablespoon one saltspoon salt, one-half pepperspoon pepper and fill with oil; mix well together and pour it over the salad; add two tablespoons more of oil and toss the salad well, lastly add one tablespoon sharp vinegar. Sufficient for six persons if used on green salad; for cooked vegetables use twice or three times the measure.

Mayonnaise Dressing.

Put into a cold bowl the yolks of three eggs and beat until they are very light and thick; add one level teaspoon of salt, half saltspoon of cayenne and a few drops of olive oil; continue beating until it is too thick to turn the beater easily, add lemon juice to thin it, alternate with more oil until two tablespoons of lemon juice have been added; then add vinegar to the same amount. Use just enough oil to make the sauce of the right consistence. Mayonnaise will keep indefinitely if kept air-tight in a dark place. If preferred, use all vinegar and no lemon juice, or all lemon juice and no vinegar.

White Mayonnaise.

One-half cup highly seasoned veal jelly whipped to a stiff froth. Add slowly one-half pint oil, six tablespoons tarragon vinegar, one-half teaspoon salt, one-quarter teaspoon white pepper, one-half saltspoon sugar, dust of cayenne. Set into a bowl of ice water and beat till stiff enough to keep its form when dropped from a spoon.

Salad Dressing Without Oil.

Two eggs, one tablespoon mixed mustard, one-half teaspoon salt, a piece of butter the size of an egg, three tablespoons of vinegar, one tablespoon sugar. Beat the eggs, then add the mustard, salt and sugar, beat a little more, then add the melted butter and the vinegar. Set the bowl over boiling water and stir constantly until thick and smooth. Use cold; add a cup of whipped cream, the last thing.—Mrs. Isaac Gale, Natick, Mass.

Bacon Fat Dressing.

Cut one-fourth pound very fat bacon or ham into small dice. Fry gently till the oil burns a light brown color; remove from the fire and add one-third vinegar to two-thirds bacon fat. Pour over a salad already seasoned with pepper, salt and such herbs as are wished. If the bits of bacon are objectionable pour through a strainer, but their savory crispness is generally an improvement.

Chicken Salad.

Cut cold chicken, roasted is best, into quarter inch dice. Use only the breast and tender fillets from the thighs. Marinate a pint with once the measure of French dressing and set away to season and chill. At serving time add an equal bulk of diced celery, and enough mayonnaise to moisten thoroughly. Arrange on a bed of torn lettuce and garnish with cress or tiny gherkins or stoned olives. Drop a large spoon of mayonnaise on top and fringe it round with the finest celery tips.

Veal Salad.

The meat may very well be the remainder of a roast of the previous day. Trim away carefully all fat and gristle and cut in dice. Serve with lettuce and a French dressing, or a more elaborate mayonnaise, as one prefers. Garden cress or pepper-grass is a good addition.

Oyster Salad.

For a pound can or a solid pint of oyster use the following dressing: Beat well two eggs, add to them one-fourth cup each of cream and vinegar, one-half teaspoon each of mustard, celery salt and salt, a dust of cayenne, one tablespoon butter. Put into double boiler and cook like soft custard. Parboil the oysters, drain them and add the dressing. Set away to cool and at serving time add one pint diced celery.

Deep Sea Salad.

Make ready a block of ice as for raw oysters, only with a deeper hole, to contain the salad. Prepare an oyster salad as directed. Arrange a bed of parsley and celery tips around the block of ice, placing large clam shells at each end to hold extra mayonnaise; pour the salad into the hole and garnish with brussels sprouts and olives cut in spirals.

Cream Salad Dressing.

Rub the yolks of three hard-boiled eggs to a smooth paste; add gradually to them one teaspoon salt, one-fourth teaspoon sugar, one-half saltspoon cayenne, one teaspoon mustard and two tablespoons vinegar; have one pint cream very cold and whip till thick and smooth; beat this, a tablespoon at a time, into the mixture with a whisk.

Melted Butter Dressing.

Put the yolks of two raw eggs with an ounce of butter in a sauce-pan and set by the side of the fire, stir rapidly until the butter is melted and the sauce begins to thicken; draw the pan away from the fire, add another ounce of butter and continue working to a cream, repeat with two more ounces of butter, add pepper and salt to taste and pour into a sauce-bowl. A few leaves of tarragon finely chopped and a squeeze of lemon should be added just before serving.

Lobster Salad.

Chop the meat rather fine, season highly, especially with salt and mustard. Pour over French dressing or some mayonnaise well thinned with vinegar, and set away to season through. At serving time add about one-half its bulk of lettuce stalks and firm leaves broken small, mix in plenty of mayonnaise and serve in the cleaned shells. Garnish with small lettuce leaves and the small claws, or if canned fish is used, serve on a bed of torn lettuce, garnishing as before. Shrimps, crabs and crawfish are prepared in the same way.

Fish Salad.

Break cold cooked halibut or any white delicate fish into convenient pieces, removing all skin, bones and fat, marinate with tarragon or spiced vinegar and set one side for an hour; arrange on leaves of lettuce and serve with mayonnaise or sauce tartare.

Chopped Cabbage.

Select a fine, white cabbage, or if preferred, use a red cabbage. Shred very fine with a sharp knife. Heap in a dish, pour over it a dressing made by stirring together one tablespoon salad oil or melted butter, a little salt and pepper, and one-half tea-cup good vinegar. Mix well through the cabbage when ready to serve. Or use boiled dressing.

Bean Salad.

One cup of beans soaked over night, in the morning pour off the water, put enough fresh water on them to boil until thoroughly done. When cool, add an onion about the size of an English walnut chopped very fine, and moisten the whole with a mayonnaise dressing seasoned rather highly with salt, pepper, cayenne and mustard.

Potato Salad.

For each quart of cold baked or boiled potatoes, allow one cucumber, one cup of diced celery, and one measure of boiled dressing. In mixing do not stir, but lift carefully and turn over.

Hungarian Potato Salad.

Take small potatoes, boil, and peel while warm. Slice very thin. To every pint of potatoes mince one small onion, one pickled beet, one fresh cucumber sliced, a Dutch herring, four sardines, and a spoonful of minced cold boiled ham. Mix all together and pour over a teacup of vinegar. Garnish with walnut pickles.

German Potato Salad.

Choose small potatoes; imported ones are best, but new potatoes will do if carefully cooked and well drained. Peel them and set aside to cool while making the following dressing: Cut one-quarter pound fat bacon into smallest possible dice, put them into a frying pan over a slow fire; shred an onion into a large bowl, add a small tablespoon of salt, one cup of vinegar and hot water (half and half). When the fat is a light brown color and the dice well crisped, add two tablespoons of salad oil and pour it into the vinegar and onion, turning in slowly at first lest it spatter. Slice the potatoes as thin as possible, stirring often; if the salad is too dry, add a little hot water from time to time. It should have a glossy look, without being either lumpy or greasy. If it looks good, it is pretty sure to taste good. Best eaten as soon as made.

Mixed Vegetable Salads.

Vegetable salads can be made of any kind of cooked vegetables, but some kinds combine better than others. Peas, string or shell beans, cauliflower, asparagus and young carrots combine well, turnips, carrots, beets, cabbage, spinach, tomatoes, make another combination, but it is generally best to use potatoes for the body of the salad, adding other vegetables to give color and flavor. A large variety of vegetables is known as "Salade Macedoine," or sometimes Russian salad. Each vegetable should be cooked and cut separately, then mixed lightly in a bowl with French dressing and set on ice to cool before serving. Rub the salad bowls with a cut onion before arranging the salad, and if it is liked very moist and highly seasoned, double the quantity of dressing or send a bowl of mayonnaise to the table with it. Garnish with nasturtium in the season and cut them up with the salad. Sliced gherkins, pickled beets, marinated eggs, Thon Marine make savory garnishes.

Waldorf Salad.

One cup sour apples, one cup celery, one tablespoon lemon juice, one-half cup walnut meats broken in pieces. Cut apples in thin slices; cut celery in small pieces. Dust with salt and pepper. Mix with mayonnaise or boiled dressing.

Cauliflower Salad.

Separate the sprigs of cold boiled cauliflower, put into the salad dish a head of lettuce and cover it with mayonnaise. Arrange the cauliflower sprigs around the dish heads outward and serve.

Artichoke Bottoms.

Those prepared by Dunbar and sold at all well supplied groceries will answer as well as the fresh. Drain from the liquor in the can and season with oil, salt, pepper and vinegar, set on ice and at serving time lay a small shape of truffled pate de foie gras (also canned) on each one, or sprinkle with grated cheese. Good either with or without mayonnaise.

Breakfast Salad.

Scald two ripe tomatoes, peel them, put them in cold water or fine ice to become cold; drain, and either slice or divide into sections. Peel and slice very thin one cucumber; line a salad bowl with crisp lettuce leaves, add the tomatoes and cucumber, a teaspoon of minced parsley, with a few blades of chives, if possible add a few green tarragon leaves. Over all pour a plain salad dressing of olive oil, vinegar, salt and pepper.

Tomato and Cucumber Salad.

Peel as many small ripe tomatoes as there are to be covers. Remove the hearts and set on ice to become cold. Pare cucumbers quite close to the seeds and chop them coarsely. Pour over a French dressing and fill them lightly into the tomatoes. Serve each on a crisp lettuce leaf.

Farmers' Salad.

In spring and early summer the tender plants of dandelion are a most appetizing and wholesome salad. Pick over and wash carefully, lay in ice cold water four hours to become crisp. Break coarsely and serve with bacon dressing.

Murrey recommends adding fresh made cottage cheese, salt, pepper, vinegar and young onions.

Water Cress Salad.

Water cress is a very acceptable spring salad plant, and its pungent flavor is considered a good whet for jaded palates. A plain salad dressing is the most appropriate. Small herbs, such as chives, borage, chervil, etc., may be added if liked.

Chicory Salad.

Select two fine heads of chicory; cut off the root end and reject all green and all decayed leaves; wash the white leaves in cold water and dry them in a napkin. Rub a salad bowl with a clove of garlic, put the crisp white leaves in the bowl. Toss the salad gently with French dressing, then add a tablespoon of vinegar, toss again and serve. A little chervil, borage or chives will improve it for many palates.

Salad in Jelly.

Make aspic jelly No. 1. Fill bottom of salad dish with a little of the jelly and set on ice. When hard set in the salad dish on top of the jelly, a bowl large enough to hold the desired amount of salad, and fill bowl with ice; pour jelly around until almost reaching the top of bowl, when the jelly is hard remove ice from bowl and fill with warm water for a moment only; then remove bowl from jelly, being careful not to break the jelly. Make any of the ordinary salads, such as chicken, veal, lobster, shrimp or nice red tomatoes sliced with a little green, as celery, lettuce, etc., mixed through here and there. Place salad in the space left in the jelly and cover salad with the remaining jelly; after it has become a little hard set aside in ice box. When wanted set dish in warm water a moment and turn salad out on a platter; have a mayonnaise dressing ready to serve with salad. Remember in making this salad the bottom of dish will be the top when turned out.

This is especially pretty to be arranged in a border mold, and after turning out fill the center with more of the meat mixed with mayonnaise.

Devonshire Salad.

Choose soft, yet firm curd of cottage cheese, cut in inch dice, season with salt, pepper and cayenne and serve on lettuce with mayonnaise. Garnish with nasturtium.

Strawberry Salad.

Choose the heart leaves of head lettuce, heap a few strawberries in each and dust them lightly with powdered sugar; lay a teaspoon of mayonnaise on each portion and serve cut lemons with them; delicious for lunch.

Orange Salad.

For six persons pare four rather acid oranges, slice them very thin, cutting down the sides instead of across, and sprinkle sparingly with sugar. Mix one tablespoon sherry with one of yellow Chartreuse and one of lemon juice and pour it over the fruit. Set on ice an hour before using. Serve before the game course.

Fruit Salad.

Half pound of almonds, blanched and grated, four oranges, pared and sliced, one can of pineapple grated, three bananas, or peaches, pears, French cherries, strawberries or other fruit, in like proportion. Alternate the layers of fruit with layers of powdered sugar, and reserve the almonds for the top layer, to be garnished with strawberries or other small bright fruits; then add the following dressing and cool:

Half cup of lemon juice, two tablespoons of sherry and two tablespoons of liqueur, preferably Maraschino.

Cranberries can be used instead of strawberries, if stewed until quite soft, with a good deal of sugar.

Grated cocoanut can be used instead of almonds.

 SAVORIES.

Digestibility of Cheese.

The digestibility of cheese depends a great deal, according to Klenze, on its physical properties. All fat cheeses are dissolved or digested with great rapidity, because the molecules of casine are separated by the fat, and so the solvent juice can attack a large surface of the cheese at one time. Whether the cheese be hard or soft does not appear to matter, and there is no connection between the digestibility and the percentage of water present in the cheese. The degree of ripeness and the amount of fat have, however, considerable influence; for both these conditions render the cheese more friable, and so allow intimate contact with the juices of digestion. Chedder takes the shortest time to digest, four hours; while unripe Swiss cheese took ten hours for solution.

In cooking cheese in any form it is well to add bi-carbonate of potash in the proportion of one-fourth saltspoon to four ounces of cheese. This restores the potash salts lost from the milk in the process of cheese making, and renders it more digestible.

Cheese Soufflé.

Make a thin, white sauce, with one teaspoon butter, two and one-half tablespoons flour, three-quarters pint milk; add four ounces cheese grated and mixed with the yolks of four eggs, fold in the stiffly beaten whites and bake at once in paper cases or scallop shells.

Cheese au Gratin.

Three slices bread, trim off the crust and butter well. Place in a deep pudding dish, buttered side down, and lay one-quarter pound of chipped or grated cheese between the slices and on top, seasoning with salt and pepper to taste (about one-quarter teaspoon salt and a dust of cayenne). Beat four eggs, add three cups milk, pour it over the bread and let stand one hour or more. Bake twenty to thirty minutes in a rather quick oven.

Cottage Cheese. (Schmier-Käse.)

Set a gallon or more of thick sour milk into warm water or in a warm oven until it reaches a temperature of 180 degrees (Fahr.). Let it stand at that temperature for an hour or more, until the whey is well separated and the curd feels firm all the way through. Turn gently on to a coarse thin cloth and hang up to drain several hours. Turn from the bag and chop in dice, dressing with salt and cream, either sweet or sour, according to taste; or mix salt and cream through the mass, working it fine with the hands.

Welsh Rarebit.

Take one-half pound cheese (American cheese preferred), three tablespoons ale, a thin slice of toast; grate the cheese fine, put it to the ale, and work it in a small saucepan over a slow fire till it is melted, spread it on toast and serve hot. (If ale is not at hand, use beer or milk.)

Welsh Rarebit au Gratin.

Prepare six thin slices toast. Cover each slice with Swiss cheese, cut half an inch thick. Lay them in a dripping pan and dust lightly with pepper or spread made mustard over. Set in a hot oven till well melted, about ten minutes. The addition of a dropped egg to each slice makes what is called a Golden Buck.

Nalenikis.

Prepare as above, but dip each one in fritter batter and fry to delicate brown. Dry for a few minutes in the oven.—Helen Campbell.

Cheese Fritters.

Prepare fritter batter, add to it eight heaping tablespoons of dry grated cheese, fry according to directions and serve with a little grated cheese sprinkled over.

Ramaquins.

4 tablespoons grated cheese.
2 tablespoons butter.
1 gill milk.
Yolks two eggs.
2 ounces bread, grated.
⅓ teaspoon mustard.
Cayenne and salt to taste.
Whites three eggs.

Put bread and milk to boil until smooth, stirring often; add cheese and butter and remove from the fire. As soon as the butter has melted stir in the yolks of the eggs and seasoning. Let cool a little before adding the stiffly beaten whites. Bake in small china dishes and serve at once as they soon fall.—Mrs. Henderson.

Cheese Balls.

1 cup grated cheese.
Whites of three eggs, well beaten.
A little bit of red pepper.
½ teaspoonful salt.

Let stand, after mixing, 15 minutes. Make into balls the size of a walnut, fry in deep fat until golden brown.

Anchovy Toast.

Six anchovies, two hard boiled eggs, two ounces butter, six croutes of bread, cayenne, lemon juice. Wash and bone the anchovies, and pound them to a paste with the egg yolk, butter and cayenne; for extra fine ones, run through a puree sieve. Fry rounds of bread, spread with the above paste, and spread over them the whites of the egg chopped very fine.

Ham Toast.

Three ounces lean ham, one ounce butter, chopped parsley, pepper and salt to taste. Mince ham very fine, put it into a stewpan with the butter and seasoning. Shake until it comes to the boiling point. Serve at once on buttered toast.

Clam Toast.

Chop two dozen small clams into small pieces; simmer a few minutes. Beat the yolks of two eggs, add a little cayenne and a gill of warmed milk. Pour into the clams, let come to the point of simmering, pour over buttered toast and serve.

Cheese Toast.

Mince the cheese fine, season to taste with salt, cayenne and mustard, and spread thickly over buttered bread. Set under the gas broiler or into a very hot oven until well browned. Serve at once.

Tomato Toast.

Two tomatoes, two eggs, one ounce butter, one ounce ham, a scrap of onion, pepper and salt. Six small rounds of buttered toast. Wipe and chop the tomatoes well. Mince the onion and ham, and cook them with the butter in a saucepan about ten minutes, remove from the fire to add the beaten egg, stir over the fire till it sets, then serve on the toast.

GOLD MEDAL FLOUR—It's a Biscuit Flour—It's a Bread Flour.

Vegetables

IF the housekeeper who is so tired of the same old way of preparing vegetables would only study the art of cooking she need never want for variety.

A little patience and skill, the use of good judgment, and a proper degree of industry will render the task easy.

Such a number of dishes may be readily made that all housekeepers should see that several vegetables appear daily on their tables.

Artichokes.

Cut the stalks close and clip the sharp points from the leaves; wash in vinegar and water and lay in cold salted water for an hour to drive out insects. Cook in boiling salted water till tender enough to draw out the leaves easily, about forty minutes, but they must not go to pieces. Turn them upside down to drain. Serve hot with Bechamel or Hollandaise sauce, or cold with French dressing. To keep them green tie some charcoal in muslin and boil with them.

Artichokes à la Barigoule.

Wash as above, parboil just long enough to remove the choke and throw them into cold water for five minutes. Put them to drain while preparing a forcemeat. Mince fine four ounces fat pork and fry it a little with two tablespoons chopped shallots; then add a pint of chopped mushrooms and parsley and simmer ten minutes. Blend with it one tablespoon flour kneaded with butter, one-half cup Spanish sauce, salt, pepper and a speck of nutmeg. Fill the artichokes and tie them with a string. Brown the outside well with a little olive oil in a sautoir; then add one-half pint broth and a small glass white wine. Cover and cook forty minutes in a moderate hot oven. Serve in a hot dish, pouring the sauce over and around them. Place a whole mushroom on top of each.—Adapted from "The Table."

Jerusalem Artichokes.

Wash and boil with the skins on in salted water till tender (about thirty minutes). Drain, peel and serve in cream sauce No. 1, seasoning very well. Let them lie in the sauce for fifteen minutes to season before serving.

Au Gratin.

Boil as above and proceed as for cauliflower.

Baked.

Boil until about half done, then peel and put into a baking-dish with one tablespoon butter, salt and pepper to taste. Dust with one teaspoon powdered sugar and bake a good brown. Baste with butter after it begins to brown.

Purée.

Cook in strong broth instead of water. Peel and put through a puree sieve, season with salt, butter and pepper and serve with braised beef, veal or chicken.

Asparagus, No. 1.

Wash carefully two bunches green asparagus, cut the ends until the tender part is reached. Arrange in one large bundle and fasten with a broad band of coarse muslin, pinned at each side. Boil gently in salted water until done, about twenty minutes. Serve with Hollandaise sauce.

Asparagus, No. 2.

Cut the tender parts in bits as long as the stems are thick and boil till tender. Drain and add to two bunches one-half cup cream, one quarter teaspoon salt. Simmer till reduced to a thick sauce and serve like green peas.

Asparagus with Eggs.

Boil two pounds of the vegetable; cut off the tender tops and lay them on a buttered pie-dish, seasoning with pepper and salt and two tablespoons of melted butter. Beat four eggs just enough to break the yolks, and pour over the asparagus. Bake eight minutes in a good oven and serve with slices of tender broiled ham.

"Asparagus in Ambush."

Have ready some small, light rolls—one for each guest. Cut off the tops to serve as covers; take out all the crumb and lay the rolls in the oven for their tops to crisp. Meanwhile heat a cup of milk to boiling point and pour it into two beaten eggs, beating well to prevent curdling; add a spoon of butter, cut in bits and rolled in flour, and the soft parts of two pounds of asparagus that has been boiled and cut fine. Stir the mixture, seasoning to taste; fill the roll, put on the tops and serve hot.

String Beans.

Snap, rather than cut with a knife, into pieces one-half inch long. Unless they are very fresh they will be improved by lying in ice-cold water an hour or more before cooking. Throw into fast boiling water and cook rapidly, *uncovered*, for an hour at least; they will generally need much more. Change the water at the end of the first half hour and they will season better if an ounce or two of fat salt meat is cooked with them. The water should be allowed to nearly all cook away and the remainder may be used to make a drawn butter sauce to pour over them; or they may be seasoned with only butter and salt. If the water is very hard, a bit of bi-carbonate of soda as large as a pea will make them more tender.

String Beans German Fashion.

Remove the strings from one quart of beans. Cut each pod through twice lengthwise, then cut into two-inch lengths. After parboiling, put into the stewpan an ounce of butter, a teaspoon sugar, pepper and salt to taste. Saute a few minutes till the butter is absorbed, then add a very little stock or water, a little lemon juice, and simmer until perfectly tender.

Shelled Beans.

Wash, and cook in boiling soft water. Add salt about ten minutes before they are done. Drain, and season with butter and salt. Lima and other white beans are improved by adding a little butter or fat salt pork.

Lima Beans.

Add to a pint of young Lima beans previously boiled and seasoned with butter, salt and pepper, half a pint of freshly gathered mushrooms. Put a tablespoon of butter in the saucepan; when melted add beans and mushrooms, with half a gill of cream; let it all simmer for about ten minutes, and serve hot.

Dried Lima beans can be made quite palatable by soaking them in cold water for 48 hours, and then cooking like the green ones. They will do very nicely for succotash.

Mother's Baked Beans.

One quart of navy beans; pick over carefully and soak over night. In the morning, put on the back of the stove, and cover with boiling water. After they have parboiled half an hour, take up a spoonful and blow on them; if the skin curls back, they are done. Put them in a colander, and pour a dipper of cold water through them. Take a deep earthen bean pot holding two quarts; put in some of the beans, then half a pound of salt pork,—"a streak of fat and a streak of lean" (the pork must be washed with warm water and gashed across the top) —then fill up with beans. Take one teaspoon of salt, half a teaspoon of mustard, and two teaspoons of molasses; dissolve in hot water and pour over the beans; then fill the pot with hot water. They must be baked six hours, and as much longer as you please. Whenever the water cooks away, fill the pot again, until nearly done, then let the water cook away.

Beets.

Brush and scrub well, but do not cut. Lay into boiling water and boil rapidly till tender, for new beets about 45 minutes, for old beets two to three hours. Plunge into cold water and slip the skins off by hand. Cut in eighths lengthwise, and pour over a sauce made with two tablespoons butter, four tablespoons lemon juice, one-half teaspoon salt, sprinkle cayenne, boil up once and pour hot over the beets just before they go to the table.

Brussels Sprouts.

Cut the sprouts from two medium sized stalks, pick off all tarnished leaves, and lay them for an hour in salted water. Drain them well and cook in plenty of boiling water, uncovered, till tender, from ten minutes to half an hour, according to their age. Drain in a colander and serve with a Bechamel or Hollandaise sauce.

Brocculi.

Cook like Brussels sprouts, and while draining prepare three-fourths pint of yellow Bechamel. Lay a slice of buttered toast in a deep platter, arrange the largest head in the middle and smaller ones around it. Pour the sauce over and around them.

Cucumbers Stuffed and Stewed.

Cut in half lengthwise, scoop out the seeds and fill the hollow with a bread or meat stuffing, or with quenelle mixture. Lay in a sautoir, with butter enough to keep from sticking. Simmer till the juice flows freely, then add a little good broth, and boil gently till very tender. Lift the slices, reduce the juice to a glaze, which may be dissolved in enough velvet sauce to cover.

Fried Cucumbers.

Slice, sprinkle with salt and pepper, dip in egg, then in cracker dust; fry brown.

Cabbage.

Choose a cabbage like an orange, by its weight. Remove the outside coarse leaves, cut in quarters, take out the inner stem, especially the coarse fibers that run between the leaves and the stem; lay it face down in salted water for an hour—longer if old and wilted; boil in plenty of water, three quarts of water to two pounds of cabbage, drain and fill again with boiling water, cook till tender, when young and crisp forty minutes, longer if old. Drain in a colander; cut, turn and press repeatedly, keeping hot in an oven. Dress as desired.

No. 1. Allow one tablespoon butter to each pound of cabbage; salt, vinegar and cayenne to taste.

No. 2. One cup of cream sauce No. 1 to each pound.

No. 3. One cup brown sauce (made like white sauce), but let the butter and flour brown a little and use good brown stock for milk.

No. 4. Put the cooked cabbage in a buttered baking dish after chopping fine and seasoning with salt, pepper and two beaten eggs diluted with three tablespoons cream, bake in a quick oven till brown. Serve hot.

No. 5. Au gratin. Put one pint plain boiled cabbage in a baking dish well buttered, pour over one good cup white sauce, cover with buttered crumbs and grated cheese if liked. Serve in the same dish.

No. 6, stuffed. Parboil till thoroughly wilted, drain, cool, unfold leaf by leaf until the heart is reached. Chop the tender leaves and add to the stuffing. Two ounces fat salt pork, two ounces tender beef, both chopped fine, one ounce butter, two egg yolks, a scant teaspoon each of salt, parsley and minced onion, one pepperspoon cayenne, one French roll soaked in milk and pressed dry. Beat the egg and bread together, add the creamed butter and work in the meat and seasoning. Make into a ball and place in the cabbage head, refold the leaves to good shape and bake three to four hours, basting often with butter and a little water. Serve on a round platter with the gravy from the pan, dashed with lemon juice. Cut like a round loaf cake.

Spring Carrots.

Wash and scrape them, parboil for ten minutes and dry them on a cloth. Return to the saucepan with one heaped tablespoon sugar, one cup stock, one tablespoon butter, and boil gently about half an hour or until perfectly tender then remove the cover and boil fast until the stock is reduced to glaze. Sprinkle with a little chopped parsley and serve with the glaze on them.

These can be reheated in a white sauce and are even better than at first.

Purée of Carrots.

Slice fine the outer part of a dozen carrots, one and a half pints is enough, parboil ten minutes, drain, and cook gently again till tender with one pint water, one teaspoon each salt and sugar, and one-fourth teaspoon white pepper; add one-half pound stale bread, broken into bits, and one quart veal or chicken broth, simmer another hour, put it through a puree sieve; if too soft allow it to cook away longer, if too dry add a little broth or milk. Serve with breast of lamb, chops, or veal cutlets.

Cauliflower.

Trim off outside leaves and lay blossoms down in cold salted water. Slugs and other insects will drop out, especially if gently shaken in the water. Tie in a piece of mosquito netting and lay in boiling salted water till very tender. Drain and serve with Hollandaise Sauce or Cream Sauce No. 1. This makes a delicious garnish for fried spring chicken or fried sweet breads.

Cauliflower with Parmesan cheese is made as above, adding a teaspoon of Parmesan cheese to the sauce before it is poured over the cauliflower; sprinkle melted butter over it and bake a few minutes in a hot oven.

Fried Squash.

Peel squash and slice about one-half inch thick. Sprinkle with pepper, salt and flour; then fry in half butter and half lard until brown. The slices should be about a finger long. This is good for either summer or winter squash. A half hour or less should be enough to fry. Cook slowly with cover over frying-pan.

Stewed Celery.

Cut the coarse pieces of celery and ends of stalks, using the fine leaves also, into inch (or less) pieces. Pour over boiling water to nearly cover. Boil until tender (about one hour). If water is not all absorbed pour off and add one pint white sauce. Season to taste with salt and pepper.

Green Corn.

This most delicious of summer vegetables is frequently spoiled by over-cooking. If the corn is fresh and tender as it should be fifteen minutes is enough. Wrap at once in a thick napkin and send to table covered, as the skin toughens if allowed to dry while hot. It is sometimes cooked in the inner husk, but this is not necessary except for roasting.

Corn Pagout.

Cut scraps of ham or bacon in small squares; fry brown, add six ripe tomatoes peeled and sliced, and the grains cut from six ears of corn; cover with boiling water, season with red pepper and salt, and cook slowly half an hour. Serve hot with toast or slices of fried bread.

GOLD MEDAL FLOUR—It's a Pastry Flour—It's a Cake Flour.

Succotash.

Cut the grains from ten ears of corn, mix with one quart of shelled Lima beans, and boil until tender, and drain. Melt two tablespoons of butter and pour on the corn and beans. Season with pepper and salt. Let simmer ten minutes; pour in a cup of sweet cream; when hot serve.

Cymlings, or Summer Squash.

Take them when young and tender. Wash, cut in thick slices and boil till tender (they should not be old enough to have seeds of any size); and prepare as follows:

Mashed.—Press out all the water possible. Make it fine and smooth, season to taste with sweet butter, white pepper and salt, return to stove and simmer fifteen minutes, stirring often.

Puree.—To each pint of mashed cymling add one cup rich milk. Stew until thick; do not let it burn.

Dolmas.—Prepare the squash as above, making the sections two inches thick. Scoop out the soft center and fill with this mixture: Take equal measures of minced raw mutton and raw rice, season to taste—it needs cayenne—and put a bit of butter on each. Range them in a buttered sautoir, in which a half dozen wafers of onions have cooked. Simmer till tender. Beat the yolks of five eggs, dilute with the juice of one lemon, pour over the dolmas and shake to mix well with the stock. Set over hot water till thick like custard.

Dandelions.

Gather only the freshly grown plants—best when the dew is on them. The tenderest leaves make an excellent salad with Bacon Dressing. The whole plant, after thorough washing, may be boiled until tender, drained, chopped fine, seasoned with salt, vinegar and a liberal measure of butter. Those who think it too bitter may use half spinach or beet, or sorrel, in which case the dandelion should be partly cooked before the more succulent plant is added. It cannot be too well recommended.

Egg Plant Fried.

Peel and cut them in half inch slices, sprinkle with salt and pepper, pile them and place a weight over for an hour or more, tipping the plate slightly that the juice may drain away. Dry each slice by rolling in seasoned flour, and fry crisp in plenty of sweet dripping, or dip in fritter batter No. 1 before frying.

Greens.

There is an almost unlimited number of plants used as greens. The general treatment is the same for all. See spinach.

Lentils.

May be used for soup or stewed and served with butter the same as beans.

Lentil Sarmas.

One-half cup lentils, one-half cup rice, one-half cup chopped ham, twelve vine leaves, one-half cup chopped raw veal or chicken, one-quarter teaspoon powdered coriander seed, salt and cayenne to taste; mix well and tie like Sarmas. Serve with a thickened sauce made from the stock in which they were boiled, adding well beaten yolks of two eggs and a tablespoon tarragon vinegar to each half pint.

Baked Macaroni.

One-half pound Macaroni broken in pieces. Pour over boiling water, add a little salt. Boil hard twenty minutes; drain and put in a pudding dish and pour over the following mixture: Two tablespoons flour, two teaspoons dry mustard, one-half pound grated cheese, one pint new milk. Mix mustard and flour into a smooth paste, with some of the cold milk; set the rest on the stove. When boiling add flour, mustard and cheese; cook until it looks smooth, taking care that it does not burn. When done pour over macaroni and bake until a nice brown. Twenty minutes ought to be enough. Be sure and use new milk as the cheese will cause it to curdle otherwise.

Macaroni.

One-fourth pound macaroni broken into bits two inches long will need at least three quarts of boiling salted water. Boil fast, *uncovered*, until tender, at least half an hour and some macaroni takes longer. Drain in a colander and rinse with cold water; it is then ready to finish in any way preferred.

With Cheese.—Arrange alternate layers of cheese and macaroni in a heavily buttered baking dish, pour over a thin white sauce or cream, or poulette, or bechamel, or tomato, according to taste. Cover with buttered crumbs and bake till the crumbs are brown.

In Cheese Shells.—Fill the empty shell of an Edam or pineapple cheese with cooked macaroni, seasoning with grated Parmesan, moisten well with thin white sauce and set into a hot oven till hot through. Replace the cover and serve very hot.

With Brown Sauce.—Arrange as for serving with cheese, but use Spanish sauce instead of other seasoning. Spaghetti, vermicelli and noodles are all prepared and served like macaroni.

Hominy.

Soak one cup over night in cold water. In the morning drain and put to cook in three cups of boiling salted water and boil gently till soft, it ought to take about three hours. Fine hominy can be cooked in one hour if soaked in warm water, changing it once or twice for warmer. Boil in the last water.

Onions.

Peel under warm water, cut a small slice from each end and let lie in cold water with a pinch of soda for an hour. Put into boiling water to cook adding one saltspoon of soda to each quart. As soon as they begin to soften change the water and finish cooking in salted water. Drain thoroughly and serve with bread sauce, or a bechamel, or with only butter, salt and pepper. They are excellent baked; for this, choose large ones, and after they are parboiled in the soda water, dry them carefully, wrap each one in a buttered paper, lay in a baking-pan and cook in a very hot oven till thy can be pierced with a straw. Serve with Spanish sauce.

Okra.

Cut stems to the tender part of the pod, cook whole in boiling salted water (if cooked in iron they will blacken), until tender, drain and return to the sauce pan with plenty of butter, a taste of vinegar, salt and pepper; simmer slowly until they are thoroughly seasoned. They are nice sliced and stewed with an equal bulk of tomato, seasoned with one sweet pepper, one teaspoon salt and one ounce of butter to each pint. Sometimes one-quarter cup rice and one-quarter pound of diced ham are added to a quart of the above stew.

Fried Okra.

Slice two onions, and fry with bits of fat bacon. Cut a quart of okra and stir in; fry brown. Sprinkle with salt and cayenne pepper.—Eliza R. Parker.

Parsnips.

Brush clean and lay in cold water to become crisp. Cook in boiling salted water till tender. Throw into cold water to slip the skins, and serve either plain or mashed; season with butter, salt and pepper, or with a thin cream sauce.

They are more savory if they can be cut in round slices, sprinkled with salt, pepper and sugar, and browned in a little ham or bacon fat, or dipped in fritter batter No. 2 before frying.

Peas.

Green peas should never grow to fill the pods quite full. If taken while still young and shelled at the last moment before cooking, and cooked the same day they are picked, they are rightly esteemed one of the best of summer vegetables. If the pods are gritty, wash them before shelling, as much of the fine flavor is lost by washing the peas. Have ready boiling salted water enough to float them, and boil rapidly uncovered for fifteen to twenty minutes. Try them and take up the instant they are done. For one pint of peas, put into the water in which they were cooked one ounce of butter, a saltspoon each of salt and sugar. Let it reduce until there is just enough to moisten the peas well and serve hot. Two or three tablespoons of sweet rich cream are sometimes used instead of the butter and pea-broth, but it makes them too rich and cloying to serve with meat.

Stuffed Green Peppers.

Wash half a dozen large green peppers, put them in boiling water five minutes, rub off the skins with a wet cloth, cut off the stem, remove the seeds and stuff the peppers with any kind of cold meat minced fine and an equal quantity of stale bread. Replace the stems, set the peppers in a deep dish, pour in as much cold gravy as the dish will hold and bake in a moderate oven for half an hour. They may be stuffed with sausage meat and bread. Serve in the dish in which they are baked.

Corn Chowder, No. 2.

1 quart raw sweet corn.	¼ cup butter.
1 pint potato dice.	2 tablespoons flour.
1 teaspoon salt.	1 pint milk.
1 saltspoon pepper.	1 pint croutons.
	2 hard-boiled eggs.

Cut each row of kernels, and scrape the raw corn from the cob. Boil the cobs twenty minutes in water to cover. Pare and cut the potatoes into small dice. Pour boiling water over them, drain and let them stand while the corncobs are boiling. Remove the cobs, add the potatoes, salt and pepper. When the potatoes are nearly done, add the corn and milk and cook five minutes. Cook the flour in the hot butter, add one cup of the corn liquor, and when thick stir it into the chowder. Add the eggs, whites chopped fine, and yolks rubbed through a strainer. Serve with croutons.—Mrs. D. A. Lincoln.

Potato. (New.)

Wash and scrub well, but do not peel. Put into boiling salted water, enough to cover two inches, and cook rapidly for fifteen to twenty minutes. Pour off all the water, and if the potatoes are not quite tender, set them in a hot place, covered, to steam until they are. When they are done, sprinkle with salt, shake them till the skins crack and serve in a folded napkin. It is better to pare winter potatoes before cooking them, and they are usually better for lying some time in cold water; otherwise cook like new potatoes.

Baked potatoes should have a thin slice cut from each end, as this helps them to become mealy and take away the strong earthy taste of "the eyes."

Potato Au Gratin.

Cut cold potato in one-quarter inch dice and arrange in a dish, seasoning each layer. Pour over an equal bulk of thin Bechamel sauce and bake in a very hot oven till brown.

Potato Lyonnaise.

Put two tablespoons of butter into a frying pan, when melted add an onion, chopped fine; cook two or three minutes; add six cold boiled potatoes, sliced, well seasoned with pepper and salt; saute a nice light brown. Just before serving, add a teaspoon of finely chopped parsley and a few drops of lemon juice.

Potato. (Fried.)

Cut cold boiled potatoes in slices and season with salt and pepper. Have frying pan hot, with just enough dripping to cover the bottom. Brown the slices on both sides and keep hot till all are fried. These are a delightful garnish for breakfast ham.

Potato, French. (Fried.)

Pare the potatoes and throw into cold water for at least an hour. Cut in slices, blocks, strips, balls or any fancy shape, and dry them on a towel. Drop quickly into fat hot enough to brown them by the time they come to the surface. They are done when they float. Skim into a draining basket and set in the oven to keep hot, either as a garnish or for a vegetable.

Hashed Potatoes.

Chop cold boiled potatoes, new ones are best, into bits the size of a peanut. Season with salt, pepper and chopped parsley, and for one quart potato allow three tablespoons butter. Heat the butter and toss the potatoes in it till they begin to show a little brown, then add one-quarter cup thin cream, and set back to brown on the bottom. Fold like an omelet and serve, or gather into a mound with the brown crust on top.

Potato Puff.

Take two cups mashed potato, stir into it two tablespoons of melted butter, beat to a white cream; add two eggs, beaten very light; a teacup cream or milk, and salt to taste. Bake in a deep dish, in a quick oven, until nicely browned. Take four eggs, add the yolks first, then fold in the whites as for omelet and it will be an elegant souffle.

Potato Croquettes en Surprise.

Prepare as usual, but fold in the center of each croquette a roll of very creamy chicken croquette paste.

Plantation Sweet Potato.

Cut cold cooked sweet potatoes in rather thick slices. Put them in a deep dish with pepper, salt and butter, pour on a little milk, enough to barely show between the pieces, and bake in a moderate oven one hour.

Sugar Potato or Candied Yams.

Parboil, peel and cut in quarter inch slices. Put the slices into a heavy syrup made in the proportion of one cup white sugar to one-quarter cup water, and one teaspoon butter. Simmer gently for an hour, then let the syrup boil away till it is almost dry. Serve with meats.

Rice, Steamed.

Pour two cups of boiling water on one cup well washed rice, add one level teaspoon of salt. Cook in double boiler thirty minutes, or till soft. If too dry at the end of twenty minutes add a little more boiling water.

Rice, Boiled.

Have ready four quarts of boiling salted water. Throw in one cup rice and let boil fast, uncovered, until the kernels open. Drain in a colander, cover with cloth, keep warm twenty minutes, shake up light three times.

Curried Rice.

Mix one teaspoon curry powder with one cup gravy or white sauce and pour over rice boiled as above. Good with veal or mutton in any style.

Tomatoes

To be served raw should be peeled and set on ice at least an hour before using. Have boiling fast a kettle of water large enough to immerce four tomatoes at once. Plunge them in long enough to count five, then remove instantly to cold water. Let the water come to a boiling point before putting in another set, and they will be found to be firm and smooth when the thin outer skin is peeled off. For serving, see Salad. They are also eaten as a fruit with sugar.

Stewed.—Cut in slices across the grain and boil gently about fifteen minutes. Season to taste with salt, pepper and butter.

Baked.—Do not peel, but cut a small slice from the stem end, leaving the stem on the piece for a handle. Scoop out the middle and mix with an equal bulk of raw rice. Season well with butter, salt, pepper, cayenne and a speck of sugar, fill each tomato moderately full, replace the stems and bake in a quick oven half an hour or till soft. This stuffing may be varied by using crumbs, chopped and seasoned meat (ham or chicken is best), or macaroni.

Fried.—Cut them in halves and dust each cut surface with salt, pepper, sugar and enough very fine bread crumbs to dry them. Have some hot butter in the frying pan and brown the tomatoes on both sides. Drop bits of butter between them and stand over a moderate fire to cook very slowly. When tender take up carefully with a cake turner and serve on a heated platter. They are somtimes finished with a cream gravy as follows: Pour over them enough cream to nearly cover, let come to a boil, and simmer five minutes. Lift the slices carefully and thicken the gravy with two egg yolks beaten with a little cold cream. Do not let it quite boil, but serve as soon as thickened.

Broiled.—Slice and broil over a hot fire. Serve with melted butter.

Scolloped.—Put in a dish alternate layers of buttered bread crumbs with sliced tomatoes, sprinkled with pepper, salt and sugar. Spread bread crumbs and butter over the top. Bake one hour.

Turnips

Are wholly deficient in salt, fat and starch, and are therefore desirable to serve plain boiled or mashed and seasoned only with salt and pepper, with boiled bacon, roast pork and mutton. They are most palatable when cut into half inch cubes, boiled in plenty of well salted water, and served in a rich white sauce.

Salsify or Oyster Plant.

Boiled.—Wash, scrape and throw into cold water. Cut into inch pieces and boil rapidly uncovered in a granite stew pan. A little vinegar will help to keep it white. Drain them well and serve with plenty of butter and lemon juice, salt and pepper to taste, or dressed with cream or Bechamel sauce.

Fried.—Cut cold boiled salsify into convenient lengths, coat each with fritter batter No. 2, and fry in deep fat until well crisped.

Sarmas.

Prepare equal measure of finely minced meat, lamb or veal, and washed rice. Season to taste with salt, pepper, onion and cayenne. Scald grape leaves till they are well wilted. In each leaf roll a little of the meat and rice, making small oval balls, stew in just enough water to keep them from browning. Blanched lettuce or cabbage leaves will do; in this case add a few drops lemon juice to the meat.

Spinach.

Pick over carefully while dry, throw a few plants at a time into a large pan of cold water, wash well on both sides to dislodge insects, and pass to another pan. They should have at least three separate waters. Put the spinach into a large kettle without water, set it on the stove where it will cook slowly till the juice is drawn, then boil till tender, drain and chop fine. For half a peck of spinach add one ounce butter, one-half teaspoon salt. Reheat and serve on buttered toast.

Yams

Are treated and served like sweet potatoes.

NOTES ON BREAD MAKING
Requisites.

First.—The best flour, fresh sweet yeast, pure water or milk scalded, clean salt, sweet butter or lard, if any shortening is used, and a good oven.

Second—Milk should not be used in any kind of bread without being scalded or brought to boiling point before using.

Third—A cook who knows how to use these things, or one willing to learn and constantly practice with the needed skill, strength and patience.

Given these and good bread is assured. Flour should be kept in a dry place; it should be brought to the same temperature as the milk or water used for mixing, 70 degrees. Remember that the temperature of the body is over 95 degrees, so that the dough should always feel cool to the hand. Keep doors and windows shut while mixing or kneading or shaping bread or rolls; cover with a cloth, especially when shaping into loaves or rolls; it never recovers from a chill then. Keep it at an even temperature not less than 60 degrees, not over 80 degrees. It is very desirable to have a high shelf where the air is warm and where it is out of the way of draughts. If a tin bread pan is used cover closely with the usual tin cover and then with a woolen cloth or several layers of linen. Use this cover for nothing else. A novice might set the kneaded dough to rise in an earthen crock, it is very easy to tell in this when the mass has doubled in bulk; butter it lightly and have it evenly warmed.

Use only good yeast; if it is dry or discolored it is too old, if rank smelling it is not properly made and will spoil the bread.

Beat vigorously while the sponge is soft to fill it with bubbles; remember that yeast is a plant and needs air to make a good growth as well as water and an even temperature. Do not let it get too warm; if it is necessary to make bread in less than the usual time increase the quanitiy of yeast, double it if necessary, but keep it cool. It will not be so good, but better than it would if made too warm. Do not let it over rise, especially when shaped in loaves or rolls; this is fatal. Do not try to mix stiff in the bowl or pan; it is easier to do it on a well floured table. Use a stiff palette knife to help in turning and shaping to a ball. Knead by pushing the dough with the palm of the hand, curving the fingers to keep the ball from flattening too much; with every push turn the ball one-quarter round and half fold it over. Do not make it too stiff. A soft dough makes a tender bread, and one that will keep better than a stiff one. Knead until the dough has a silky smoothness, is full of blisters and does not stick to the hands or board. Work fast but lightly; the time required will vary with the manner of working and the method of mixing, usually about twenty minutes.

If dough does not rise fast enough, set the crock in warm water; this will give it an even temperature; add warm water every half hour. Bread should double its bulk at the first rising in four hours and at the second in one hour.

The proper size for bread pans is four inches deep, four and a half wide, ten long; they are best made of Russia iron. These will bake a two-pound loaf, but it is better to use not more than one and a half pounds. A new baking pan should always be baked blue in the over before it is used. For greasing baking tins use butter, lard, flour or a piece of laundry wax, rubbing on the pan while it is hot. Do not grease tins for white bread.

After the loaves or rolls have been in the pans a half hour the temperature may be increased; slip a warm, not hot, board under them and set a pan of warm water over them. Attend to the fire if coal is used (the oven can be heated with a wood fire in fifteen minutes); shake out ashes, see that the fire box is evenly filled half way up, and that the dampers are set right; brush off the outside of oven and see that the inside is ready for use; in ten minutes check the draught so that the oven shall not be too hot at first. When the loaves are nearly ready scatter a spoon of flour on paper and set in the oven; if it takes a good color in five minutes the oven is right for loaves; it should be quite brown in three minutes for rolls.

To prevent bread from raising unevenly in the oven, turn the loaf end for end when it has been in the oven just five minutes without regard for the way it looks at that time.

When loaves are baked the heat should be slightly increased for ten minutes, then gradually reduced. Rolls should have their greatest heat at first. Watch the oven, looking at the bread every ten minutes. In ordinary small ranges the loaves need frequent turning to ensure an even baking. In forty or fifty minutes the loaf will shrink somewhat and slip easily from the pan; it should have an evenly browned crust; one good test is to lay the hand on the bottom of the loaf and if the escaping steam is too hot to bear it shows that the interior needs more cooking. When safe to handle it is safe to take out. Take from the pans as soon as done and wrap in a thick cloth used for no other purpose. Lay on a rack, set where it will cool quickly and do not put away until entirely cold. Sift all meal and flour before measuring.

Always pulverize salt, cream of tartar, soda or baking powder before using.

For shortening a mixture of dripping, lard and the fat of veal or chicken is very nice.

Keep the bread box or jar sweet by frequent scalding and sunning.

Dry old rolls and pieces and keep in a separate place.

Do not throw away bread; it does not take much sense to find some way to use if there is no one who would be glad to eat the carefully kept odds and ends of good bread.

Always use a wooden spoon for stirring batter, soups, or fruits, as it will not wear out a sieve, stain nor spoil the flavor; to keep it white always dip in hot water before using, as that will fill the pores so they cannot absorb much of anything else.

BREAD RECIPE

To one quart of lukewarm (not hot) wetting (composed of equal portions of water and sweet milk, or water alone), add two half-ounce cakes (1 oz.) of compressed yeast and stir until completely dissolved, then add one teaspoonful of salt and three tablespoonfuls of sugar. When salt and sugar are thoroughly dissolved, stir in well-sifted flour with a wooden spoon until a dough is formed sufficiently stiff to be turned from the mixing bowl to the moulding board in a mass. The quantity of flour used to above wetting should be about three quarts; to this flour may be added, with excellent results, about two tablespoonfuls lard, if shortening is desired. Knead this dough, adding, if necessary, a little flour, from time to time until it becomes smooth and elastic and ceases to stick to the fingers

BE SURE AND READ THE ARTICLE ON WHITE BREAD APPEARING ON PAGE 70.

or mouldboard. Then put it into a well-greased earthen bowl, brush lightly with melted butter or drippings, cover with a bread towel or blanket and set to rise in a warm place for two hours, or until light. As soon as light, knead well and again place in earthen bowl, covering as before, and set for another rising of an hour, or until light. As soon as light, form gently into loaves or rolls, place in greased bread or roll pans, brush with melted butter or drippings, cover again with the towel or blanket and let stand for one and one-half hours, and then bake.

Water Bread.
READ NOTES ON BREAD MAKING.

One quart flour sifted, one-half teaspoon salt, one-half teaspoon sugar, one tablespoon butter or lard, one-half ounce compressed yeast (dissolved in one-half cup tepid water), one pint warm water. Measure flour, sugar and salt into a six-quart mixing bowl. Pour hot water enough to dissolve it onto the shortening, then add cold water to make just one pint of water at the right temperature (about 70 degrees), mix in the dissolved yeast and make a batter with the flour, beating well. Add more flour till the mixture is stiff enough to handle on the moulding board and knead, using as little flour as possible to keep it from sticking. Cover closely with a plate and let rise till it doubles its bulk. Cut it down and let rise again; divide into four parts and shape into round loaves, putting two in each pan, or shape part as biscuit. Cover and let rise to double its bulk. Bake as directed about forty-five minutes.

A different quality of bread is made by using milk to mix with, omitting the shortening, or by taking half milk and half water and part of the shortening; and still another by using skimmed milk. Always scald the milk thoroughly and cool before adding the yeast.

Milk Bread, with a Sponge.
Pour one pint of scalding milk on one tablespoon each of butter and sugar and one-half teaspoon salt; when lukewarm add one-half ounce yeast and let it rise. Stir in three and one-half cups of flour and beat well. Let it rise till very light, then add enough more flour to knead and work it till smooth and fine grained. Let it rise in the bowl, cutting down two or three times. This makes an excellent rule for tea biscuit, or rolls, and by doubling the measure of butter and adding the white of an egg well beaten you have the delicious White Mountain rolls.

Milk Rising Bread.
Boil one-half cup of new milk at night and add to it enough Southern corn meal to make a soft batter. Let it stand over night at a temperature of about 75 degrees. In the morning boil another half-cup of new milk and add cold water till about milk warm, and mix thoroughly with the batter made at night, adding one tablespoon sugar, one teaspoon salt and enough flour to make a soft batter. Set this mixture in a very warm place (not less than 100 degrees), and let it rise to double its bulk; it will take about three hours. As soon as well risen add an equal bulk of water in which has been dissolved one-half teaspoon soda, one rounded tablespoon of lard, more salt if liked, and flour enough to knead quite soft. Put it into the pans, let rise again to double its bulk, and bake as usual.—Mrs. J. B. S. Holmes, Rome, Ga

Graham Bread.

1 pint milk.	½ ounce yeast.
2 tablespoons brown sugar.	1 pint Graham.
1 teaspoon salt.	1 pint white flour.

Scald and cool the milk, add the sugar and crumbled yeast; when it floats and is frothy make a batter with the flour and meal, beating vigorously, let it rise till spongy, add the salt and more meal gradually until it is as thick as can be worked with a stiff knife, put one and a half pounds in each pan, smoothing the tops; cover and raise again. It should be set in a quick oven and the heat reduced in ten minutes. It is sometimes liked made stiff enough to knead, but should not be made as stiff as ordinary wheat bread; bake as usual, with heat increasing for ten minutes. Good baked as muffins.

Christmas Bread.
Dough enough for one medium-sized loaf.

1 cup of sugar.	1 egg.
½ cup lard.	1 teaspoonful spices (mixed).
1 cup raisins (seeded).	cloves and cinnamon.
½ cup currants.	Soda—the size of a bean.

Bake two loaves in one tin.

Graham and Rye Bread.
One pint Graham, one pint rye meal, one tablespoon molasses, one tablespoon shortening, one teaspoon salt, one-half ounce compressed yeast dissolved in two and one-third cups water. Make a sponge with the Graham, when light make stiff with the rye. It does not require long kneading, and will always be slightly sticky, but it is both palatable and nutritious. Put not more than one and a half pounds in a loaf and bake an hour and a quarter in a moderate oven. This is the "brown bread" of the English bakeries, and needs only a brick oven to be as good as theirs.

Graham and Rye Bread Steamed.
Two cups buttermilk, one-third cup molasses, one teaspoon salt, one teaspoon soda, one pint wheat Graham and one pint rye Graham. Beat well, put in two well-buttered two-pound tomato cans, (melt the top off at the gas jet) set over cold water and bring to a boil, this gives the loaf time to rise. Steam two hours, dry in a moderate oven one-half hour.

Rye Bread.
Three pints of rye flour; if the coarse rye meal is used take one quart rye and one pint white flour; dissolve one-half ounce yeast in three cups milk or water, one teaspoon salt and two tablespoons molasses, if liked. Treat like Graham. Bake moderately but thoroughly.

"Rye'n Injin."
Scald one cup corn meal with one quart boiling milk and let it cook fifteen minutes, add two tablespoons molasses, one teaspoon salt and let it cool; meanwhile dissolve one ounce of yeast in two tablespoons water, and beat thoroughly into the corn meal batter; mix in three cups of rye meal, not flour; if very coarse sift out some of the bran, but keep three cups to mix with, put into an iron or steel pan, bake in a sponge cake oven, but let it stay in two hours at least, covering closely if there is danger of browning. The old way was to put it in for the last baking of the brick oven and let it stand all night. If the upper crust was too hard it was evenly sliced from the loaf, well browned and used for crust coffee or brewis, either of which needs only to be known to be appreciated.

"Boston Brown Bread" Steamed.
Two cups rye meal, one cup corn meal, one-third cup molasses, one teaspoon salt, one teaspoon soda dissolved in two tablespoons water, one pint sour milk, steam four hours.

Graham Bread Steamed.
Three cups Graham, one teaspoon salt, one rounding teaspoon soda, one-third cup molasses, one pint sour milk, beat well, steam three hours in one tall mould or two tomato cans well buttered, set in oven to dry fifteen minutes.—Miss Ellen Munro, Milwaukee, Wis.

ROLLS.

For ordinary breakfast use take one and a half pounds bread dough when ready to shape into loaves, make a long even roll and cut into twelfths, shape with thumb and fingers into round balls set in an eleven by six-inch pan if liked without crust, or two inches apart on a sheet if wanted crusty all around, brush with butter, cover closely and let rise slowly for thirty or forty minutes, then raise the temperature slightly for another half hour; they should more than double their bulk and should have even, dome-shaped tops; bake in a quick oven fifteen to twenty-five minutes.

Finger Rolls.
Make "Milk Bread with a Sponge," putting in a generous measure of butter; proceed as usual, but cut down twice. Make a pound and a half of dough into two rolls, cut each into twelfths and make two rows in a biscuit tin, rise and bake as before.

For Pocket Books roll out the same dough after the second cutting to less than a half inch, spread thinly with butter, cut in strips four or five inches wide, fold down an inch or two at one end and then over again, cut off square and begin again, bake separately.

Folded Rolls are cut from the same sheet of buttered dough with a two-inch cutter, folded a trifle unevenly and set with edges up three rows of ten each in a biscuit tin.

Sticks.
These are used with soups and salads. Use the same material as for "Tea Biscuit with Potato," omitting the potato. Knead thoroughly and shape after the first rising, eighteen ounces of dough will make two dozen sticks. Make two even rolls and cut into twelve each, roll as even as a lead pencil and set in stick pans; they come in sets of one dozen. If the hands are dry dampen them with a wet towel, cover the rolls closely while rising; when making several dozen cover

with a damp cloth and put a thick dry one over. If wanted soft inside bake five minutes in a quick oven, or ten to fifteen in moderate oven if wanted crisp all through.

White Mountain Rolls.

Are made with four ounces dough, each six inches long and tapering somewhat to the ends; they may be laid on a sheet, but are nicer baked in French roll pans; these are half cylinders of Russia iron.

Thumb Rolls.

Are one and a half ounces made about two inches long and baked separately in French roll pans.

French Twists.

These require twenty ounces for each pair. Divide in fourths, roll nearly as long as the pan, lay a knife across the ends of two strands and fold one over the other to make a shapely twist. Braids are made in the same way with three or four strands, but are better baked in a pan.

Tea Biscuit.

One cup milk scalded and cooled, one tablespoon sugar, two tablespoons shortening, one-half teaspoon salt, one-half ounce yeast dissolved with the sugar in one-fourth cup water, three cups flour, beat well; let rise till light, add one cup flour and raise again, shape, butter, cover, raise till light and bake in quick oven.—Miss Ellen Mevrick, Milwaukee, Wis.

Tea Biscuit with Potato.

Three-fourths of a cup of hot, sifted potato, one-fourth cup butter, one teaspoon sugar, one teaspoon salt, mixed well together. One cup milk that has been scalded and cooled, one-fourth ounce compressed yeast, white of one egg slightly beaten. Mix the above ingredients well and add enough flour to knead it smooth. It will take about one quart.

If this is set at ten o'clock in the morning, it will be ready to shape and bake for tea.

Cut the sponge down once and when it has risen the second time shape in rather small biscuit, set them well apart in the pan and let it rise in a cool place till very light. Bake in a quick oven. These are excellent to use for croustades.—Mrs. Cheney, Ft. Wayne, Ill.

Sweet Potato Biscuit.

Boil and mash a large sweet potato while hot; work in two eggs and flour enough for a dough. Add one-quarter ounce yeast, and let it rise over night. In the morning work in a spoon of butter, mould in small biscuit, let them rise to double their size, and bake in a quick oven. Good for breakfast or tea.

Parker House Rolls.

Put one quart of flour in a large mixing bowl, make a hollow in the center, add one teaspoon salt, one tablespoon sugar, two large tablespoons butter, and pour on one pint of milk, boiling hot; let it alone until cooled to 70 degrees; add one-half ounce yeast dissolved in two tablespoons water; stir gently to make a thin batter, leaving a shell of flour around the batter; when full of bubbles mix stiff, using three cups flour, more or less; let it rise to twice its bulk, cut down, rise again, roll or pat out one-half inch thick, cut, butter, fold so that the upper edge overlaps the under one or they will spread apart too much in rising, cover closely, give them plenty of time to rise and do not let them be too warm, bake ten or fifteen minutes in hot oven.

Lancashire Tea Cakes.

1½ pounds flour.	½ pound currants.
¼ pound butter.	2 ounces candied lemon.
1 pint new milk.	2 eggs.
½ ounce yeast.	2 tablespoons sugar.

A little grated nutmeg.

Put the sugar and currants with the flour; melt the butter in the milk which must be scalded, and when cool enough mixed with the well-beaten eggs and yeast. Add the dry ingredients beating all well and set away to rise. When light put in cake pans to rise again to double its bulk. Bake in a moderately hot oven. These are delicious when fresh, and equally good split and toasted the second day.—Mrs. W. S. Turner, Asheville, N. C.

"To Make Wigs."

Take three pounds and a half of flour, and three-quarters of a pound of butter, and rub it into the flour till none of it be seen; then take a pint or more of new milk and make it very warm and half a pint of new Ale-yeast; then make it into a light paste. Put in caraway seeds and what spice you please; then make it up and lay it before the fire to rise; then

work in three-quarters of a pound of sugar, and then roll them into what form you please, pretty thin, rise again before the fire and bake in a warm oven.—The Compleat Housewife.

Crumpets.

One pint milk, scalded and cooled, one-half ounce yeast, dissolved in the milk with one teaspoon sugar and one-half teaspoon salt; when light, from two to four hours, add one-half cup melted butter, let stand twenty minutes, bake in rings on a large griddle; best when one or two days old and toasted.

Buns and Rusk.

One pint milk, scalded and cooled, one-half cup butter and lard mixed, one-half cup sugar, one-half cup sifted potato, one ounce yeast dissolved in the pint of milk with one teaspoon sugar, three eggs. Mix in the order given, adding flour to make a thin batter, about one quart; beat well; when full of bubbles, add flour to stiffen and knead well. Raise again, cut down, and when light again shape one-half the dough into small balls, like breakfast biscuit; place them close together in the pan, raise slowly at first, and when very light brush them over with this syrup: One tablespoon cream and one of sugar, boiled one minute. Currants or raisins seeded and quartered, may be added, or one teaspoon cinnamon. Bake the other half in two two-pound loaf pans. Set it in moderate oven so that the loaf will be nearly level; the next day cut in half-inch slices, set in a very moderate oven until perfectly crisp and of a bright yellow color. These are delicious with milk or chocolate for lunch. There are many variations of this rule. If a soft flour is used make simply a bread sponge, and after the second rising add the butter and sugar, creamed and beaten as for cake. This must be done with the hand, and when smooth add one, two or three eggs. Some recipes double the butter and sugar, and they are good with one-half as much.

Hot Cross Buns have two gashes cut across them with a sharp knife, or have deep folds pressed into them with a long pencil. When baked separately and shaped like French rolls they are called Quebecs. Roll to a thin sheet, brush with soft butter, sugar and spice, or fine dried fruit. Then fold over like jelly cake and cut in half-inch slices; let rise again till light, brush again with butter or sweetened milk and bake separately for Swedish Rolls.

Soft Kringles.

One-half pound dough from "Milk bread with a sponge." Pound two cardamon seeds to a powder with two good tablespoons sugar and work into the dough with two eggs and two tablespoons butter; add just enough flour to knead well. Roll into long sticks and cut into sections, shape in rings, links or pretzels.

Prune Kringles.

One-half pound dough, one tablespoon each butter and sugar kneaded into it. Chop six or eight good prunes in four tablespoons sugar, chop first, the meat of three or four of the stones very fine, mix, shape the dough into sticks the size of the little finger, roll in the prunes bake in oblong rings.

Sugar Kringles are made in the same way, substituting a dozen blanched and chopped almonds for the prunes, roll the sticks rather smaller, make oblong rings with one end crossing at the middle to the opposite side.

Giffles.

Take one-half pound Soft Kringle dough, roll one-quarter inch thick, cut in eight equal squares, put a spoonful of any firm jelly near one corner, roll over and over, stretching a little and curve like a Vienna roll. When very light glaze and bake ten minutes in a hot oven.

 BISCUIT, SHORTCAKE, MUFFINS, ETC.
WITH BAKING POWDER.

Baking Powder Biscuit.

One quart sifted flour, one teaspoon salt, four level teaspoons baking powder sifted together four times, two tablespoons butter, enough cold milk to make a stiff dough (patent flour will require about one pint). Rub the butter between the thumb and fingers to make it into fine flakes, add the milk gradually, mixing and cutting through with a knife till the whole is a light spongy mass. Turn on a well-floured board and press out with the hands to one inch thick, use a two-inch cutter and bake at once in a very hot oven; this will make just eighteen and fill one biscuit tin.

GOLD MEDAL FLOUR—It's a Biscuit Flour—It's a Bread Flour.

For Twin Biscuit make as above and roll only one-half as thick. Spread the rounds with soft butter, put two together and bake quickly.

For Sandwich Biscuit, make as before, but add one teaspoon shortening, roll less than one-half inch thick, cut in four inch rounds, bake separately on an iron sheet, cool, split and use for salad sandwiches with plain lettuce dipped in French dressing.

Dropped Biscuit.

One quart flour, one teaspoon sugar, one teaspoon salt, and four teaspoons baking powder sifted together four times. Rub in two tablespoons of butter and mix with one pint of milk; beat vigorously for one minute, drop by tablespoons in hot iron gem pans and bake ten minutes in a quick oven. Excellent made with Rye or Graham.

Short Cake, No. 1.

One pint flour, one-half teaspoon salt, two teaspoons baking powder, sifted together four times, one-quarter cup butter rubbed in, one egg beaten and mixed with one scant cup milk. Spread on a biscuit tin and bake in quick oven. Pull apart after cooling five minutes, spread with softened butter and fill with fruit.

Short Cake, No. 2.

One quart flour, one teaspoon salt, four teaspoons baking powder, sifted together four times, rub in one-half cup butter and lard and one-quarter cup milk. Bake in two long biscuit tins, making off in squares before baking. Bake in a very quick oven till a good brown. Use a generous quart of fruit for each layer, dust thick with powdered sugar. Pile whipped cream on the top layer just before serving. If it is wanted very crisp and short like pastry the amount of shortening is doubled and water used to mix rather stiffer than before. All butter makes it more crisp than lard.

Old Fashioned Short Cake, No. 4.

One large cup rich sour cream, one-half teaspoon salt and the same of soda, sifted four times with one pint flour, mix, beat well for two minutes. If there is no old fashioned spider take a twelve inch frying pan, have it buttered and hissing hot, spread in the short cake, cover with a flat tin and set hot griddle over. Do not burn, turn in less than ten minutes, when done break in pieces and send to table folded in napkin.

Doughnuts.

One cup sour cream, one cup sugar, three eggs well beaten, one level teaspoonful soda, a little salt, one-half grated nutmeg. Flour to roll to proper consistency, roll flat and cut into shape with tin circular form. Roll in confectioners sugar before serving.

Dumplings for Stews.

One pint of flour, one-half teaspoon salt, two teaspoons baking powder, sifted together four times; mix with one cup rich milk, drop by spoonsfuls into the boiling stew. Cover tight and do not open for ten minutes, when they should be done. These may also be dropped on a buttered plate and cooked in an ordinary steamer over fast boiling water.

When cooked with stewed fruit made very rich, this is called Fruit Pot Pie. Peach, pear, plum, apple highly flavored with quince, and cranberries are good. Crabapple is better to use with the rich crispness of a short cake.

Apple Dumplings, No. 1.

Fill a two quart granite ware pan two-thirds full of tart apples, pared, quartered and cored, add one-half cup water, cover and set on stove to heat while preparing crust. Make one-half the rule for short cake No. 1. Roll out to exactly fit the pan, cut several gashes to let the steam escape, lay it over the hot apples and cover with a deep pie plate; cook on top of the stove for half an hour, setting the pan on a trivet if necessary to keep the apples from burning; then lift the cover and brown the crust in a hot oven. Serve with hard sauce. Excellent also when steamed forty minutes. Invert on a large plate and serve with brown sugar sauce.

Apple Dumplings, No. 2.

Make crust as in short cake No. 1, but use scant measure of milk, roll out and cut in five inch squares, core and halve three large apples, fold each piece of apple in a square of paste,

bringing the corners to the core; turn the dumplings upside down in a well buttered dripping pan, dot them with bits of butter and sprinkle over four tablespoons of sugar; set the pan in a quick oven and after ten minutes pour on boiling water to half cover. Baste often and bake about thirty minutes in an oven hot enough to have them browned in that time. Serve with hot sauce, cream or the syrup from the pan.

Apple Cake.

Core, pare and cut in eighths four or five tender sour apples. Make the rule for short cake No. 2. Lay the apples closely in rows the long way of the biscuit pan, sift over two tablespoons sugar, in which a half teaspoon of cinnamon has been mixed if liked; work fast; bake in a rather quick oven about thirty minutes. It may be used plain for tea or with hot sauce for dessert. This is a very good and quickly made substitute for the true German dish, that has the rich, delicate coffee bread for a foundation, but which requires more time and care.

Peach Cobbler.

Prepare a rich short cake crust, using cream to mix it if possible. Fill a granite baking dish about one-half full with pared and stoned peaches. Allow one pint sugar to each quart of fruit. Cover and bake for an hour or longer until the peaches show a dark red color. Cool and serve with sugar and cream.

Peach Dumplings.

Make one-half the rule for short cake No. 1, roll out one inch thick, cut three inch rounds and make a large hollow in the biscuit with a cup, leaving just a rim around the edge, fill with fresh peaches cut in quarters, or nice canned peaches; sprinkle white sugar over the top enough to season well, set the dumplings in a pan and bake thirty minutes in a moderate oven; ten minutes before taking out pour over one pint boiling hot syrup (use the juice from the can) and baste twice, increase the heat to glaze the dumplings; if they brown a little all the better.

Corn Muffins, No. 1.

One-half cup corn meal, one and one-half cups flour, one cup sweet milk, two eggs; butter the size of small egg, three tablespoonfuls sugar (even full), three teaspoonfuls baking powder. Beat eggs together until very light, add milk and sugar, then flour, meal and butter (melted but not hot), the very last thing.

Corn Muffins, No. 2.

One cup corn-meal, two tablespoons sugar, one teaspoon salt, one even tablespoon butter, five cups boiling water. At night mix the meal, salt, sugar, in top of double boiler; add the boiling water and butter and cook one hour. Turn into a mixing bowl and pour over it one-quarter cup water to keep a crust from forming. In the morning beat it up soft and smooth, mix one and one-half cups fine yellow corn flour, one and one-half cups white flour, two even teaspoons baking powder and stir into the mixture. Add one egg well beaten, bake in iron gem pans in a hot oven; or, in the morning add one cup each of corn, rye and wheat flour; or, one and one-half corn, one graham, one-half cup wheat flour. These are good enough to pay for the extra trouble of cooking the evening before using. This rule makes sixteen muffins.—Boston Cook Book.

Loaf Corn Bread.

One pint yellow meal, one-half pint flour, one teaspoon salt, two teaspoons baking powder, all sifted together; one tablespoon sugar, three tablespoons melted butter, three eggs, one pint sweet milk. Beat long and hard, and bake in a large round loaf. The oven must not be too hot.

Togus Muffins.

1 cup sweet milk,	1½ cup corn meal,
1 cup sour milk,	½ cup flour,
¼ cup molasses,	1 teaspoon soda,
	½ teaspoon salt.

Steam in cups two hours.

White Corn Bread.

Put one quart of cream-white meal into a bowl, pour over sufficient boiling water to scald it through; the meal must be moist, but not wet; add to this a tablespoon of butter and teaspoon of salt. Beat three eggs without separating until light;

GOLD MEDAL FLOUR—It's a Biscuit Flour—It's a Bread Flour.

add them to the meal; then add one pint of thick sour milk; beat until smooth. Dissolve one teaspoon of soda in a tablespoon of boiling water, stir into the mixture, turn into a greased pan and bake in a moderately quick oven forty-five minutes. If you use sweet milk, baking powder must be used but your cake will not be so good.

Corn and Rice Cakes.

One pint white corn meal, one teaspoon salt, one tablespoon flour, one cup cold boiled rice, three eggs well beaten, one pint of milk, two tablespoons melted butter, one heaping teaspoon baking powder, bake in muffin pans about twenty minutes.

Hominy and Corn Meal Cakes.

Mix two tablespoons fine uncooked hominy, one-half teaspoon salt, one tablespoon butter, one-half cup of boiling water. Set over the boiling teakettle till the water is all absorbed, pour one cup boiling milk on one scant cup of cornmeal, add two tablespoons sugar and the hominy, cool and whisk in two eggs (yolks and whites beaten separately), one heaping teaspoon baking powder. Bake in gem pans twenty minutes.—Boston Cook Book.

Johnny Cake.

One quart of watermilled corn meal, one teaspoon salt, two tablespoons molasses, three cups buttermilk, two level teaspoons soda, crushed and stirred into the meal. Beat two eggs to a cream, add to the milk and meal, and beat fast for two minutes with a broad wooden spoon. Bake in two pans for one-half hour in a rather quick oven. This old-fashioned bread can only be properly made with old-fashioned meal. The usual kiln-dried meal makes a different quality, and the proportion should be three cups meal and one of flour, while if one has the golden granulated, which is so nice for mush and steamed bread, it will do to take one pint of flour to one pint of corn meal. In this case take one pint sour milk and use four tablespoons melted shortening.

Corn Cake with Suet.

One cup corn meal, one cup flour, one-half teaspoon salt and one-half teaspoon crushed soda, sifted together. Add one-half cup finely chopped suet and one pint sour milk; beat well and bake in moderate oven one-half hour. It may be eaten with syrup, but is recommended only for zero weather.

Muffins, No. 1.

One pint milk, one tablespoon sugar, half ounce yeast, make a sponge with three cups flour, beat well. When light add two eggs, two tablespoons butter melted, half teaspoon salt, one cup flour, more or less; raise till light, fill rings or gem pans, raise again and bake in a rather quick oven for twenty or twenty-five minutes. If baked in a buttered dish and sent to the table in the same pan it is called Sally Lunn. It used to be the custom to cut them in two as soon as out of the oven, butter freely, replace and eat at once, but happily this villainy is now out of fashion.

Muffins, No. 2. (English.)

One quart flour, one teaspoon salt, one-third ounce yeast, one and one-half cups of warm water. Dissolve the yeast in one-third cup of cold water, add it with the salt and the warm water and gradually stir it into the flour. Beat the dough thoroughly; cover and let rise in a warm place until spongy, about five hours. Then shape the dough on a floured board into balls about twice as large as an egg. Flatten to one-third of an inch thick. Lay these on a warm griddle which has been lightly greased and set on the back of the stove to rise slowly. As soon as they have risen a little draw them forward and cook slowly, turning often. They should take about twenty minutes to rise and fifteen minutes to bake. Tear them apart and butter them while hot.—Miss Parloa.

Yorkshire Toasted Tea Cakes.

Make a sponge with three pints of sifted flour, one teaspoon of salt, one pint warm milk, one-half pound of butter melted in it, half an ounce of yeast dissolved in a little warm water. Beat these smooth and let rise until very light, add a beaten egg and enough flour to knead smooth. Make this into flat cakes the size of a teaplate, let them rise an hour and bake in a moderate oven. The next day split and toast, butter at once and serve hot.

Graham Muffins, No. 1. (Raised.)

Make the same as for bread but fill well-buttered gem pans

instead of making loaves, raise until light, bake twenty minutes in quick oven.

Graham Muffins, No. 2. (With Baking Powder.)

Make like drop biscuits but take only half the shortening, none is needed if creamy milk can be had; use a little more milk.

Graham Muffins No. 3 (With Baking Powder).

1 cup Graham Flour,	1 teaspoon salt,
1 cup Flour,	1 cup milk,
¼ cup sugar,	1 egg, well beaten,
2 teaspoons Baking Powder,	1 tablespoon melted butter.

Sift together thoroughly the flour, sugar, baking powder and salt. Add gradually the milk, egg and butter. Bake in hot buttered gem pans twenty-five minutes.

Brown Muffins.

One cup corn meal, two cups rye meal, one-fourth cup molasses, one-half teaspoon salt. Dissolve one-fourth yeast cake in a little tepid water, add enough more to make a soft dough. Rise over night. In the morning add one saltspoon soda dissolved in as little warm water as possible. Drop into muffin pans, let stand till light. Bake in a rather moderate oven.

Oat Meal Muffins.

One large coffee cup freshly cooked oat meal, one tablespoon butter, one tablespoon sugar, one teaspoon salt, mix well together, add one-fourth to one-half yeast cake dissolved in as little water as possible, and enough flour to mould very stiff. Rise till light, drop in warm gem pans, rise again until soft. Bake in a quick oven about twenty minutes.

Rice Muffins, No. 1.

One coffee cup of warm boiled rice, half tablespoon sugar, one tablespoon butter well worked into the rice while warm, add one scant cup milk and flour enough to make a very stiff dough. One-quarter to one-half yeast cake dissolved in a little of the milk. Rise till light, then add two eggs beaten to a cream, drop into well buttered muffin pans, rise till very light. Bake about ten minutes in the hottest kind of an oven.

Rice Muffins, No. 2.

Use the same ingredients as in No. 1, but scant the measure of flour so as to make it a drop batter and add two teaspoons baking powder instead of the yeast.

Cream Muffins.

One pint flour, half teaspoon salt, two teaspoons baking powder sifted four times, yolks of two eggs beaten lightly, one and a quarter cups cream, beat thoroughly then fold in lightly the beaten whites of the two eggs. Bake in muffin pans and serve hot.—Mrs. Lincoln.

Pauline Muffins.

One pint flour, one pint milk, two eggs, one tablespoon sugar, one tablespoon butter, two teaspoons baking powder, one-half teaspoon salt. Mix and sift the flour, baking powder and salt, rub the butter and sugar, then mix the flour with it to cream, add the eggs and beat till smooth, then mix it with the flour, pour in the milk and beat rapidly till very light. Pour into buttered gem pans or muffin rings with bottoms, about two-thirds full, and bake in a quick oven.

Harrison Bread.

One pint of milk, one tablespoon of lard, four eggs well beaten, flour for a thick batter, half ounce of yeast. Pour the milk boiling hot on the lard; when cold, stir in the eggs, flour and yeast; set to rise, and when light bake in a loaf. Serve it hot, and slice it at the table, like cake.

Quick Sally Lunn.

One quart flour, one teaspoon salt, three teaspoons baking powder, three eggs well beaten with two tablespoons sugar, one pint milk, two tablespoons butter, softened. Beat well; makes two square pans of sixteen muffins.

Quick Coffee Bread.

Same as above, using half cup less milk, five eggs and sprinkling sugar on top with a little cinnamon, instead of mixing it with the dough.

GOLD MEDAL FLOUR—It's a Pastry Flour—It's a Cake Flour.

Blueberry Tea Cake.

One quart flour, one teaspoon salt and three of baking powder sifted with the flour. One cup sugar, two eggs, one pint sweet milk, one-half cup butter, melted, beat all well together; then add one pint blueberries that have been picked over and well dusted with flour. Stir carefully not to break the berries. Fill pans about three-quarters full and bake about one-half hour in a moderate oven. Serve with stewed berries.—Mrs. Helen Campbell.

Squash Muffins.

Cream, one-half cup butter, add one-half cup sugar and beat two minutes, then add one and a half cups sifted squash, it should be very dry, dilute with one and a half cups milk in which has been dissolved one-half ounce yeast, mix stiff with flour, perhaps five cups; knead well and let rise till light. Shape into biscuit, raise slowly. It will take a half hour longer than for plain rolls and they must not be too warm. Bake half an hour in oven not so hot as usual.

Squash Muffins, No. 2.

One pint flour, two teaspoons baking powder, two eggs, one teaspoon salt, four tablespoons sugar, one cup sifted squash, and milk enough to make a drop batter (about one cup). Bake like Tea Cake.

Popovers.

One egg, one cup flour, one saltspoon salt, add gradually one cup milk and beat furiously five minutes; have iron gem pans or stone cups hissing hot, fill half full, set in a white bread oven and do not open the door for fifteen minutes. (They may also be made with graham). Mix with milk and cream, half and half, or add one tablespoon melted butter in the last two minutes' beating, and the popovers can be served with any rich hot sauce for dessert and called Sunderland pudding.

Graham Puffs.

For one dozen puffs use three eggs, one pint of milk, one pint of graham, one teaspoon of sugar, half a teaspoon of salt and three eggs. Butter the muffin pans and place them where they will get warm. Mix the graham, flour, sugar and salt; beat the eggs till very light, and add the milk to them; pour it upon the dry ingredients, and beat well for three minutes; turn the batter into the muffin pans, and bake in a rather hot oven for half an hour. If the taste of rye be liked, half a pint of rye meal may be substituted for the graham.

Whole Wheat Puffs.

Beat the white of one egg to a stiff froth, add to the yolk one-half cup of rather thin, sweet cream and one cup of skim milk; beat together until perfectly mingled and foamy with air bubbles; then add gradually, beating well at the same time, one pint of flour; continue the beating vigorously without interruption eight or ten minutes; then stir in lightly the white of the egg. Do not beat after the white of the egg is added, but turn at once into heated irons and bake. If properly made and carefully baked, they will be of fine, even texture and as light as bread raised by fermentation. Fill the irons full.

Corn Popovers.

Scald one pint of milk, add an even tablespoon butter, stir in a generous half pint of sifted corn meal. When cool, add three well beaten eggs, put in hot iron gem pans and bake as above.

Graham Rolls.

These rolls properly made are excellent. Mrs. Susanna Dobbs gives the following directions for a perfect gem: Mix graham or whole wheat flour with ice-cold water in the proportions of two-thirds of a cup of water to a pint of flour; more wetting must be used if the flour is very coarse. Stir fast until a moderately stiff dough is formed, and knead thoroughly from ten to fifteen minutes, till the dough is fine and elastic to the touch. Roll half of it at a time into long rolls a little over an inch in diameter; cut off and shape into rolls three or four inches long and three-quarters of an inch thick. Work quickly and place a little apart in a pan; prick them with a fork and put the pan in a hot oven. When done they should not yield to pressure between the thumb and finger. They are to be eaten warm or cold and are just as good re-warmed as when new. To do this dip in cold water, cover with cloth and set in a moderate oven, when they will puff up lighter than at first. These require slow mastication, and are sweet as a nut and very nutritious.—Hester M. Poole.

Rye Breakfast Muffins.

One cup rye meal, one cup flour, one cup milk, one-quarter cup sugar, one-half teaspoon salt, two teaspoons baking powder, one egg well beaten. Mix all the dry materials. Add milk to the beaten egg and beat well together. Bake twenty minutes in muffin tins in a quick oven.—Miss Parloa.

Wafers.

One pint whole wheat flour, one-half teaspoon salt; rub in a tablespoon butter and make into a stiff dough with milk. Take bits of double the size of an English walnut and roll them the size of an eight inch plate. Bake in a hot oven till a golden brown.

Gluten Wafers.

One-half cup good cream, one saltspoon salt, and gluten to make a stiff dough; knead well, shape in long rolls, lay on unbuttered baking sheet and roll as thin as letter paper. Bake in quick oven till lightly brown.—Mrs. Lincoln.

Beaten Biscuit.

Three pints pastry flour, one cup lard, one teaspoon salt, rub lard and flour together and make into a very stiff dough with milk or milk and water, knead and beat with rolling-pin (or mallet) an hour, or work in machine for half that time. The dough should be smooth and glossy, bits should break off with a snap. Shape in thin flat cakes, pick all over with a sharp fork and bake in a moderate oven to a delicate brown and till the edges crack a little. They must have time enough to bake thoroughly, or they will be heavy in the middle.

Dodgers.

Put one cup Indian meal in the upper part of double boiler with one-half teaspoon salt, when it boils pour on one cup boiling water, beat smooth, cook one hour, add one tablespoon butter; drop by spoonfuls on a buttered griddle, pat them down flat and when browned put a dot of butter on each before turning. They are a good accompaniment to broiled ham, and may be used for a winter breakfast cooked in the frying pan after sausage or bacon.

Hoe Cake.

Put one quart of white corn meal into a bowl, add one teaspoon of salt, add to it sufficient boiling water to moisten, stirring all the time to make a stiff batter. Moisten the hands in cold water. Take a tablespoon of the batter in your hand and press it into a thin round cake.

If you have an open fire, have before it an oak plank, well heated. Place the cakes against the board in front of the fire. Bake on one side and turn and bake on the other until thoroughly done, about three-quarters of an hour. These can also be baked on a griddle on top of the fire.

When done pull apart, butter and send to the table hot. Good.—Mrs. Rorer.

Thin Corn Cake. "Splits."

One cup corn-meal (yellow), one-quarter teaspoon salt, one round tablespoon butter, one and one-half cups boiling water, one teaspoon sugar. Pour the boiling water on meal, sugar and salt. Beat thoroughly. Add the butter and when well mixed spread very thin on buttered tin sheets. Bake slowly about twenty minutes. Pull apart and butter while hot.

Corn Meal Scones.

Put two cups of corn meal into a bowl. Add a teaspoon of sugar, a teaspoon of salt, two teaspoons of baking powder and mix it well together. Add a large teaspoon of butter. With your hands rub it into the flour. Add to this sufficient cold milk to make a batter that will drop, not pour from the spoon. Bake on a griddle in muffin rings, as you would ordinary muffins.—Mrs. Rorer.

Soft Johnny Cake.

Put to boil one pint water in a saucepan, one saltspoon salt. When it boils add one gill rolled oats and boil fifteen minutes. Then stir in well half-pint corn-meal. Spread out on a small frying pan. Cover close and bake twenty minutes. Turn and bake ten or twenty minutes more according to its thickness;

with raisins, currants or chopped dates, children will often relish it without butter. Serve warm. It can be baked in an oven. If spread out in a thin loaf it can be baked in a harder crust, which some prefer.

Oatmeal Scones.

Oatmeal scones are made from the left-over porridge from breakfast, which is often thrown away. Put a piece of butter the size of a walnut into a cup, add quarter of a teaspoon of bi-carbonate of soda; pour over this a gill of hot water; stir until the soda is melted, then quickly turn it over the porridge in the bowl. Mix well, turn it out on a bake board, knead it into a round, flat mass, just as you would bread. Roll out the dough to about a quarter of an inch thick; divide it into three and bake it on a hot griddle. This must be baked exceedingly slow; when baked carefully on both sides, remove them from the fire, and when ready to use toast them slowly for ten minutes.

Oatmeal Breakfast Cakes.

Wet a pint of No. 2 oatmeal or granulated oatmeal with sufficient water to saturate it well and pour into a shallow pan, making it half an inch thick or less. Bake twenty minutes in quick oven. Break it like sponge cake and eat warm. It can be made either crisp or moist. Corn meal cooked in the same manner and eaten at once, is equally good. One would not believe without trying, how palatable and satisfying such simple dishes can be made. Without butter, sugar or eggs and slightly salted, the true flavor of the grain is developed.

Pan Cakes.

To bake pan cakes with comfort do not grease the griddle, if the cakes stick add a teaspoon of butter to the batter; it is much better to have it there than on the hot griddle, where it burns and fills the house with vile smoke. Turn the griddle often to keep the heat even. When using a gas range set the cake griddle on two open griddles instead of one. Keep the cake turner free from batter and clear off all drops and crumbs before putting on fresh batter. Let each cake bake until full of holes and dry at the rim, turn only once and let it stand till it has done puffing. Cakes made with a large proportion of cooked material like rice, crumbs, etc., can be cooked more quickly than when made wholly of flour.

French Pan Cakes.

Two cups flour, three eggs, one tablespoon sugar, a little salt, one cup of milk. Beat well together for five minutes and fry in hot butter, roll up and fill with any kind of fruit, sprinkle a little powdered sugar over the top and serve hot.

Scotch Short Bread.

1 pound flour,	¼ ounce caraway seeds or ¼
½ pound powdered sugar,	pound caraway comfits.
½ pound butter,	

Beat butter to a cream, add flour, sugar and seeds mixed; knead the paste smooth, roll out one-half inch thick and cut in oblong cakes. Prick all over and bake in moderate oven one-half hour.

Pan Cakes, No. 1.

Make a batter with one pint of flour and one heaping teaspoon baking powder well sifted, add one and one-half cups milk, beat two eggs, one-half cup melted butter, a little salt, mix well and bake by the spoonful on hot griddle.

Pan Cakes, No. 2.

One pint flour, one-half teaspoon salt and one teaspoon crushed soda sifted together, add one pint sour milk, two tablespoons butter melted and two well beaten eggs, beat well with broad spoon, drop from the point of a tablespoon. Try one-half graham or one-third corn meal for a variety. Cook the last more slowly.

Add one pint huckleberries, cleaned and rolled in flour, or one cup peaches cut fine, laid in sugar for one hour, or cherries stewed sweet and drained. These are quite as nice as the French pancakes and more digestible.

When eggs are scarce the cakes may be made with less or even with none, but the amount of milk should be diminished and the beating, not stirring, increased.

Pan Cakes with Rice.

No. 1. One pint soft boiled rice, stir in while hot two tablespoons butter and let cool, add one-half cup milk, one-half cup flour and two well beaten eggs.

No. 2. One pint soft boiled rice, if cold heat with two tablespoons milk, mixing thoroughly with a fork; add one cup sour milk, one cup flour in which there is one scant teaspoon of soda and two well beaten eggs.

No. 3. One-half pint boiled rice, crushed and beaten gradually into one quart milk, three cups flour sifted with three teaspoons baking powder and one-half teaspoon salt, add two ounces softened butter and two eggs beaten separately, folding the whites in carefully the last thing.

These three rules are a very good epitome of the countless variations one sees in cook books and newspapers. With these for a standard one can vary at pleasure with crumbs, hominy, oatmeal, sweet corn, etc.

Crumb Pan Cakes.

Into a double boiler put one tablespoon of butter, one and a half cups coarse crumbs and one pint sweet milk; steam till tender and rub through a sieve or Henes press. When cool add the beaten yolks of two eggs and one cup flour in which two teaspoons baking powder have been sifted. Beat the whites stiff with a pinch of salt and fold in lightly; they should be baked rather more slowly than the ordinary pancakes. If they stick add a little melted butter, stirring in very carefully.

Graham Pan Cakes.

Make a sponge as for bread with one pint milk, scalded and cooled, one-quarter ounce yeast dissolved in the milk, with one teaspoon sugar and one of salt, one cup graham or whole wheat flour, one cup flour. Let it rise over night in a cool place. Add one saltspoon soda dissolved in two tablespoons milk, beat well, try a spoonful, and add milk or soda to make it right. Wheat bread sponge may be used in the same way.

Buckwheat Cakes.

Mix one-half cup of corn meal and one-half teaspoon of salt with one pint boiling water, beat well and when cool add one-half cup white flour and one cup buckwheat, with one-quarter ounce dissolved yeast; in the morning pour off the discolored water that lies on top of the batter and dilute with one-half cup of milk in which is dissolved one saltspoon of soda. Butter the griddle lightly and bake in small cakes quickly; the batter is so thin that they do not need much time. They should be thin, crisp and full of bubbles. Beat the batter and add more milk or soda if needed before sending to the table. They will brown better if made with milk, but will not be so crisp; a tablespoon of molasses may be added. Save a cup of the batter to serve as yeast for the next time, they improve with repeated use. The griddle for these cakes as well as a waffle iron must be well greased; fold a five inch strip of cotton, roll it around the end of a pine stick, fasten it with a tack and when the cakes are baked burn it.

Potato Pan Cakes.

Peel large potatoes over night and keep them in cold water; grate, drain, and for every pint allow two eggs, beaten separately, one-half teaspoon salt, a dust of pepper and one tablespoon flour, more or less according to the quality of the potatoes. Brown in thin cakes in butter. In winter use with meat, in summer try tomato or any brown sauce.

Waffles.

Any of the recipes for pancakes can be cooked in a waffle iron by adding more butter to make the proportion equal two ounces butter to each pint of flour. Yolks and whites are best beaten separately.

French Waffles.

One cup butter, one cup sugar, beaten together as if for cake, add singly yolks of seven eggs, one tablespoon brandy, and the grated peel of one-half lemon or one saltspoon mace. Add alternately three cups flour and one pint of milk, beating until it is full of bubbles, then add one ounce yeast, dissolved, and the stiff whites of the eggs; let it rise three hours.—Mrs. Bayard Taylor.

German Waffles. (Pfann-Kuchen.)

One-half cup butter, rub to a cream, add one cup powdered sugar and the yolks of eight eggs, one at a time; add alternately a scant cup milk, and two cups flour, in which two teaspoons baking powder, one-half teaspoon salt and some grated lemon peel have been sifted.—Mrs. Bayard Taylor.

GOLD MEDAL FLOUR—It's a Biscuit Flour—It's a Bread Flour.

Hello! Hello!

"Give me the best Flour please!" But you may not get it — you are disappointed. Next time you order

Specify

PASTRY.

Puff Paste.

One pound flour (one quart), one teaspoon salt, one-third pound butter, well rubbed together till like meal. If your hands are hot, chop it together without touching it with the hands. Mix stiff as possible with ice water and pat this out on the board to about one-third of an inch thick; lay this sheet of paste on ice while two-thirds pounds butter is washed and worked in cold water until waxy. Divide it in four parts and pat each out to as thin a cake as you can, it is no matter if it is broken through in holes. Set these sheets of butter on ice also. Now dust the board and pin slightly with flour, place the sheets of paste on it and one sheet of butter on the middle of the paste; fold the paste over the butter in such a way as to divide the paste in thirds, then turn over the ends letting them meet in the middle; the paste is now in rectangular shape, and with a little care in rolling can be kept so through all the subsequent foldings and rollings. Roll out to one quarter inch thick and fold as before, but without butter. The third time of folding enclose the second piece of butter, and continue adding it at every alternate rolling until it has all been used; as there were four sheets of butter that will make eight times folding and rolling the paste. Finally give one, two or three extra turns, as your patience holds out; lay on ice until needed for use; it is better to lie for several hours before being baked. If the paste sticks to the board or pin lay on ice until chilled through, scrape the board clean, polish with a dry cloth and dust with fresh flour before trying again. A stone slab is a comfort but not at all necessary. Use as little flour in rolling as possible, but use enough to keep the paste dry. Roll with a light, even, long stroke in every direction, but never work the rolling-pin back and forth, as that kneads the paste and toughens it, besides breaking the bubbles of air. The number of layers of butter and paste makes it flaky, but every bubble of air that is folded in helps it to rise and puff in baking.

To Bake Puff Paste

The dough should be ice cold when put into the oven. If it softens while being cut into the desired shape, place it on the ice again until hard. The oven should be as hot as for baking white bread; set it on the floor of the oven at first until risen to its full height, then slip a grate under to keep from burning while baking through and browning; if the oven is too hot the paste will set and scorch before it is risen; if too cold it will melt and spread or slip out of shape. The exact temperature can only be learned by practice.

For Pies.

Roll the paste out about one-third of an inch thick, then roll up and cut from the end of the roll. Turn each piece on the side so that the folds show the rings, pat out flat, then roll a trifle larger than the plate. This should be used for the upper crust only, and for a rim if desired; if used for under crust it is always sodden and indigestible.

Tarts

Are rolled as thin as convenient and cut with a fluted cutter. They are served cold, filled with jelly or jam.

Chopped or Rough Puff Pastry.

One pound flour, fourteen ounces butter, one teaspoon salt, one cup ice water. Have flour, salt and butter ice cold and chop the butter into it until there are no bits larger than a bean. Pour in the water slowly, tossing the mass together until a little more than half of the flour is moistened. Turn on the rolling-board, gather with a long knife into a square mound and press down with a cold rolling-pin, rolling gently till the mass is three times as long as it is wide. With a broad-bladed knife turn over the ends so as to fold it in thirds and roll out again; repeat, gathering all the loose crumbs between the folds at each turn, until the loose pieces form a consistent sheet of paste. It will usually need four turns, though three are sometimes enough. This can be shaped and baked at once, but is more flaky if allowed to chill on ice for an hour or more.

Plain Pastry.

One cup of flour, heaping, one saltspoon baking powder, one saltspoon salt, one-quarter cup lard, one-quarter cup butter mix baking powder and salt with the flour; rub in the lard and butter till fine and dry like meal. Mix to a stiff paste with ice water; this makes a tender, crispy crust, but not in the least flaky. If baked quickly and thoroughly it is as little hurtful to the digestion as any pastry can be. To make it somewhat flaky rub in only the lard, pat and roll out to one-third inch thick, dot on one-half the butter in thin pieces, dust on flour and fold in thirds; pat and roll out again, dot with remainder of butter and roll up like a jelly roll; cut from the end as directed for puff paste and it will give a fairly handsome crust if properly done. All pastry needs a quick oven at first to keep it from melting. Never grease the pie plate. All pies made with an upper crust should have holes cut to let the steam escape or the crust will be likely to be sodden on the under side. Tin or granite ware plates are much the best, as they cannot soak grease and they bake the under crust more quickly and perfectly. The English fashion of baking all fruit pies in deep dishes, with no under crust, is admirable, being far more delicious as well as more wholesome. Their meat and game pies, made in the same way, win favor wherever they are introduced.

Apple Pie

Line a plate with plain paste, fill with apples that have been pared, cored and cut in eighths. Pile as high above the edge as the bottom of the plate is below. Cover with either chopped or puffed paste, and bake till apples are soft, about thirty minutes. (Try them with a straw.) When done boil three-quarters cup sugar in one-quarter cup of water five minutes. Pour this syrup boiling hot through the holes in the crust. Tilt the pie a little until the syrup shows through on every side. If you choose to put in the sugar before baking, sprinkle three-quarters cup over the apples when the pie is little more than one-half full, cover with remainder of apples and put on crust as usual. Cut a bias strip of cotton one inch wide and long enough to go around the plate, wring it out in cold water and bind the edge of the pie with it. If pulled from the pie as soon as taken from the oven, it will leave no mark.

Creamed Apple Tart.

Line a small, deep pudding dish, with pastry, pack in one and a half pint cut apples, with three-quarters cup of brown sugar and grated rind and juice of one-half lemon. Cover and bake till well done. Lift the crust and pour in one pint boiled custard. Return the cover and let it be ice cold when served. This is an old fashioned, Dutch dish. Whipped cream may be used for a filling; in this case heap it high and do not put the cover on again.

Pie Plant Pie.

Wash the stalks and cut into inch bits without peeling, pour boiling water over it and let it stand ten minutes, drain and dredge lightly with flour; for a ten inch plate allow a heaping cup of sugar, dot with one tablespoon butter cut in bits the size of a pea, cover and bake in a quick oven for the first ten minutes, then more slowly until done, about thirty minutes in all.

Custard Pie.

Line a deep plate with a rim. Heat one pint of milk, rub one teaspoon flour smooth with one-half cup cold milk, add to the boiling milk and cook five minutes. Pour upon three beaten eggs, one-half cup of sugar, one saltspoon salt and flavor to taste, one-half teaspoon lemon or one teaspoon vanilla. Strain hot into the plate, bake slowly, never letting it boil. It is done when a knife blade makes a clean cut.

Pumpkin Pie.

One cup of stewed and sifted pumpkin (or squash), one level teaspoon salt, one saltspoon mace, one teaspoon cinnamon, two-thirds cup sugar, one beaten egg well mixed together, pour over one cup each of cream and milk boiling hot, fill the plate and set into oven as quickly as possible; if pumpkin is watery add one teaspoon flour. It is done when it rises well in the middle. A rim of puff paste can be laid around the edge of the plate if liked, if used it should be at least one inch

GOLD MEDAL FLOUR—It's a Pastry Flour—It's a Cake Flour.

wide and the edge that goes down into the squash rolled very thin. For potato pie use boiled and sifted sweet potato in place of pumpkin.

Sliced Potato Pie.

Boil sweet potatoes until well done. Peel and slice them. Line a deep pie pan with good plain paste and arrange the sliced potatoes in layers, dotting with butter and sprinkling sugar, cinnamon and nutmeg over each layer, using at least one-half cup sugar. Pour over three tablespoons whiskey, about one-half cup water, cover with pastry and bake. Serve warm.—Mrs. J. B. S. Holmes, Rome, Ga.

Lemon Pie, No. 1.

One cup of milk, one cup of sugar, one tablespoon cornstarch cooked over hot water for at least fifteen minutes, one saltspoon salt, the yolk of three eggs and the white of one egg, grated rind and juice of one lemon. Fill the paste while hot and bake quick. Beat the whites of two eggs stiff, add slowly two tablespoons of sifted powdered sugar, spread over the pie as soon as it comes out of the oven and return it to dry and brown slightly.

N. B. Leave the door ajar.

Lemon Pie, No. 2.

Grated rind and juice of one lemon, one cup sugar, one-half cup of milk, two tablespoons cracker dust, two eggs, one saltspoon salt. Good baked in old fashioned way between two crusts, but better used to fill shallow muffin pans that have been lined with rough puff paste; cover with a meringue.

Cherry Tart.

Pick over one and one-half pounds of cherries; turn a tiny cup upside down in the middle of a deep pie dish, fill around it with the fruit, add sugar to taste. Lay a wide strip of plain paste around the edge of the dish, cover and press the edges firmly together with a pastry jagger, bake in hot oven and serve with powdered sugar sprinkled thickly on top. All juicy fruits are most excellent cooked in the same way.

Mirlitons.

Pound and sift six macaroons, add one tablespoon grated chocolate and one pint hot milk. Let stand ten minutes and then add the yolks of three eggs well beaten, one tablespoon sugar, one teaspoon vanilla. Line patty tins with puff or chopped paste, fill with the mixture and bake in a quick oven twenty minutes.

Brambles.

One lemon grated whole, one cup raisins, seeded and chopped fine, one-half cup sugar, one egg, one tablespoon cracker dust, bake in "turnovers" or patty pans, or better still, roll trimmings of puff paste as thin as possible, put a layer on a baking sheet, spread with above mixture and cover with another flat of paste. Mark off with a pastry jagger in strips four inch long by two inch wide and bake in a quick oven. These are nice with a thin icing and are delicious with cocoa for lunch. Another richer filling is made by chopping very fine one-quarter pounds figs, two ounces citron, one-quarter cup pistachio nuts (or almonds), two ounces seeded raisins, add one egg well beaten and use like the above.

Mince Pies, Plain.

Two coffee cups chopped beef and small piece, about four ounces, of fat salt pork, four coffee cups sugar, one nutmeg, one coffee cup molasses, two lemons, rind and juice, or sour orange, four teaspoons salt, two cups cider, boiled with the molasses, four teaspoons cinnamon, four cups of chopped fruit (raisins, citron, currants), one teaspoon cloves, one cup suet, finely chopped. Mix and scald, pack down in jars and pour a little brandy on top. When used add six cups apple and stoned raisins ad lib.

Mince Pies, Richer.

One pound fresh beef, one pound tongue, one-half pound salt pork (scalded) chopped very fine, one pound large raisins, seeded, one pound Sultana raisins, one pound currants, three-quarter pound "A" sugar, three-quarters pound granulated sugar caramel, one pint of rich stock, one pint of boiled cider, fruit juice or soft jelly, simmer till well blended. Add one tablespoon salt, two teaspoons cinnamon, one teaspoon allspice, one teaspoon clove, one teaspoon mace, one teaspoon nutmeg,

one-half pound citron, shredded. Cool and taste; add more seasoning if liked. Pack in glass jars, pouring two tablespoons brandy on the top of each. When ready to use, add two and one-half cups of chopped raw apples to each cup of the mince; partly cook and put into the pies hot, adding lemon (grated rind and juice) and rose water, if liked.

Sour Cream Pie.

1　cup sour cream,	¼ teaspoon cloves,
½ cup seeded raisins, chopped fine,	
½ teaspoon cinnamon,	3　yolks of eggs,
1　cup sugar,	1　white of egg.

Bake like lemon pie, using the whites of two eggs, with two tablespoons sugar. Put on after pie is baked and brown in oven. If not liked that way, stir all three whites in together before baking.

Mock Cherry Pie.

Cover the bottom of a pie plate with paste. Reserve enough for upper crust. For filling use one cup of cranberries cut in halves, one-half cup raisins seeded and cut in pieces, three-quarter cup of sugar, one tablespoon flour, lump of butter size of walnut. Bake thirty minutes in moderate oven. Some like a little more sugar.

Genoese Pastry.

Four ounces of flour, three of butter, four of almond paste, four of sugar and five eggs. Melt the butter in a bowl, taking care it does not get very hot. Break the eggs into bowl, add the sugar to them, stand the bowl in a saucepan of boiling water and whip eggs and sugar for twenty minutes, but they must not get very hot, take the bowl from the water, add the almond paste, crumbled fine, to it, beat till smooth, then add the butter and last of all sift in the flour, stirring lightly all the time. Line a round jelly-cake pan with buttered paper, neatly fitted and standing an inch above the edged bake in a rather quick oven for half an hour. When it is done, no mark should remain on it when pressed with the finger.

THE EASIEST WAY TO MAKE A CAKE.

Make ready all the materials before beginning to put any cake together; that is, see that flour, butter and sugar are weighed or measured as the recipe calls for. Let the fire be in good condition to finish baking without putting on fresh coal. If the fire is too hot, discourage it by leaving the griddles open for five minutes or less, then sprinkle on a little fresh coal without increasing the draft. Leave the oven doors open a few minutes before putting in a sponge cake, if it is still too fierce. If too hot on top, set a pan of cold water on the grate above the cake—never lay a paper over it. Thin cakes need a hotter oven than loaves and should bake in ten minutes; sheets of cakes in from fifteen minutes to one-half hour; loaves from one-half hour to an hour, while fruit cake will require from two to four hours. Do not attempt to bake a fruit cake weighing over fifteen pounds in an ordinary stove oven. Send it to some first-class baker unless you are so fortunate as to have an old-fashioned brick oven in your house. Whatever kind of cake you are baking, divide the time into quarters; during the first quarter it should not change except by rising; during the second it should finish rising and begin to brown; during the third and fourth finish browning, settle a very little and shrink from the pan. On first taking from the oven, set for a few minutes on a stove hearth or shelf where you can barely hold your hand. A very light, delicate cake will fall if cooled too quickly, or shaken while hot.

Pans should be greased with sweet lard or unsalted beef fat, as butter scorches so easily; line them with paper and grease the paper very little; if the paper is thin, not at all. In baking pound or fruit cake, line the pan with more than one thickness of paper; on the bottom there may be as many as six, but in such cases only the layer next to the cake needs to be greased.

Mix cake in an earthen bowl and always with a wooden spoon (or the hand). Use only the best materials; it is better to go without cake than try to make it, or eat it when made with "cooking" butter, second rate eggs or low grade baking powder.

Coarse texture with large holes shows insufficient beating and too large a measure of baking powder. Brown sugar may be used for fruit cake, but finest granulated (or sifted) is the best. Coarse granulated sugar makes a heavy cake with a hard sticky crust, powdered sugar makes a tight, close-grained cake, and measure for measure is not as sweet as the granulated, if weighed, there is not much, if any, difference. The recipes in this book are proportioned for patent flour; if pastry flour is used, take about one-eighth more. All flour should be sifted once before measuring.

Never beat eggs until the last possible moment before using! in beating whites of eggs with a Dover beater, hold it as nearly as possible to the horizontal instead of perpendicular and there will be nearly one-half greater bulk of foam than when beaten as usual. Eggs will beat up lighter if laid on ice till chilled through before using. Baking powder should be sifted with a part of the flour and added with the white of an egg at the last.

Measure exactly, and use all the materials. A teaspoon of butter left sticking to the measuring cup, a tablespoon of milk spilled on the table, one-half an egg left not wiped from the shells or at the bottom of the bowl in which it was beaten, does make a difference in the cake. With a small palette knife it is possible to scrape out the last speck of butter, every atom of egg, each grain of sugar and flour.

In making butter cake mixtures observe the following order. Warm the bowl, and scald wooden spoon with boiling water, then wipe dry. Rub butter to a cream, add sugar and beat again until light. If the proportion of sugar is more than double the butter, beat a part of it with the yolks of the eggs. Add a tablespoon of flour to prevent curdling before putting in any liquid; beat in the beaten yolks, then add milk and flour alternately, taking care not to let the mixture become very stiff nor very soft; lastly add the beaten whites, and beat long and hard to make sure of having it smooth and fine grained. Fruit should be added last, or if in thin large pieces, it may be put in layers as the dough is put into pans.

Cake is baked when it shrinks from the pan and stops hissing; or when a straw thrust into the center comes out clean. Let stand on a warm surface five minutes or less, then turn out on a sieve or wire netting (a window screen will do), remove paper at once, peeling it back in narrow strips to avoid taking off the brown crust. If the cake should happen to burn, rasp the too brown portion with a coarse grater.

There are really but two elementary forms of cake—that made with butter, known as pound cake, and that made without butter, known as sponge cake. The modification of pound cake, in which the proportion of flour is increased with the addition of milk, is called cup-cake, and this makes the basis of almost all the plain loaf and layer cakes. Whenever the measure of butter is made scant, the flour should be diminished in proportion; if the quantity of egg is lessened, the milk must be lessened also, or the flour increased.

In the following recipes proportions only will be given, full directions for putting together having been already given. The few exceptions to the general rule will be given in detail.

Sponge Cake, No. 1.

Six eggs, once their weight in finest granulated sugar, one-half their weight in flour, one-half teaspoon salt, the grated rind and juice of one lemon. Beat the eggs, yolks and whites together, with a spoon-whisk for twenty minutes, beating with a long steady stroke; sift in the sugar with the left hand, keeping up the beating with the right, then add lemon juice and rind and lastly fold in the flour, not beating any more. If it has been put together right it will have a light spongy texture and seem rather dry. Bake in a rather deep tin about fifty minutes. Do not open the oven door for the first fifteen minutes, at the end of that time it should begin to rise, at the end of the next fifteen minutes it should double its bulk and by the end of the next twenty minutes it should be sufficiently browned and baked through.

Sponge Cake, No. 2.

Three eggs beaten to a cream, one and one-half cups of sugar, add one-half cup of cold water, two cups of flour in which has been sifted two teaspoons baking powder, one saltspoon salt and flavoring to suit the taste. (N. B. Try grated rind of one-half lemon). Beat hard for two minutes and bake thirty to forty minutes in a rather quick oven.

Berwick Sponge.

Same recipe as above but the cake is beaten five minutes for each ingredient added.

Jelly Roll.

One cup flour, one cup sugar, one and one-half teaspoons baking powder, three eggs well beaten. Mix in order given,

beat well and pour into a smooth, well-greased pan; bake slow, spread jelly over and roll it up.

Note.—Have ready a smooth sheet of brown paper well dusted with powdered sugar, turn your cake on it and spread quickly with the jelly which should be well broken with a fork if at all stiff. With a sharp knife trim off all the crusty edges and roll it by lifting one side of the paper. The cake will break if allowed to cool before rolling. To keep the roll perfectly round hang it up in a cloth till cool.

Children's Sponge Cake.

One and one-half cups flour, two teaspoons baking powder, one cup sugar, two eggs broken into a cup and the cup filled with milk or cream. Stir all together in a mixing bowl, beat hard for five minutes and bake about ten minutes in muffin pans or a large pan with a chimney.

Graham Sponge Cake.

Use recipes either No. 1 or 2, substituting sifted graham meal for flour and making the measure round instead of level.

Sunshine Cake.

Eleven whites of eggs, six yolks of eggs, one teaspoon cream of tartar, one and one-half cups sifted granulated sugar, one cup patent flour, one teaspoon extract orange. Beat whites till stiff and flaky, then whisk in one-half the sugar, beat yolks very light and add flavor and one-half the sugar, put yolks and whites together and fold in flour and cream of tartar, mixing as quickly as possible. Bake fifty to sixty minutes in a slow oven, using Angel Cake pan.

Angel Cake.

One and one-half cups granulated sugar, measured after sifting, one cup of pastry flour, one teaspoon cream tartar, sift together eight times, then sift flour and sugar together three times. Beat the whites of eleven eggs with a wire beater, until they are dry and flaky. Pour over one teaspoon vanilla, fold in the mixture of flour and sugar. Get into a moderate oven as quickly as possible and bake about one hour. The pan should have a chimney and little legs on top so that when turned over a current of air can pass under it. Do not grease the pan. Never try to take it out, but stand upside down till it drops of itself.—Mrs. Lincoln.

Note.—Some authorities advise sifting the cream of tartar into the eggs when about half beaten. This prevents the cake from falling, but makes a closer grain than when mixed with the flour.

Orange Cake, No. 1.

2 cups sugar,	2 teaspoons baking powder,
½ cup butter (scant),	5 eggs (omit one white),
2 cups flour,	Grated rind of one orange.
½ cup orange juice.	

Filling and Frosting.

White of one egg beaten stiff; add alternately powdered sugar and orange juice till the juice of one large orange and one-half a lemon has been used. It will take from one and one-half to two cups XXX sugar.

Orange Cake No. 2.

Two eggs, one cup of sugar, one tablespoon melted butter, one-half cup of milk, one and one-half cups of flour, two teaspoons baking powder, one tablespoon of orange juice, one teaspoon grated rind, mix in order given, bake in square pan, split and fill with orange cream.

Orange Cream.

Put into a cup the rind of one-half and the juice of one orange, one tablespoon of lemon juice, and fill with hot water. Strain and put on to boil, add one tablespoon corn starch, wet with cold water and cook ten minutes, being careful not to scorch. Beat yolk of one egg with two heaping teaspoons sugar, add to the mixture with one teaspoon butter, let cook until the butter is dissolved, and cool. Fill the cake with cream and front with orange icing.—Boston Cook Book.

Lemon Cake

Is made by the above recipe, using lemon instead of orange.

GOLD MEDAL FLOUR—It's a Biscuit Flour—It's a Bread Flour.

Pineapple Cake.

Same recipe using pineapple juice and pulp instead of orange, and frosting the top and sides with five-minute frosting.

Pineapple Cake, No. 2.

One-half pound butter, one-half pound sugar beaten to a cream; add the well beaten yolks of three eggs, two cups flour, in which has been sifted two teaspoons baking powder. Flavor with two tablespoons pineapple juice; or use two tablespoons water and one-fourth teaspoon mace with one-half teaspoon vanilla. Bake in three jelly cake tins.

Filling.—Boil two cups sugar with two-thirds cup cream for ten minutes. Take from the fire and beat till thick and smooth. To one-third of this add one cup grated pineapple to spread between the layers. To the remaining two-thirds add enough pineapple juice to make it spread smoothly for an icing.

Ashland Cake.

½ cup butter,	½ cup milk,
1 cup sugar,	1 cup flour,
4 eggs, whites,	½ cup corn starch,
10 drops lemon extract.	1 teaspoon baking powder.

Bake in two deep jelly cake tins.

Filling for Above.—Two cups granulated sugar, one-quarter cup of boiling water. Boil till it will spin, then pour slowly boiling hot on the well beaten whites of two eggs beating all the time. Beat till thick enough not to run, then add one-half teaspoon citric acid (powdered), one teaspoon each of lemon and vanilla, spread between the layers and over the cake, or, ice with maple fondant.

Plunkets.

Cream one-half pound butter, add gradually one-half pound granulated sugar. Separate six eggs. Beat whites until stiff, beat yolks, add them to the whites, then to butter and sugar. Sift together twice six ounces cornstarch, two ounces flour and one teaspoon baking powder and add gradually to the other mixture; add one teaspoon vanila. Bake in patty pans fifteen minutes.—Mrs. Rorer.

Quisset Cake.

One-half cup butter rubbed to a cream with one and one-half cups sugar, add yolks of three eggs well beaten with two tablespoons of milk, one and one-half cups flour (heaping) in which has been sifted two level teaspoons baking powder, one-half cup milk, six tablespoons chocolate melted over hot water, and lastly three whites of eggs. Bake in two narrow loaves.

Frosting.—Two cups granulated sugar, three-fourths cup milk, one ounce butter. Boil fifteen minutes, beat till thick, spread while warm. Is best after the third day.

One-Egg Cake.

One-half cup butter, one cup of sugar, one egg, two cups of flour, one cup of sweet milk, two teaspoons baking powder. Mix well and bake in a hot oven.

Cup Cake.

1 cup butter,	1 cup milk,
2 cups sugar,	4 eggs,
3½ cups flour,	1 heaping teaspoon baking powder.

Put together according to general directions, bake in two brick loaves or one large one.

Using but half a cup of butter and a scant measure of sugar makes a plain cup cake that is useful for layer.

A heaping tablespoon of yellow ginger makes this cake a most delicious ginger bread. Omit the milk and add enough flour to roll out and it can be baked as jumbles or with half the milk and flour to roll out, as cookies.

White Cup Cake.

Same as above, using eight egg whites instead of four whole eggs. The yolks of six eggs with one whole one makes an excellent gold cake.

Delicate Cake.

½ cup butter,	½ cup milk,
1½ cup sugar,	4 eggs (whites only),
2 cups flour,	1 teaspoon baking powder.

Almond, vanilla or lemon extract for flavoring. Makes one sheet.

Layer Cakes.

Make once the rule for pound cake, adding grated rind and juice of one-half lemon, and divide it into quarters; into the first put three large tablespoons vanilla chocolate grated, into the second one cup almonds blanched and grated, into the third one-fourth pound each raisins and currants, or one-quarter pound citron, into the fourth one cup butternut meats cut fine. Put the layers together with boiled icing and ice the sides and top thickly.

Marsh Mallow.

Make once the rule for white cup cake, baking in three layers; make a boiled frosting with one and one-half cups sugar, one-half cup water, three egg whites, one-half teaspoon citric acid and one teaspoon vanilla. Spread a layer of icing between the cakes, and into each layer of icing press marsh mallows cut in halves, setting them as thick as possible; after the top is iced set marsh mallow thickly around the edge. If they are put in while the cake and icing are warm they will soften enough to blend well.

Chocolate.

Once the rule for cup-cake—bake in three layers. Filling No. 1. Three teaspoons corn starch, quarter pound grated chocolate, one cup sugar, heaping, one ounce butter, mixed; when melted add one cup boiling milk, cook fifteen minutes in double boiler, beating hard until glossy, cool five minutes, add two teaspoons vanilla, a speck of salt and spread while warm.

Filling No. 2.

Melt one-quarter pound baker's chocolate over warm water and stir it into twice the rule for boiled icing, spread while warm as it stiffens quickly. If too firm, beat in slowly sweet cream until as thin as desired.

Fig.

Make one-half the measure of cup-cake and one-half the white cup cake. Bake in square cake tins and put together alternately with the rule for boiled frosting. Add three-quarters pound of figs chopped fine. Ornament the top with choice figs cut in slices or strips.

Fig No. 2.

Split the figs and lay them flat in the layers of white cake before baking. Put the layers together with one pound figs, chopped fine and stewed till soft in syrup made with one cup water and one-half cup sugar and juice of one lemon.

Fruit Filling.

One cup stoned raisins, one-half pound blanched almonds, one-half pound figs, one-half pound citron, all chopped fine, add enough frosting to make a soft paste.

Lemon Filling.

The grated rind and juice of one large lemon, one cup sugar, two eggs (or four yolks), one-half ounce butter; simmer all together for ten minutes and use when cool.

Almond Cream Filling.

The whites of two eggs beaten stiff, with two cups of XXX sugar, one teaspoon extract vanilla, one pint blanched almonds chopped fine. Walnuts, pecans, hickory and butternuts are used in the same way.

Almond Filling, No. 2.

1 cup XXX sugar,	½ cup thick sour cream,
1 cup blanched almonds (pounded or grated),	1 tablespoon vanilla.

Chocolate Filling for Cake.

Yolk of 1 egg,	¼ cake chocolate,
1 gill sweet milk,	1 cup sugar.

Flavor with vanilla and cook like custard.

Pound Cake.

Wash and dry half a pound of butter. Beat it with the hand until it is quite creamy, then add half a pound of sugar. Beat it until it is like the lightest and whitest hard sauce, then add one egg, beat until it is quite incorporated, then add another and beat again, and so on until five eggs are used.

Take great care that each egg is completely incorporated before the next is added; this requires from three to five minutes' beating between each egg, according as your strokes are vigorous or slow, and on sufficient beating the success of the cake depends.

When eggs, sugar and butter look like thick yellow cream, add gradually a small sherry-glass of wine or brandy, and half a wine-glass of rose water. Mix well together, then sift to the ingredients half a pound of finest flour, well dried, and very slightly warmed, to which half a saltspoon of salt has been added. Line a round cake pan with upright sides with buttered paper, neatly fitted, and pour the batter into it, and sift powdered sugar over the surface.

Bake this cake one hour and a half in a very slow oven. It should have a cardboard cover laid on the top for the first hour, which may then be removed and the cake allowed to brown slowly. In turning, be very careful not to shake or jar it.

Pound Cake, No. 2.

1 pound sugar,	14 oz. flour,
1 pound butter,	10 eggs,
1 lemon, grated rind and ½ the juice, if large.	

Soda the size of a pea, dissolved in one tablespoon of cold water. Beat eggs separately and very thoroughly adding whites last, folding them carefully in. Citron or other fruit may be added, making yellow fruit cake.

White Pound Cake.

1 pound flour,	¾ pound butter,
1 pound sugar,	Whites of 16 eggs
	Flavor to taste.

Emma's Wedding Cake.

1 lb. flour.	3 tablespoons cinnamon.
1 lb. butter.	2 tablespoons mace.
1 lb. citron.	2 tablespoons nutmeg.
1¼ lb. dark brown sugar.	1 tablespoon ginger.
1 lb. lemon and orange peel	1 tablespoon allspice.
(½ lb. each.)	1 dessert spoon of cloves.
2 lbs. currants.	1 cup molasses.
6 lbs. raisins.	1 pint brandy. 12 eggs.

Bake slowly until a straw will come out clean. This is a very delicious cake and will keep indefinitely.

Recipe for Scripture Cake.

4½ cups of I Kings iv:22 (Flour).
1 cup of Judges v:25, last clause (Butter).
2 cups of Jeremiah vi:20 (Sugar).
2 cups of I Samuel xxx:12 (Raisins).
2 cups of Nahum iii:12 (Figs).
2 cups of Numbers xvii:8 (Almonds).
6 cups of Jeremiah xvii:11 (Eggs).
1 cup of Judges iv:19, last clause, (Milk).
6 tablespoons I Samuel xiv:25 (Honey).
2 teaspoons Amos iv:5 (Baking Powder).
A pinch of Leviticus ii:13 (Salt).
Season to taste of II Chronicles ix:9 (Spice).

Queen's Cake.

2 lbs. sugar.	8 eggs.
4 lbs. raisins.	½ pint wine.
2 lbs. currants.	½ pint brandy.
2 lbs. flour.	1½ lbs. butter.
1 teaspoon soda.	2 nutmegs.
½ pint sweet cream.	1 tablespoon orange peel or marmalade.

Election Cake.

4 lbs. flour.	4 nutmegs.
3 lbs. sugar.	1 quart sweet milk.
2 lbs. butter.	1½ lbs. raisins.
Whites of 6 eggs.	½ pint home-made yeast.
Juice and rind of 2 lemons.	

Cream thoroughly the butter and sugar, then divide; with ½ mix all the flour, milk and yeast; when light add the other half of butter and sugar, eggs, raisins and flavoring. Beat thoroughly; put in pans and let rise till light and bake with great care.

White Fruit.

One cup butter, two cups sugar, three cups flour, eight eggs, whites, three level teaspoons baking powder, one-half glass white wine, one-quarter pound citron, one-half pound almonds, three-quarters cup dessicated cocoanut, one cup light Sultana raisins. This makes two brick loaves.

Domestic Fruit Cake.

2 cups dried apples soaked over night, in the morning chop fine and boil one hour in 1 cup of molasses, then add:

1 cup of sugar.	4 cups flour.
1 cup sweet milk.	1 heaping teaspoon soda.
1 cup butter.	1 teaspoon (each) cinnamon,
1 bowl raisins, or more if wanted rich, also currants, etc.	mace, nutmeg, cloves, ginger and allspice.

Butternut Fruit Cake.

2 cups flour.	2 tablespoons molasses.
1 cup brown sugar.	Butter the size of a large egg.
1 cup sour cream.	2 eggs.
1 cup chopped raisins.	1 teaspoon soda.
1 cup chopped butternuts.	1 teaspoon (each) cinnamon,
¼ lb. citron cut very fine.	cloves and nutmeg.

Spice Cake.

2 cups sugar.	5 eggs.
1 cup molasses.	2 nutmegs.
1½ cups butter.	1 lb. raisins.
1 cup sour milk.	5 cups flour.
2 tablespoons cinnamon.	1 large teaspoon soda.
1 tablespoon cloves.	½ lb. currants, (1½ lb. citron, if wanted rich).

Ellen's Nut Cake.

2 small cups sugar.	4 tablespoons melted butter.
3 cups flour.	3 eggs.
1 cup sweet milk.	

2 heaping teaspoons baking powder mixed in last cup of flour. Bake in layers.

Filling for Cake.

1 cup seeded raisins. 1 cup English walnut meats, each chopped very fine. Yolks of 2 eggs, using whites for frosting. 1 cup Sherry or Port wine or a little less wine, filling up cup with 2 tablespoons sweet cream, which will make it richer. 1 teaspoon vanilla. After spreading mixture on cake sift over it a little sugar, add layer of cake, and so on until all are used.

Ice top and ornament with walnut meats. This is a very delicious cake.

Marguerites.

White of 1 large egg.
1 cup sugar—enough water to moisten.

Boil together slowly until a soft ball can be made. Then pour slowly over the well beaten egg, beating all the time. Stir thick with shelled walnuts (English) chopped fine, and spread over salted wafers; place in oven to brown. Delicious to serve with coffee, chocolate or lemonade. Nice if crackers not salted are used to serve hot with ice cream.

Macaroons.

½ lb. nuts.	½ lb. sugar.
Whites of 2 eggs.	

Pound the meats of the nuts in a mortar with a little rose water. Beat the eggs very light, then add the sugar and the nuts and make into balls the size of nutmegs. Lay on paper and bake in a cool oven 30 minutes.

½ teaspoon bitter almond.	½ teaspoon nutmeg.
This makes 2½ dozen.	

Lemon Cake.

2 cups flour.	4 tablespoons milk.
2 cups sugar.	2 teaspoons cream tartar.
6 eggs.	1 teaspoon soda (or two of
6 tablespoons butter.	baking powder).

JELLY FOR CAKE.

¾ lb. sugar.	4 eggs.
¼ lb. butter.	Rind of 3 lemons grated and the juice.

Beat the butter, sugar and eggs together. Set into a dish of boiling water until heated; then add the lemon and stir until thick. Spread between layers of cake.

GOLD MEDAL FLOUR—It's a Pastry Flour—It's a Cake Flour.

Hickory Nut.

One cup butter, two and a half cups sugar, one cup milk, five eggs, three and a half cups flour, two teaspoons baking powder, one pint hickory nut meats, one-half pound citron, one pound raisins, one ounce each candied lemon and orange peel. This makes two sheets. Bake one hour.

Soft Jumbles.

1½ cups sugar.
1 cup sour milk or cream.
2-3 cup butter.

1 teaspoon soda.
3 cups flour.
3 eggs.

Flavor to taste.
Drop by teaspoonfuls on greased tin and bake.

Bedford Jumbles.

Two cups sugar, one cup butter, beaten well together; add one-half cup flour and four well beaten eggs, one tablespoon vanilla and flour enough to roll out. One-half cup grated co-coanut is a delicious addition, or finely shred almonds laid on each cake.

One-half cup stoned and chopped raisins makes Hermits. Bake them one-quarter inch thick.

Ginger Drops.

1 cup light brown sugar.
2-3 cup butter.
½ cup cold water.

1 egg.
2-3 cup molasses.
1 large tablespoon ginger.

1 large teaspoon soda.
Flour to make thick batter. Drop by teaspoonfuls on a well greased pan, bake in moderate oven. These are very nice if properly made.

Ginger Snaps.

One cup molasses, one teaspoon soda, one-half cup sugar, one-half cup butter, one tablespoon ginger, flour to roll very thin. Mix molasses, sugar, ginger and butter, stir over the fire until the butter is melted, then stir in quickly four cups of flour in which has been sifted the pulverized soda. Knead the dough until it becomes smooth and set on ice, over night if possible. Roll as thin as pasteboard and bake in a quick oven.

Ginger Cookies.

One cup molasses, two tablespoons warm milk or water, one tablespoon ginger, one-half cup of soft butter, one teaspoon soda, flour to mix soft as can be handled on the board. Mix in order given, dissolving soda in the milk. Shape on a floured board into balls the size of a hickory nut. Lay on a sheet and flatten with a tin cup or smooth tumbler to one-half inch thick.—School Kitchen Text-Book.

Ft. Atkinson Ginger Bread.

1 cup New Orleans molasses.
1 cup boiling water.
2 cups flour, heaped.
½ cup butter.

1 egg.
1 teaspoon soda.
1 teaspoon ginger.
2 tablespoons sugar.

Stir butter and sugar together, then rub it into the flour till fine, add molasses and yolk of egg and beat well; lastly, add the boiling water and white of egg beaten stiff. Makes a thick sheet in a biscuit pan. "Easiest Way."

1 cup molasses.
1 cup sour cream.
2½ cups flour.
½ teaspoon nutmeg.

½ cup sugar.
1 egg—beaten.
1 teaspoon ginger.
1 rounding teaspoon soda.

Wafers.

½ cup butter.
2 cups sugar.

1 cup sweet milk.
3 eggs.

3 heaping teaspoons baking powder.   Nutmeg to taste.
Flour to shape stiff.—Mrs. J. A. Noyes.

Eclairs.

Put one cup of boiling water and half a cup of butter in a large saucepan, and when it boils turn in one pint of flour. Beat well with the vegetable masher. When perfectly smooth and velvety to the touch, remove from the fire, and as soon as cold break into it five eggs, one at a time, beating hard with the hand. When the mixture is thoroughly beaten (it will take about twenty minutes), spread on buttered sheets in oblong pieces about four inches long and one and a half wide. These must be about four inches apart. Bake in a rather quick oven for about twenty-five minutes. As soon as they are done, ice with either chocolate or vanilla frosting. When the icing is cold, cut the eclairs on one side and fill them.

Make an icing with the whites of two eggs and a cup and a half of powdered sugar. Flavor with one teaspoon vanilla extract. Frost the eclairs; and when dry, open, and fill with a cream, the same as Chocolate Eclairs. They may be filled with cream sweetened, flavored with vanilla, and whipped to a stiff froth. Strawberry and raspberry preserves are sometimes used to fill eclairs. They are then named after the fruit with which they are filled.

Chocolate Éclairs.

Put two squares of scraped chocolate with five tablespoons of powdered sugar and three of boiling water. Stir over the fire until smooth and glossy. Dip the tops of the eclairs in this as they come from the oven. When the chocolate icing is dry, cut open, and fill with this. Put one and a half cups of milk in the double boiler. Beat together two-thirds cup of sugar, one-fourth cup of flour, two eggs, and one-fourth teaspoon of salt. Stir the mixture into the boiling milk. Cook fifteen minutes, stirring often. When cold, flavor with one teaspoon of vanilla. If chocolate is liked with the cream, one tablespoon of the dissolved chocolate may be added to it.

Méringue Shells.

The whites of two eggs, beaten until it will not slip out of the bowl, fold into it very gently three ounces of powdered sugar, remembering the rule that anything to be mixed with white of egg must be done with a light lifting motion of the spoon, rather than stirring, which may liquify the eggs. Fill a tablespoon with the mixture and turn on to a sheet of white paper placed on a board which has been made a little damp, the mounds should be oval like half an egg. Put them in a very cool oven for fifteen or twenty minutes, then open the door and leave them ten minutes longer, the idea is to make the crust as thick as possible which is done by the long slow drying; if firm enough remove them from the paper, take out the moist center very carefully, and when cold fill them with cream, flavored, sweetened and whipped solid, then put two together; they should be over full, and the cream show considerably between the two sides.—Catherine Owen.

Doughnuts.

Two eggs beaten light, one cup sugar, one cup sour cream, four cups flour, one-half teaspoon soda, one teaspoon each of cinnamon and salt. Have board well floured and take on it one large spoon of dough, kneading gently till firm enough to roll out and cut. Mix the trimmings with a fresh spoon and roll again, repeating until all are used. Cook in fat hot enough to make them rise instantly to the top.—Mrs. Henderson.

Note.—It is more satisfactory to have two teaspoons baking powder sifted with the flour, and scant the measure of soda.

Dropped Doughnuts.

1 gill milk.
1 gill sugar.
Grated rind of 1 lemon.
3 gills flour.

1 egg, beaten separately.
1-3 teaspoon salt.
1-3 teaspoon nutmeg.
1 heaping teaspoon baking powder.

Hold teaspoonful of batter close to fat and the doughnuts will come up in round balls.

❊   **FROSTING.**   ❊

Five Minute.

The white of one egg, one teaspoon lemon juice, one scant cup of powdered sugar stirred together until the sugar is all wet, then beat with a fork for just five minutes; spread quickly on the cake while warm.—Boston Cook Book.

Boiled.

Boil one cup granulated sugar, a speck of cream of tartar, and one-third cup water until it spins a thread when dropped from the spoon, then pour in a fine stream into the white of an egg beaten stiff, beating as you pour; continue beating until stiff enough to stand alone, add flavoring and spread quickly on the cake with a knife dipped in warm water.

Ornamental.

One cup sifted, powdered sugar, one teaspoon lemon juice, the white of an egg; beat the egg until it is all frothy but not dry, then sprinkle over three teaspoons sugar and beat five minutes; add one teaspoon each five minutes till quite thick, then put in the lemon juice. Beat with a fork and when a point of it will stand in any position it is ready to press through a pastry tube upon the cake, which should be already covered with a smooth plain frosting and dry.

Golden.

Beat two yolks of egg with one cup sugar and one-half teaspoon old Jamaica rum, add more sugar if not stiff enough to hold its place.

Chocolate.

Melt one ounce chocolate, add one teaspoon powdered sugar, and add to the boiled frosting till it is dark as you wish.

Orange.

Grate the thin rind of an orange and soak it one-half hour in three teaspoons lemon juice. Squeeze the juice through a fine muslin and use like the lemon in five-minute frosting.

Gelatine.

Dissolve one teaspoon gelatine in three tablespoons warm water, add one cup pulverized sugar and beat until smooth. Flavor to taste.

Sugar Glaze.

One cup powdered sugar, one tablespoon lemon juice, about one tablespoon boiling water; beat hard till smooth and semi-transparent. Spread on the cake as soon as taken from the oven.

Chocolate Glaze.

Omit the lemon juice from the above recipe and add three heaping tablespoons of pulverized chocolate and one teaspoon vanilla.

Fondant.

Two cups sugar, one cup water, a bit of cream of tartar half as large as a pea. Boil without stirring until a little dropped into ice water can be gathered into a ball and rolled like wax between the fingers. Cool and stir to a soft cream. Add flavor or coloring while cold, then soften over hot water and spread while warm.

Maple Fondant.

1 cup yellow or maple sugar, one-half cup thin cream; boil together fifteen minutes, take from fire and stir constantly till it stiffens, spread quickly on warm cake as it hardens very fast.

 PUDDINGS AND SAUCES.

English or Christmas Plum Pudding.

One and one-half pounds bread crumbs, two ounces citron, one-half pound flour, two ounces almonds, blanched and shredded, two pounds suet, chopped fine, two small nutmegs, grated, two pounds currants, two pounds raisins, one lemon, juice and grated rind, two pounds sugar, one teaspoon salt, two ounces candied lemon peel, sixteen eggs, one wine glass of brandy, and enough milk to make stiff paste. Mix in order given and let rest over night. In the morning put into buttered moulds and steam for twelve hours and as much longer as convenient. When it is to be used, steam for two hours more. Stick a sprig of holly in the top, pour two tablespoons brandy over and bring it to the table blazing. Serve with English sauce.

Pudding Sauce, No. I.

One heaping teaspoonful corn starch. Rub smooth in a little cold water. Do this in a teacup. Pour on slowly, stirring all the while, boiling water, as if making starch until the cup is full. Add a pinch of salt and set it on the back of the stove to keep hot. Then take same sized cup of sugar and one egg. Beat together until very light in a quart bowl. Then pour in slowly the hot starch, stirring well. Flavor to suit taste. If desired cold, place on ice.

Creamy.

One heaping teaspoon butter, softened, two cups powdered sugar, one well-beaten egg rubbed to a cream together, add one-half cup thick cream and one teaspoon vanilla. If it should separate set it over hot water and stir until smooth again. Keep on ice till wanted.

Hard Sauce.

One-half cup butter well beaten; stir in slowly one cup fine sugar, and beat to a cream. Pile on a plate and grate over a little nutmeg. Keep cool and add wine or flavoring.

Plain.

Two cups water, one cup sugar, boiling; stir in one tablespoon cornstarch, wet with cold water, one teaspoon butter, one lump sugar well rubbed on lemon rind, or any flavoring preferred. Care must be taken to cook corn starch well or it will taste raw.

Baked Bananas.
Sauce for Six.

Two tablespoons melted butter, two tablespoons lemon juice, one-third cup sugar. Pour over bananas one-half the sauce. Bake 20 minutes in a slow oven, baste with remainder of sauce.

Caramel or Browned Sugar.

Brown one cup of sugar and dissolve in half a cup of hot water. This makes a nice sauce for waffles also.
The above will make a serving for twelve or fourteen people.

Strawberry.

One large tablespoon butter beaten to a cream. Add gradually one and one-half cups powdered sugar, and the beaten white of one egg. Beat till very light, and just before serving add one pint mashed strawberries.

Soft Custard.

One pint milk scalded, yolks of four eggs, two tablespoons sugar, one-half saltspoon salt. Cook over hot water till it will mask the spoon, strain, cool and flavor. Is improved for some things by having the sugar browned as for caramel sauce.

Maple Sugar.

One-fourth pound maple sugar, one-half cup water, boiled together till it will spin. Whisk boiling hot into the beaten whites of two eggs add one-half cup thick cream and a little lemon juice to taste.

Suet Pudding.
(Equal to Plum Pudding.)

1 cup suet, chopped fine.	1 cup currants.
1 cup sweet milk.	¼ cup each of citron, lemon
2 cups seeded raisins.	and orange peel.
1 cup molasses.	1 teaspoon soda, cinnamon,
2 cups flour.	cloves and nutmeg (each).

Steam two hours. This is a very nice pudding. If not wanted so rich, omit fruit entirely or use one cup raisins. Serve with any good sauce either hard or liquid.

Angel Pudding.

1 lb. Eng. Walnuts (shelled).	9 ounces dates.
7 ounces powdered sugar.	Whites of 5 eggs.
3 teaspoons baking powder mixed with sugar.	

Break walnuts fine and cut dates in small pieces. Add sugar and whites of eggs last. Bake in very moderate oven 20 to 30 minutes. Serve with whipped cream.

Yorkshire Pudding.

Beat two eggs very light, add one scant teaspoon of salt and two-thirds pint of milk, pour half a cup of this mixture on one-half cup of flour, and stir to a smooth paste, add the remainder of the mixture and beat well. Bake in hot gem pans 45 minutes. Baste with the drippings from the beef. This is a more convenient way than to bake in the pan under the beef, and gives more crust. Serve as a garnish for roast beef.

GOLD MEDAL FLOUR—It's a Biscuit Flour—It's a Bread Flour.

Sunderland Pudding.

Six eggs, one pint milk, salt, three tablespoonsful flour. Beat the yolk well, mix them smoothly with the flour; then add the milk and lastly the well beaten whites. Bake immediately.

Whole Wheat Pudding.

Two cups of whole wheat meal, half a teaspoon of soda, half a teaspoon salt, one cup of milk, half a cup of molasses and one cup of stoned dates. Put the fruit into the meal and mix until they are thoroughly floured; add soda, salt, milk and molasses; this will make a very soft batter, but the dry fruit absorbs a great deal of moisture. Steam three hours in a closed mould. Serve with any plain pudding sauce, wine sauce, or whipped or beaten cream. If sour milk is used, add one level teaspoon of soda. Raisins, figs, stewed prunes, or other preserved fruits, or chopped sweet apples, make a pleasing variety.

Batter Pudding.

6 tablespoons flour.   3 eggs.
1 tablespoon butter (melted). 1 quart sweet milk.
Bake one hour.

Steamed Batter Pudding.

1 cup milk.   ½ cup sugar.
8 tablespoons melted butter. 4 eggs.
2 teaspoons baking powder.
Make stiff with flour, as soft cake. Steam one hour.

Poor Man's Pudding.

One cup rice, well picked and washed, one-half cup sugar, two quarts milk, one teaspoon salt, one-half teaspoon cinnamon; bake very slowly for three to four hours, keeping covered as much as possible until the last fifteen minutes, then lift the cover to brown the top. It should be creamy and not dry when done.

Cottage.

One cup of milk, three-fourths cup of sugar, one egg, three tablespoons melted butter, two teaspoons baking powder sifted with two and one-half cups flour. Bake one-half hour and serve with liquid sauce.—Boston Cook Book.

Put in the bottom of a round pudding dish, one pint of firm fruit, sliced apples, bananas, peaches, cherries, etc., if very acid, sweeten to taste, add one tablespoon salt, let them heat through, pour over the above mixture, bake thirty-five to forty minutes, invert on round plate, serve with cream or sauce. The fruit may also be stirred into the batter and baked in a round loaf. If the fruit is very juicy scant the measure of milk a little, if bananas are used make banana sauce.

Delicate Pudding.

One and one-half cups water, one-half cup sugar, and one-half saltspoon salt, well mixed and brought to the boiling point. Wet three tablespoons corn starch in a little cold water, stir into the boiling syrup and cook ten minutes.

Beat the whites of three eggs to a dry froth and whip the boiling mixture into them; return to the fire one minute to set the egg, adding one-half cup lemon juice and a little of the grated rind.

Turn at once into a border mould that has been wet in cold water, and set away to become ice cold. Serve with strawberries or other fruit piled high in the center; or pour a soft custard around as a sauce.—Mrs. S. T. Rorer.

Huckleberry Pudding.

1 pint molasses.   3 pints berries.
1 tablespoon cinnamon. A little salt.
1 teaspoon cloves.
1 teaspoon soda dissolved in hot water and stir into the molasses and berries till it is very light.
Add flour enough to make a very stiff batter. Then add the other ingredients and steam three hours.

 CREAMS, CUSTARDS, ETC.

Devonshire Cream.

Let the milk stand twenty-four hours in winter (twelve in summer), then set it on the stove till almost at the boiling point. It must not bubble, but should show wrinkles and look thick. The more slowly it is done the firmer it will be. On the following day skim it by folding over and over in small rolls, and set them on ice till wanted. This is also known as "clotted cream."

Blanc Mange.

One-half cup Irish moss. Wash in tepid water, pick over and put into double boiler with one quart milk. Boil until it thickens when dropped on a cold plate. Add one-half saltspoon salt, strain, not allowing bits of moss to pass, add flavoring and turn into a mould that has been wet with cold water. Sea Moss Farina may be used—one level teaspoon to a quart of milk. Heat slowly and stir often.

Boiled Custard.

One quart milk, four eggs, four tablespoons sugar, one saltspoon salt, one teaspoon corn starch, one teaspoon vanilla. Dissolve corn starch in a little of the cold milk, add to the remainder of the quart boiling hot and cook ten minutes. Beat eggs and sugar together, pour the boiling milk over them and return to the fire until thick enough to mask the spoon, take off at once, set into cold water and stir often until almost cold. Add the flavoring and strain into the dish from which it is to be served. This custard may be used at discretion with cake sliced or crumbled, macaroons, fruit, singly or combined to make a great variety of dishes.

Cocoanut Custard.

Add one cup grated cocoanut after straining.

Chocolate Custard.

Melt one ounce of chocolate over hot water, rub well with a little of the hot custard and add before straining.

Orange Custard.

Cook like soft custard. Just before serving, add the juice of two and the lightly grated rind of one orange.

Baked Custard.

Make a custard, using one quart milk, one-half cup sugar, six eggs, speck salt; strain into a mold or cups, set in a deep pan and fill two-thirds of the way to the top of the mould with water. Bake in a very moderate oven. Test often with a knife and take out the instant the knife blade comes out smooth and clean. These two recipes are the foundation for numberless varieties of desserts, according to the fancy of the cook.

For Caramel Custard brown the measure of sugar as for caramel sauce, dissolve it in the milk and finish according to directions for baked custard given above. This is often served as a pudding with caramel sauce.

Bavarian Cream.

Whip one pint cream to a stiff froth; it ought to make two quarts; if too rich to whip add a little milk. Make a custard with the cream that drains from the whip, adding milk enough to make one pint, one scant cup sugar, one-half box gelatine softened in cold water, the yolks of four eggs and one teaspoon vanilla. Cook one minute and strain into a broad pan set in ice water. Watch it carefully and as soon as it begins to thicken add the whipped cream, folding it in as for an omelet. Put into moulds and set on ice to harden. This, too, is the foundation for a large variety of creams.

Coffee Bavarian Cream.—Use one cup clear strong coffee and one cup milk to make the custard.

Chocolate.—Add one ounce chocolate, melted, to the hot custard before straining.

Pear, Pineapple or Peach.—Take one pint sifted pulp instead of one pint milk and omit the eggs.

Strawberry or any other small fruit.—Three pints berries mashed fine, strain the juice, add one cup sugar, gelatine soaked as above and dissolved in one cup boiling water. Add whipped cream and mold as before.

Almond.—Add one pint sweet almonds blanched and pounded to a paste, soak the gelatine with milk.

Pistachio.—As above.

Orange.

Make the custard with the yolks of six eggs, one-half pint of cream drained from the whip, add the grated rind of one orange and a pint of orange juice with an extra half cup sugar add an ounce (one-half box) soaked gelatine, cool and fold in whipped cream as usual.

GOLD MEDAL FLOUR—It's a Biscuit Flour—It's a Bread Flour.

JELLIES, ETC.

Wine.

½ box gelatine.   1 cup wine.
½ cup cold water.   1 cup sugar.
1 pint boiling water.   1 lemon.

Soak the gelatine in cold water until soft. Add the boiling water, wine, sugar and lemon juice. Strain. Keep on ice until ready to serve.

Orange.

½ box gelatine.   1 pint orange juice.
½ cup cold water.   1 cup sugar.
1 cup boiling water.   1 lemon.

Soak the gelatine in the cold water twenty minutes or until soft. Add the boiling water, sugar, orange and lemon juice. Strain. Keep on the ice until ready to serve. Cut the orange rinds in baskets and fill with the jelly broken irregularly just before serving.

Lemon.

Same as above, except one cup lemon juice and one pint boiling water.

Coffee Jelly.

One-half box Cox's gelatine, soaked one hour in one-half cup cold coffee. Add one quart strong coffee and one cup sugar, one teaspoon vanilla. Cool in a crown mould, letting it stand on ice over night if possible. Turn on a large platter and heap whipped cream in the center as high as possible. The cream is often flavored with kummel or other cordial.

Calf-Foot.

4 calf feet.   2 lemons.
4 quarts cold water.   2 inch stick cinnamon
½ box gelatine.   3 eggs.
1 cup sugar.   1 pint wine.

Wash and split the feet, add the water and cook slowly until the flesh separates from the bones and the stock is reduced to three pints. Strain. When cold remove the fat, add the whites and shells of the eggs, the cinnamon, sugar, the gelatine which has been soaked in one-half cup cold water twenty minutes, and the juice of the lemons. Stir until hot. Let it simmer fifteen minutes. Add the wine. Skim and strain through a fine napkin into tumblers.

Orange Charlotte.

One-third box gelatine, one-third cup cold water, one-third cup boiling water, one cup orange juice and pulp, juice of lemon (more or less according to the sweetness of oranges), whites of three eggs.

Line a bowl with the sections of oranges, lady fingers or sponge cake. Soak the gelatine in cold water until soft; pour on the boiling water, add sugar and lemon juice; strain and add the orange juice and pulp with a little of the grated rind. Cool in a pan of ice water. Beat the whites of the eggs stiff, and when the orange-jelly begins to harden, beat light, add the whites and beat until stiff enough to drop; mold and cool on ice. One pint whipped cream may be used instead of the whites of eggs, or it may be piled on top after the charlotte is removed from the molds; loosen thoroughly all around the edges with a palette knife; place a dish firmly over the mould and turn quickly upside down. This will keep for several days if the seeds and white core of the oranges are removed.

Another pretty way to fill the dish is to make the center filling of strawberry juice, or line the dish with strawberries by dipping them in soaked gelatine (which should be quite stiff and flavored with strawberry juice), and sticking them to the sides, and fill with a plain charlotte russe.

To make a Snow Pudding, beat the gelatine and whites of eggs separately, let the gelatine stiffen first, then beat in the white of eggs.

Charlotte Russe, No. 1.

1 pint cream,   1 speck salt,
½ cup powdered sugar,   ½ dozen lady fingers,
                1 teaspoon vanilla.

Mix the cream, vanilla and sugar. Set into ice water and when chilled whip to a thick froth. Drain and fling into a dish that has been lined with the cake. Keep on ice till wanted. Serve in the same dish.

Charlotte Russe, No. 2.

Soak one-third box of gelatine in 1 cup of water, dissolve slowly, put over teakettle to heat. In another dish put 1 cup of milk, 1 egg well beaten, 1 cup sugar, and cook like custard. When done add gelatine, flavor with vanilla and wine (sherry is best), when cool stir in 1 pint of whipped cream, pour over any stale cake, or better still line a mold or glasses with sponge cake, fill with the mixture; when set, turn out. If you choose to make a meringue of whites of eggs and put on top, it makes the charlotte russe look handsome

Currant Jelly.

5 pints currant juice.
2 pints water, boil 5 minutes.

After it begins to boil, skim well, add 1 lb. sugar to each pint (counting water also). Boil 3 minutes.

Do not cook more than this amount at once.

DIRECTIONS:

Put currants in kettle, mash with potato-masher, using 1 pint of water (out of the 2) to cook currants in, do not stem currants.

Currant Preserves.

3 lbs. currants,   1½ cups water,
                3 lbs. sugar,
2 oranges sliced thin, skin and all.

Put in an earthen dish over night, then put over fire in kettle and boil just 15 minutes after boiling begins.

Orange Marmalade.

Take the whole of the peel of ½ of the oranges and only the thin outer peel of the other half; chop; cut up the pulp; put pulp and peel together and cover with water in the pro portion of one quart water to one pound of the fruit. Let stand over night, put on to boil until the peel is perfectly tender, about 2½ hours. Measure and take pint for pint of fruit and sugar and boil until it jellies, about 2 hours. Just before it is done, add lemon juice, in proportion one lemon to three oranges. One doz. oranges makes about 15 glasses of marmalade. The peel from the half of oranges is to be cut thin with a sharp knife, so only the yellow rind is used. If the marmalade is wished thick, boil a little longer than 2 hours. This is nice to be eaten with toast for breakfast or luncheon. Use large oranges with a thin rind.

Raspberry and Currant Preserves.

2 lbs. raspberries,   3 lbs. sugar,
                1 pint currant juice.

Cook 20 minutes and no more fruit at a time.

PICKLES, CATSUP, ETC.

Tomato Catsup.

For gallon strained tomatoes put,
4 tablespoons salt,   ½ tablespoon allspice,
3 tablespoons black pepper,   1 tablespoon red pepper,
3 tablespoons mustard,   3 garlic,
½ tablespoon cloves,   1 pint vinegar.

Boil until of the required thickness; put the dark spices and garlic into a cloth to prevent the catsup from being dark.

Tomato Sauce.

To 2 gal. strained tomatoes add 1 doz. onions, 8 green peppers, chopped fine with the onions, add after the juice has been boiled down somewhat; 10 tablespoons brown sugar, the same of salt, 6 large cupfuls white vinegar, or 8 of other vinegar. Boil all together 1 hour. Bottle and seal.

Spanish Pickles.

1 pk. green tomatoes, 1 doz. onions. Slice, sprinkle with salt and let stand over night and strain off the juice. Allow 1 lb. sugar, ¼ lb. whole white mustard seed, 1 oz. ground black pepper, 1 oz. ginger and one of cinnamon. Mix dry.

Put a layer of tomatoes and onions in a kettle and sprinkle with spice, then tomatoes and so on until all are used. Cover with vinegar and let boil 2 hours, after which pack in small jars and set in the cellar.

GOLD MEDAL FLOUR—It's a Pastry Flour—It's a Cake Flour.

Currant Catsup.

5 lbs. currants,   ½ pint vinegar,
3 lbs. sugar,   1 teaspoon cloves,

One teaspoon cinnamon, one of salt and of allspice and one of black and red pepper mixed. Boil one half hour.

Green Tomato Pickles.

½ bu. green tomatoes,   6 large peppers,
6 large onions,   ¼ lb. white mustard seed,
2 tablespoons celery seed or more if liked.

Chop all together fine, put in layers, one of tomatoes and onions and one of salt, using in all ½ cup of salt. Let stand over night, in the morning squeeze dry and put on to boil in 2 qts. vinegar. Cook until tender; when nearly done, add 1 lb. sugar; put in cans.

Oil Pickles.

Slice 100 uniform medium sized cucumbers without paring, slice very thin like shavings. Lay in salt 3 hours, using two-thirds sack of table salt; drain off all this liquor and if too salty, wash off with cold water; add 3 pints of small white onions sliced first in water with a piece of alum size of a small nut dissolved in it; prepare onions same time as cucumbers.

3 oz. white mustard seed,   1 oz. celery seed.
2 oz. white ground pepper,   1 pt. pure olive oil.

Mix all together with the hands, then cover with cold vinegar. Can be used in a few days. Put in Mason jars. This makes nearly if not quite two gallons.

Peach Pickles.

8 lbs. peaches,   4 lbs. sugar,
1 pt. vinegar.

Stick 2 or 3 cloves in each peach. Add a few sticks of cinnamon. Cook till tender. Take them out on platter to cool. When cold put in jars. Pour the cold syrup over. Let them stand 24 hours then seal up. This is a good rule for all kinds of fruit pickles, if wanted rich; if not, use less sugar.

 ICE CREAM, ICES, SHERBETS, ETC.

DIRECTIONS FOR FREEZING.

A freezer holding four quarts is the most satisfactory size for family use, and it is well worth while to invest in a crown ice chip at the same time. The hole for draining away water should be about three-quarters of the distance from bottom to top and should never be plugged, lest the water rise high enough to enter the can. About ten quarts of ice and three pints coarse salt will be needed for a gallon freezer. "Diamond C" rock salt is the best grade to use, and if drained from the water and dried will serve for several freezings. After adjusting the can in the freezer pack fine ice about five inches deep at the bottom. Sprinkle this with one cup of salt and add another layer of ice; alternate salt and ice till even with top of can, packing it down solid every time salt is added. Pour on one quart cold water and begin turning the handle, slowly at first, but after five minutes as fast as convenient, in order to insure a fine, smooth cream. More salt will freeze it quicker, but the cream will be coarse grained or even lumpy. Remove the beater as soon as the cream is frozen, and work the frozen mass together with a wooden spoon, packing it solid in a mould if desired. Cover closely, corking the hole in the cover, and if it is to stand very long, repack with fresh ice and salt. Cover the whole freezer with a blanket or piece of carpet and set in a cool place, tipping it slightly to let extra water run from the drainage hole.

At serving time, lift out the mould, hold for two or three minutes under the cold water faucet, wipe dry and turn quickly on to a napkin folded on an ice cold platter.

To keep over night or for several hours butter the joint of the mould and also cut a strip of cloth an inch wide, spread it with soft butter and wrap around the joints where the cover fits the mould, drawing as tight as possible and lapping the ends well. This will keep out salt water.

Ice Cream.

Whip and drain one pint cream, to the thin part that drains from the whip, add one scant cup sugar, one cup cream, one cup milk, and scald thoroughly. Cool and add one tablespoon vanilla or any flavoring preferred, freeze till like soft mush, then put in the whip and turn the freezer as fast as possible for five minutes; pack and let stand thirty minutes before serving. This is the best and simplest way to make it if you can get cream.

Ice Cream, No. 2.

One pint milk, two eggs, one cup sugar, one pint cream (or more), one level teaspoon flour, one-half cup sugar, one saltspoon salt, one tablespoon flavoring. Boil the milk, mix the sugar, flour and salt, and stir into it. Cook twenty minutes, stirring constantly; pour boiling hot on two well beaten eggs, beating well. Strain, add cream, sugar and flavoring, and freeze as usual.

Ice Cream, No. 3. (With Gelatine.)

One quart cream, one pint milk, one tablespoon vanilla, one cup sugar, one-eighth package gelatine soaked till perfectly soft and then drained; one-half saltspoon salt. Scald the milk and sugar, pouring boiling hot over the gelatine, add salt, strain and cool. Whip the cream, add it to the milk and freeze as usual. This has the merit of packing easily into fancy forms and holding its shape in a warm room better than pure cream.

These three standard preparations form the basis of almost all the varieties of frozen creams.

Chocolate.—Melt three ounces baker's chocolate over hot water and stir it into No. 2.

Coffee.—Substitute one pint strong coffee for the milk in No. 3.

Fruit Creams.

Prepare No. 1, omitting the cup of milk; when half frozen, beat in one pint to one quart fruit pulp sweetened to taste and finish as usual. Peach is improved by the addition of a little Maraschino, and other fruits by some flavoring or cordial to accent their natural flavor.

Nut Creams.

Pistachio, almonds, filberts, etc., should be blanched, pounded fine with a little water, and simmered in the milk of No. 3, till the flavor is well extracted. It may be strained for a smooth cream, or the bits of nut left in.

Frozen Puddings

Are usually prepared with No. 3, using four or more egg yolks in addition to the gelatine. Let the custard cook two minutes, then strain over the gelatine; when dissolved strain again into the freezer. Wine, cordials or other flavorings should be added when half frozen, and the fruit or nuts stirred in as it is packed. Preserves of any kind cut in small pieces, French candied fruit, chestnuts blanched and simmered in a thick syrup till tender, almond paste rubbed fine, Canton ginger, powdered macaroons, cake crumbs, etc., are all used singly and in combination at the whim of the confectioner. The following is given for illustration and suggestion.

Nesselrode Pudding.

One-half pound almond paste, thirty French chestnuts, one pint cream, a pint can pineapple, the yolk of ten eggs, half a pound of French candied fruit, one tablespoon vanilla extract, four of wine, one pint water, one of sugar. Blanch the chestnuts and pound to a paste. Rub almond paste smooth. Boil the sugar, water and juice from the pineapple twenty minutes. Beat the yolks of the eggs, and stir them into the syrup. Put the saucepan in another of boiling water, and beat the mixture with an egg beater until it thickens. Take off, place in a basin of cold water, and beat ten minutes. Mix the almonds and chestnuts with the cream. Add the candied fruit and the pineapple, cut fine. Mix this with the cooked mixture. Add the flavor and half a saltspoon salt. Freeze the same as ice cream. Pack in a chimney mould. In serving, fill the hole with preserved chestnuts; lay thick beaten cream around the form and garnish with preserved cherries and pieces of other fruit.

Orange Straws.

Cut orange peel into strips with scissors. Put into cold water and boil 20 minutes. Change water, boil 20 minutes.

GOLD MEDAL FLOUR—It's a Pastry Flour—It's a Cake Flour.

Change again and boil 20 minutes, making 3 boilings. Take 1 cup orange and 1 of sugar and water to cover and boil till it hairs, roll in granulated sugar, place on platter to dry; handle with sugar tongs.

Candied Orange Peel,

Dip oranges in hot water, wipe with soft cloth, then rub with lump sugar to extract oil. Roll sugar fine and set aside; peel oranges, throw skins into boiling water and cook until tender, changing water twice; drain well; cut into strips and weigh, allowing 1 lb. sugar and ½ cup of water to every pound of peel. Boil sugar and water together a moment; add peel; simmer until transparent; drain and roll each piece in the sugar. Put in warm oven to dry.

Candied Watermelon Rind,

Cut watermelon into pieces 1½ inches square. Boil in alum water until tender. Then drain well. Make a thick syrup and cook the melon until clear and the syrup nearly cooked down. Then spread on plates and partly dry in oven. Now sprinkle granulated sugar on both sides and drop 2 or 3 drops Jamaica ginger on each piece. Then dry until you can handle without sticking to fingers and so that pieces will not stick together when put into jars.

Cream Nectar.

Six lbs. sugar, pour over 2 qts. warm water, 4 oz. tartaric acid. Stir well. When the sugar is dissolved stir in the beaten whites of 4 eggs. When cool flavor with lemon and vanilla. Do not let the mixture boil. Put in bottles or jugs and keep well corked.

Directions for use: Put 2 tablespoons in glass of icewater, add soda size of pea, stir until foamy. A nice drink in hot weather.

Chocolate Chips.

First make a candy of molasses for the filling. One cup New Orleans molasses, two-thirds cup sugar, butter the size of a butternut. Flavor with vanilla. Boil until hard, pull thin, cut in small pieces. When cold dip in hot chocolate flavored with vanilla, if you like, sweetened a little.

Grape Juice.

Ten lbs. of grapes, 2 qts. water. Boil ten minutes, strain and add 2 lbs. of sugar. Let it come to a boil, bottle in patent cork bottles. When you strain the juice do not squeeze.

 ## MISCELLANEOUS.

Furniture Polish.

1 tablespoonful sweet oil.   1 tablespoonful lemon juice.
1 tablespoonful corn starch.

Compound for Cleaning Carpets.

2½ bars Ivory soap   ½ lb. borax,
¼ pint acqua ammonia,   3 oz. soap bark,

Shave soap fine, boil until dissolved in 1½ qts. water. Borax added, boil 10 minutes; steep soap bark in 1 qt. water for ½ hour. Add ammonia and 1 qt. cold water, mix together and add water to make 6 gallons. This is a very valuable recipe not only for carpets, but draperies, clothing, etc.

Liniment.

1 cup vinegar,   1 cup turpentine,
1 raw egg.

Put in bottle and shake well.
A most excellent liniment for man or beast.

Liniment for Rheumatism.

To be applied externally, must not be bound on with cloths as it will blister.

½ oz. gum camphor,   ½ oz. sulphuric ether,
½ oz. ammonia,   ½ pint alcohol.

Mix together in a bottle, shake before using; does not grease clothing. Can be applied 2 or 3 times a day. This has never been known to fail if used regularly.

Senna Prunes (For Constipation.)

24 prunes,   1 pint of boiling water,
2 tablespoons senna leaves.

Steep senna in the water, where it will keep hot 2 hours, then strain, wash stew pan and put in the senna water and prunes. Cover and simmer until the prunes have absorbed all the water, then put in a jar and use as required. These are delicious and will keep for months.

Fostoria Fruit Tablets.

2 oz. raisins,   2 oz. dates,
2 oz. figs,   2 oz. prunes,
1 oz. senna leaves.

Put these ingredients in water, removing all seeds and hard portions of fruit; chop them fine; spread thin and cut in squares and wrap each in wax paper and put in a glass or tin can where they will keep fresh and are convenient for use. Take two at night. Excellent for constipation.

For Quinsy.

Guaiac Lozenges.

Take one three times daily.

For Diarrhœa.

3 oz. cinnamon water,   1 oz. subcarbonate of bismuth.
Dose—One tablespoonful every 3 or 4 hours.

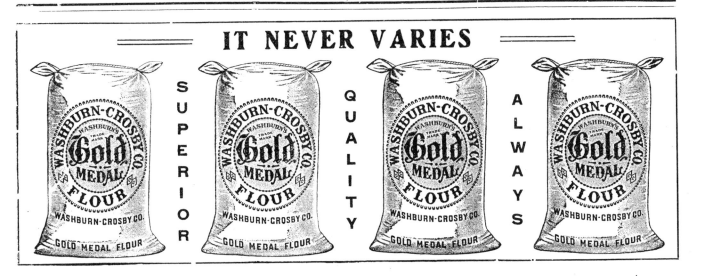

WHITE BREAD.

A PAPER on "Bread" was recently read before the Natural Science Association of Toronto University, by the chemist of the Provincial Board of Health. He said in part :

White bread is more nearly a perfect ration, and will maintain life longer than any other single food; because its tissue-forming constituents, the proteids (gluten), and its energy yielding portion, the carbohydrates (starch), are nearly in the proportions demanded by the system. The human body demands from the food daily about a hundred grains of protein, 50 grams of fat, and 450 grams carbohydrate. In 100 grams of bread there are 7.8 grams of assimilable protein, 1.3 grams of fat, and 53.1 grams of carbohydrate, so that to get the necessary amount of protein from bread a man would have to eat about 1,300 grams of bread—about three pounds—a day. This would give 35 grams too little fat, and 240 grams too much carbohydrate, but since fat and carbohydrate are both energy-formers, and to certain extent interchangeable, the variation from a standard diet is not great. We have instinctively recognized these facts by eating our bread with butter —a fat—or taking it with milk, which contains a large amount of proteid and fat.

Brown breads are inferior to white bread, because they contain much less available nutriment, weight for weight, than it does. Text-books and medical men religiously reiterate the statement disproved years ago, that the best part of the wheat grain is milled out and thrown away in the bran. There is absolutely no foundation for the wild claims made by the whole wheat "crank;" in fact, all the evidence is in favor of the white article.

It is true, that whole wheat contains more protein than white flour, but then, "we live not by what we eat, but by what we digest." We can eat hay, but not digest it. The fact is, that the protein in the bran and so-called aleuron layer is enclosed within cellulose walls; human beings cannot digest cellulose, and therefore the enclosed food is not available to us. I have digested thin sections of wheat grain with artificial gastric juice for two days, and have invariably found the cell contents to be unaltered when examined under the microscope. Similarly investigators have allowed thin sections to pass through the alimentary tract with precisely the same results. It has also been found, from numerous experiments on human beings, that there is not much food absorbed from whole wheat or graham flour bread as from white. For instance, a number of people were fed on bread and milk, and by accurate physiological chemical methods, it was found that on the average 85 per cent of the protein, and 97 per cent of the carbohydrate of the best white flour is digestible. In whole wheat 80.5 per cent of the protein and 94 per cent of the carbohydrate is digested; white in graham bread only 77.6 per cent of the protein, and 88½ per cent of the carbohydrate is digested.

In one case, for example, a student aged 23 was fed on bread made from patent flour and milk, for a space of two days, gaining two pounds in weight in that time. He consumed 1.9 pounds of bread and 4¾ pounds of milk per day, digesting 85.6 per cent of the protein and 06.7 per cent of the carbohydrate of the bread. Numerous experiments always yield exactly the same results.

Obviously, then, any one who says that white bread is poor food is ignorant of the subject in question; experimental evidence proves that white bread yields eight per cent more nourishment to the body than graham bread, which is made from the whole wheat; not only so, but the branny particles, by irritating the intestinal walls, and thus promoting peristalis, hastens other foods too rapidly through the intestine, so that complete absorption cannot take place, and considerable loss occurs. Of course, in certain affections of the alimentary tract this increased peristalsis is of benefit, and many people take brown bread for this reason. As with every other food, eat what agrees with you; it is literally a fact that "what is one's meat may be another's poison."

The workingman demands, and always has demanded, white bread, not as the great physiologist Bungs imagined, from a perverted instinct, but because he has found by experience that he "can work better on it." Public opinion always has endorsed the white loaf, evidently for good reasons; less than fifteen per cent of the bread made in Toronto to-day is brown bread. Sedentary people are often benefited by using brown bread, but the active person will be yielded more energy from the white.

White flour is obtained by grinding the endosperm of the wheat grain, that is, all of the wheat grain left when the branny coats and germs are milled out, and thrown away. Whole wheat flour is white flour plus the inner branny coats, especially the aleuron layer. Graham flour consists of the entire grain ground up.

A great deal is made of the loss to the system of the calcium, iron and phosphorous salts which are undoubtedly present in the bran. But no one has as yet proved that we require abnormal quantities of these salts, and since they are present in oatmeal, breakfast foods, and, in fact, almost every vegetable and animal food we eat, the so-called loss is immaterial.

EVERY POUND OF GOLD MEDAL FLOUR IS TESTED CAREFULLY

Invitation

The Famous Brands Cookbook Library invites you, the modern cook, to a new experience in your own kitchen. Have you ever wished you had a larger repertoire of company's-coming menus? Ever searched for a different and exciting way to prepare favorite products? Ever felt that if you could just have a certain technique explained simply, you could master an entire new world of cooking?

The solutions to these dilemmas and others are the cornerstone of the twelve volumes that comprise *The Famous Brands Cookbook Library*. Whether you are just getting to know your kitchen—or have a long-standing relationship with it—the recipes and hints provided here offer the very best and latest information available from the test kitchens of many of America's finest food companies. Once you have had a chance to discover the treasures inside this volume, you'll want to collect each of the other volumes in this series—and an invaluable home cooking library will be yours.

Famous Brands Desserts

Famous Brands Every Oven Microwave Cookbook

Famous Brands Great Vegetable Dishes

Famous Brands Meat Cookbook

Famous Brands Chicken & Poultry

Famous Brands Breads, Quick Breads, & Coffee Cakes

Famous Brands Soups & Salads

Famous Brands Pasta Dishes

Famous Brands Fish & Seafood Cookbook

Famous Brands Cooking with Eggs & Cheese

Famous Brands Main Dishes

Famous Brands Chocolate Classics

Front cover: *Shrimp Mousse (page 20)*. Photograph is compliments of SARAN WRAP™ brand plastic film.

A Splendid Catch

Grandma called fish "brain food." Perhaps so, perhaps not. But we can be certain of this: Fish and shellfish are enjoying a greater popularity today than ever before. And no wonder, for these delicious foods answer the two all-important culinary questions with a resounding affirmative. Is it good? Yes! Is it good for you? Yes, indeed!

These days, when we are learning to be guided by nutritional considerations as well as those of taste and texture, fish and shellfish claim a place of honor on our menu plans. And these fine foods are easy to come by. If you are lucky enough to live close to the ocean, an excursion to the docks when the fishing boats come in can be a treat for the whole family. If not, never mind—fish is readily available in dozens of fish stores in cities of any size, and in supermarkets, too—fresh or frozen or canned. You can have mild-tasting boneless fillets of flounder and haddock, assertive flavors such a mackerel or shad, big whole fish, such as salmon or sea bass or red snapper, to poach or stuff and bake, or small fish, such as perch or sunnies or trout, to bread and sauté. There are just-right fish for any dish you'd like to make: fragrant soups and stews and chowders, fish-sauced pasta and rice, refreshing salads when hot weather drives you away from the stove, delicate mousses and timbales and soufflés for occasions when you're going to entertain.

And we haven't even mentioned shellfish! There are succulent clams and oysters, meaty lobsters, everybody-loves-them shrimp sized from tiny to huge, shiny-shelled mussels and sweet little crayfish. And if you're adventure-minded, sample the cockles and winkles and sea urchins that appear every now and again in the fish market. Try shad roe in its brief late-winter season, or abalone for new taste sensation.

Whatever you do, don't confine your fish eating to can after can of tuna. Tuna is good, fine in its place, but it's only the smallest fraction of the great eating that fish and shellfish offer you. In this the *Famous Brands Fish & Seafood Cookbook*, you'll find many ways to prepare fish, from simple to elaborate. If you're not a great fish cook, it's time to turn yourself into one. Begin with quick/easy scampi or baked fillets; graduate to the subtle flavors of poached salmon or bouillabaisse. Plan to serve fish twice a week, then learn the many ways to prepare it so that your family will never be tempted to moan, "Oh no—fish again?"

Contents

Tantalizing Tidbits

Your next party will be a seafood success when you tempt your guests with spreads, dips, pâtés, and fabulous finger foods carefully chosen, easily prepared—and enthusiastically enjoyed.

Seafood Cocktail Sauce
Makes 1½ cups
- 1 can (6 ounces) Hunt's Tomato Paste
- 1 cup water
- 1 teaspoon Worcestershire sauce
- ¼ cup minced pickle or pickle relish
- 2 teaspoons lemon juice
- 1 teaspoon horseradish
- ½ teaspoon salt
- ¼ teaspoon sugar
- ⅛ teaspoon pepper
- Crab, shrimp, or mixed seafood cocktail

Combine all ingredients in a bowl. Chill thoroughly to blend flavors. Serve with crab, shrimp, or mixed seafood cocktail.

Variation
Mix this sauce half and half with mayonnaise; use to dress any kind of seafood salad.

Potted Shrimp
Makes 1⅔ cups
- 1 package (8 ounces) cream cheese, softened
- 2 tablespoons minced celery
- 1 teaspoon grated onion
- 2 tablespoons beer or cream
- ¼ teaspoon Worcestershire sauce
- ⅛ teaspoon dry mustard
- ½ cup coarsely chopped cooked pink shrimp
- ½ cup chopped shelled California pistachios
- Assorted crackers or raw vegetables

Blend together cream cheese, celery, onion, beer, Worcestershire sauce, and mustard. Stir in shrimp and pistachios. Pack into serving container; chill. Serve with crackers or vegetables.

Russian Herring Spread
Makes about 2 cups
- 1 cup Lipton California Dip (recipe follows)
- 1 jar (11 ounces) herring fillets, drained and finely chopped
- ¼ cup white wine
- 1 tablespoon dill weed
- ¼ teaspoon pepper
- Pumpernickel bread or crackers

In medium bowl, blend all ingredients; chill. Serve on party-size pumpernickel bread or crackers.

Lipton California Dip
Makes about 2 cups
- 1 envelope Lipton® Onion Recipe Soup Mix
- 2 cups sour cream

In small bowl, blend Lipton Onion Recipe Soup Mix with sour cream; chill.

Hot Crab Spread
Makes 1¾ cups
- 1 package (8 ounces) cream cheese, at room temperature
- 1 tablespoon milk
- 2 teaspoons Worcestershire sauce
- 1 can (7½ ounces) crab meat, drained and flaked
- 2 tablespoons chopped green pepper
- 2 tablespoons toasted slivered almonds
- Assorted crackers

Combine cream cheese, milk, and Worcestershire sauce. Add crab meat and pepper to cream cheese mixture. Turn into a small shallow baking dish. Top with almonds. Bake in a preheated 350°F oven for 15 minutes, or until heated through. Keep warm over candle warmer. Serve with crackers.

Seafood Cocktail Sauce. Photograph provided by Hunt-Wesson Foods, Inc.; photo by Tom Kelley Studios

Tuna Spread

Makes 3 cups

    2 cans (7 ounces each) tuna, drained
    2 packages (3 ounces each) cream cheese, at room
       temperature
    2 teaspoons horseradish
    ½ teaspoon Worcestershire sauce
    ¼ cup finely chopped onion
    1 clove garlic, minced
    ½ teaspoon celery salt
    3 tablespoons mayonnaise
    ¼ teaspoon pepper
       Assorted crackers

Flake tuna in a bowl. Add cream cheese and mix
well. Add remaining ingredients except crackers, and
blend. Refrigerate. Serve with crackers.

Sherried Crab Dip

Makes 10 servings

    1 package (8 ounces) cream cheese, softened
    3 tablespoons medium-dry sherry
    1 teaspoon Worcestershire sauce
    1 teaspoon lemon juice
    ⅛ teaspoon hot pepper sauce
       Salt to taste
    1 can (6½ ounces) crab meat, drained
    ¼ cup toasted sliced almonds
       Assorted crackers

Preheat oven to 350°F. Stir cream cheese in 3-cup
glass bowl until smooth. Add sherry, Worcestershire
sauce, lemon juice, hot pepper sauce, and salt. Stir
well. Pick over crab meat, discarding any pieces of
cartilage and shell. Stir into cream cheese mixture.
Spoon mixture into small baking dish and bake 15 to
20 minutes, or until hot and bubbly. Sprinkle with
almonds and serve with crackers.

This recipe was provided by the makers of Saran
Wrap™ brand plastic film.

Smoked Salmon Spread

Makes 16 servings

    1 package (8 ounces) cream cheese, at room
       temperature
    ½ cup finely diced smoked salmon
    1 teaspoon freshly ground black pepper
    2 tablespoons lemon juice

Combine ingredients, blending thoroughly with a
fork until of a good spreading consistency.

Dip Delights

The day someone thought of mixing dry onion soup
mix and sour cream and serving the mixture with
chips to dunk in it, the whole appetizer/snack world
turned upside down. There had been few-and-far-be-
tween dips before, notably one made of cream cheese
softened with sour cream and liberally laced with
snipped chives, but dip on a scale that swept the country, dip you met everywhere you turned? Never—and,
if heaven smiles on us, never again. Good as it is, that
onion soup mix got pretty tiresome before it began to
occur to people that there must be other combinations
that would make great dunks. And so there are, so
there are.

Dips are thinner than the canapé spreads from which
they sprang, but should be thick enough not to be a
threat to clothes and carpets when used by speeding,
starving dunkers, especially the stand-up ones of the
cocktail party circuit. Sour cream makes a fine base.
So does softened cream cheese. So does mayonnaise—
in some cases. So do, less calorically, plain yogurt and
lowfat cottage cheese whirled smooth in the blender.
As the flavoring, the dip maker has wide scope. Make
any dips as above, add fish selection from the column
on the left, then a zipper-upper from the column on
the right, season to taste, and you're ready to let the
party get underway.

drained minced clams	grated onion
chopped shrimp	snipped fresh dill
chopped lobster	snipped chives
flaked smoked whitefish	chopped parsley plus onion
fish roe or caviar	juice
chopped anchovies	thinly sliced small scallions
	finely chopped raw
	mushrooms
	chopped chutney plus curry
	powder
	crumbled blue cheese
	sharp cheddar plus bacon bits

And those are only to get you started on ideas of
your own.

As for dippers and dunkers, there are dozens available—corn or potato chips, toasted bread strips, sautéed bread shapes, pretzel sticks, commercial (flavored
or not) small bread sticks, shredded-wheat wafers,
crackers by the dozens of all shapes and flavors. Vegetables of many sorts are fine, too—thin strips or sticks
or slices of carrot, celery, zucchini, jicama, turnip, cucumber, cauliflower and young broccoli flowerets,
whole radishes, and scallions.

Caviar Spread

Makes 12 servings

    3 slices white bread, crusts trimmed
    1 jar (8 ounces) red caviar
    ⅓ cup finely chopped onion
    ¼ cup lemon juice
    ¾ cup olive oil
      Thinly sliced crusty white bread chunks

Soak the bread in 1 cup water for 5 minutes; squeeze out all the water and mash bread until smooth. Add caviar, onion, and lemon juice; mix until smooth. Mix in olive oil very gradually until mixture is pale pink. Chill. Serve with white bread chunks.

Thousand Island Salmon Spread

Makes about 5 cups

    2 envelopes Knox₈ Unflavored Gelatine
    ½ cup cold water
    1 cup boiling water
    2 cups (16 ounces) sour cream
    ¾ cup Wish-Bone₈ Thousand Island Dressing
    1 tablespoon lemon juice
    1 can (16 ounces) salmon, drained and flaked
    1 teaspoon dill weed

In a medium bowl, mix Knox Unflavored Gelatine with ½ cup cold water. Add 1 cup boiling water and stir until gelatine is completely dissolved. Add sour cream, Wish-Bone Thousand Island Dressing, lemon juice, salmon, and dill weed. Turn into a 5½-cup mold and chill until firm, about 4 hours.

Tuna Dip

Makes 3½ cups

    2 cans (6½ ounces each) Chicken of the Sea®
       Chunk light tuna, drained★
    2 cups sour cream
    ⅓ cup chili sauce
    1 enevelope (1¼ ounces) dehydrated onion soup
       mix, dry
      Snack crackers

Place tuna in medium-size mixing bowl. Break into small pieces with fork. Add sour cream, chili sauce, and soup mix. Stir until very well mixed. Cover. Chill at least 3 hours to blend flavors. Serve with snack crackers.

★Tuna packed in oil or water may be used, based on personal preference.

Clam Dip with Crisp Vegetables

Makes 2 cups

    2 packages (3 ounces each) cream cheese
    1 teaspoon salt
    ½ teaspoon Tabasco pepper sauce
    1 tablespoon grated onion
    1 can (7½ ounces) minced clams
    1 cup sour cream
      Assorted vegetables: celery, cucumbers, white
        turnips, carrots, scallions, and Belgian endive

Place cream cheese in a small bowl and let soften at room temperature. Blend in salt, Tabasco sauce, and onion. Drain clams, reserving 2 teaspoons of the clam juice. Add clams and the reserved juice to cream cheese. Stir in sour cream and blend well. Turn into a serving dish and chill at least ½ hour before serving. Serve with crisp sticks of celery, cucumber, white turnip, carrot, small whole scallions, and blades of Belgian endive.

Clam Dip

Makes 12 servings

    1 can Doxsee Minced Clams
    1 package (3 ounces) cream cheese
    ½ tablespoon chopped scallions or onions
    ½ teaspoon Worcestershire sauce
      Assorted crackers, potato chips, or vegetable
        dippers

Drain clams, reserving 1 tablespoon clam juice. Soften the cream cheese with clam juice. Add remaining ingredients and beat into cream cheese mixture. Mix in clams. Chill and serve on crackers or with chips or vegetable dippers.

Zesty Clam Dip

Makes 1¼ cups

    1 can (6 ounces) minced clams
    1 tablespoon clam juice
    6 drops Tabasco pepper sauce
    ½ teaspoon Worcestershire sauce
    ¼ teaspoon salt
    ½ teaspoon onion salt
    1 cup creamed cottage cheese

Drain clams and put into blender with remaining ingredients. Cover and process at Beat until smooth. Chill before serving.

Cream Cheese Caviar Mold (page 15)

Tuna Dip (page 9). Ralston Purina Company

Salmon Supreme Cheese Ball (page 13). Photo courtesy of Thomas J. Lipton, Inc.

Skinny Clam Dip
Makes 2½ cups
  2 cups Colombo Original Plain Yogurt
  1 cup minced clams, drained
  2 tablespoons green onions, minced
  1 tablespoon lemon juice
  ½ teaspoon salt
  ¼ teaspoon white pepper

For perfect results, drain yogurt 1 hour in colander. Mix together all ingredients until well blended. Chill. Serve with bread sticks, crackers, or potato chips.

Shrimp Dip
Makes 2 cups
  ¼ cup milk
  1 cup mayonnaise
  1 tablespoon Worcestershire sauce
  ¼ teaspoon garlic salt
  3 drops Tabasco pepper sauce
  1 small onion, quartered
  1 can (5 ounces) shrimp, drained
  ½ pound cheddar cheese, cubed

Put all ingredients into blender; cover and process at Chop until smooth. Chill.

Smoky Tuna Dip
Makes about 2 cups
  1 package (8 ounces) cream cheese
  1 tablespoon milk
  1 can (6½ ounces) tuna in water, undrained
  ½ teaspoon Wright's Condensed Smoke or 2 teaspoons Wright's Mild Smoke—Table Shaker
  1 teaspoon lemon juice
  1 teaspoon Worcestershire sauce
  ½ teaspoon salt
  2 drops Wright's Smoky Hot Sauce
  ¼ cup pickle relish (optional)

In mixing bowl, combine softened cheese with milk; beat until light and fluffy on medium speed. Add remaining ingredients. Mix on low speed of mixer. Serve chilled as a spread or pour into chafing dish and heat over burner. Serve with toast rounds or crackers.

Shrimp Pâté
Makes about 2 cups
  2 cups cooked shelled shrimp
  3 tablespoons mayonnaise
  2 tablespoons dry sherry
  1 tablespoon lemon juice
  ½ teaspoon Dijon-style mustard
  ¼ teaspoon garlic salt
  ¼ teaspoon onion salt
  ¼ teaspoon ground nutmeg
  Dash hot pepper sauce

Put shrimp into blender container. Cover; blend at medium speed until chopped. Add remaining ingredients to blender container in order listed. Cover; blend at high speed until thoroughly mixed. If necessary, stop blender during processing and push ingredients toward blades with rubber spatula. Turn into serving dish. Chill. Serve on bread or crackers.

Shrimp-Cucumber Dip
Makes 10 servings
  1 medium-size cucumber, unpared
  1 cup creamed cottage cheese
  2 tablespoons minced onion
  2 teaspoons white vinegar
  ½ teaspoon horseradish
  1 can (4½ ounces) shrimp, drained and chopped
  Crisp crackers or vegetable sticks

Cut cucumber in half lengthwise; remove seeds and discard. Shred enough cucumber to make 1 cup. Drain well. Combine shredded cucumber, cottage cheese, onion, vinegar, and horseradish. Beat until smooth. Fold in shrimp. Serve with crisp crackers or vegetable sticks.

On the Half Shell
To enjoy to the fullest the taste of fresh raw oysters and clams, don't insult the little bivalves by loading them with red sauce, horseradish, red-pepper sauce, mayonnaise, or other gunk. If you truly like the flavor and texture of raw oysters and clams, eat them plain or with simply a squirt of lemon juice. If you don't like the flavor, all the sauces and seasonings in the world won't disguise it.

Crab Meat Pâté

Makes 16 canapés

- 1 can (6 ounces) crab meat
- ¼ cup shelled chopped almonds
- ¼ cup Pompeian Olive Oil
- 2 tablespoons finely minced parsley
- ¼ teaspoon salt
- 1 tablespoon dry sherry
  Patty shells or toast rounds

Clean crab meat. Sauté almonds in 2 tablespoons of the olive oil until browned; drain, cool, then chop fine. Combine crab meat, nuts, parsley, and salt in blender container and blend at low speed; slowly add 2 tablespoons olive oil and dry sherry; blend until smooth. Serve in tiny patty shells or on toast rounds, or in bowl for guests to make their own canapés.

Salmon Party Log

Makes 12 servings

- 1 can (1 pound) salmon
- 1 package (8 ounces) cream cheese, softened
- 1 teaspoon prepared horseradish
- ¼ teaspoon Wright's Natural Hickory Liquid Smoke
- 1 tablespoon lemon juice
- 2 teaspoons finely chopped onion
- ¼ teaspoon salt
- ½ cup chopped pecans
- 3 tablespoons fresh parsley

Drain and flake salmon, removing skin and bones. Combine salmon, cream cheese, Wright's Natural Hickory Liquid Smoke, lemon juice, onion, and salt. Combine pecans and fresh parsley. Shape salmon mixture in 8 x 2-inch log. Roll in nut mixture and chill well.

Gravad Lax

A triumph of the Swedes, those splendid kitchen innovators, this is raw pickled salmon. As an appetizer delicacy, it puts lox (smoked salmon), even the elegant Nova Scotia variety, to shame.

Scout around for a Scandinavian delicatessen to find gravad lax. Serve on small squares of dense, dark bread with a squirt of lemon and a bit of dill or a few capers. Or soften cream cheese, add fresh snipped chives, and spread on slices of the salmon; roll, chill, cut into ¼-inch slices, and impale on a food pick. Or make a sandwich (again, dark bread) of cream cheese or sliced hard-cooked egg and gravad lax. Or fold slivers into soft scrambled eggs just before you serve them. Sometimes you will find the name shortened to gravlax.

Shrimp in Tomato Aspic

Makes 9 to 10 servings

- 1 pound shrimp, uncooked
- 1 carrot, sliced
- 1 stalk celery and leaves, sliced
- 1 large onion, sliced
- 1 bay leaf
- 6 peppercorns
- 2 envelopes unflavored gelatin
- 2 cans (10¾ ounces each) Campbell's Condensed Tomato Soup
- ¼ cup dry sherry

Rinse shrimp; place in saucepan; cover with water. Add carrot, celery, onion, bay leaf, and peppercorns. Bring to a boil; simmer about 5 minutes, or until tender. Strain ¾ cup cooking liquid; chill. Meanwhile, shell and devein shrimp; cut in pieces. Soften gelatin in cold cooking liquid. Dissolve over low heat; stir in soup and sherry. Chill until slightly thickened. Fold in shrimp. Pour into a single mold or individual molds.

Holiday Tuna Tree

Makes 4 cups

- 2 packages (8 ounces each) cream cheese, softened
- 1 can (12½ ounces) *and* 1 can (6½ ounces) Chicken of the Sea® Chunk light tuna, drained and flaked
- 1 tablespoon lemon juice
- 2 tablespoons capers, drained
- ¼ cup finely chopped ripe olives
- ½ cup finely chopped walnuts
- ¼ teaspoon salt
- ⅛ teaspoon pepper
- 1½ teaspoons dry mustard
- ½ teaspoon thyme
  Parsley
  Whole pimiento, cut into small circles
  Bread rounds, melba toast, or crackers

In large bowl, combine cream cheese and tuna. Add lemon juice, capers, olives, walnuts, salt, pepper, mustard, and thyme; stir well. With hands, shape into tree about 6 inches high and 4 inches in diameter at base. Refrigerate. At serving time, transfer to serving plate. Decorate with garlands of small parsley leaves and pimiento circles. Serve with bread rounds, melba toast or crackers.

Crab-Stuffed Mushrooms

Makes 12 servings

12 large mushroom caps
    Lemon juice
 2 tablespoons butter
 1 can (6½ ounces) crab meat, drained and flaked
 ¼ cup La Choy Water Chestnuts, finely chopped
 1 tablespoon dry whole wheat bread crumbs
 1 tablespoon finely chopped green onion
 1 teaspoon lemon juice
 1 teaspoon La Choy Soy Sauce
 1 tablespoon finely chopped parsley
 1 egg, lightly beaten

Trim stems from mushrooms. Sprinkle caps with lemon juice. Chop stems fine. Cook stems in butter for 2 minutes. Stir in remaining ingredients, mixing well. Fill mushroom caps with mixture. Place in a buttered 8-inch square pan. Bake at 350°F. for 20 minutes. Serve hot.

Curried Tuna-Stuffed Celery

Makes 2 dozen appetizers

 1 can (6½ ounces) Chicken of the Sea® Chunk
    light tuna, drained and flaked
 ¼ cup mayonnaise
 ¼ to ½ teaspoon curry powder
 ¼ teaspoon garlic powder
 ⅛ teaspoon garlic salt
 ⅛ teaspoon cayenne
 1 tablespoon lemon juice
 1 cup chopped apple
 ¼ cup white raisins
 2 tablespoons chopped green onion
 ¼ cup chopped peanuts
 6 large ribs celery, cut into 6 chunks

In medium bowl, combine tuna, mayonnaise, curry powder, garlic powder, garlic salt, cayenne, lemon juice, apple, raisins, onion, and peanuts. Blend well. Spoon mixture into celery. Serve at once or refrigerate.

Salmon Supreme Cheese Ball

Makes about 3 cups

 1 package (8 ounces) cream cheese, softened
 1 cup (4 ounces) shredded cheddar cheese
 ¼ cup Wish-Bone® Creamy Cucumber Dressing
 1 can (7 ounces) salmon, drained and flaked
 ½ teaspoon dill weed
 ½ teaspoon garlic salt
 ¼ cup finely chopped parsley

In medium bowl, combine all ingredients except parsley; chill until firm. Shape into ball and roll in parsley.

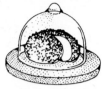

Tuna Devils

Makes 2 dozen appetizers

12 hard-cooked eggs
 1 can (9¼ ounces) Chicken of the Sea® Chunk
    light tuna, drained and flaked
 ⅔ cup mayonnaise
 2 tablespoons chili sauce
 2 tablespoons finely chopped green pepper
 1 tablespoon grated onion
 1 tablespoon prepared mustard
 ¾ teaspoon seasoned salt
 5 to 6 drops bottled hot pepper sauce
    Chopped pimiento
    Parsley

Cut eggs in half lengthwise. Remove yolks. Mash. Add tuna, mayonnaise, chili sauce, green pepper, onion, mustard, salt, and pepper sauce. Mix well. Divide mixture among egg whites, heaping high. Garnish with pimiento and parsley.

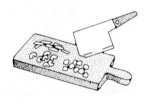

Smoked Salmon Pinwheels

Makes about 16 servings

 1 package (3 ounces) cream cheese, softened
 2 tablespoons minced onion
1½ teaspoons Lea & Perrins Worcestershire Sauce
 2 ounces (about 4 slices) thinly sliced smoked
    salmon
    Pumpernickel bread rounds
    Sliced black olives or minced onion (optional)

In a small bowl, blend cream cheese, onion, and Lea & Perrins. Spread about 2 tablespoons of the cheese mixture over each slice of salmon. Roll up, jelly roll fashion. Refrigerate until firm, about ½ hour. Cut each roll into 4 crosswise slices. Place each slice on a bread round. Garnish with sliced black olives or minced onion, if desired.

Shrimp in Tomato Aspic (page 12). Campbell Soup Company

Cream Cheese Caviar Mold

Makes 1 mold

    1 cup cream cheese, softened
    ½ cup sour cream
    2 tablespoons chopped onions
    1 tablespoon chopped dill
    1 teaspoon salt
    1 teaspoon pepper
    ½ tablespoon unflavored gelatin, softened in 1
        tablespoon lemon juice
    2 ounces red salmon caviar
    2 ounces black lumpfish caviar
    2 green onions, chopped
      Crackers or dark bread slices

Mix cream cheese, sour cream, onions, dill, salt,
and pepper. Add softened gelatin. Pack into 2-cup
mold and chill until firm.

Unmold cream cheese mixture onto serving plate.
With a toothpick, mark off the top of the mold in
wedge-shaped thirds. Spread one-third with red caviar, one-third with black caviar, and one-third with
chopped green onions. Serve with crackers or dark
bread slices.

Hot Crab Meat Canapés

Makes 4 dozen canapés

    3 tablespoons butter
    3 tablespoons all-purpose flour
    1 cup hot chicken broth
    ¼ cup light cream
      Dash pepper
    1 teaspoon lemon juice
    1 can (7 ounces) crab meat, drained and flaked
   48 bread rounds (2-inch), toasted
      Grated Swiss cheese

Melt butter in a heavy saucepan. Stir in flour. Remove from heat and stir in broth and cream. Cook,
stirring constantly, until mixture comes to a boil and
thickens. Remove from heat. Blend in pepper, lemon
juice, and crab meat and mix well. Spread mixture on
toasted bread rounds. Sprinkle with cheese. Arrange
on a baking sheet and broil about 4 inches from
source of heat for 2 to 3 minutes, or until lightly
browned. Serve hot.

> **Q.** *We love anchovies, but sometimes they're very salty. Is
> there anything I can do to reduce the salt and let the flavor
> through?*
> **A.** You can soak them in lukewarm water or, even
> better, in milk. Ten to 20 minutes will do it. Dry well
> between paper towels.

Fried Shrimp in Beer Batter. Hamilton Beach Scovill Inc.

Fried Shrimp in Beer Batter

Makes 6 servings

    1 cup beer
    2 eggs
    2 tablespoons vegetable oil
 1¼ cups all-purpose flour
    1 teaspoon salt
      Dash cayenne
    2 pounds shelled shrimp
      Vegetable oil for deep frying

Put beer, eggs, vegetable oil, flour, salt, and
cayenne into blender container. Cover; blend at high
speed until smooth. Let stand 5 minutes. Heat 3-inch
depth of oil in deep heavy pan to 365°F on deep-fat
thermometer. Dip shrimp into batter; let excess drip
off. Add to hot oil a few at a time; fry until golden
brown, turning once. Drain on paper towels.

South Seas Party Puffs

Makes 48 puffs

½ cup butter or margarine
1 tablespoon soy sauce
1 cup water
1 cup all-purpose flour
¼ teaspoon salt
4 eggs
  Tuna Filling (recipe follows)

Preheat oven to 400°F. In a saucepan, combine butter, soy sauce, and water. Bring to a boil. Add flour and salt all at once. Stir over medium heat until mixture leaves sides of pan, about 1 minute. Remove from heat. Blend in eggs, one at a time, beating vigorously after each addition until mixture is smooth and glossy. Drop by rounded teaspoonfuls onto an oiled baking sheet. Bake 25 or 30 minutes, or until golden brown and dry. Remove from sheet immediately and cool. Split and fill with chilled Tuna Filling just before serving.

Tuna Filling

Makes 4 cups

1 can (8 ounces) crushed pineapple
2 packages (3 ounces each) cream cheese, softened
½ cup chopped green pepper
2 tablespoons finely chopped onion
½ teaspoon paprika
2 teaspoons soy sauce
1 cup chopped celery
1 can (6 ounces) Chicken of the Sea® Chunk light tuna, drained and flaked
1 can (5 ounces) water chestnuts, drained and chopped

Drain pineapple, reserving liquid. Combine cream cheese, green pepper, onion, paprika, and soy sauce. Stir until creamy. Add celery, pineapple, tuna, and water chestnuts. Mix just to blend. Refrigerate. Serve as a sandwich or appetizer.

Clam Fritters

Makes about 4 dozen fritters

2 cups all-purpose flour
2 teaspoons baking powder
1½ teaspoons salt
1 can (8 ounces) minced clams
¼ cup chopped onion
2 eggs, lightly beaten
½ cup milk
4 teaspoons Lea & Perrins Worcestershire Sauce
  Oil for shallow frying

In a medium bowl, combine flour, baking powder, and salt; set aside. Combine undrained clams with onion, eggs, milk, and Lea & Perrins. Stir into flour mixture just until blended. In a large skillet, heat about 2 tablespoons oil. Drop batter by the teaspoonful, about 6 at a time, into the hot oil. Fry over moderate heat until golden, about 2 minutes on each side. Drain on paper towels. Repeat, using more oil, until all of the batter is used.

Shrimp Cocktail Bites

Makes 8 servings

4 envelopes Knox® Unflavored Gelatine
2 tablespoons sugar
½ teaspoon salt
1½ cups boiling water
2 cups tomato juice
½ cup Wish-Bone® Low-Calorie Russian Dressing
1½ tablespoons prepared horseradish
1 tablespoon lemon juice
1½ cups chopped cooked shrimp
1 cup finely chopped green pepper
  Lettuce (optional)
  Lemon wedges (optional)

In a medium bowl, combine Knox Unflavored Gelatine, sugar, and salt. Add boiling water and stir until gelatine is completely dissolved. Stir in tomato juice, Wish-Bone Low-Calorie Russian Dressing, horseradish, and lemon juice. Pour into a shallow baking pan, about 13 × 9 inches. Sprinkle with shrimp and green pepper. Chill until firm, about 3 hours. To serve, cut into bite-size squares. If desired, arrange on lettuce-lined plates and garnish with lemon wedges.

Roe

Eggs, still enclosed in the thin membrane in which they occur in the female fish, are called roe. The roe of many kinds of fish is sold—limited availability—in various fish markets, but the most familiar kinds are the roe of sturgeon, shad, and salmon. Sturgeon roe is caviar; salmon roe—much larger and colored red orange—is called salmon caviar and is usually sold in small jars, to be used as an appetizer, often in combination with sour cream. Shad roe is generally lightly sautéed, served with bacon or just a wedge of lemon, but may be deviled or, suitably seasoned, used as a filling for small, elegant reception- or tea party-type sandwiches.

Stamp-and-Go Fritters

Makes 20 servings

 1 package (4 ounces) shredded salt codfish
 ½ cup sifted all-purpose flour
 ½ teaspoon baking powder
 ¾ teaspoon thyme
 ⅛ teaspoon ground red pepper
 1 teaspoon minced onion
 ⅓ cup finely chopped fresh tomato
 2 teaspoons lime juice
   Oil or shortening for deep-fat frying

Prepare codfish as directed on package and set aside. Sift together flour, baking powder, thyme, and red pepper. Blend in onion. Add tomato, lime juice, ½ cup cold water, and codfish. Mix well. Drop from a teaspoon into deep oil heated to 370°F and fry until very crisp and brown. Serve piping hot on tooth-picks.

Favorite Tuna Fritters

Makes 4 servings

 ⅔ cup rice
   Vegetable oil
 1 can (6 ounces) Chicken of the Sea® Chunk light
   tuna, drained and flaked
 ¼ cup milk
 2 eggs, separated
 2 tablespoons all-purpose flour
 ⅛ teaspoon pepper

Cook rice according to package directions. Preheat oil in deep fryer or skillet to 375°F. Combine tuna, milk, egg yolks, flour, and pepper. Add to rice and mix well. Beat egg whites until stiff; fold into mixture. Drop by tablespoonfuls into oil and fry until brown. Drain on paper towels.

Crab Louis "En Blox"

Makes about 100 squares

 6 envelopes Knox® Unflavored Gelatine
 ¼ cup sugar
 2½ cups boiling water
 1 cup mayonnaise
 ½ cup Wish-Bone® Deluxe French or Thousand
   Island Dressing
 ½ cup chili sauce
 2 cups flaked cooked crab meat
 ½ cup chopped celery
 1 hard-cooked egg, chopped (optional)

In a large bowl, mix unflavored gelatine with sugar. Add boiling water and stir until gelatine is completely dissolved. With wire whip or rotary beater, blend in remaining ingredients. Pour into a shallow baking pan, about 9 × 13 inches; chill until firm. To serve, cut into 1-inch squares.

Salmon "Lox Blox"

Makes about 80 squares

 4 envelopes Knox® Unflavored Gelatine
 ¾ cup cold water
 1¼ cups boiling water
 1 cup (8 ounces) sour cream
 ¾ cup Wish-Bone® Thousand Island Dressing
 2 teaspoons lemon juice
 1 can (7¾ ounces) salmon, drained and flaked
 3 tablespoons finely chopped onion

In a large bowl, mix Knox Unflavored Gelatine with cold water. Add boiling water and stir until gelatine is completely dissolved. With wire whip or rotary beater, blend in remaining ingredients. Pour into a 9-inch square pan; chill until firm. To serve, cut into 1-inch squares.

Herring Appetizer

Makes 10 to 12 servings

 2 salt herrings
 3 boiled potatoes, peeled and diced
 2 sour apples, peeled and diced
 2 dill pickles, diced
 1 large cooked beet, shredded, or 1 can (8 ounces)
   diced beets, drained
 1 cup finely diced cooked veal
 ½ green pepper, diced
 2 tablespoons minced onion
   Dash black pepper
 1 teaspoon sugar
 ¼ teaspoon dry mustard
 ¼ cup olive oil
 ½ cup wine vinegar
 1 can (10½ ounces) Campbell's Condensed Beef
   Broth
   Lettuce leaves
 3 tablespoons drained capers
 3 hard-cooked eggs, sliced

Rinse herring; cover with cold water and let soak overnight. Drain; remove skin and slice fillets from bones. Pull out fine bones. Chop herring into ½-inch pieces. Combine herring with all ingredients except lettuce, capers, and eggs. Let stand in refrigerator overnight. Drain mixture well. Spoon herring salad on top of lettuce leaves. Sprinkle with capers and garnish with hard-cooked egg slices.

Swiss-Tuna Quiche (page 28); Salmon-Flounder Roulades (page 28).
Hellmann's/Best Foods Real Mayonnaise

Seafood Starters

An elegant fish or shellfish first course sends a meal on its way to rave reviews. Choose from among magnificent molded mousses, super stuffed shellfish, zesty sauced appetizers, mouth-watering fish sticks, croquettes, and quiches—and no one will be disappointed.

Shrimp Mousse Elégante

Makes 4 to 6 servings

 - 2 egg whites
 - 2 cups heavy cream
 - 1 teaspoon salt
 - 1 teaspoon white pepper
 - ¼ teaspoon ground nutmeg
 - 1 pound raw shrimp, shelled and cleaned
   Sauce Elégante (recipe follows)

Butter a 1-quart mold. Combine egg whites, cream, and seasonings. Pour ⅓ of this mixture into blender and add ⅓ of shrimp. Cover and process at Cream to a smooth paste. Empty into prepared mold. Repeat until all ingredients are used. Cover mold with aluminum foil. Place in pan with 1 inch water and bake 45 minutes in a preheated 350°F oven. Let stand in mold 5 minutes. Turn out on warm platter and cover with Sauce Elégante.

Sauce Elégante

Makes 2 ¼ cups

 - 1 can (10½ ounces) condensed cream of
     mushroom soup
 - ⅓ cup dry white wine
 - 1 tablespoon butter
 - ½ teaspoon tarragon (optional)
   Dash black pepper
 - 2 sprigs parsley
 - ¼ pound cooked shrimp, cleaned

Combine ingredients in blender. Cover and process at Grate only until shrimp are chopped. Pour into saucepan. Heat slowly until hot. Pour over Shrimp Mousse.

Grapefruit Escabèche

Makes 6 to 8 servings

 - ½ cup plus 3 tablespoons olive oil, divided
 - 1¼ pounds king mackerel, cut into ½-inch steaks
 - 1½ cups sliced onions
 - 1 cup thinly sliced pared carrots
 - ½ cup thinly sliced red pepper
 - 1 garlic clove, sliced
 - 1 bay leaf, crumbled
 - 1½ teaspoons pickling spices
 - ⅔ cup Florida grapefruit juice
 - 2 to 4 tablespoons white wine vinegar
 - 1 teaspoon salt
 - 1 Florida grapefruit, peeled and sectioned
 - 2 tablespoons finely minced parsley

In a large skillet, heat 3 tablespoons olive oil; add fish steaks and cook over medium heat for 2 to 3 minutes on each side. Transfer to plate. Add the remaining ½ cup oil to the pan. Add onions, carrots, pepper, garlic, bay leaf, and pickling spices; cook 5 minutes. Add grapefruit juice, wine vinegar, and salt; simmer 5 minutes. Place half the mixture in a deep serving dish. Remove the skin and bones from the fish and cut into ¾-inch squares; place on top of the vegetable mixture. Cover and refrigerate for 12 to 48 hours. Bring to room temperature before serving. Add grapefruit sections and sprinkle with parsley.

Seviche with Avocado

Makes 6 servings

  1 pound scallops or whitefish fillets
  ¾ cup lime or lemon juice
  ⅓ cup Sun-Maid® Seedless Raisins
  1 medium-size onion, minced
  1 medium-size tomato, minced
  4 tablespoons chopped parsley, divided
  2 tablespoons olive oil
  ½ teaspoon salt
  ¼ teaspoon crushed red pepper
  3 avocados, peeled and halved lengthwise

Cut the scallops or fish into small, thin slices and combine with the lime juice. Cover and refrigerate for 2 to 4 hours. Gently fold in the raisins, onion, tomato, 2 tablespoons of the parsley, oil, salt, and crushed red pepper. Return to the refrigerator to chill. Spoon into the avocado halves. Garnish with remaining chopped parsley.

Shrimp Mousse

Makes 6 servings

  2 envelopes unflavored gelatin
  3 tablespoons lemon juice
  1 teaspoon salt
  1 pound shrimp, peeled and cleaned
  1 cup finely chopped celery
  2 tablespoons minced onion
  ½ teaspoon dill weed
  1¼ cups sour cream
  ½ cup mayonnaise
  ¼ cup chopped parsley
    Lettuce leaves
    Lemon wedges

Sprinkle gelatin over 1 cup cold water in saucepan. Let stand 3 minutes to soften. Stir in lemon juice and salt. Heat to boiling. Add shrimp, cover, and cook 3 minutes, or until shrimp turn pink. Remove shrimp from cooking liquid with a slotted spoon, reserving liquid. Coarsely chop shrimp, place in bowl, cover with Saran Wrap, and refrigerate. Add celery, onion, and dill to reserved cooking liquid. Cover and simmer 6 minutes. Place mixture, covered, in refrigerator to thicken, about 30 minutes. Lightly oil 6-cup mold. Blend sour cream and mayonnaise until smooth. Stir into gelatin mixture. Add shrimp and parsley. Pour into prepared mold. Cover with Saran Wrap and chill until set, about 4 hours. Unmold onto platter. Tuck lettuce around molded gelatin and serve with lemon wedges.

Salmon Mousse

Makes 6 servings

  3 tablespoons lemon juice
  2 tablespoons cold water
  2 envelopes unflavored gelatin
  ⅔ cup boiling water
  2 stalks celery, cut up
  ¼ medium cucumber, pared and cut up
  1 thin slice onion
  ½ cup mayonnaise
  1 cup heavy cream
  1 can (16 ounces) salmon, drained, boned, and flaked
  ¾ teaspoon salt
    Dash cayenne
    Salad greens
    Ripe olives and pimiento (optional)

Put lemon juice and cold water into blender container. Sprinkle on gelatin; let stand 1 minute. Add boiling water. Cover; blend at low speed until gelatin is dissolved. Add remaining ingredients except salad greens, olives, and pimiento to blender container in order listed. Cover; blend at high speed until mixture is smooth. Pour into 5-cup fish or other mold. Chill several hours, or until firm. Unmold on salad greens. Garnish with olive slices and pimiento strips, if desired.

Coquilles St. Jacques

Makes 6 servings

  ½ cup fresh bread crumbs
  5 tablespoons margarine
  1½ cups (6 ounces) shredded process gruyère cheese
  1 cup Hellmann's or Best Foods Real Mayonnaise
  ¼ cup dry white wine
  1 tablespoon chopped parsley
  1 pound sea scallops, quartered
  ½ pound mushrooms, sliced
  ½ cup chopped onion

Toss bread crumbs with 1 tablespoon melted margarine; set aside. Stir together next 4 ingredients; set aside. In medium skillet over medium-high heat, cook scallops in 2 tablespoons margarine until opaque. Remove; drain well. Cook mushrooms and onion in 2 tablespoons margarine 3 minutes, or until tender. Add to cheese mixture with scallops. Spoon into 6 individual baking dishes or shells. Sprinkle with bread crumbs. Broil 6 inches from source of heat 2 to 4 minutes, or until browned.

Stuffed Clams

Makes 12 appetizers
- **12 large clams**
- **¾ cup spaghetti sauce**
- **½ teaspoon oregano (optional)**
- **1 clove garlic, minced (optional)**
- **¾ cup fresh bread crumbs**
- **3 tablespoons snipped fresh parsley**
- **2 tablespoons grated Parmesan cheese**

Scrub clams with stiff brush. Place in water to cover and soak 15 minutes. In steamer or saucepot over high heat, place enough water to cover bottom and heat to boiling. Place clams on rack in pot, cover pot tightly, and reduce heat to low. Cook just until the clams open, about 5 to 10 minutes. Discard any clams that do not open. Remove from pot and cool clams slightly; twist off top shells and discard. Remove clams from bottom shells, reserving shells, and chop coarsely. Combine with spaghetti sauce and, if desired, oregano and garlic. Spoon mixture into shells. Place stuffed clams in large baking dish. Combine bread crumbs, parsley, and cheese; sprinkle over clam mixture. Bake 15 to 20 minutes in preheated 350°F. oven until hot and lightly browned.

Refrigerator Storage

From the time you buy it until the time you use it, keep fresh fish tightly enclosed in moisture- and vaporproof material, constantly refrigerated. Plan to use the fish within 2 days. Store cooked fish in a tightly closed container in the refrigerator; plan to use within 2 days.

Seaside Loaf

Makes 6 servings
- **¼ cup lemon juice**
- **1 tablespoon gelatin**
- **1¼ cups hot water**
- **3 tablespoons sugar**
- **½ teaspoon salt**
- **¼ cup cider vinegar**
- **¾ cup diced celery**
- **¼ cup sliced sweet pickles**
- **1 medium avocado, peeled, seeded, and sliced**
- **1 cup flaked tuna fish**
  Mayonnaise

Put lemon juice and gelatin into blender; add water, sugar, salt and vinegar. Process at Stir until gelatin is dissolved. Add celery, pickles, and avocado; blender-chop vegetables. Stir in tuna. Pour into oiled loaf pan. Chill until firm. Slice and serve with mayonnaise.

Clams Casino

Makes 8 servings
- **2 dozen cherrystone clams in the shells**
- **½ cup finely chopped onion**
- **½ cup finely chopped green pepper**
- **1 clove garlic, crushed**
- **¼ cup chopped pimiento**
- **⅛ teaspoon Tabasco pepper sauce**
- **1 cup salted cracker crumbs, divided**
- **1 egg, beaten**
- **¼ cup butter, melted**
- **8 strips bacon, partially cooked and drained**

Remove clams from shells; wash and save shells. Cook clams in boiling water for 10 minutes. Reserve a small amount of clam liquid. Drain and chop clams. Combine with onion, green pepper, garlic, pimiento, Tabasco sauce, and ¾ cup of the cracker crumbs. Stir in beaten egg, melted butter, and enough of the reserved clam liquid to moisten well. Spoon lightly into clam shells. Sprinkle with remaining crumbs. Cut bacon into 1-inch pieces. Top each clam with a piece of bacon. Bake in a preheated 350°F oven for 15 to 20 minutes. Serve piping hot.

Zesty Seafood Appetizer

Makes 6 servings
- **2 envelopes Knox₈ Unflavored Gelatine**
- **½ cup cold water**
- **2 cups clamato juice, heated to boiling**
- **¼ cup chili sauce**
- **3 tablespoons lemon juice**
- **1 tablespoon prepared horseradish**
- **1 can (8 ounces) minced clams, drained**
  Lettuce

In a medium bowl, mix Knox Unflavored Gelatine with water. Add clamato juice and stir until gelatine is completely dissolved. Stir in chili sauce, lemon juice, and horseradish. Chill, stirring occasionally, until mixture is the consistency of unbeaten egg whites. Fold in clams. Turn into individual ½-cup molds; chill until firm. Unmold onto lettuce-lined plates.

Fish Sticks with Herb and Butter Sauce (page 33). ©1983 Joe Long

Scallops Elégante

Makes about 4 servings

⅓ cup Lipton Onion Butter (recipe follows)
½ pound mushrooms, sliced
1 pound scallops
½ cup dry white wine
1 tablespoon chopped parsley
2 tablespoons grated Parmesan cheese
  Toast points or rice

In medium skillet, melt Lipton Onion Butter and cook mushrooms until golden. Add scallops, wine, and parsley; simmer 5 minutes, or until scallops are tender. Turn mixture into 4 individual serving dishes or a 1-quart baking dish; sprinkle with cheese and broil until golden brown. Serve with toast points or over rice.

Lipton Onion Butter

Makes about 1¼ cups

1 envelope Lipton® Onion Recipe Soup Mix
1 container (8 ounces) whipped butter or soft
    margarine, or ½ pound butter or margarine,
    softened

Throughly blend Lipton Onion Recipe Soup Mix and butter. Store covered in refrigerator.

Scalloped Oysters Casseroles

Makes 6 servings

2 cans (10 ounces each) oyster soup
1 quart shucked drained oysters
¼ cup flour
¾ cup coarsely crushed crackers
6 tablespoons butter
  Paprika

Drain liquid from oyster soup and reserve. Mix oysters from soup with fresh oysters. Place oysters in 6 individual casseroles. Stir drained oyster soup into flour gradually. Cook over low heat, stirring constantly, until mixture bubbles and thickens. Simmer 5 minutes. Spoon hot sauce over oysters. Sprinkle tops of casseroles with cracker crumbs. Dot with butter. Bake in a preheated 400°F. oven 15 minutes, or until bubbly and browned. Sprinkle with paprika.

Scallops Elégante. Photo courtesy of Thomas J. Lipton, Inc.

Edam-Shrimp Appetizer

Makes 4 to 8 servings

 1 15-ounce Edam cheese, divided
 ½ pound shrimp, thawed if frozen, shelled and
   deveined
 ¼ cup minced onion
 2 tablespoons butter or margarine
 1 medium-size tomato, finely chopped
 1 cup fresh bread crumbs
 ⅓ cup Sun-Maid® Seedless Raisins
 2 tablespoons capers or chopped pimiento-stuffed
   green olives
 ¼ teaspoon salt
 ⅛ teaspoon freshly ground pepper
 1 egg, lightly beaten
 1 slice lemon
   Watercress

Grease a 1-quart soufflé dish or straight-sided casserole. Remove wax coating from cheese. Cut into ¼-
inch slices. Use about two-thirds of the slices to line
the bottom and sides of the baking dish. Dice the
remaining cheese and set aside. Reserve 1 or 2 shrimp
for garnish. Finely dice the remaining shrimp. Preheat the oven to 350°F. Sauté diced shrimp, whole
shrimp, and onion in butter until shrimp turn pink.
Reserve the whole shrimp. Stir in ½ cup of diced
cheese, the tomato, bread crumbs, raisins, capers,
salt, pepper, and egg. Spoon into cheese-lined baking
dish. Sprinkle remaining diced cheese over shrimp
mixture in dish. Bake in preheated oven 30 minutes.
Let stand 15 to 20 minutes in dish. Invert onto a
platter. Garnish top with the whole shrimp, lemon
slice, and watercress. To serve, cut into wedges.

Shrimp and Avocado Appetizers

Makes 4 to 6 servings

 ½ pound small shrimp, thawed if frozen, shelled
   and deveined
 3 tablespoons vegetable oil
 1 large onion, chopped
 1 clove garlic, minced
 2 large tomatoes, peeled and diced
 ½ cup Sun-Maid® Seedless Golden Raisins
 1 tablespoon white vinegar
 1 teaspoon ground ginger
 ½ teaspoon turmeric
 ¼ teaspoon ground cumin
 ¼ teaspoon hot pepper sauce
 ½ teaspoon salt
 1 large avocado
   Lemon juice

Sauté the shrimp in hot oil just until they turn
pink. Remove from the oil with a slotted spoon. Add
the onion and garlic and sauté until the onion is soft
but not browned. Stir in the tomatoes, raisins, vinegar, ginger, turmeric, cumin, hot pepper sauce, and
salt and bring to a boil. Meanwhile, peel and pit the
avocado; cut into quarters or sixths, depending on
the number of servings. Brush each wedge lightly
with lemon juice, sprinkle with salt, and arrange on a
serving dish. Drain any liquid that may have col-
lected on the shrimp and add the shrimp to the
tomato mixture. Cook for 1 to 2 minutes to heat.
Spoon the shrimp and sauce over the avocado wedges
and serve immediately.

Smart Shopping

When you buy fresh fish, partonize a store that has
a large number of customers—high turnover means
both fresh fish (stocks must be replenished often) and
high quality (people don't return to buy from a store
whose products don't satisfy). Make certain the fish
are stored in refrigerated cases, displayed on beds of
ice. Take a deep breath: Fresh fish smells clean, with a
faint ocean aroma, but stale fish has a garbagy odor.
The eyes of fresh fish are not sunken, the skin is not
sticky to the touch. Shells of oysters, clams, and mussels should be tightly closed; shrimp shells—which can
vary in color from gray to pink—should be firm and
tight, not loose and spreading. Live lobsters should be
lively, moving about, and when picked up their tails
should curl under.

Crab à la Dewey

Makes 4 servings

 ½ cup mayonnaise
 2 tablespoons all-purpose flour
 1 can (4 ounces) mushrooms
 ¼ cup milk
 2 tablespoons butter or margarine
 4 scallions, chopped
 1 pound cooked crab meat, picked over
 1 cup dry white wine
 4 slices bread

Combine mayonnaise and flour in a small saucepan. Stir in liquid from mushrooms and milk. Cook
over very low heat, stirring constantly, until mixture
thickens. Stir in mushrooms. Keep warm over very
low heat. Melt butter in Sunbeam Multi-Cooker
Frypan at 280°F. Add scallions and cook about 5 minutes, stirring frequently. Add crab meat and wine.
Turn heat to 300°F and cook 5 minutes. Pour mayonnaise mixture over crab meat and mix gently. Simmer
gently 5 minutes. Toast bread in Sunbeam Toaster.
Serve crab meat hot over toast points.

Scampi

Makes about 4 servings
  1 cup Wish-Bone® Creamy Italian Dressing
  2 teaspoons garlic salt
  1 pound uncooked medium shrimp, cleaned
  Chopped parsley (optional)
  Lemon wedges (optional)

In small bowl, blend Wish-Bone Creamy Italian Dressing and garlic salt. Arrange shrimp on broiler pan without rack and spoon on dressing mixture. Broil 5 to 7 minutes, turning once and basting with dressing mixture. If desired, sprinkle with chopped parsley and serve with lemon wedges.

On Being a Fussy Cook
Whether you cook crab at home or buy precooked crab meat at the fish market, make certain to pick it over carefully before using it in a soup or salad or any other dish. Those small, elusive pieces of crab cartilage can be very off-putting to bite down on, just when you're enjoying a delicious crab concoction.

Gefilte Fish

Makes 10 servings
  3 pounds mixed fish (1 pound each whitefish, pike, and carp)
  1 quart water
  1 medium onion
  2 stalks celery, cut up
  2 carrots, pared and cut up
  3 teaspoons salt
  1 medium onion, cut up
  1 cup cold water
  2 eggs
  4 slices dry bread or ¼ cup matzo meal
  1 teaspoon salt
  ¼ teaspoon pepper
  Prepared horseradish

Remove heads from fish; skin and bone fish; cut fish into 1-inch cubes (or have market man do all this for you). Put heads, skin, and bones into large saucepan. Add 1 quart water, whole onion, celery, carrots, and 2 teaspoons salt. Bring to a boil; lower heat; simmer 30 minutes. Put 1 cup cubed fish and cut-up onion into blender container. Cover; blend at medium speed until finely chopped. If necessary, stop blender during processing and push ingredients toward blades with rubber spatula. Empty into large mixing bowl. Put ½ cup cold water, eggs, 2 slices bread torn into pieces or half the matzo meal, and half the remaining cubed fish into blender container. Cover; blend at medium speed until almost smooth. Add to fish in mixing bowl. Repeat with remaining water, bread or matzo meal, and cubed fish; add remaining salt and pepper. Mix ingredients in bowl thoroughly. Wet hands; shape mixture loosely into balls, each about the size of an egg. Strain fish stock; remove and reserve carrots; discard other vegetables. Return stock to saucepan; bring to a boil. Add fish balls to boiling stock; reduce heat; simmer 1½ hours. Cool. Remove fish balls from stock with slotted spoon; chill. Strain stock; chill until jelled. Slice reserved carrots for garnish. Serve with jellied stock and horseradish.

Eggs with Oysters and Bacon

Makes 4 servings
  1 jar (12 ounces) small oysters, drained
  ½ teaspoon salt
  1 egg
  1 cup minced filberts
  ½ cup all-purpose flour
  6 slices raw bacon, chopped
  8 eggs
  1 teaspoon Worcestershire sauce
  2 dashes Tabasco pepper sauce
  2 tablespoons brandy
  1 tablespoon snipped chives

Sprinkle oysters with salt. Beat 1 egg with 1 tablespoon water and add oysters. In a bag, combine nuts and flour; lift oysters with a fork, a few at a time, from egg and drop into bag. Shake to coat well. Arrange oysters in a single layer on a small tray; sprinkle any remaining nut mixture over them. Cover lightly and chill at least 30 minutes. In a large skillet, cook the bacon over medium-high heat until crisp. Remove bacon and reserve. To drippings, add the oysters and brown on each side; do not crowd. (If necessary, remove a few of the cooked oysters from the pan to make room for the remaining ones.) While oysters are cooking, break 8 eggs into a bowl and beat with Worcestershire sauce and Tabasco sauce. Add brandy to oysters and ignite; pour the eggs into pan around the oysters. Reduce heat and cook until eggs are set. Slide a wide spatula under oysters to let egg flow to bottom of pan. Sprinkle with snipped chives and cooked bacon. Serve directly from skillet.

Individual Tuna Loaves

Makes 8 servings

   6 tablespoons butter or margarine, divided
   1 cup finely chopped onion
   1 cup finely chopped celery
   3 tablespoons finely chopped parsley
   1 cup fine dry bread crumbs, divided
   2 hard-cooked eggs, chopped
   ⅔ cup evaporated milk
   3 tablespoons lemon juice
   2 eggs, well beaten
1½ teaspoons salt
   ¼ teaspoon pepper
   1 can (12½ ounces) and 1 can (6½ ounces)
      Chicken of the Sea® Chunk light tuna,
      drained and flaked
      White Sauce (see index) (optional)

Preheat oven to 350°F. Melt 4 tablespoons butter in a large skillet and cook onion, celery, and parsley until onion is golden, about 5 minutes. In large bowl, combine onion mixture, bread crumbs, hard-cooked eggs, milk, lemon juice, beaten eggs, salt, pepper, and tuna. Mix thoroughly. Shape mixture into 8 loaves. Place on lightly oiled 15½ x 10½ x 1-inch jelly roll pan. Melt remaining 2 tablespoons butter. Brush on loaves. Bake 25 minutes, or until loaves are lightly browned. Serve with White Sauce.

Tuna Creole in Rice Ring

Makes 4 servings

   1 green pepper, chopped
   ½ cup chopped onion
   ½ cup sliced celery
   1 clove garlic, crushed
   2 tablespoons pure vegetable oil
   1 can (6 ounces) Hunt's Tomato Paste
1¼ cups water
   1 teaspoon salt
   1 teaspoon dill weed
   1 bay leaf
      Dash Tabasco pepper sauce
   2 cans (6½ to 7 ounces each) chunk-style tuna,
      drained and flaked
   4 cups hot cooked rice

Sauté vegetables and garlic in oil until tender. Add Hunt's Tomato Paste, water, and seasonings. Simmer 30 minutes, stirring occasionally. Stir in tuna; heat through. Pack hot cooked rice in buttered ring mold; turn out onto serving platter. Spoon Tuna Creole into center.

Scampi (page 25). Photo courtesy of Thomas J. Lipton, Inc.

Q. *Even tuna, which our family enjoys and which I use often for economy meals, is going up in price. Any suggestions?*
A. Buy chunk light rather than solid-pack white for casserole dishes—same nutrients, same flavor, lower price. For sandwiches, use the flaked kind. Have you thought of trying canned mackerel on your family? The flavor is excellent—use it in place of tuna, or substitute it for half the tuna a recipe calls for.

Seviche with Avocado (page 20). Sun-Maid Growers of California

Scalloped Oysters Casseroles (page 22)

Swiss-Tuna Quiche

Makes 6 servings

    1 frozen 9-inch pastry shell, thawed, or 1 8-inch
        unbaked pastry shell
    1 can (7 ounces) tuna, well drained and flaked
    1 cup (4 ounces) shredded Swiss cheese
    ½ cup sliced green onions
    2 eggs
    ½ cup Hellmann's or Best Foods Real Mayonnaise
    ½ cup milk

Pierce pastry shell thoroughly with fork. Bake in 375°F. oven 10 minutes; remove. In large bowl, toss together tuna, cheese, and onions; spoon into pastry shell. In small bowl, beat together eggs, mayonnaise, and milk. Pour over cheese mixture. Bake in 375°F. oven 35 to 40 minutes, or until golden and knife inserted in center comes out clean.

Tuna Croquettes

Makes 4 servings

    ¼ cup butter or margarine
    ½ cup chopped onion
    ½ cup chopped green pepper
    2 teaspoons curry powder
    1 can (12½ ounces) Chicken of the Sea® Chunk
        light tuna, drained and flaked
    2 cups fresh bread crumbs
    1 cup (4 ounces) shredded cheddar cheese
    2 eggs, lightly beaten
    2 tablespoons chopped parsley
    ½ teaspoon salt
    ¼ teaspoon pepper
    ¼ cup all-purpose flour
    ½ cup fine dry bread crumbs
    1 egg
    1 tablespoon water
    ¼ cup butter or cooking oil

In skillet, melt ¼ cup butter. Add onion, green pepper, and curry powder and cook until onion is transparent, about 5 minutes. Turn into large mixing bowl. Add tuna, bread crumbs, cheese, 2 eggs, parsley, salt, and pepper. Mix thoroughly. Divide tuna mixture into 8 equal portions. Shape each to form an oblong. Place flour and dry bread crumbs on 2 separate pieces of waxed paper. In shallow bowl, beat remaining egg and water. Roll each croquette in flour, coat evenly with egg, and roll in bread crumbs. Place on baking sheet. Cover with waxed paper. Refrigerate until ready to cook. To cook, sauté croquettes in butter or oil until evenly browned on all sides.

Lasagna Maritime

Makes 6 to 8 servings

    1 can (9½ ounces) tuna, packed in oil
    1 clove garlic, minced
    ½ cup chopped onion
    1 can (15 ounces) Hunt's Tomato Herb Sauce
    ½ cup water
    1 teaspoon salt
    1½ cups cottage cheese
    1 egg, beaten
    ¼ cup grated Parmesan cheese
    1 teaspoon leaf basil
    8 ounces lasagna noodles, cooked and drained
    ½ pound mozzarella cheese, shredded

Drain oil from tuna into 10-inch skillet. Cook garlic and onion in tuna oil until onion is soft. Add Hunt's Sauce, water, and salt. Simmer 10 minutes; then add tuna in chunks. Meanwhile, combine cottage cheese, egg, Parmesan cheese, and basil. Arrange half of cooked noodles in bottom of 7½ × 12 × 1½-inch baking dish. Add layers of half of cottage cheese mixture, half of mozzarella, and half of tuna and sauce. Repeat layers. Bake at 375°F. for 30 to 35 minutes. Let stand 10 minutes before serving.

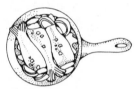

Salmon-Flounder Roulades

Makes 4 servings

    1 medium onion, thinly sliced
    4 flounder fillets
    ¼ teaspoon salt
    ⅛ teaspoon pepper
    1 can (7¾ ounces) salmon, drained and flaked
    ½ cup Hellmann's or Best Foods Real Mayonnaise
    ½ cup sour cream
    ¼ cup chili sauce
      Watercress, lemon slices, cooked shrimp
        (optional)

Line bottom of 8 × 8 × 2-inch baking dish with onions. Sprinkle fish fillets with salt and pepper. Place one-quarter of the salmon on each fish fillet. Roll up lengthwise; place on onions. Bake covered in 350°F. oven 25 minutes. Remove from oven. In small bowl, stir together mayonnaise, sour cream, and chili sauce until smooth. Spoon over fish fillets. Bake uncovered 5 to 10 minutes longer, or until fish flakes easily. If desired, garnish with watercress, lemon slices, and cooked shrimp.

Salmon and Wild Rice Roma

Makes 6 servings

    1 small onion, cut into ¼-inch wedges
    1 tablespoon butter or margarine
 2¼ cups water
    1 package (6 ounces) Uncle Ben's® Original Long
        Grain & Wild Rice
    1 can (16 ounces) whole tomatoes, well drained
        and chopped
  ⅓ cup sliced ripe olives (optional)
    1 can (7 ounces) salmon, drained and separated
        into chunks
    1 small zucchini (about 6 ounces), cut into 1 × ½-
        inch sticks
    1 cup shredded mozzarella cheese

Cook onion in butter in 10-inch skillet until tender but not brown. Add water, contents of rice and seasoning packets, tomatoes, and olives. Bring to a boil. Cover and simmer until all liquid is absorbed, about 25 minutes. Stir in salmon; heat through. Remove from heat. Stir in zucchini; top with shredded cheese. Cover and let stand until cheese is melted, 1 to 2 minutes.

Lemon Fish and Rice Amandine

Makes 6 servings

 2¼ cups water
  ¼ cup lemon juice
    1 cup Uncle Ben's® Converted® Brand Rice
    1 teaspoon salt
  ⅛ teaspoon ground nutmeg
    4 green onions with tops, sliced
    1 pound frozen fish fillets, thawed
        Salt (optional)
        Paprika (optional)
  ¼ cup butter or margarine, melted
    1 lemon, thinly sliced
  ¼ cup toasted sliced almonds

Bring water and lemon juice to a boil in a saucepan; stir in rice, salt, and nutmeg. Cover tightly and simmer 20 minutes. Remove from heat. Let stand covered until all liquid is absorbed, about 5 minutes. Stir green onions into rice. Spoon rice into 12 × 8-inch baking dish. Arrange fish over rice; sprinkle lightly with salt and paprika, if desired. Pour butter evenly over fish; arrange lemon slices over fish. Sprinkle almonds around lemon slices. Cover loosely with aluminum foil. Bake at 400°F 12 to 15 minutes, or until fish flakes easily.

Boning Basics

Cutting a fish into servings is more a matter of boning than of carving. Here a carving knife is excess baggage, although in some cases you may need a fork—but use it very carefully, or you will tear the tender fish. A small, blunt knife—such as a butter knife—is fine for small fish, a table knife for larger ones. In a large fish, the choice portions are in the center. When you serve a portion of a large fish, or of a piece of such a fish—a poached center cut of salmon, for example—lift the meat away from the bones, preserving it in sizable sections and using the natural flakes as your guide. A large server or, in a pinch, a pancake turner, is useful here.

Boning a whole cooked fish: Anchor the fish by holding it with a fork placed—not too deeply—in the gill section. Use a butter knife or some other short, blunt-tipped knife; slip it through the skin and—gently—along the entire length of the backbone. Lift the entire top piece (this is a fillet), including the backbone and tail, away from the bottom fillet; place it, skin side down, on the platter. By sliding the knife closely underneath them, lift away and discard the tail, the backbone with its attached lateral bones, and the head. If this is a small fish—one serving—replace the top fillet over the bottom one and serve. If a large fish, cut each fillet into serving pieces gently, using the natural lines of the flakes as a guide. The skin is left on a small fish, such as a trout; it can be removed or left in place on a large fish, as you wish.

Boning fish steaks for medallions: Lay a raw steak, ¾ to 1 inch thick, flat on a cutting board with the open end toward you. With the point of a small, sharp knife, remove the skin and discard (or save skin and bones to make court bouillon, if the medallions are to be poached). Working with the knife tip, cut and gently pry away the central bone and the sets of long, thin bones that are attached to it, making certain not to break off and leave behind any of these bones. You now have two boneless, skinless halves. Turn one of these upside down and place it very close to the second. Press the large ends together and wrap the small ends around them, until you have a solid, circular piece. Secure with food picks, which will stay in place during cooking but be removed before the medallions are served.

Stuffed Clams (page 21). Caloric Corporation

Tuna Rice Creole Skillet

Makes 4 to 6 servings

- ½ cup chopped green pepper
- 2 tablespoons butter or margarine
- 1 can (1 pound) stewed tomatoes
- 1 cup Uncle Ben's® Converted® Brand Rice
- 1¼ teaspoons salt
- 1 tablespoon instant minced onion
- 1 can (6½ ounces) tuna, drained and flaked

Sauté green pepper in butter in 10-inch skillet 2 or 3 minutes. Drain tomatoes, reserving juice. Add water to juice to make 2½ cups liquid. Add tomatoes, liquid, rice, salt, and onion to skillet; stir. Bring to boil. Reduce heat, cover, and cook over low heat until liquid is absorbed, about 25 minutes. Fold in tuna and heat through.

Variations

Add sliced fresh mushrooms, sauté with green pepper.

Use ¼ cup dry white wine for ¼ cup of the liquid.

Tuna Stroganoff

Makes 6 servings

- 1 chicken bouillon cube
- 1 cup boiling water
- ¼ cup butter or margarine
- ½ cup chopped onion
- ½ pound fresh mushrooms, sliced
- 2 tablespoons all-purpose flour
- 1 can (12½ ounces) Chicken of the Sea® Chunk light tuna, drained and flaked
- ¼ teaspoon Worcestershire sauce
- 2 tablespoons catsup
- ⅛ teaspoon pepper
- ½ cup sour cream
- 2 cups hot cooked rice

Dissolve bouillon cube in boiling water. Melt butter in saucepan and cook onion and mushrooms until tender. Stir in flour and brown. Add bouillon gradually and cook, stirring constantly, until sauce is thickened. Add tuna, Worcestershire sauce, catsup, pepper, and sour cream. Heat through. Serve over rice.

Tuna Enchiladas. Ralston Purina Company

Tuna-Stuffed Artichokes

Makes 4 servings
    6 tablespoons lemon juice or vinegar
    4 small artichokes, washed and trimmed
    2 cans (6½ ounces each) tuna, drained and flaked
    2 tablespoons finely minced onion
    ½ cup olive or salad oil
    1 tablespoon lemon juice
    2 tablespoons wine vinegar
      Salt and pepper to taste
    2 tablespoons snipped parsley
    1 tablespoon snipped dill weed

In a large soup pot, bring 2 quarts water and 6 table-spoons lemon juice to a boil. Place artichokes in boiling water and cook 20 minutes. Remove from water; invert on paper towels to cool and drain. When artichokes are cool, remove fuzzy choke and several inner leaves, forming a hollow. Reserve leaves and save choke for another use.

Chop the tender, meaty part of the reserved leaves, discarding the tips. In medium bowl, combine tuna, artichoke meat, onions, olive oil, 1 tablespoon lemon juice, 2 tablespoons wine vinegar, salt, pepper, parsley, and dill. Mix together until well blended. Spoon mixture into artichoke. Refrigerate at least 30 minutes before serving.

Tuna Enchiladas

Makes 4 servings
    1 can (14 ounces) enchilada sauce, divided
    ¾ cup sour cream, divided
    ¼ teaspoon salt
    ¼ cup chopped onion
    ¼ cup chopped green pepper
    4 tablespoons chopped green chilies
    1 cup chopped fresh tomato, divided
    1 cup (4 ounces) shredded cheddar cheese,
      divided
    1 can (12½ ounces) Chicken of the Sea® Chunk
      light tuna, drained and flaked★
    8 flour tortillas (6 or 7 inches)
      Sliced pitted ripe olives

Preheat oven to 350°F. In medium-size bowl, combine 2 tablespoons enchilada sauce, ½ cup sour cream; add salt. Stir in onion, green pepper, chilies, ⅔ cup tomato, ½ cup cheese, and tuna. Set aside. In small bowl, combine remaining enchilada sauce and remaining ¼ cup sour cream. Pour 1 cup sauce mixture into bottom of shallow 2-quart baking dish. Set aside.

Heat and soften tortillas according to package directions. Fill each tortilla with ⅓ cup tuna mixture. Roll. Place seam side down in baking dish. Pour remaining sauce over top. Sprinkle on remaining ½ cup cheese. Bake 25 to 30 minutes, or until bubbly. Garnish with olives and remaining tomato. Allow to set 5 minutes before serving.

★Tuna packed in oil or water may be used, based on personal preference.

Salmon Stack-up Supper

Makes 6 servings

 1 can (16 ounces) stewed tomatoes
 1 can (4 ounces) chopped green chilies
 1 cup Uncle Ben's® Select Brown Rice
 1 tablespoon butter or margarine
 1 teaspoon salt
 1 can (7 ounces) salmon or tuna, drained and
    flaked
1½ cups shredded Monterey Jack cheese
    Sour cream (optional)

Drain tomatoes and chilies, reserving juice. Add enough water to juice to make 2⅔ cups liquid. Bring liquid to a boil. Stir in rice, butter, and salt. Cover tightly and cook over low heat until all liquid is absorbed, about 50 minutes. Stir in tomatoes and chilies. Spread half of rice mixture onto bottom of 8-inch square baking dish; top with salmon. Sprinkle with 1 cup cheese. Top with remaining rice mixture; sprinkle with remaining cheese. Bake at 450°F about 15 minutes. Serve with dollops of sour cream, if desired.

Tuna Chip Casserole

Makes about 6 servings

 1 envelope Lipton® Onion-Mushroom Recipe
    Soup Mix
 3 tablespoons all-purpose flour
 2 cups milk
 2 tablespoons diced pimiento
 3 cups cooked egg noodles (about 8 ounces
    uncooked)
 2 cans (7 ounces each) tuna, drained and flaked
    Crushed potato chips or buttered bread crumbs

Preheat oven to 350°F In medium saucepan, blend Lipton Onion-Mushroom Recipe Soup Mix with flour; stir in milk. Simmer, stirring constantly, until sauce is thickened, about 5 minutes; add pimiento. In greased 1½-quart casserole, combine sauce, noodles, and tuna; top with potato chips. Bake 25 minutes, or until bubbling.

Note: Elbow macaroni can be substituted for the egg noodles.

Canned Fish

There is no federal inspection program for fresh fish—as there is for meat and poultry—but canned and frozen fish may be, at the option of the processor, inspected by the Department of Commerce National Marine Fisheries Service. Such products will carry one or both of two inspection marks. The first is round and carries the words "US Dept. of Commerce, Packed Under Federal Inspection." The mark is given only to inspected fish and means that the product has been sampled and found to be of good quality, wholesome and safe. The second mark is a shield, similar to the USDA's meat and poultry inspection shields, bearing the words "US Grade A." This mark is given only to top-quality products that are uniform in size, free of blemishes and defects, and possess fresh flavor and odor.

Handling canned fish. Store on pantry shelf, at room temperature but away from a source of heat. After opening, store in glass or plastic containers, tightly covered, in the refrigerator up to 3 days.

Before you buy, check the condition of the can. If it is bulging, something has broken the seal—the fish may be spoiled. If the can is dented or rusty, there is no way to tell if the seal has been broken—don't buy.

At home, when you open the can, check to make sure the flesh is firm. If the meat is overcooked, the flesh next to the can will be darker than that in the middle—if so, return the can to the store. If the fish is packed in oil, the oil should be clear, not milky. The can should be properly filled to the top.

Most tuna is packed in vegetable oil; some is packed in water, and there is a diet pack in distilled water, without salt. Read the tuna label.

Canned salmon labels will also tell you a good deal. The color of the salmon is an indication of the oil content of the fish, and also determines the price. The deeper red the color, the higher the oil content will be. Sockeye salmon, a deep red color, has the highest oil content. Pink varieties are paler in color, lower in oil. Salmon is packed in 7- and 16-ounce cans. Years ago, before food processing was regulated, an enterprising canner put out a pale pink salmon the label of which carried the legend: "Guaranteed not to turn red in can" and charged a fancy price for this "special" product.

Sardines come in a variety of packs, but virtually always in flat cans, most of which have to be opened with a key. They can be whole—heads, tails, skin, and bones—or skinless and boneless (also, although the label doesn't say so, headless and tailless), packed in oil, in tomato sauce, in mustard sauce, sometimes in wine sauce.

Tuna Florentine

Makes 6 servings

    4 ounces egg noodles
    1 package (10 ounces) frozen chopped spinach
    1 can (9¼ ounces) tuna
    1 can (10½ ounces) cream of mushroom soup
    1 tablespoon Wright's Natural Hickory Liquid
        Smoke
    1 onion, chopped
    ½ cup celery, chopped
    ½ cup green pepper, chopped
    ⅓ cup butter
    1 cup Swiss cheese, grated

Cook noodles and spinach according to package directions. Spread drained noodles over bottom of greased casserole dish. Cover with tuna and drained spinach. Sauté onion, celery, and green pepper in butter; stir in mushroom soup and Wright's Natural Hickory Liquid Smoke. Pour sauce over casserole and bake in 325°F. oven for 20 minutes; top with Swiss cheese and bake additional 3 minutes.

Fish Sticks with Herb and Butter Sauce

Makes 6 servings

    1 package (12 ounces) Gorton's® Crunchy Fish
        Sticks
    2 tablespoons finely chopped onion
    ½ clove garlic, finely chopped
    ¼ cup margarine or butter
    1 cup water
    1 tablespoon cornstarch
    2 teaspoons dried parsley flakes
    1 teaspoon dried tarragon leaves
    1 teaspoon instant chicken bouillon
    1 teaspoon vinegar
    ½ teaspoon prepared mustard
    ½ teaspoon salt
        Dash pepper

Heat oven to 400°F. Bake fish sticks as directed on package. Cook and stir onion and garlic in margarine in 1-quart saucepan over low heat until tender; cool slightly. Stir in remaining ingredients. Heat to boiling, stirring constantly. Boil and stir 1 minute. Pour over fish; serve immediately.

Cautionary Note

Unless you are extremely skillful, let the fishmonger fillet fish for you, rather than doing it at home. It takes an expert to release a totally boneless fillet from the fish without mangling it. Stray bones are annoying at best, dangerous at worst.

Savory Sauces for Fish

Lime butter is a simple and simply delicious fish sauce. First, clarify the butter by cooking it gently over low heat, until it foams—but don't let it begin to brown. Let stand about 3 minutes. Then skim off and discard the foam. Slowly and gently pour out the butter, leaving behind the milky residue in the bottom of the pan. Flavor the clear butter with lime juice and grated rind to taste.

When you poach fish, use some of the fumet—the stock in which it was poached—to make a light **lemony sauce**. Strain the stock and measure 2 cups into a saucepan. Add 2 tablespoons butter; cook over low heat until stock is warm and butter melted. Stirring constantly, add 2 tablespoons cornstarch dissolved in 3 tablespoons water; continue to stir until mixture bubbles and thickens. Stir in 1½ tablespoons lemon juice; season to taste with salt and white pepper, and serve at once. If you wish, add 1 tablespoon chopped fresh dill or 1 teaspoon dried dill weed, or 2 tablespoons snipped fresh parsley. For a richer-looking, golden sauce, add ½ teaspoon turmeric along with the salt and pepper.

To serve with cold fish—anything from canned tuna to poached fresh salmon—a cold **cucumber sauce** can be just the right thing. Peel lengthwise strips from a cucumber, leaving alternate strips of the green peel in place. Cut cucumber in half lengthwise and cut the resulting strips into thin slices. Salt lightly; refrigerate, covered and weighted, at least 2 hours. Drain very well. Mix with just enough unflavored yogurt to bind. Stir in 1 tablespoon snipped fresh or thawed frozen chives. Season to taste with salt and white pepper.

In old-fashioned English novels, there was often mention of **lobster mayonnaise** when the upper classes had luncheon on the terrace. To duplicate this delicacy in your kitchen, you will need to stockpile lobster shells in the freezer. In a heavy-duty food processor, or in a bag and using a meat pounder, chop the shells of 2 lobsters. To the shells, add ¼ cup rich fish stock and ¼ cup white wine; let stand, covered and refrigerated, 2 hours. Press through a fine sieve. Add 6 tablespoons of this lobster essence to 1 cup mayonnaise. Stir gently to combine well, and refrigerate until needed. Use to top a lobster, crab, or shrimp salad.

New York Chowder
Makes 12 servings
- ¼ pound salt pork, diced
- 1 large onion, diced
- 3 stalks celery, diced
- 1 green pepper, diced
- 2 carrots, diced
- 2 medium potatoes, cubed
- 2½ teaspoons salt
- ¼ teaspoon pepper
- 2 cups water
- 1 can (29 ounces) tomatoes (3½ cups)
- Small bay leaf
- ¾ teaspoon thyme
- 3 cans Doxsee Minced Clams
- ½ cup bread or cracker crumbs

Place diced salt pork in saucepan and cook until brown. Add onion and sauté until golden. Add remaining vegetables, salt, pepper, water, tomatoes, and herbs. Cover and simmer gently 1 hour. Add clams. Cook 3 minutes. Add crumbs. Stir well and serve steaming hot.

Hearty Fish Chowder
Makes 4 to 6 servings
- ¼ cup butter or margarine
- 6 tablespoons all-purpose flour
- 1 envelope Lipton® Country Vegetable Recipe Soup Mix
- 2 cups water
- 2 cups milk
- 1 package (16 ounces) frozen flounder fillets, thawed
- 1 cup shredded cheddar cheese
- ½ teaspoon salt

In medium saucepan, melt butter and blend in flour. Stir in Lipton Country Vegetable Recipe Soup Mix, water, and milk. Cook, stirring constantly, until soup thickens. Add flounder, cheese, and salt and cook until flounder flakes, about 5 minutes.

Miss Edna's Seafood Bisque
Makes 6 servings
- 1 can (11¼ ounces) Campbell's Condensed Green Pea Soup
- 1 can (10¾ ounces) Campbell's Condensed Tomato Soup
- 1½ cups milk mixed with 1½ cups light cream
- ½ cup sherry
- 1 cup flaked crab meat
- Lemon peel

Combine soups. Gradually stir in milk and cream. Cook over low heat, stirring occasionally, until soup bubbles. Stir in sherry and crab meat. Reheat slightly. Add a twist of lemon peel to each bowl of soup.

Fish Chowder
Makes 4 servings
- 6 slices bacon
- 1 medium-size onion, chopped
- 2 stalks celery, diced
- 2 medium-size potatoes, cut into chunks
- ½ teaspoon thyme
- 1 teaspoon salt
- ¼ teaspoon pepper
- 1 can (8 ounces) tomatoes
- 1 pound fish fillets
- 2 cups half and half
- 2 tablespoons chopped parsley
- Croutons

Sauté bacon, onion, and celery in Dutch oven until onion is transparent. Add 2½ cups water, potatoes, and seasonings. Heat to boiling. Reduce heat, cover, and simmer 15 to 20 minutes, or until potatoes are tender. Add tomatoes and fish. Cover and simmer 10 minutes. Add half and half. Stir gently to break fish into large flakes. Ladle into soup bowls and sprinkle with parsley and croutons. Serve piping hot.

This recipe was provided by the makers of Saran Wrap™ brand plastic film.

Manhattan Clam Chowder
Makes 4 servings
- 3 slices bacon, cut into ½-inch pieces
- ½ cup chopped onion
- ½ cup diced celery
- 1½ cups water
- 1 cup diced potatoes
- 1 carrot, shredded
- 1 teaspoon salt
- 1 can (8 ounces) Hunt's Tomato Sauce
- 1 can (8 ounces) minced clams, undrained
- ¼ teaspoon leaf thyme

In 3-quart saucepan, brown bacon until crisp. Add onion and celery; sauté until onion is soft. Drain fat. Add water, potatoes, carrots, and salt. Cover; simmer 20 minutes. Add Hunt's Sauce, clams, and thyme. Heat through.

King Crab Bisque

Makes 4 to 6 servings
   1 can (11¼ ounces) Campbell's Condensed Green
        Pea Soup
   1 can (10¾ ounces) Campbell's Condensed
        Tomato Soup
   1 soup can light cream
   1 soup can milk
   2 cups flaked cooked crab
   ½ cup bourbon
     Chopped parsley

Blend soups until smooth. Gradually stir in cream and milk; add crab. Heat, stirring often. Do not boil. Add bourbon; reheat. Garnish with parsley.

Crab Meat Bisque

Makes 4 to 6 servings
   2 tablespoons butter or margarine
   ½ small onion, sliced
   1 package (6 ounces) frozen crab meat, thawed,
        or 1 can (6 ounces) crab meat, boned and
        flaked
   1 cup milk
   1 tablespoon all-purpose flour
   ¼ teaspoon salt
     Dash pepper
   1 cup light cream
   3 tablespoons dry sherry
     Chopped parsley

Heat butter in medium-size saucepan. Add onion and cook over medium heat, stirring occasionally, until soft. Add crab meat; cook over medium heat, stirring occasionally, for 1 minute. Put mixture into blender container. Add milk, flour, salt, and pepper. Cover; blend at medium speed until smooth. Return mixture to saucepan. Stir in cream; heat, stirring, until simmering. Remove from heat and stir in sherry. Garnish with chopped parsley.

Hearty Corn and Fish Soup

Makes about 4 servings
   1 can (1 pound) stewed tomatoes, broken up
   1 bottle (8 ounces) clam juice
   1 package (12 ounces) frozen fish fillets, thawed
        and chunked
   1 package (10 ounces) frozen succotash, thawed
   1 tablespoon Lea & Perrins Worcestershire Sauce
   ¼ teaspoon salt

In a medium saucepan, combine all ingredients. Simmer uncovered until fish flakes when tested with a fork, about 15 minutes.

Quick Clam Bisque

Makes 4 servings
   2 cups light cream or half and half
   1 teaspoon celery salt
   ¼ teaspoon dried tarragon
     Few drops hot pepper sauce
   2 cans (7½ ounces each) minced clams with liquid

Put all ingredients into blender container in order listed. Cover; blend at medium speed until clams are finely chopped. Pour into saucepan; heat, stirring, until simmering. Serve warm or refrigerate and serve chilled.

Clam-Tomato Consommé

Makes 3 servings
   2 cups clam juice
   1 medium tomato, cut up
   ½ small onion, cut up
   1 thin slice lemon
   ½ teaspoon celery salt
     Dash pepper

Put all ingredients into blender container in order listed. Cover; blend at high speed until smooth. Pour into saucepan; simmer 3 minutes.

Clam Bisque

Makes 4 to 6 servings
   1 tablespoon butter
   1 onion, finely chopped
   2 tablespoons all-purpose flour
   1 bottle Doxsee Clam Juice
     Dash salt and pepper
     Dash celery salt
   ⅔ cup cream or milk
   1 tablespoon parsley, finely chopped

Melt butter in saucepan. Add onions and cook until tender. Add flour and blend. Add bottle of Doxsee Clam Juice and an equal amount of water. Cook until thickened, stirring constantly. Season with pepper and celery salt, and simmer slowly 10 minutes. Heat cream or milk and add just before serving. Top with parsley.

Turtle Soup au Sherry

Makes 8 servings

 1 can (2 pounds 1 ounce) green turtle meat
 ½ cup butter
 1½ cups chopped white onions
 ½ cup all-purpose flour
 1 can (10¾ ounces) Campbell's Condensed
   Tomato Soup
 ½ cup sherry
 ¼ cup Worcestershire sauce
 2 hard-cooked eggs, finely chopped
 ½ cup finely chopped parsley
 ½ lemon, thinly sliced

Drain turtle meat and reserve liquid. Add enough water to liquid to make 5 cups. Dice turtle meat into ½-inch cubes. In a large kettle, melt butter and sauté onions until transparent but not brown. Stir in flour and cook until flour turns pale golden brown. Stir in tomato soup, turtle liquid, sherry, and Worcestershire sauce. Let simmer, stirring occasionally, for 15 minutes. Add eggs, parsley, lemon slices, and turtle meat. Simmer another 15 minutes. Serve at once. If desired, serve with extra sherry at the table: Spoon 1 or 2 tablespoons into each serving and stir lightly.

Potato-Tuna Chowder

Makes 8 servings

 2 tablespoons butter or margarine
 ½ cup chopped onion
 6 medium potatoes, washed, peeled, and diced
 2 medium carrots, peeled and diced
 ½ cup diced celery
 2 cups water
 1 can (9¼ ounces) tuna, undrained
 4 cups milk
 2 teaspoons salt
 ¼ teaspoon white pepper
 ¼ cup minced parsley

Melt butter in 3½-quart saucepan. Sauté onion until transparent. Add potatoes, carrots, celery, and water; bring to a boil. Cover and simmer 25 to 30 minutes, or until vegetables are tender, stirring occasionally. Add tuna and milk; heat through. Stir in salt and pepper. Sprinkle parsley on each serving.

Herb-Shelf Harmony

Ever wonder which herb would bring out the flavors of your fish or shellfish selection? Here are some suggestions:

basil	bay leaves	chervil	dillweed	majoram	oregano	parsley
crab	poaching medium	poaching	halibut	clams	clams	poaching
halibut	for shellfish	medium for	salmon	crab sauté	creamed lobster	liquids
mackerel	halibut	fillets	shrimp	creamed tuna	*or* crab	
salmon	salmon		sole	halibut	shrimp	
shrimp				salmon		
tuna						

peppermint	rosemary	saffron	sage	savory	tarragon	thyme
shrimp	poaching	baked	baked	halibut	salmon	cod
prawns	liquid for	halibut and	halibut	shrimp	crab	crab
	salmon,	sole	and sole	sole	halibut	creamed tuna
	halibut		poached	crab	lobster	halibut
	broiled salmon		salmon	salmon	shrimp	scallops
					sole	sole

Italian Fish Stew

Makes 8 servings

¼ cup olive oil
1 medium onion, finely chopped
2 cloves garlic, crushed
1 can (1 pound 12 ounces) whole tomatoes, cut up
2 cans (8 ounces each) tomato sauce
2 packages (1½ ounces each) Lawry's Spaghetti Sauce Seasoning Blend with Imported Mushrooms or 1 package (3 ounces) Lawry's Economy-Size Spaghetti Sauce Seasoning Blend with Imported Mushrooms
1 teaspoon Lawry's Seasoned Salt
¼ teaspoon Lawry's Seasoned Pepper
2 cups water
1 cup dry white wine
1½ pounds whitefish, such as halibut, cut into large chunks
1 pound uncooked shrimp, shelled and deveined
4 uncooked lobster tails (about 6 ounces each), fins and soft undershell removed and cut into large chunks, shell and all
1 dozen clams
   Crusty bread or rolls

In Dutch oven or large kettle, heat oil; sauté onion and garlic until tender. Add tomatoes, tomato sauce, Spaghetti Sauce Seasoning Blend with Imported Mushrooms, Seasoned Salt, Seasoned Pepper, and water; blend well. Bring to a boil; reduce heat, cover, and simmer 30 minutes, stirring occasionally. Add wine, fish, shrimp, lobster, and clams. Cover and simmer about 15 minutes, stirring occasionally. Clam shells will open during cooking. Serve in large shallow soup bowls with crusty bread or rolls.

Note: To prepare clams, scrub shells and allow to stand in cold salted water (⅓ cup salt to 1 gallon water) about 15 to 20 minutes. Drain water and repeat salt water soaking process twice. Refrigerate until ready to use.

If lobster, shrimp, and clam prices are prohibitive, use more whitefish.

Hearty Fish Stew

Makes 4 to 6 servings

- ¼ cup butter or margarine
- 6 tablespoons all-purpose flour
- 1 envelope Lipton® Country Vegetable Recipe Soup Mix
- 2 cups water
- 2 cups milk
- 1 pound fish fillets
- 1 cup (about 4 ounces) shredded cheddar cheese
- ½ teaspoon salt

In medium saucepan, melt butter and blend in flour; stir in Lipton Country Vegetable Recipe Soup Mix, water, and milk. Heat but do not boil, stirring constantly, until soup is slightly thickened. Add fish, cheese, and salt; cook until fish flakes, about 5 minutes.

Variation

Two cans (6 to 7½ ounces each) crab meat can be substituted for the fish fillets.

Seafood Jambalaya Supreme

Makes 4 to 6 servings

- ¼ cup butter or margarine
- ½ cup chopped green pepper
- ¼ cup chopped onion
- ¼ cup chopped celery
- 1 envelope Lipton® Ring-O Noodle Recipe Soup Mix with Real Chicken Broth
- ½ teaspoon thyme
  Dash cayenne
- 2¼ cups water
- 2 cups instant rice
- 2 cans (4½ ounces each) shrimp, drained
- 1 can (7½ ounces) crab meat, drained and flaked

In large saucepan, melt butter and cook green pepper, onion, and celery until tender. Add Lipton Ring-O Noodle Recipe Soup Mix, thyme, and cayenne blended into water; cook, stirring occasionally, 5 minutes. Stir in rice, shrimp, and crab meat. Cover, remove from heat, and let stand 5 minutes.

Bouillabaisse Marseillaise (page 44). Campbell Soup Company

Boatman's Stew

Makes 6 servings

 2 pounds firm-fleshed whitefish (cod, haddock, or halibut), cut in large chunks
   Salt
 2 onions, sliced
 2 tablespoons pure vegetable oil
 1 can (6 ounces) Hunt's Tomato Paste
 3 cups water
 ¼ teaspoon *each* red pepper and black pepper
 1 cup finely chopped parsley
 ⅓ cup dry white wine
 6 slices Italian bread (toasted, if desired)

Sprinkle fish with ½ teaspoon salt; let stand 1 hour. Meanwhile, lightly brown onion in oil; pour off fat. Stir in Hunt's Tomato Paste, water, red pepper, 1½ teaspoons salt, black pepper, parsley, and wine. Simmer 20 minutes. Add fish; simmer about 10 minutes longer, or just until fish flakes easily with a fork. To serve, place a slice of bread in each soup bowl; ladle soup over.

Sunday Night Supper

In New England and in many parts of the country to which New Englanders have emigrated, chowder is the dish of choice for supper on Sunday. All fish chowders call, naturally, for fish; most call for onion, celery, and potato. Manhattan-style adds tomatoes and sometimes other vegetables, calling down the scorn of New England folks who want their chowder pale and richly creamy. Almost any kind of white-fleshed nonfat fish will do splendidly for chowder. But if you want authenticity and best-of-all flavor, never skip the first chowder-making step that all truly good recipes call for: "trying out" small cubes of salt pork. Once one of the diet mainstays of sailors at sea as well as of the colonists during long winters, salt pork is belly meat preserved in salt. It is very fat, with some strips of lean—much less lean than good bacon—and imparts a like-no-other flavor to dishes in which it is used. Buy salt pork at a butcher shop or supermarket. Cut off and discard the rind. Cut the pork into ¼- to ½-inch cubes and place in a cold heavy skillet or soup kettle. Heat and cook slowly until the cubes have expressed their fat, turned golden brown and crisp. Remove the pork with a slotted spoon and set aside—it will be returned to the soup later. In the expressed salt-pork fat (or part of it), sauté the onions and celery the recipe calls for, and you're on your way to delicious, authentic chowder.

Bouillabaisse

Makes 10 servings

 1 cup chopped celery
 ½ cup chopped green pepper
 ⅓ cup chopped onion
 1 medium clove garlic, minced
 1 large bay leaf
 ½ teaspoon thyme leaves, crushed
 ¼ teaspoon crushed red pepper
 3 tablespoons butter or margarine
 2 cans (11 ounces each) Campbell's Condensed Tomato Bisque Soup
 2 soup cans water
 2 tablespoons lemon juice
 2 tablespoons chopped parsley
 1 pound fillets of halibut, cut in 2-inch pieces
 1 package (6 ounces) frozen Alaskan king crab meat, thawed and drained
 ½ pound medium raw shrimp (about 16), shelled and deveined
   Sea toast or bread

In large saucepan, cook celery, green pepper, and onion with garlic, bay leaf, thyme, and red pepper in butter until tender. Add remaining ingredients. Cook 10 minutes, or until done. Stir gently occasionally. Remove bay leaf. Serve with sea toast or bread.

Bouillabaisse Marseillaise

Makes 6 servings

 ¼ cup olive oil
 1 can (1 pound 12 ounces) tomatoes, chopped
 ½ cup chopped onion
 3 cloves garlic, chopped
 ¼ teaspoon fennel seed
 ½ teaspoon crushed thyme
 1 bay leaf
 2 tablespoons chopped parsley
 ½ teaspoon crushed rosemary
 ¼ cup minced celery
 2 slices orange
 2 slices lemon
 1 cup dry white wine
 2 cans (10½ ounces each) Campbell's Condensed Chicken Broth
 ¼ teaspoon crushed saffron
 4 pounds assorted raw seafood (lobster, crab meat, red snapper, cod, clams, whiting), cut into bite-size pieces
   Salt
   Toasted French bread slices or croutons
   Chopped parsley

In a Dutch oven or deep kettle, heat olive oil. Add remaining ingredients except fish and salt. Bring to a boil, lower heat, and simmer until vegetables are tender, about 15 minutes. Remove bay leaf, lemon, and orange slices. If you are using lobster, drop into boiling water and cook only until shell turns red. Drain and drench with cold water. Cut the seafood—including lobster shell—into 1-inch pieces. Add fish pieces to soup. Simmer 10 minutes or until fish is cooked. Season to taste with salt. Serve bouillabaisse in soup bowls topped with toasted French bread slices or croutons and chopped parsley.

Supermarket Shopper—Shellfish

Use your eyes, but also your nose and your fingers when making your purchase of fresh shellfish. Lobster and crab should show signs of life—movement, wriggling of claws—or don't buy; if they are dead, it's impossible to determine how long they've been dead. Crab and lobster are also sold cooked, in which condition they are red in color. Smell them—there should be no high, unpleasant odor. You can also buy crab and lobster "picked"—the meat removed from the shell. Oysters, hardshell clams, and scallops should all close their shells when tapped with a finger; if they don't, they are not alive. However, all of these are also sold shucked—removed from their shells—and in this case your sense of smell should guide you. Shrimp are sold headless; they can be "green"—shell in place, not cooked—cooked but not shelled, or cooked, shelled, and with the central back vein removed. Each process done by the fish market raises the per-pound price of the shrimp, but take into consideration that when they are shelled you are not paying for the weight of the shell. Here, too, let your nose guide your purchases. Shrimp occur in a number of sizes, from very small to very large.

Shellfish of most kinds are also available frozen, in shell or out, cooked or uncooked. They can also be had canned, in which case they are always shelled; they may be vacuum-packed or in a brine or their own juices. Look for the USDA inspection shield on canned and frozen products.

Crab Meat Stew
Makes 6 servings
- 2 tablespoons Planters® Peanut Oil
- 1 small onion, grated
- ¼ pound fresh mushrooms, thinly sliced
- 2 medium tomatoes, skinned and chopped
- ½ pound flaked crab meat
- ½ teaspoon salt
  Dash ground red pepper
- 1 cup milk
- 1 cup heavy cream
- 1 tablespoon parsley, chopped
- 1 teaspoon chopped chives
- ¼ cup Dry Sack® Sherry

Heat Planters® Peanut Oil in a saucepan over medium heat; add onion and cook, stirring for about 1 minute. Add mushroom slices and continue cooking for about 3 minutes. Mix in tomatoes and cook for 5 minutes. Stir in crab meat, salt, red pepper, milk, and cream; heat until mixture just comes to a boil. Mix in parsley, chives, and Dry Sack® Sherry. Serve at once.

Poor Man's Cioppino
Makes 8 servings
- 1 cup chopped onion
- ½ cup chopped green pepper
- ½ cup chopped carrot
- ½ cup chopped celery
- 1 clove garlic, minced
- 2 tablespoons pure vegetable oil
- 1 can (15 ounces) Hunt's Tomato Sauce
- 2½ cups water
- ½ cup dry red wine
- 1 vegetable bouillon cube
- ½ teaspoon Italian herb seasoning
- ½ teaspoon salt
- ⅛ teaspoon seasoned pepper
- ½ pound halibut, cut into 1-inch pieces
- 6 ounces cooked shrimp
- 1 package (6 ounces) frozen snow crab, thawed
  Minced parsley

In Dutch oven, sauté onion, green pepper, carrot, celery, and garlic in oil until onion is soft. Stir in Hunt's Sauce, water, wine, bouillon cube, Italian seasoning, salt, aad pepper. Cover; simmer 15 minutes. Stir occasionally. Add halibut, shrimp, and crab. Cover; simmer 20 minutes longer. Sprinkle with minced parsley.

Easy Paella

Makes 6 servings

1 package (12 ounces) frozen peeled shrimp
1 can (7 to 8 ounces) minced clams
2 cups diced cooked chicken
1 can (16 ounces) tomatoes
1 package (10 ounces) frozen green peas, broken apart
2½ cups uncooked instant rice
3 tablespoons instant minced onion
1 teaspoon paprika
2 chicken bouillon cubes
¼ teaspoon cayenne
⅛ teaspoon saffron

Combine all ingredients in large skillet; add ½ cup water. Heat, stirring occasionally, to boiling. Reduce heat and simmer 5 minutes. Remove from heat; cover and let stand about 10 minutes.

Cioppino

Makes 8 servings

1 large onion, chopped
1 medium-size green pepper, seeded and chopped
½ cup sliced celery
1 carrot, pared and shredded
3 cloves garlic, minced
3 tablespoons olive oil
2 cans (1 pound each) tomatoes
1 can (8 ounces) tomato sauce
1 teaspoon crumbled basil
1 bay leaf
1 teaspoon salt
¼ teaspoon pepper
1 pound whitefish
1 dozen mussels or littleneck clams in the shells
Cornmeal (optional)
1½ cups dry white wine
½ pound shrimp, cleaned
½ pound scallops
Snipped parsley

Cook onion, green pepper, celery, carrot, and garlic in olive oil in a Dutch oven until soft. Stir in tomatoes, tomato sauce, basil, bay leaf, salt, and pepper. Heat to boiling. Reduce heat, cover, and simmer 2 hours. Discard bay leaf. While sauce is simmering, cut whitefish into serving pieces. Using a stiff brush, thoroughly scrub the mussels, cutting off their beards, or soak clams in cold water to which cornmeal has been added and then scrub under running water to remove any residue of mud and sand. Stir wine into tomato mixture. Add whitefish, shrimp, and scallops. Cover and simmer 10 minutes. Place mussels or clams in a layer on top of fish in kettle. Cover and steam 5 to 10 minutes, or until the shells are fully opened. Discard any mussels or clams that are unopened. Ladle soup into soup plates or bowls. Sprinkle with parsley.

New Orleans Jambalaya

Makes 4 servings

¼ cup chopped onion
2 tablespoons butter or margarine
1 cup cubed Armour's Pork Shoulder Picnic
1 cup cooked shrimp
1½ cups cooked rice
1 cup hot water
3 tablespoons tomato paste
2 tablespoons chopped parsley
1½ teaspoons all-purpose flour
¼ teaspoon garlic powder
Pitted ripe olives

Cook onion in butter 5 minutes. Stir in remaining ingredients. Cook over low heat 10 minutes, or until thoroughly heated. Garnish with olives.

Shrimp Gumbo

Makes 5 to 6 servings

1 cup Uncle Ben's® Converted® Brand Rice
2 cups sliced fresh okra
⅓ cup fat or bacon drippings
⅔ cup chopped green onions and tops
3 cloves garlic, finely chopped
1½ teaspoons salt
2 teaspoons black pepper
2 pounds shrimp, shelled and deveined
2 cups hot water
1 cup stewed tomatoes
2 whole bay leaves
6 drops hot pepper sauce

Cook rice according to package directions. Meanwhile, sauté okra in fat, stirring constantly, about 10 minutes, or until okra appears dry. Add onion, garlic, salt, pepper, and shrimp. Cook about 5 minutes. Add water, tomatoes, and bay leaves. Cover and simmer 20 minutes. Remove bay leaves. Add hot pepper sauce. Spoon over rice and serve.

Easy Paella (page 46)

Shrimp Gumbo (page 46). Submitted by Uncle Ben's, Inc.

New Orleans Jambalaya (page 46). Armour Food Company

Riceland's Special Seafood Gumbo

Makes 8 to 10 servings

½ cup all-purpose flour
½ cup Chef-way Oil
1 cup chopped onion
1 cup chopped celery
3 cloves garlic, minced
½ cup chopped green pepper
½ gallon warm water
2 cups sliced okra
8 ounces tomato sauce
1 tablespoon salt
½ teaspoon black pepper
½ teaspoon cayenne
2 pounds fresh shrimp
1 pound crab meat
1 tablespoon dried parsley
¼ cup chopped green onion tops
4 cups cooked Riceland Rice
Gumbo file powder (optional)

Combine Chef-way Oil and flour in a heavy iron pot over medium heat; cook, stirring constantly, until roux is the color of copper penny, about 10 to 15 minutes. Add onion, celery, garlic, and green pepper to roux; cook, stirring constantly until vegetables are tender, being careful not to burn the roux. Gradually add warm water, blending well after each addition. Add okra and tomato sauce. Bring mixture to a boil. Reduce heat; simmer, stirring occasionally, 1 to 1½ hours. Stir in salt, peppers, and seafood. Bring gumbo to a boil and simmer 10 minutes. Add parsley and green onion; simmer 5 minutes longer. Remove from heat and stir in cooked rice. Gumbo can be further thickened, if desired, by adding a small amount of file powder in the gumbo or in each individual serving.

Seafood Méditerranée

Makes 4 to 6 servings

½ cup olive oil
3 cloves garlic, minced
6 small rock lobster tails, cut into thirds
1 teaspoon oregano
1½ teaspoons salt
½ teaspoon pepper
1 can (1 pound) Italian plum tomatoes
1 cup dry white wine
2 bay leaves
1½ dozen cherrystone clams, scrubbed
1 pound shrimp, shelled and deveined
1 cup snipped parsley
French bread

Preheat Sunbeam Multi-Cooker Frypan to 300°F. Add oil and garlic and cook, stirring, 1 minute. Add lobster pieces and cook, stirring, 3 minutes. Add oregano, salt, pepper, tomatoes, wine, and bay leaves. Bring to a boil. Cover, lower heat to Simmer, and cook 5 minutes. Add clams, shrimp, and parsley. Bring mixture to a boil. Reduce heat to Simmer, cover, and cook 5 minutes, or until shrimp are cooked and the clams are open. Serve in soup bowls with French bread.

Seafood Louisiana

Makes 4 servings

2 tablespoons Planters® Peanut Oil
¾ cup chopped onion
¼ cup finely chopped celery
2 medium cloves garlic, crushed
1 tablespoon all-purpose flour
1 can (28 ounces) crushed plum tomatoes in tomato purée
1 teaspoon sugar
½ teaspoon salt
¼ teaspoon black pepper
¼ teaspoon thyme leaves
¼ teaspoon marjoram leaves
1 bay leaf
½ pound swordfish, cut into bite-size pieces
½ pound bay scallops
Hot cooked rice

Heat Planters® Peanut Oil in a Dutch oven over medium heat. Add onion, celery, and garlic; sauté until vegetables are tender. Blend in flour. Cook 1 to 2 minutes, stirring constantly. Mix in tomatoes, sugar, salt, pepper, thyme, marjoram, and bay leaf. Bring mixture to a boil. Reduce heat; simmer uncovered until thick, about 1½ hours, stirring occasionally.

Mix swordfish and scallops into tomato sauce. Bring mixture to a boil; reduce heat and simmer 10 to 15 minutes, or until fish is done. Serve over hot cooked rice. Best when prepared 1 day before serving.

Fish Stock (Fumet)

Use this flavorful fish stock as a base for soups and chowders, or in sauces and aspics.

- 2½ cups cold water
- ½ cup chopped onion
- ¼ cup chopped carrot
- ½ cup chopped celery
- 6 white peppercorns
- 3 whole cloves
- Bouquet garni
- ½ cup dry white wine or 3 tablespoons lemon juice
- 1½ pounds lean fish bones, skins, tails, trimmings, and heads (remove gills)
- Leftover shrimp, lobster, and/or crab shells (optional)

Place all ingredients in a pan. Heat until liquid begins to simmer; continue simmering uncovered 15 minutes—no longer, or bitter flavors may develop. Skim, strain, and refrigerate covered unless it is to be used immediately. May also be frozen.

Oyster Stew

Makes 4 servings

- 4 cups half and half
- 1 onion, minced
- ¼ cup butter or margarine
- 2 tablespoons all-purpose flour
- 2 cups shucked oysters, undrained
- 1 tablespoon Worcestershire sauce
- 1¼ teaspoons salt
- ¼ teaspoon freshly ground pepper
- Oyster crackers or diced buttered toast
- Chopped parsley

Heat half and half in small saucepan over low heat until hot but not boiling, about 10 minutes. Cover and set aside. In large saucepan, sauté onion in butter until onion is transparent, about 5 minutes. Stir in flour until smooth. Cook 1 minute. Add oysters, Worcestershire sauce, salt, and pepper. Reduce heat to low, cover, and cook 8 minutes, or until edges of oysters begin to curl. Add half and half. Cover and simmer over very low heat 20 minutes to blend flavors. Ladle into soup bowls and sprinkle with oyster crackers and chopped parsley.

This recipe was provided by the makers of Saran Wrap™ brand plastic film.

Simple Seafood Creole

Makes 4 servings

- ½ green pepper, chopped
- 1 clove garlic, minced
- 2 teaspoons pure vegetable oil
- 1 can (15 ounces) Hunt's Tomato Sauce Special
- 1 teaspoon salt
- 1 bay leaf
- ¼ teaspoon thyme
- ⅛ teaspoon pepper
- 1 package (6 ounces) frozen crab meat, thawed
- 1 pound fresh or frozen halibut or whitefish, cut into bite-size pieces
- 3 cups hot cooked rice

In a 10-inch skillet, sauté green pepper and garlic in oil until tender. Add Hunt's Sauce, salt, bay leaf, thyme, and pepper. Simmer 5 minutes, stirring occasionally. Add seafood; simmer 5 minutes longer. Remove bay leaf. Serve over hot cooked rice.

Nutritionally Speaking

Fish varies somewhat in nutrients and considerably in calories, depending on the kind. However, all fish is high in protein; it's also low in calories compared to other main-dish foods.

It's helpful to know that some fish are classified as fat, others as lean. This makes a certain amount of difference in the best cooking methods for each type—lean fish, if broiled, must be basted with butter or other fat, if baked, should be cooked in milk or a sauce; fat fish are sufficiently moistened by their own fat so that basting or sauce is not necessary to keep them from drying out during the cooking process. Lean fish include catfish, yellow perch, cod, flounder, sole, halibut, red snapper, sea and striped bass (rockfish). Among the fat fish are lake and rainbow trout, whitefish, eel, herring, mackerel, pompano, salmon, and tuna.

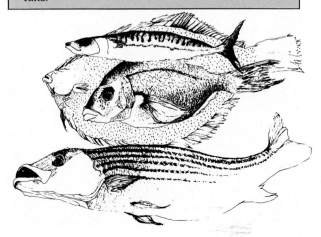

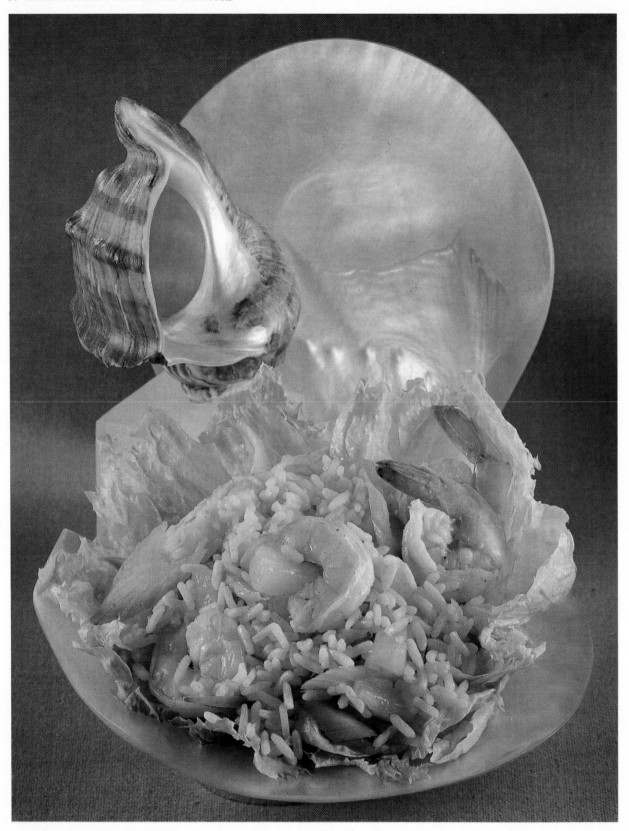

Rice and Shrimp Salad. Uncle Ben's, Inc.

Salads by the Sea

What could be more refreshing—and more nutritionally sound—than a salad, tossed, molded, or arranged, graced with the delicately sweet meat of your favorite fish or shellfish? Combine it with greens, crunchy vegetables, or fresh fruit, and your table will explode with color, texture, and great taste.

Rice and Shrimp Salad

Makes 6 to 8 servings

  2 cups cooked Uncle Ben's® Converted® Brand
     Rice, cooled
  2 cups cooked shrimp, halved lengthwise
  1 cup celery, thinly sliced crosswise
  ⅔ cup green pepper, cut in thin julienne strips
  1 can (15½ ounces) pineapple chunks, drained
  3 tablespoons vinegar
1½ tablespoons salad oil
  1 teaspoon Worcestershire sauce
  1 teaspoon sugar
  ½ teaspoon salt
  ½ teaspoon curry powder
  ⅛ teaspoon ginger powder
     Dash black pepper
     Watercress sprigs

Combine rice, shrimp, celery, green peppers, and pineapple. Combine remaining ingredients to form dressing. Pour over rice mixture and stir. Let chill and marinate at least 3 hours. Serve garnished with more shrimp, watercress sprigs.

Shrimp Salad

Makes 4 to 6 servings

  ¼ cup lemon juice
  ¼ teaspoon tarragon
  1 pound small or medium-size shrimp, thawed if
     frozen, shelled, and deveined
  ½ cup Sun-Maid® Puffed Seeded Muscat Raisins
  1 small head iceberg lettuce, coarsely shredded
  1 small bunch watercress
  1 small cucumber, sliced very thin
  3 tablespoons butter or margarine
  ½ teaspoon salt
     Freshly ground pepper to taste
     Avocado-Raisin Dressing (recipe follows)

Combine lemon juice and tarragon. Add shrimp and raisins and refrigerate covered for 2 to 3 hours. When ready to prepare, drain shrimp and raisins and discard marinade. Pat the shrimp dry with paper towels. Toss the lettuce, watercress, and cucumber slices to combine and arrange on salad plates. In a large skillet, sauté the shrimp and raisins in the butter for 3 to 5 minutes, or until shrimp are pink and firm. Sprinkle with salt and pepper. Mound the shrimp mixture on the lettuce, and spoon dressing over all. Garnish with watercress.

Avocado-Raisin Dressing

Makes about 1½ cups

  1 large very ripe avocado
  1 tablespoon lemon juice
  ¾ teaspoon salt
     Dash freshly ground pepper
  ¼ cup Sun-Maid® Seedless Raisins
  ¼ cup mayonnaise

Peel the avocado; remove the pit and set it aside. Coarsely mash the avocado with a potato masher or fork. Combine with the remaining ingredients and mix well. Place in a serving dish and put the pit in the center of the dressing to keep it from discoloring; remove the pit before serving. This dressing may be stored in the refrigerator for up to 3 days.

Avocado Raisin Dip

Grate one small onion and add to the Avocado-Raisin Dressing. Serve with cauliflowerets, carrot and celery sticks, blanched green beans, and green pepper strips.

Shrimply Delicious Cocktail Ring

Makes 12 servings

- 2 envelopes Knox® Unflavored Gelatine
- 1 cup cold water
- 1½ cups tomato juice, heated to boiling
- 1 cup chili sauce
- ¼ cup lemon juice
- 2 to 3 tablespoons prepared horseradish
- ⅛ teaspoon hot pepper sauce
- ½ cup chopped celery
- ½ cup chopped green pepper
- 2 pounds shrimp, cleaned, cooked, and chilled

In a medium bowl, mix Knox Unflavored Gelatine with water. Add hot tomato juice and stir until gelatine is completely dissolved. Add chili sauce, lemon juice, horseradish, and hot pepper sauce; chill, stirring occasionally, until mixture is the consistency of unbeaten egg whites. Fold in celery and green pepper. Turn into a 6-cup ring mold; chill until firm, about 4 hours. To serve, unmold onto a serving plate; fill center with shrimp.

Savory Fish Salad

Makes 6 servings

- 2 packages (12 ounces each) frozen fish fillets, thawed
- 1 cup diced celery
- ¼ cup chopped onion
- 2 tablespoons diced pimiento
- ¼ cup oil
- 1 tablespoon lemon juice
- 1½ teaspoons Lea & Perrins Worcestershire Sauce
- ½ teaspoon salt
  - Lettuce leaves, tomato wedges, radish roses (optional)

In a medium skillet, bring 1 inch of water to boiling point. Add fish; poach for 6 to 8 minutes. With a slotted spoon, remove fish from the water to a mixing bowl. Cool and flake. Chill thoroughly. Add celery, onion, and pimiento. Mix oil with lemon juice, Lea & Perrins, and salt. Pour over fish mixture. Toss well. Serve on lettuce leaves garnished with tomato wedges and radish roses, if desired.

Herring Salad

Makes 6 servings

- 1 jar (12 ounces) pickled herring in wine sauce, drained
- 2 medium-size cooked potatoes, coarsely chopped
- ¾ cup pickled beets, coarsely chopped
- 1 small onion, minced
- ¼ cup Sun-Maid® Zante Currants
- 2 tablespoons capers
- ¼ teaspoon salt
  - Dash freshly ground pepper
- ¼ cup white wine vinegar
- ½ cup sour cream (optional)

Cut the herring into 1-inch pieces and combine with remaining ingredients, tossing lightly to mix. Cover and refrigerate for 2 to 3 hours to blend the flavors.

Idea: Serve on lettuce with sliced hard-cooked eggs and apples; serve with dark pumpernickel bread.

Cosmopolitan Lobster Salad

Makes 4 servings

- 1½ cups cubed cooked lobster meat
- ½ cup chopped celery
- 2 hard-cooked eggs, chopped
- 2 tablespoons chili sauce
- 1 cup mayonnaise
- 1 tablespoon lemon juice
  - Salt and pepper to taste
  - Lettuce leaves
- 6 stuffed olives, sliced

Combine lobster, celery, and eggs. Add chili sauce to mayonnaise. Stir in lemon juice. Season, pour over salad, and toss lightly. Line a serving bowl with lettuce leaves. Place salad in bowl and garnish with olives.

Creamy Goodness

Cream cheese is one of the best friends a fish—to say nothing of a cook—ever had. Use it as a stretcher to combine with any kind of flaked fish to make a sandwich spread. Use it as a flavor-tamer to tone down fish, such as sardines and anchovies, or any of the smoked fish, whose smoked flavor may be too high for your taste. Use it to "butter" the bread for fish sandwiches. Or melt it in milk, season well, and use to sauce almost any fish.

Jambalaya Rice Salad

Makes 6 servings

2½ cups water
1 cup Uncle Ben's® Converted® Brand Rice
2 teaspoons salt
½ teaspoon red pepper sauce
¼ cup vegetable oil
1 garlic clove
½ pound cooked shrimp or 1 to 2 cans (4½ ounces each) shrimp, drained
1 cup diced cooked ham
4 green onions with tops, sliced
½ medium green pepper, cut in 1 × ¼-inch strips
2 medium tomatoes, coarsely chopped

Bring water to a boil in large saucepan. Stir in rice, 1 teaspoon salt, and red pepper sauce. Cover and simmer 20 minutes. Remove from heat. Let stand until all liquid is absorbed, about 5 minutes. Transfer rice to large bowl. Combine oil, remaining salt, and garlic, mixing well; stir into rice. Stir in shrimp, ham, onions, and green pepper. Chill at least 3 hours. Stir in tomatoes to serve.

Grapefruit Asparagus Salad with Emerald Sauce

Makes 6 servings

Bibb or butter lettuce
2 packages (10 ounces each) frozen asparagus spears, cooked and chilled
1 package (6 ounces) frozen crab meat, thawed and drained
2 to 3 Sunkist® grapefruit, peeled, sectioned, seeded, and chilled (1½ to 2 cups)
Emerald Sauce (recipe follows)

Arrange lettuce leaves on 6 individual salad plates. Divide asparagus spears among plates; add crab meat and grapefruit sections. Top with Emerald Sauce or pass separately. Serve very cold.

Emerald Sauce

1 cup mayonnaise (not salad dressing)
2 tablespoons finely chopped chives
2 tablespoons finely chopped watercress or parsley
2 tablespoons finely diced cucumber
2 tablespoons fresh-squeezed lemon juice
Several drops green food coloring

Combine all ingredients, adding enough green food coloring to tint sauce a bright green; chill thoroughly.

Spicy Shrimp Luncheon Mold

Makes 6 to 8 servings

2 cans (15 ounces each) Hunt's Tomato Sauce with Tomato Bits
1 package (6 ounces) raspberry-flavored gelatin
1 teaspoon instant minced onion
1 teaspoon celery seed
1 teaspoon salt
¾ teaspoon prepared horseradish
⅛ teaspoon cayenne
3 drops Tabasco pepper sauce
1½ cups shredded cabbage
½ cup sweet pickle relish
1 pound cooked small shrimp or 2 cans (4½ ounces) shrimp, drained
Assorted greens
Sour cream

In a medium saucepan, bring Hunt's Sauce to a boil. Add raspberry-flavored gelatin and stir until dissolved. Add onion, celery seed, salt, horseradish, cayenne, and Tabasco sauce. Cool. Add cabbage, relish, and shrimp. Pour into a 7-cup mold. Chill until firm. Unmold on bed of greens. Serve with sour cream.

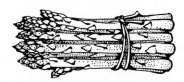

Other Ways, Other Forms

Many supermarkets, particularly those near large bodies of water, have fresh-fish departments. And all of them sell fish processed in various ways.

On grocery shelves, in cans: Canned tuna, salmon, sardines, and mackerel; fish cakes and fish balls; kippered herring; in jars, gefilte fish—airy quenelles of pike and other fish in jellied fish stock that you definitely don't have to be Jewish to enjoy; anchovies, anchovy paste; soups, stews, and chowders of several kinds.

In grocery frozen-food section: Frozen raw fish fillets of many kinds; fish sticks, ready to heat and eat; whole trout; breaded raw or cooked fillets; fish dinners.

In delicatessens or supermarket deli counters: Fillets of herring in wine, in sour cream with onions, other ways; many kinds of delicately cured and/or smoked fish.

Fisherman's Favorite Cioppino Salad

Makes 6 to 8 servings

  1 cup Wish-Bone® Italian Dressing
  ¼ cup dry white wine
  ¼ teaspoon dry basil or ¾ teaspoon chopped fresh
      basil
  2 cups (about ¾ pound) cooked crab meat
  ¾ pound large shrimp, cleaned and cooked
  2 quarts mixed salad greens
  3 cups coarsely chopped tomatoes
10 artichoke hearts, halved, or 1 can (15 ounces)
      artichoke hearts, drained and halved
  1 medium red onion, cut into rings
    Chopped parsley (optional)

In large shallow baking dish, blend Wish-Bone Italian Dressing, wine, and basil; add seafood. Cover and marinate in refrigerator, turning occasionally, at least 2 hours. Meanwhile, in salad bowl, arrange salad greens, tomatoes, artichoke hearts, and onion; chill. Just before serving, add seafood with marinade and toss. Garnish, if desired, with chopped parsley.

Crab-in-Tomato Aspic

Makes 6 servings

  2 envelopes unflavored gelatin
1½ cups water
  1 package (6 ounces) frozen crab meat, thawed
  2 cans (8 ounces each) Hunt's Tomato Sauce with
      Onions
  2 beef bouillon cubes
  1 bay leaf
  ¼ teaspoon celery salt
  2 tablespoons lemon juice
  1 cup chopped celery
    Assorted greens

Soften gelatin in ½ cup water; set aside. Drain crab, reserving liquid. In medium saucepan, combine crab liquid, remaining 1 cup water, Hunt's Sauce, bouillon cubes, bay leaf, and celery salt; bring to a boil. Remove bay leaf. Add softened gelatin and lemon juice; stir until gelatin is dissolved. Chill until mixture is slightly thickened. Fold in celery and crab meat. Turn into 6-cup mold; chill until firm. Unmold on bed of greens.

> **Q.** *The shrimp I cook are often tough, although I cook them only 6 or 7 minutes. What am I doing wrong?*
> **A.** Six minutes should be all right for shrimp in their shell. If you shell them first (which is easier and less messy), place the shelled shrimp in a saucepan and cover them with boiling water. Put the cover on the pan. Exactly 5 minutes later, drain the shrimp. They will be cooked to perfection.

Fisherman's Favorite Cioppino Salad. Photo courtesy of Thomas J. Lipton, Inc.

Niçoise Salad (page 61). Wisconsin Potato Growers Auxiliary

Keeping and Cooking Shellfish

All of these creatures are very perishable indeed, and speed must be the watchword. Cook live shellfish as soon as you get them home; refrigerate the meat and use it as soon as possible. It's best to buy shellfish the same day that you are going to eat them. For storage longer than the second day, freeze them. Shuck oysters, clams, and scallops before freezing; plan on using within 3 months. Cook lobster and crab; use within 1 month. Uncooked shrimp, shelled or not, can be freezer stored up to 3 months. Plan on using commercial, packaged frozen shellfish within 4 months.

Most shellfish are tender, and overcooking toughens them. Mollusks in shell are done when the shells open—if the shell does not, the mollusk was dead before cooking and must be discarded. Out of shell, they are cooked when the edges of the meat curl, a matter of a very few minutes.

Crustaceans are done when they turn pink or red—from 2 to 5 minutes for shrimp to 10 or even 15 or even 20 for lobster, depending on size.

Mollusks such as clams, oysters, and scallops, can be eaten raw; all shellfish may be boiled, steamed, broiled, baked, or fried.

Molded Crab Meat Salad

Makes 6 to 8 servings

⅓ cup vinegar
2 envelopes unflavored gelatin
½ cup boiling water
2 cups sour cream
2 teaspoons salt
2 cans (6 ounces each) crab meat, drained and boned
2 small cucumbers, pared and cut up
2 thin slices onion
  Salad greens
  Cucumber and radish slices (optional)

Put vinegar into blender container. Sprinkle on gelatin; let stand 1 minute. Add boiling water. Cover; blend at low speed until gelatin is dissolved. Add sour cream and salt. Cover; blend at medium speed until smooth. Add crab meat, cucumber, and onion. Cover; blend at medium speed just until vegetables are chopped. Pour into 1½-quart mold. Chill several hours, or until firm. Unmold onto salad greens. Garnish with cucumber and radish slices, if desired.

Fruited Crab Salad

Makes 4 servings

3½ cups cooked crab meat
½ cup chopped celery
1 cup halved pitted Bing cherries
⅔ cup mayonnaise
1 tablespoon lemon juice
¼ teaspoon ground ginger

Combine crab, celery, and cherries. Blend mayonnaise, lemon juice, and ginger. Add to crab mixture and toss lightly to mix well. Chill until serving time.

Variations

Shrimp, tuna, or chicken may be substituted for the crab meat, cut-up peeled oranges or whole green seedless grapes for the cherries.

Clam-Tomato Ring

Makes 6 servings

1 can (10¼ ounces) minced clams
2 envelopes Knox₋ Unflavored Gelatine
½ cup cold water
1 teaspoon Worcestershire sauce
2¾ cups tomato juice
1 cup thinly sliced celery
¼ cup sliced green onions
2 cups (16 ounces) lowfat cottage cheese
2 tablespoons snipped chives

Drain clams, reserving liquid. In a medium bowl, mix Knox Unflavored Gelatine and cold water. To reserved clam liquid add enough water to make ¾ cup; add Worcestershire sauce. Heat to boiling; pour over gelatine and stir until gelatine is completely dissolved. Stir in tomato juice. Chill, stirring occasionally, until mixture is the consistency of unbeaten egg whites. Stir in clams, celery, and green onions. Turn into a 5-cup ring mold. Chill until firm. Combine cottage cheese and chives. To serve, unmold gelatine ring, fill center with cottage cheese.

Variations

Omit cottage cheese and chives; fill center of the unmolded ring with chilled cooked green beans, broccoli, or cauliflower, lightly dressed with bottled low-calorie Italian dressing. For a flavor change, substitute canned vegetable juice cocktail for the tomato juice. Another time, instead of tomato juice, use 2¾ cups of hot instant chicken-flavor broth; cool before stirring into gelatine mixture.

Seaside Salad

Makes 16 servings

  6 envelopes Knox® Unflavored Gelatine
  6 cups tomato juice, divided
  ⅔ cup lemon juice
1½ teaspoons salt
  1 tablespoon Worcestershire sauce
  ⅓ cup prepared horseradish
  3 cups mayonnaise
  6 cups cooked seafood (shrimp, crab meat, or
      lobster)
  3 cups chopped celery
    Salad greens (optional)

In a medium saucepan, mix Knox Unflavored Gelatine with 3 cups tomato juice. Let stand 1 minute. Stir over medium heat until gelatine is completely dissolved, about 5 minutes. Remove from heat; stir in remaining 3 cups tomato juice, lemon juice, salt, Worcestershire sauce, horseradish, and mayonnaise. Beat until smooth. Chill, stirring occasionally, until mixture mounds slightly when dropped from a spoon. Fold in seafood and celery. Turn into two 8-cup molds; chill until firm. Unmold to serve. Garnish with salad greens, if desired.

Variation

Solid-pack white tuna or chunk-pack light tuna, both well drained and flaked, can be substituted for the shellfish in this recipe.

Tuna in a Can

Cans of tuna on the pantry shelf, even though considerably more expensive than they used to be, are a home cook's ace in the hole for emergencies. The fish may be served creamed or à la king (stashed-away frozen patty shells are fine with these), or in any one of a number of casserole and skillet dishes and salads that can be put together quickly and with little fuss.

There are several species of tuna. Only albacore may be labeled "white meat"—the others (such as bluefin and skipjack) are labeled "light meat." Three packs are available; the differences lie in the size of the pieces of fish and do not relate to quality.

- *solid pack*—contains 3 or 4 large pieces of fish; the most expensive of the canned tunas, it is ideal for cold plates, or in any recipe where appearance is important.
- *chunk pack*—convenient-size pieces for mixed salads and casseroles; moderately priced.
- *flake pack*—pieces smaller than the chunk style; good for sandwich spreads and for appetizers where the fish is blended with other ingredients; lowest in price.

Packed in water or oil, tuna can be had in 3¼-, 3½-, 6-, 6½-, 7-, 9¼-, 12½-, and 13-ounce cans.

Anchovy Delights

This sardine-anchovy butter is easy to make. If you have canned fish in your pantry, you're equipped to serve something delicious to droppers-in. In the food processor or blender, purée 1 can (4⅜ ounces) sardines with their oil, 4 flat anchovy fillets, and ½ cup softened unsalted butter. Add 2 minced scallions, 1½ teaspoons Dijon-style mustard, 1½ teaspoons lemon juice, ½ teaspoon Worcestershire sauce. Blend until well combined. Refrigerate at least 30 minutes. Serve with crackers or small bread shapes for canapés, or use to make finger sandwiches on pumpernickel bread.

These savory sandwiches make a delicious luncheon or supper dish, or may be served as an appetizer at dinner: Cut 3-inch rounds from firm white bread. Sandwich 2 rounds with a slice of mozzarella cheese, trimming to fit; press edges of the sandwich together. Dip in an egg-milk mixture, as for French toast; sauté until golden in a half-and-half mixture of butter and vegetable oil. Top each sandwich with 2 crisscrossed anchovy fillets and drizzle with the following anchovy-butter sauce. In 6 tablespoons unsalted butter, cook 1 minced clove garlic 3 minutes. Remove from heat; stir in 1 tablespoon minced anchovy fillet, 1 tablespoon minced capers, 2 tablespoons snipped fresh parsley, 2 teaspoons lemon juice, and ⅛ teaspoon coarse-grind pepper.

Creamy Tuna Salad

Makes 4 servings

  1 envelope Knox® Unflavored Gelatine
  ¼ cup cold water
  2 envelopes instant chicken flavor broth
1¼ cups boiling water
  1 teaspoon lemon juice
  ⅓ cup mayonnaise
  ¼ small onion
  1 stalk celery, cut into 1-inch pieces
  3 pimiento-stuffed olives (optional)
  1 can (6½ or 7 ounces) tuna, drained

In 5-cup blender container, sprinkle Knox Unflavored Gelatine over cold water; let stand 3 to 4 minutes. Add broth powder and boiling water; cover and process at low speed until gelatine and broth are completely dissolved. Add remaining ingredients; cover and process at high speed just until vegetables are chopped. Turn into a 3- or 4-cup mold. Chill until firm. Unmold to serve.

Pineapple-Seafood Salad

Makes 6 servings

  6 strips bacon
  1 pineapple
  **3 cups mixed seafood (crab meat, shrimp, lobster
    meat, fish fillets), cut in bite-size pieces**
¼ cup lemon juice
  Salt and pepper to taste
  Lemony Dressing (recipe follows)

Fry bacon until crisp; drain on paper towels. Cut pineapple in half lengthwise. Hollow out shells and cut fruit into cubes. Invert hollow pineapple shells on paper towels to drain.

Cut bacon into strips; toss with seafood, lemon juice, salt, and pepper. Arrange salad in pineapple shells. Serve on individual plates with Lemony Dressing.

Lemony Dressing

¼ cup mayonnaise
4 tablespoons lemon juice
1 tablespoon snipped dill weed
1 tablespoon snipped parsley
¼ teaspoon garlic powder
  Salt and pepper to taste

Mix all ingredients until well blended. Chill.

Fish-and-Flavor Love Affairs

Many flavors have an affinity for fish and shellfish. We're all familiar with the lemon-and-fish partnership, but did you know that other citrus fruits go well with fish, too? Try a shrimp and grapefruit salad with a mild vinaigrette dressing. Make Hollandaise sauce to serve with fish, using lime or orange juice instead of lemon for a change. Or make a simpler sauce by folding grated orange rind into sour cream. Finocchio (it may be labeled fennel or anise in the market) is excellent with fish—try baking a whole fish or fillets on a bed of chopped finocchio, basting the fish with butter as it cooks; when it is done, remove the fish, salt and pepper the finocchio, stir in a little more butter and about ½ cup heavy cream, and serve this sauce with the fish. Herbs/spices and fish are go-togethers, too. Marjoram and thyme and tarragon all go well. Curry is a bit strong for delicate fish, but try golden turmeric, which is one of the components of curry powder, to impart lovely flavor and color. Parsley and fish live well together, too—try a light bread stuffing with lots of parsley and a little grated lemon rind in a baked sea bass.

Herbed Rainbow Trout in White Wine

Makes 4 servings

  4 boned or dressed Clear Springs Trout (5 ounces
    each)
  3 tablespoons minced shallots or white part
    scallions
¼ cup butter
  1 teaspoon minced parsley
  1 teaspoon dried chervil, crumbled
  1 teaspoon dried thyme, crumbled
  1 teaspoon dried tarragon, crumbled
  1 teaspoon salt
⅛ teaspoon white pepper
1½ cups dry white wine
  2 cups heavy cream

If desired, remove heads from trout. Cook shallots
in butter over low heat until soft. Add remaining
ingredients except trout and cream. Remove from
heat. Arrange trout over herb mixture. Cover and
simmer about 5 minutes until fish flakes with fork.
Remove trout to heated platter. Reduce liquid to thin
film in skillet. Add cream; cook and stir until thick.
Serve at once over trout.

Sauce Sorcery

Tartar Sauce: Chop 5 stuffed green olives, 3
sprigs parsley, 1 medium dill pickle, 1 thin slice
onion. Fold into 1 cup mayonnaise, along with 1
tablespoon drained capers, 1 teaspoon lemon juice, a
few dashes hot pepper sauce, and salt and pepper to
taste.

Green Goddess Sauce: Mix 4 tablespoons snipped parsley, 2 tablespoons snipped dill, 1 tablespoon
chopped onion, 2 chopped scallions, into 1 cup sour
cream. Fold in ¼ cup mayonnaise. Add 2 tablespoons
lemon juice, salt and pepper to taste

Caper Sauce: Melt ¼ pound butter. Add ½ cup
snipped parsley, 2 tablespoons chopped capers, 1 teaspoon lemon juice, salt and pepper to taste. Serve at
once.

Chili-Cream Sauce: Combine ½ cup sour cream,
½ cup chili sauce, 1 teaspoon lemon juice, salt to
taste. Serve at once or refrigerate until needed.

Almond Sauce: Melt 2 tablespoons butter. Add ½
cup chopped blanched almonds; brown lightly. Add
2 tablespoons flour, stirring as you go. Blend well
and stir in 1 cup light cream. Season to taste. Stir in 1
lightly beaten egg yolk. Do not boil. Serve at once.

White Sauce: Melt 2 tablespoons butter in heavy saucepan over low heat. Add 2 tablespoons all-purpose flour,
½ teaspoon salt, ⅛ teaspoon pepper, ⅛ teaspoon paprika
and stir together until smooth. Gradually stir in 1 cup
milk or half and half and stir constantly until thick and
smooth.

Fish Fillets with Shrimp

Makes 6 to 8 servings

  2 Herb-Ox Vegetarian Style Bouillon Cubes, or 2
    teaspoons Herb-Ox Instant Vegetarian
    Bouillon
½ cup boiling water
  1 cucumber, thinly sliced
  1 teaspoon basil
  2 pounds fish fillets
  1 pound shrimp, cleaned and deveined
  1 tablespoon lemon juice, or to taste

Dissolve bouillon cubes in boiling water; add cucumber slices and basil; simmer 3 minutes. Arrange
fish fillets in shallow baking pan. Add broth; arrange
shrimp on top. Cook in hot oven (400°F) for 15
minutes, until fish flakes easily with fork and shrimp
is pink. Add lemon juice.

Catch of the Day

If you're lucky enough to be faced with a fresh-
caught fish, you'll need to clean and dress it before
you can enjoy it.

First, scale the
fish.

Place it on a
board and run a
sharp knife from
tail to head,
scraping off the
scales. Repeat on
other side.

Slit open the belly of the fish and remove the
entrails; rinse the cavity thoroughly. Make sure the
fish is clean, inside and out.

To fillet a whole
fish, cut along
backbone to tail.

With clean, even
strokes, cut the
flesh away from
the backbone,
being careful not
to cut into flesh.

Lift the fillet out
in one piece.

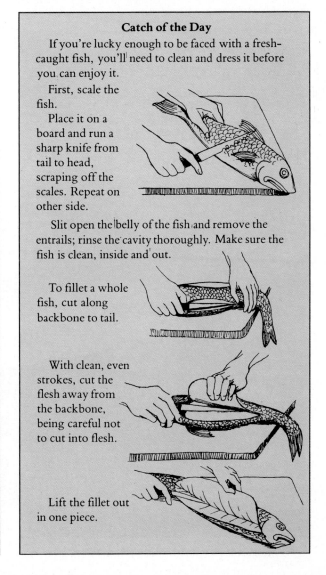

Poached Salmon with Easy Mock Hollandaise. Campbell Soup Company

Crisp-Fried Fish

Makes 6 servings

2 pounds fish fillets
1 cup buttermilk
  Salt and pepper
1 cup packaged biscuit mix
  Shortening

Soak fillets in buttermilk 30 minutes. Drain; sprinkle with salt and pepper. Dip fish in packaged biscuit mix. Fry in preheated shortening at 375°F. in Sunbeam Multi-Cooker Frypan until brown and tender. Drain on paper towels.

Fish-Fry Idea

Hush puppies, made of onion-flavored yellow cornmeal, are traditional fish-fry fare. But lots of people don't care for the onion-cornmeal combination, or would simply like to serve something different for a change. In such a case, try Rhode Island johnnycakes. Make them by combining in a large bowl, 1 cup white stone-ground cornmeal, 1 teaspoon salt, 1 teaspoon sugar. Stir in 1½ cups boiling water; mix well. This will make a thick batter and, consequently, thick cakes—if you prefer them thinner, add more water. Let stand 30 minutes. Grease a large frying pan or griddle with bacon fat; heat to medium low. Drop batter by tablespoons on griddle; cook until golden brown, about 6 minutes; turn and cook the other side until golden, about 5 minutes. Serve hot with butter, bacon, and fried panfish, such as sweet, fresh-caught little sunfish.

Beer Batter Fish

Makes 4 servings

1 pound fish fillets, fresh or frozen, thawed
1½ cups Homemade Mix (recipe follows)
⅓ cup ReaLemon® Lemon Juice from Concentrate
⅔ cup beer
1 cup vegetable oil
  ReaLemon® Lemon Juice from Concentrate

Place fish on paper towels; pat dry. Coat fish with ½ cup Homemade Mix. In large bowl, combine remaining Homemade Mix, ReaLemon, and beer. (This mixture will foam.) Stir until consistency of pancake batter. In large skillet, heat oil over medium heat. Dip fish into batter; fry about 3 minutes on each side, or until golden brown. Drain on paper towels. Serve immediately; sprinkle with additional ReaLemon. Refrigerate leftovers.

Homemade Mix

1½ cups all-purpose flour
2¼ teaspoons baking powder
¾ teaspoon baking soda
1 teaspoon salt

Combine all ingredients and mix well.

Wrap It Up

Large whole fish or large pieces of fish are often difficult to handle without having them break apart—which doesn't spoil the flavor, but detracts considerably from the appearance. To avoid such mishaps, wrap the fish in cheesecloth before cooking, tying the cloth at the top or at either end and use these knots as handles.

Stuffed Fish Mornay (page 81). Campbell Soup Company

Corn Meal Batter-Coated Fish

Makes 6 servings

　2　pounds fish fillets, cut into serving-size pieces
　⅓　cup Martha White All-Purpose Flour
　　　Oil for deep-fat frying
　½　cup Martha White Self-Rising Flour
　½　cup Martha White Self-Rising Corn Meal
　¼　teaspoon salt
　1　egg, lightly beaten
　⅔　cup milk
　1　tablespoon vegetable oil

Rinse fish in cold water; pat dry with paper towels. Place all-purpose flour in shallow dish. Coat fish evenly with flour; set aside. Heat oil for deep-fat frying to 350°F. Combine self-rising flour, corn meal, and salt in small bowl. Combine egg, milk, and vegetable oil in bowl. Gradually add flour mixture, beating until smooth. Dip floured fish into batter to coat. Deep-fry fish, a few pieces at a time, 4 to 6 minutes, or until golden brown, turning to brown evenly. Drain on paper towels. To keep fish warm until all pieces are cooked, place in shallow pan in 300°F. oven.

Note: If you prefer a lighter coating, simply place about ¾ cup Martha White Self-Rising Corn Meal in a shallow dish. Coat fish evenly. Deep-fry as directed above.

Smoky Cheese Fillets

Makes 4 servings

　1　pound fresh fish fillets (cod, halibut, trout, turbot, or flounder)
　1½　tablespoons minced onion
　¼　teaspoon salt
　⅛　teaspoon pepper
　1　tomato, chopped
　¼　cup butter
　1　teaspoon Wright's Natural Hickory Liquid Smoke
　½　cup grated Swiss cheese

Place fillets in an oiled baking dish. Combine onion, salt, pepper, and tomato pieces. Sprinkle mixture over fillets. Melt butter and add Wright's Natural Hickory Liquid Smoke. Pour butter mixture over fillets. Broil 12 to 15 minutes. Sprinkle cheese over fillets and broil 2 minutes longer.

Mediterranean Fish Rolls

Makes 6 servings

　2　pounds fillets of flounder, sole, or perch
　　　Juice of ½ lemon
　　　Salt and pepper
　¼　cup chopped onion
　1　clove garlic, minced
　2　tablespoons pure vegetable oil
　1　can (6 ounces) Hunt's Tomato Paste
　1½　cups water
　¼　teaspoon oregano
　¼　cup dry white wine (optional)
　　　Lemon wedges
　　　Parsley

Cut fillets in half lengthwise. Sprinkle with lemon juice, salt, and pepper. Roll up and fasten with toothpicks. Place in greased 10 × 6 × 2-inch baking dish. In a skillet, cook onion and garlic in oil until soft. Add Hunt's Tomato Paste, water, ½ teaspoon salt, ¼ teaspoon pepper, and oregano; mix well. Simmer uncovered 10 minutes. Add wine and pour over fish. Bake at 375°F., basting occasionally, for 35 minutes, or until fish flakes easily. Garnish with lemon wedges and parsley.

Baked Fish Fillets with Wild Rice

Makes 6 servings

　2⅓　cups water
　1　package (6 ounces) Uncle Ben's® Original Long Grain & Wild Rice
　2　tablespoons butter or margarine
　1½　pounds fresh or thawed frozen fish fillets
　　　Salt and pepper
　¼　cup butter or margarine, melted
　1　package (10 ounces) frozen chopped broccoli or spinach, thawed
　1　envelope Hollandaise or cheese sauce mix
　　　Paprika

Combine water, contents of rice and seasoning packets, and 2 tablespoons butter in large saucepan. Bring to a boil. Reduce heat, cover, and simmer 20 minutes. While rice is cooking, season fish with salt and pepper. Arrange in single layer in lightly buttered baking dish. Pour melted butter evenly over fish. Bake in preheated 350°F oven for 20 minutes, or until fish flakes easily with fork. Stir broccoli into rice. Cover and continue to simmer until all water is absorbed, about 5 minutes. Prepare sauce mix according to package directions. Transfer fish to serving platter. Spoon sauce over top; sprinkle with paprika. Serve with rice.

Marinated Fish

Makes 6 servings

¼ cup chopped onion
¼ cup catsup
1 tablespoon vinegar
1 teaspoon Worcestershire sauce
3 tablespoons lemon juice
⅓ cup tomato juice
½ teaspoon celery salt
⅛ teaspoon pepper
2 pounds fish fillets
Fine dry bread crumbs

Combine onion, catsup, vinegar, Worcestershire sauce, lemon juice, tomato juice, and seasonings. Cook mixture about 5 minutes. Cool, pour over fish, and marinate several hours, covered, in refrigerator. Remove fish from mixture, drain, and dip into bread crumbs. Fry in preheated shortening at 375°F. in Sunbeam Multi-Cooker Frypan until brown and tender, about 5 minutes. Drain on paper towels.

Lenguado Spanish Pavillion

Makes 4 servings

4 fillets of sole, cut into 1-inch strips
10 red Spanish shrimp (or regular large or extra-large shrimp)
1 shallot, minced, or 1 tablespoon minced green onion
1½ cups sherry
2 pimientos, diced
¼ pound fresh mushrooms, sliced
6 large pitted green olives, sliced
2 tablespoons butter
1 can (10½ ounces) Campbell's Condensed Cream of Chicken Soup
1 egg yolk
¼ cup heavy cream
1 teaspoon lemon juice

Combine sole, shelled and deveined shrimp (reserve 2 for sauce; mince these 2 shrimp), shallot, and sherry. Cook gently until sole and shrimp are just cooked. With a slotted spoon remove sole and shrimp and arrange in a 9-inch square shallow baking pan. Add minced shrimp to sherry mixture and simmer until liquid is reduced to ½ cup. Reserve. Sauté pimientos, mushrooms, and olives in butter until mushrooms are wilted. Spoon vegetables over sole and shrimp. Combine soup, egg yolk, reserved sherry, and cream. Heat slowly, stirring constantly, until hot, but do not boil. Remove from heat and stir in lemon juice. Spoon sauce evenly over sole and shrimp. Place under broiler and broil until top is lightly browned.

Fish Coquille

Makes 6 servings

1 can (4 ounces) sliced mushrooms
Water
¼ cup dry white wine
2 tablespoons minced onion
1 tablespoon Lea & Perrins Worcestershire Sauce
⅛ teaspoon salt
1½ pounds fresh or frozen fish fillets, cut into chunks
1 package (1 ounce) white sauce mix
1¼ cups milk
2 tablespoons grated Parmesan cheese
2 tablespoons chopped parsley
2 tablespoons diced pimiento
½ cup soft bread crumbs
1 tablespoon butter or margarine, melted

Drain mushrooms, reserving liquid; set mushrooms aside. Add sufficient water to mushroom liquid to measure 1 cup. In a medium saucepan, combine mushroom liquid, wine, onion, Lea & Perrins, and salt. Bring to boiling point. Add fish. Simmer uncovered until fish flakes, about 15 minutes. With a slotted spoon, remove fish from the saucepan; set aside. Into liquid in the saucepan, stir white sauce mix, milk, and cheese. Cook and stir until thickened. Return fish to sauce. Stir in reserved mushrooms along with the parsley and pimiento. Simmer uncovered for 5 minutes, stirring occasionally. Spoon into individual baking shells or casseroles. Combine bread crumbs with butter; sprinkle over fish mixture. Bake in a preheated hot oven (400°F.) until bubbly, about 10 minutes.

Poached-Fish Gravy

1½ cups poaching liquid
2 tablespoons butter
1½ teaspoons cornstarch
3 tablespoons water
2 tablespoons lemon juice
¾ teaspoon dried dill weed or 2 tablespoons fresh dill weed

Pour poaching liquid into small pan. Add butter; melt over low heat. Combine cornstarch and water; add slowly to liquid, stirring constantly, until mixture bubbles and thickens. Stir in lemon juice and dill weed. Pour over fish or serve separately.

Striped Bass with Mustard Sauce (page 84)

Lemon-Baked Fish with Stuffing

Makes 4 servings

  3 tablespoons butter or margarine
½ cup chopped celery
½ cup chopped onion
  3 cups fresh bread crumbs
  2 tablespoons ReaLemon® Lemon Juice from
    Concentrate
  1 egg, lightly beaten
  1 tablespoon chopped parsley
¼ teaspoon salt
¼ teaspoon Tabasco pepper sauce
  1 pound fish fillets, fresh or frozen, thawed
    Lemon Basting Sauce (recipe follows)
    Chopped parsley and paprika

Preheat oven to 350°F. In medium skillet, melt butter; cook celery and onion until tender. In large bowl, combine bread crumbs, cooked vegetables, ReaLemon, egg, parsley, salt, and Tabasco; mix well. Spoon stuffing into shallow 1½-quart baking dish. Layer fillets on stuffing. Pour half of the Lemon Basting Sauce over fillets; bake 25 minutes, or until fish flakes with fork. During last 10 minutes of baking, pour remaining sauce over fish. Remove to serving platter, reserving sauce. Garnish with parsley and paprika; serve with sauce.

Lemon Basting Sauce

Makes about ¼ cup

  3 tablespoons butter or margarine, melted
  2 tablespoons ReaLemon® Lemon Juice from
    Concentrate
¼ teaspoon Tabasco pepper sauce
⅛ teaspoon salt

Combine all ingredients; mix well.

Whole Stuffed Fish

Rinse one 2- to 3-pound fresh or frozen white-fleshed fish, drawn and boned, in cold water and pat dry. Rub cavity with salt and pepper. Prepare stuffing as for Lemon-Baked Fish with Stuffing; stuff fish; brush with Lemon Basting Sauce. Bake uncovered 50 to 60 minutes, or until fish flakes with fork. Baste occasionally during baking.

Fish Florentine with Almonds

Makes 4 servings

  1 pound whitefish fillets, fresh or frozen, thawed
  1 tablespoon lemon juice
½ teaspoon salt
  3 tablespoons butter or margarine
  2 tablespoons chopped onion
  2 tablespoons all-purpose flour
  1 cup milk
½ teaspoon dried basil
⅔ cup cooked chopped spinach, drained
½ cup chopped natural almonds, toasted

Brush fish fillets with lemon juice and ¼ teaspoon of the salt. Roll up and place, spaced apart, in buttered shallow baking dish; set aside. In 2-quart saucepan, melt butter over medium heat. Add onion. Sauté 5 minutes. Stir in flour; cook 1 minute. Gradually stir in milk. Bring to boil, stirring. Mix in remaining ¼ teaspoon of the salt, the basil, and spinach. Bring to boil, stirring. Mix in all but 2 tablespoons of the almonds. Spoon spinach mixture over fish. Sprinkle with remaining almonds. Bake in 350°F oven 20 to 25 minutes until fish flakes easily and sauce is bubbly.

Fish in Orange Juice

Makes 8 servings

  8 whitefish fillets
    Salt and pepper to taste
    Juice of 2 limes
  2 tablespoons olive oil
1½ tablespoons minced scallions
  2 tomatoes, peeled and chopped
1½ tablespoons chopped green pepper
  2 tablespoons olive oil
½ cup orange juice
  4 tablespoons drained capers
  2 oranges, sliced thinly, including peel
½ cup toasted blanched chopped almonds

Season fish with salt and pepper and marinate it in the lime juice for about 20 minutes. Oil baking pan with 2 tablespoons olive oil and place fish in pan. Top the fish with minced scallion, tomatoes, and green pepper, and drizzle 2 tablespoons olive oil over this. Place in a preheated 350°F oven, and when the fish begins to brown (about 15 minutes after it is placed in the oven), add the orange juice. Cook another 15 or 20 minutes, or until fish flakes easily when pierced with a fork. Garnish with capers, orange slices, and almonds.

Hungarian Whitefish with Mushrooms and Sour Cream

Makes 4 servings

    4 boneless whitefish fillets
    ¼ cup butter
      Paprika
    1 cup sliced mushrooms
    1 can (10½ ounces) Campbell's Condensed Cream
      of Mushroom Soup
    1 cup sour cream
      Paprika
      Sour cream (optional)

Butter a shallow baking dish large enough to hold fish fillets in a single layer. Place fillets in dish and dot with butter. Sprinkle fish with paprika. Sprinkle mushrooms over fish fillets. Bake in a preheated 350°F. oven for 15 minutes. Combine soup and sour cream. Heat just until mixture bubbles. Spoon sauce over fish and bake an additional 15 minutes, or until fish flakes. Sprinkle top with paprika. Top with additional spoonful of sour cream, if desired.

Shrimpy Flounder Turbans

Makes 6 servings

    1 medium-size onion, chopped
    1 cup sliced mushrooms
    3 tablespoons butter or margarine
    ½ teaspoon fines herbes
    ½ teaspoon salt
    ¼ teaspoon freshly ground pepper
    1 cup fresh bread cubes
    ¼ pound shrimp, cooked, cleaned, and chopped
    2 tablespoons plus ½ cup dry white wine
    6 flounder fillets (about 2 pounds)
      Hollandaise Sauce

Butter 10 × 6-inch baking dish. Preheat oven to 350°F. Sauté onion and mushrooms in butter until onion is transparent. Stir in seasonings, bread cubes, shrimp, and 2 tablespoons wine. Spoon a little stuffing onto darker side of each fillet. Roll up, starting at narrow end. Place in prepared baking dish. Pour ½ cup wine around turbans and bake about 25 minutes, or until fish flakes easily. Serve with Hollandaise Sauce.

This recipe was provided by the makers of Saran Wrap™ brand plastic film.

Stuffed Fish Mornay

Makes 4 servings

    1 can (10¾ ounces) Campbell's Condensed
      Cheddar Cheese Soup
    ½ cup flaked crab meat
    ½ cup chopped shrimp
    2 tablespoons chopped mushrooms
    2 tablespoons chopped green onions
    ¼ teaspoon salt
    ¼ teaspoon tarragon, crushed
    ½ small clove garlic, minced
    8 fillets of flounder, about 2 pounds
    8 oysters, cut in half
    2 tablespoons butter, melted
    ¼ cup water
    2 tablespoons diced tomato
      Generous dash crushed tarragon

In bowl, combine ¼ cup soup with crab, shrimp, mushrooms, onions, salt, tarragon, and garlic. Mix well. Arrange 4 fillets in shallow baking dish; spread evenly with filling. Top with oysters. Cover with remaining fillets. Brush with melted butter. Bake in preheated 375°F. oven for 30 minutes. For sauce, combine remaining soup with water, tomato, and tarragon. Heat, stirring occasionally. Serve with fish.

Variation

Fillets of sole, red snapper, ocean perch, or pompano may be substituted for the flounder.

One tablespoon finely chopped green onion may be substituted for the tomato in the sauce.

Barbecue-Baked Fish

Makes 3 servings

    1 pound fish fillets, thawed if frozen
      Salt and pepper to taste
    1 tablespoon butter or margarine
    4 thin slices lemon
    4 thin onion rings
    2 tablespoons chopped parsley
    1 can (10¾ ounces) Campbell's Condensed
      Tomato Soup

Place fish in 10 × 6 × 2-inch baking dish; sprinkle with salt and pepper. Dot with butter; top with lemon, onion, and parsley. Bake at 350°F. for 15 minutes. Pour soup over, stirring in liquid around fish. Bake 10 minutes more, or until done. Stir sauce before serving.

Baked Flounder with Clam Sauce

Makes 4 servings

1½ **pounds Gorton's® Fillet of Flounder or Sole**
 1 **onion, about 1 inch in diameter, finely diced**
 1 **cup clams, minced (reserve liquid)**
⅔ **cup dry white wine**
 2 **tablespoons butter**
1½ **tablespoons all-purpose flour**
½ **cup heavy cream**
    Salt
    White pepper

Arrange fillets in a shallow baking dish. Sprinkle with onion. To clam liquid, add enough wine to make 1 cup. Pour over fillets. Bake in a preheated 325°F. oven until just done, about 15 minutes. Carefully transfer fillets to a heatproof serving dish and keep warm. Melt butter in a saucepan and stir in flour. Gradually stir in 1 cup hot cooking liquid, the heavy cream, and the clams. Season to taste with salt and white pepper. Heat until hot but not boiling and pour over cooked fillets. Broil, about 4 inches from heat, for about 4 minutes, until the sauce bubbles and begins to glaze. Serve immediately.

Flounder Fillets Neapolitan

Makes 4 servings

 4 **flounder fillets**
    All-purpose flour
 1 **egg, lightly beaten**
    Polly-O Bread Crumbs
    Olive oil
 1 **can (8 ounces) tomato sauce**
 6 **ounces Polly-O Mozzarella, grated**
⅛ **teaspoon oregano**
    Polly-O Butter

Dredge fillets in flour, dip in egg, and coat with bread crumbs. Sauté in olive oil until golden brown on both sides. Arrange in buttered baking dish, cover with tomato sauce, sprinkle with oregano, and top with mozzarella cheese. Place under broiler until cheese melts.

Flounder Nouvelle

Makes 4 servings

    3 tablespoons Mazola Corn Oil, divided
    1 cup chopped onions
    1 clove garlic, minced or pressed
    ¼ cup dry white wine
    ½ teaspoon salt
    ¾ pound flounder fillets (4 small)
    3 medium carrots, cut in matchstick strips
    3 ribs celery, cut in matchstick strips

In medium skillet, heat 1 tablespoon corn oil over medium heat. Add onion and garlic. Stirring frequently, cook 5 minutes. Place onion mixture, wine, and salt in blender container; cover. Blend on high speed 15 seconds, or until smooth. Beginning with tail end, roll each flounder fillet lengthwise. Place in 10 × 6 × 2-inch (1½-quart) shallow baking dish. Spoon onion mixture over fish. Bake uncovered in 375°F oven 20 minutes. Meanwhile, heat remaining 2 tablespoons corn oil in skillet over medium heat. Add carrots and celery. Stirring frequently, cook 5 minutes. Spoon over fish. Bake 5 to 7 minutes longer, or until fish flakes easily.

Low-Calorie Flounder Nouvelle

Follow recipe for Flounder Nouvelle. Omit 2 tablespoons of the corn oil. In 3-quart saucepan, cook the matchstick strips of carrots and celery in boiling water about 2 minutes, or until tender-crisp. Spoon over fish. Bake 5 to 7 minutes longer, or until fish flakes easily.

Tomato Stuffed with Flounder Fillet

Makes 4 servings

    4 firm ripe tomatoes
      Salt and pepper
    1 pound flounder fillet, each fillet cut lengthwise
      into 2 long strips
    1 can (10½ ounces) Campbell's Condensed Cream
      of Asparagus Soup
    1 cup sour cream
      Pitted black olives

Core tomatoes and cut into halves, top to bottom. Scoop out about half the pulp. Sprinkle tomatoes with salt and pepper. Roll up strips of fish and place a roll, spiral side up, in each tomato. Sprinkle with salt and pepper. Combine soup and sour cream. Spoon over filled tomatoes. Place tomatoes into a shallow baking dish. Bake for 35 minutes in a preheated 350°F oven until tomatoes are tender and fish flakes easily. Serve garnished with pitted black olives.

Portuguese Fish

Makes 4 servings

    2 tablespoons olive oil
    ½ cup chopped onion
    1 clove garlic, minced
    1 can (8¼ ounces) tomatoes, broken up
    3 tablespoons tomato paste
    2 teaspoons Lea & Perrins Worcestershire Sauce
 1½ teaspoons salt
    1 teaspoon sugar
 1½ cups cooked rice
    1 package (1 pound) frozen fillet of flounder,
      thawed

In a medium saucepan, heat oil. Add onion and garlic; sauté for 2 minutes. Stir in tomatoes, tomato paste, Lea & Perrins, salt, and sugar. Bring to boiling point. Reduce heat and simmer uncovered for 5 minutes. Stir in rice; heat until hot. Arrange half the rice mixture in a buttered 10 × 6 × 1½-inch baking pan. Top with fish fillets, then remaining rice. Bake uncovered in a preheated moderate oven (350°F) until fish flakes easily when tested with a fork, about 20 minutes.

> **Q.** *What is a court bouillon and how do I make it?*
> **A.** A *court bouillon* is a medium for poaching fish; it adds a delicate flavor to any fish or shellfish poached in it. Start with water or fish broth; add fish bones and heads (especially important if you're using water rather than broth); peppercorns, parsley, dill, lemon, white wine, and other herbs and spices. Be careful not to add anything too strong, as it will overpower the flavor of the fish.

Stuffed Flounder Supreme

Makes 4 servings

    ½ cup Wish-Bone® Deluxe French Dressing
    1 pound flounder fillets
    ¾ cup seasoned croutons, crushed
    ¼ cup finely chopped celery

Preheat oven to 350°F. Brush 2 tablespoons Wish-Bone Deluxe French Dressing on top side of fillets. In small bowl, combine ¼ cup Wish-Bone Deluxe French Dressing, croutons, and celery; equally divide mixture on fillets and roll up. Brush fillets with remaining Wish-Bone Deluxe French Dressing and bake 35 minutes, or until fish flakes.

Mache Qorma

Makes 4 servings

    4 large fillets of flounder, 1 to 1½ pounds
       Salt and freshly ground pepper
    ¼ cup vegetable oil
    2 medium-size onions, sliced
    1 clove garlic, minced
    ½ cup tomato juice
    ⅓ cup Sun-Maid® Seedless Raisins
    2 teaspoons curry powder
    ½ teaspoon ground cumin
    ⅛ to ¼ teaspoon cayenne
    1 cup plain yogurt, at room temperature
    ¼ cup toasted sliced almonds
       Rice pilaf (optional)

Pat the fish dry with paper towels and lightly sprinkle with salt and pepper. Heat the oil in a large skillet and brown the fish on both sides; remove the fish and keep warm. Sauté the onions and garlic in the oil until the onions are soft but not browned. Add the tomato juice, raisins, and seasonings and bring to a boil. Reduce heat and simmer for 2 to 3 minutes. Stir in the yogurt and return the fish to the skillet, basting with the sauce. Simmer for 2 to 3 minutes, or until the fish is heated through. Sprinkle with the almonds and serve immediately. Serve with rice pilaf, if desired.

Almond Tomato Fillets

Makes 4 servings

    4 tablespoons butter or margarine, divided
    ½ clove garlic, minced
    4 cups chopped peeled tomatoes
    1 teaspoon salt, divided
    ½ teaspoon tarragon
    ¼ teaspoon pepper, divided
    ¼ cup all-purpose flour
    1 pound sole or flounder fillets
    ¼ cup blanched almonds, slivered and toasted

In a saucepan, heat 1 tablespoon butter. Add garlic and cook over medium heat about 30 seconds. Add tomatoes, ½ teaspoon salt, tarragon, and ⅛ teaspoon pepper. Cover and simmer over low heat while preparing fish. Combine flour, remaining salt, and pepper. Coat fillets with flour mixture. Melt 4 tablespoons butter in Sunbeam Multi-Cooker Frypan at 380°F. Add fillets and fry until golden brown on one side, 2 to 3 minutes; turn and brown other side until fish flakes easily when tested with a fork. Arrange tomato mixture on a shallow heated serving platter. Place fillets on top. Sprinkle with almonds and serve immediately.

Striped Bass with Mustard Sauce

Makes 6 servings

    1 sea bass (6 to 7 pounds), filleted
       Salt and pepper
    ½ cup butter, melted
    1 tablespoon minced onion
    2 tablespoons lemon juice
    2 cups white wine
    1 cup fish broth or water
    1 jar (12 ounces) oysters (reserve liquid)
    1 can (10½ ounces) condensed cream of celery soup
    1 tablespoon Dijon-style mustard (or to taste)
       Parsley

Cut each of the bass fillets into three pieces and sprinkle with salt and pepper. Place fish pieces in a shallow pan in a single layer. Add butter, onion, lemon juice, wine, and fish broth, and liquid drained from oysters. Bake in a preheated 400°F. oven 20 minutes, or until fish flakes. Remove fish carefully and place on a platter and keep warm. Transfer liquid in baking dish to a saucepan and boil until liquid is reduced to one-third of its original volume. Add celery soup and mustard and continue simmering until sauce is thick. Add oysters and reheat slightly. Spoon sauce over fish. Garnish with parsley.

Baked Sole Roll-ups

Makes 4 servings

    1 can (6½ ounces) Bumble Bee Chunk Light Tuna
       in Water
    1 large carrot, thinly sliced
    1 medium zucchini, thinly sliced
    4 sole fillets
       Salt
       Pepper
    ⅓ cup green apple, cored and diced
    ⅓ cup minced green onions
    1 egg
    2 tablespoons fresh lemon juice
    ¼ teaspoon thyme, crumbled
    ¼ teaspoon celery seed
    ¼ teaspoon salt
       Paprika

Drain tuna. Steam carrots for 5 minutes, then add zucchini and steam additional 5 minutes. Arrange vegetables in 1-quart casserole dish. Rinse fillets with water; pat dry. Sprinkle with salt and pepper. In small mixing bowl, combine tuna, apple, green onions, egg, 1 tablespoon lemon juice, and seasonings. Spread mixture evenly on fillets, then roll up. Place fillets seam side down on vegetable slices. Drizzle remaining lemon juice over fillets. Sprinkle with paprika. Cover and bake in 350°F oven for 25 minutes, or until fish flakes with a fork.

The Sociable Side

Fish and shellfish seem to lend themselves to partying. Here are two seafood-theme parties that you might enjoy trying:

The Backyard Clambake

Everything you need is cooked right on the grill. If your backyard happens to be the beach, so much the better.

Hot-Coaled Seafood Supper

Makes 1 serving

> 12 steamer clams
> 1 1-pound lobster
> ½ small broiler-fryer chicken
> 1 ear corn
> 1 potato, peeled and cut lengthwise in eighths
> 1 medium-size onion, quartered
> Salt and pepper to taste
> Melted butter

Besides the above ingredients, you will also need a 1-yard square of cheesecloth and heavy-duty aluminum foil for each serving. If lobster comes with seaweed or if you live where you can get it, have a handful of seaweed for each serving. Scrub the clams; rinse and split the lobster; remove as many sharp bones from chicken as will come out easily. Shuck the corn. Tear off a large square of heavy-duty aluminum foil, slightly smaller than the cheesecloth. Place cheesecloth on top of foil. Add seaweed if you have it. Put chicken in place in center of square; place lobster on top, surround with clams. Tuck in the corn, potato, and onion to make a tight package. Season with salt and pepper. If you have not used seaweed, add 4 tablespoons water to each package.

Tie the cheesecloth up over the food, then seal the foil to make an airtight package. Place package on grill over a medium-hot fire. Open package after 35 minutes to test chicken for doneness. Reclose and continue cooking—up to 1 hour, if necessary, depending upon the size of the chicken. Serve with individual dishes of melted butter.

The Fish Fry

At one time, the fish fry was an agreeable get-together, especially in the South. Catfish were the fish of choice for such an occasion, and crisp hush puppies (cornmeal cakes, sometimes with onion in the batter) were fried along with the fish.

Fried Fish

Makes 6 servings

> 2 pounds fish fillets or steaks
> ⅔ cup all-purpose flour
> 2 teaspoons salt
> ¼ teaspoon pepper
> 1 egg
> 1 cup fine dry bread crumbs
> Shortening or oil

Cut fish into serving pieces. Combine flour, salt, and pepper. Beat together egg and ¼ cup water. Dip fish in seasoned flour, then in egg mixture, then in bread crumbs. Place fish on a piece of waxed paper and let stand a few minutes. Fill Sunbeam Multi-Cooker Frypan at least half full with shortening or oil. Heat to 375°F. Fry fish, a few pieces at a time, 3 to 6 minutes, or until golden brown. Drain. Put on paper towels to drain thoroughly. Serve at once with desired sauce.

Fillet of Sole Werner

Makes 4 servings

> ⅓ cup butter or margarine
> 1 box (8 ounces) frozen artichoke hearts
> ½ pound mushrooms, sliced
> 1½ pounds fillet of sole, cut into strips
> 4 tomatoes peeled, seeded and minced
> ¾ cup white wine
> 1 cup clam juice
> 1 tablespoon butter or margarine
> 1 tablespoon all-purpose flour
> ¾ cup Hollandaise Sauce
> ⅓ cup heavy cream, whipped
> 1 tablespoon lemon juice
> 4 patty shells
> 4 truffles or black olives (optional)

Melt butter in Sunbeam Multi-Cooker Frypan with dial set at 325°F. Sauté artichokes in butter 5 minutes. Add mushrooms; sauté 2 minutes. Add fish, tomatoes, wine, and clam juice. Bring to a boil; turn dial to Simmer. Cook 8 to 10 minutes, or until fish flakes. Remove fish and vegetables from Frypan. Combine butter and flour; stir into liquid in Frypan. Cook until thickened, 2 or 3 minutes. Turn off heat and let mixture cool about 4 minutes. Fold Hollandaise Sauce and whipped cream into mixture. Add lemon juice. Taste and correct seasoning. Turn Frypan dial to Simmer. Return fish and vegetables to sauce. Cook just until heated through—but do not boil. Spoon into patty shells; garnish with truffles.

Handsome Sole au Gratin

Makes 6 servings

1½ pounds fillet of sole or whitefish
 2 tablespoons lemon juice
½ cup chopped onion
 2 tablespoons butter
 1 can (15 ounces) Hunt's Tomato Sauce with
   Tomato Bits
¼ cup chopped parsley
½ teaspoon *each* salt, pepper, and sugar
 2 packages (10 ounces each) frozen cut green
   beans, cooked and drained
 1 egg yolk
 2 cups prepared mashed potatoes
 2 tablespoons grated Parmesan cheese

Cut fillets into 6 serving-size pieces; sprinkle with lemon juice. Roll up; secure with toothpicks and stand on end in center of 7½x12x1½-inch baking dish. Sauté onion in butter in small saucepan. Add Hunt's Sauce, parsley, salt, pepper, and sugar; simmer 3 to 5 minutes. Pour over fillets. Spoon green beans around fillets. Blend egg yolk with potatoes; spoon in border around edge of dish. Bake at 375°F for 20 minutes, or until fish flakes with fork. Sprinkle with Parmesan cheese.

Sole in Mousseline Sauce

Makes 6 servings

 6 fillets of sole
   Salt, pepper
½ cup dry white wine
 3 egg yolks
   Dash cayenne
½ cup butter
¼ cup heavy cream

Wipe fillets with paper towels. Sprinkle with salt and pepper and roll up each fillet. Secure with toothpicks. Heat wine in Sunbeam Multi-Cooker Frypan with a dash of salt at 280°F. Add sole, cover, and simmer about 5 minutes, or until opaque. Remove sole and place in a baking dish. Boil down wine to 2 tablespoonfuls. Place in blender. Add egg yolks, a pinch of salt, and cayenne. Cover and process at Cream for a few seconds. Heat butter until it is foaming hot. Remove feeder cap and pour butter in a steady stream until mixture is thickened. Turn sauce out of blender into a bowl and cool slightly. Whip cream in blender or with a Sunbeam Mixmaster Hand Mixer at highest setting until stiff. Fold cream into sauce. Spoon over poached fillets. Bake 10 minutes in a preheated 400°F oven, or until fish flakes easily when tested with a fork.

Fish Bonne Femme

Makes 6 servings

1½ pounds fillet of sole or flounder
¼ pound fresh mushrooms, sliced (1 cup)
 2 tablespoons finely chopped onion
 2 tablespoons chopped parsley
½ cup Chablis or other dry white wine
 1 can (10¾ ounces) Campbell's Condensed Cream
   of Celery Soup
¼ cup heavy cream, whipped

In skillet, place sole on bottom; top with mushrooms, onion, and parsley. Add wine. Cover; cook over low heat 10 minutes. Carefully transfer fish and garnish to ovenproof platter. Stir soup into ¼ cup of the remaining liquid; heat. Fold in whipped cream. Pour over fish. Place under broiler until lightly browned.

Fillet of Sole Véronique

Omit mushrooms, onion, and parsley from Fish Bonne Femme recipe. Substitute 1 cup seedless white grapes.

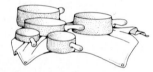

Sole in Almond Shrimp Sauce

Makes 4 servings

1½ pounds sole fillets
 1 cup dry white wine
 3 ounces baby shrimp
 4 tablespoons butter
 2 tablespoons all-purpose flour
½ cup half and half
¼ teaspoon salt
   Dash pepper
½ cup Blue Diamond® Blanched Slivered
   Almonds, toasted

Poach fillets in wine in 350°F oven until fish flakes easily with fork but is still moist, 15 to 20 minutes. Do not overcook. Reserve ¼ cup shrimp; mash remainder with 2 tablespoons butter; set aside. In small saucepan, heat 2 remaining tablespoons butter. Add flour; cook 2 to 3 minutes. Gradually stir in half and half. Cook and stir over medium heat until sauce begins to thicken. Stir in ½ cup of fish cooking liquid; continue cooking and stirring until sauce boils. Reduce heat, add shrimp butter, salt, and pepper; stir until butter melts. Stir in ¼ cup of the almonds. Arrange fillets on serving platter. Pour sauce over; garnish with remaining shrimp and almonds.

Louisiana Fish Loaf (page 93); Lemon-Baked Fish with Stuffing (page 80); Marinated Tuna and Green Beans (page 61). ReaLemon® Lemon Juice from Concentrate

Imperial Fish Casserole

Makes 4 servings

⅓ cup Sun-Maid® Zante Currants
3 tablespoons medium-dry sherry
1 pound haddock or whitefish fillets
3 tablespoons butter or margarine
3 tablespoons all-purpose flour
¼ teaspoon ground nutmeg
½ teaspoon salt
⅛ teaspoon cayenne
1½ cups half and half or light cream
2 eggs, lightly beaten
2 slices bread, cubed
¼ cup chopped parsley
2 tablespoons minced onion
   Paprika
   Melted butter
   Rice and vegetable pilaf (optional)

Grease a 1½-quart casserole. Combine the currants and sherry in a small bowl and let stand for at least 20 minutes. Bring 2 cups water to a boil in large skillet and add the fish. Reduce heat, cover, and simmer for 3 to 5 minutes, or just until the fish flakes easily with a fork. Using a slotted spatula, carefully remove the fish from the pan; drain well, flake, and set aside. Melt the 3 tablespoons butter in a saucepan. Add the flour, nutmeg, salt, and cayenne; cook, stirring, until the mixture bubbles. Gradually blend in the half and half, continuing to stir until the sauce thickens. Remove from heat and slowly whisk some of the hot sauce into the beaten eggs. Return the egg mixture to the saucepan, whisking until smooth. Preheat the oven to 375°F. Combine the bread cubes, parsley, onion, and sherried currants with the sauce and gently fold in the flaked fish. Spoon the mixture into the prepared casserole and sprinkle with paprika. Bake for 25 to 30 minutes, or until golden brown and set in the center. Remove from the oven and let stand for 10 minutes before serving. Pass melted butter to spoon over the custard. Serve with rice and vegetable pilaf, if desired.

Backyard Bonanza

For your next cookout, try a healthy—and delicious—alternative to burgers and franks. You will be delighted at what you can do on an outdoor grill. One thing to remember—fish should not be overcooked. Small fish should be grilled in a hinged grill to make them easier to handle. For large fish, a spatula or pancake turner is a big help. Plenty of fresh ingredients—lemon, butter, and olive oil—also make for best results.

Halibut Kebabs

Makes 4 servings

¼ cup salad oil
¼ cup dry vermouth or white wine
¼ cup fresh lemon juice
1 teaspoon Lawry's Seasoned Salt
¼ teaspoon Lawry's Garlic Salt
½ teaspoon leaf oregano, crushed
1 pound fresh or frozen and thawed halibut steaks, cut into 1-inch cubes
6 mushroom caps
1 green bell pepper, cut into 1-inch squares
12 cherry tomatoes
4 bamboo skewers, soaked in water 2 hours

In shallow glass or ceramic dish, combine first 6 ingredients. Add halibut and marinate 1 hour at room temperature. Drain and reserve marinade. On skewers alternate fish, green pepper, and tomato and end with mushroom. Grill kebabs over medium coals 8 to 10 minutes, turning and basting frequently with reserved marinade.

Note: Use any firm-fleshed thick whitefish, such as swordfish. Generously brush the grid of the grill with salad oil to prevent sticking.

Teriyaki Fish Grill

Makes 6 servings

½ cup Kikkoman Teriyaki Sauce
½ cup vegetable oil
½ cup dry white wine
¼ cup water
½ teaspoon dill weed
2 tablespoons lemon juice
6 fish steaks (halibut, sea bass, rockfish, sole, or flounder), 1 inch thick
2 tablespoons parsley flakes

Combine first 6 ingredients in flat shallow pan. Add fish; marinate 30 minutes. Remove fish from marinade; reserve marinade. Sprinkle both sides of fish with parsley. Cook on grill 5 inches from coals 10 to 15 minutes; baste often with marinade. Heat remaining marinade and serve with fish.

Barbecued Fish

Makes 4 servings

1½ pounds fresh or frozen fish fillets or steaks
½ cup salad oil
1 tablespoon Worcestershire sauce
½ teaspoon Lawry's Garlic Salt
½ teaspoon Lawry's Seasoned Pepper
   Lemon wedges

Thaw fish if frozen. In small bowl, combine oil, Worcestershire sauce, Garlic Salt, and Seasoned Pepper; blend well. Brush fish with oil mixture. Place in well-oiled wire grill basket. Grill 5 to 8 minutes. Turn basket over and brush fish again (through basket) with oil mixture. Grill until fish flakes easily when tested with a fork, 5 to 8 minutes more. Garnish with lemon wedges.

Note: Buy fresh fish if possible. The more you brush or baste fish with a marinade, the more flavorful and juicy the fish will be. Brush grill basket generously with oil, and fish with marinade, to prevent sticking.

Barbecued Red Snapper

Makes 6 servings

2 pounds red snapper steaks or fillets
1 can (6 ounces) Hunt's Tomato Paste
⅓ cup water
2 tablespoons lime juice
2 tablespoons Worcestershire sauce
1 tablespoon sugar
1 tablespoon pure vegetable oil
1 teaspoon salt
⅛ teaspoon garlic salt

Thaw fish if frozen; cut into serving-size portions. Combine remaining ingredients in a small bowl. Arrange fish on grill or broiler pan about 4 inches from heat source. Brush generously with sauce. Cook 6 to 10 minutes. Turn, brush with more sauce, and cook 7 to 10 minutes longer, or just until fish flakes when tested with a fork. (Length of cooking time depends on thickness of fish.) Do not overcook.

Barbecued Sea Steaks

Makes 4 servings

4 fish steaks, each about ¾ inch thick
½ cup Kikkoman Teriyaki Sauce
2 green onions and tops, chopped
1 tablespoon vegetable oil
2 teaspoons minced fresh ginger root
½ teaspoon grated orange rind

Place fish steaks in single layer in shallow pan. Combine teriyaki sauce, green onions, oil, ginger, and orange rind; pour over fish. Turn fish over to coat both sides. Marinate 45 minutes, turning over occasionally. Remove fish; reserve marinade. Place fish on grill 4 to 6 inches from hot coals. Cook 3 minutes on each side, or until fish flakes easily with fork. Brush frequently with reserved marinade.

Grilling Whole Fish

This method can be used for practically any type of fish. Small fish need a brisker heat than large fish, because of the shorter cooking time. Butter or oil the inside of a fish and season it with salt and pepper. A few slices of onion or a sprig of dill or tarragon inside the fish before broiling gives it a delicious taste. Thin, thin slices of lemon or even orange are excellent.

Oil your grill or your hinged grill well before you start to cook. If you brown the fish well on both sides and continue cooking, turning often, it will be evenly cooked. If you feel that the fish is too dry, baste with a mixture of olive oil and lemon juice.

Fish is cooked when the flesh flakes easily when you test it with a fork. Small fish will cook in 10 to 15 minutes. Larger fish will take up to 60 minutes to cook. Lemons, parsley butter, anchovy butter, Hollandaise or Béarnaise sauce are excellent complements to grilled fish. Plain boiled or crisp French-fried potatoes are traditional accompaniments.

Spitted Fish. Large fish such as salmon, haddock, cod, tuna, sturgeon, and some members of the bass family may be spitted and roasted over charcoal. The fish must be tied securely or wired to the spit. Some people make a wire basket, which they line with ferns, that will fit on the spit. Baste the fish with olive oil and lemon juice blended together.

Foil-Roasted Fish. Whole fish may be rolled in aluminum foil which has been buttered or oiled and either roasted directly in the coals or roasted on the grill. The advantage of using foil is that you may stuff the fish with any savory stuffing you desire, or with thinly sliced raw onions, peppers, tomatoes, and sprigs of parsley, well lubricated with butter or oil, and know that the juices will not run out and that you will have a perfectly flavored fish when it is finished. Note: Small fish may be cooked in the same manner, although a double coating of foil is recommended for them.

Fish Steaks and Filleted Fish. Fish steaks, especially those from the oilier fish, make delicious charcoal-broiled main courses. Choose a steak cut from 1½ to 2 inches thick. The steak as well as the grill on which it is cooked should be oiled, and the coals should be moderate. Total cooking time, allowing for turning the fish over once during the process, should be from 12 to 15 minutes, depending upon the thickness and the texture of the steak. You may brush the fish while it is cooking with hot olive oil or melted butter. Salt, freshly ground pepper, and lemon butter may also be used. Fish may be rolled in crumbs, in chopped almonds, or in sesame seed during the broiling and returned to the grill.

A Shellfish Sumptuary

Fresh-from-the-sea shellfish delights—saucy and sweet,
spicy and special—these recipes will please everyone,
from those who favor beautifully boiled lobsters or shrimp
to those who'd prefer succulent casseroles or kebabs.

Shrimp Capri

Makes 4 servings

    1 pound (16 to 20) medium shrimp
1¼ cups Seven Seas Capri® dressing, divided
    1 cup fresh white bread crumbs
    2 tablespoons melted butter
    2 tablespoons finely chopped fresh dill weed
    ½ cup buttermilk

Clean, devein, and butterfly shrimp, leaving last tail section intact. Combine ¼ cup dressing, bread crumbs, butter, and dill; cover with plastic wrap and set aside. Stir together 1 cup dressing and buttermilk; dip each shrimp into mixture and grill flat over hot coals. (Watch carefully; they cook very quickly.) Baste shrimp as they cook. Warm crumb mixture. Lay grilled shrimp on warmed platter; sprinkle crumb mixture over evenly and serve.

Shrimp with Dill Sauce

Makes 4 servings

    2 tablespoons Mazola Margarine
    1 tablespoon Argo or Kingsford's Corn Starch
    ½ teaspoon dried dill weed
    ¼ teaspoon salt
    ⅛ teaspoon pepper
    1 cup milk
    ¼ cup dry sherry
    1 tablespoon lemon juice
    1 pound shrimp, peeled, cleaned, and cooked
      Hot cooked rice

In 2-quart saucepan, melt margarine over low heat. Stir in cornstarch, dill, salt, and pepper until smooth. Remove from heat. Gradually stir in milk until smooth. Stirring constantly, bring to boil over medium heat and boil 1 minute. Stir in sherry and lemon juice until well blended. Stir in shrimp. Reduce heat to low. Stirring occasionally, cook 3 minutes, or until heated through. Serve over rice.

Louisiana Shrimp Creole

Makes 5 servings

    ¼ cup Planters® Peanut Oil
    1 cup chopped onion
    ½ cup thinly sliced celery
    ½ cup chopped green pepper
    2 tablespoons chopped parsley
    2 large cloves garlic, crushed
    1 can (16 ounces) tomatoes
    ½ cup water
    2 teaspoons salt
1½ teaspoons paprika
    ⅛ teaspoon ground red pepper
    1 bay leaf
    1 pound medium shrimp, shelled and deveined
    1 tablespoon cornstarch
    2 tablespoons water
      Hot cooked rice

In Dutch oven or large saucepot, heat Planters® Peanut Oil over medium heat. Add onion, celery, green pepper, parsley, and garlic; sauté about 5 minutes, or until tender. Stir in tomatoes, ½ cup water, salt, paprika, red pepper, and bay leaf; bring to a boil. Reduce heat to low. Cover; cook for 30 minutes.

Stir shrimp into vegetable mixture. Cook covered until shrimp are tender, about 5 minutes. Blend together cornstarch and remaining 2 tablespoons water; add to shrimp mixture. Cook and stir until sauce thickens, about 2 minutes. Serve with rice.

Shrimp with Dill Sauce. Mazola Corn Oil

Sweet Spicy Shrimp Supreme

Makes 4 servings

⅓ cup Wish-Bone® Sweet 'n Spicy French Dressing
½ cup sour cream
¼ cup white wine
1 pound shrimp, cleaned and cooked
2 cups cooked rice
¼ pound fresh button mushrooms, cooked
1 cup cooked peas
  Buttered bread crumbs

Preheat oven to 325°F. In large bowl, combine all ingredients except bread crumbs. Spoon into 4 baking shells or dishes and top with bread crumbs; bake 15 to 20 minutes.

Shrimp au Gratin en Casserole

Makes 4 to 6 servings

2 tablespoons butter
2 tablespoons all-purpose flour
1 cup milk
½ teaspoon salt
⅛ teaspoon pepper
1 can (10¾ ounces) Campbell's Condensed Cheddar Cheese Soup
1 pound shrimp, cooked, shelled, and deveined
1 cup grated Swiss or cheddar cheese

Melt butter and stir in flour. Gradually stir in milk. Add salt and pepper. Cook, stirring, until sauce bubbles and thickens. Add soup and shrimp. Stir again until sauce bubbles. Pour mixture into a greased 1-quart casserole. Sprinkle top with cheese. Bake casserole in a preheated 400°F oven for 10 minutes, or until cheese is melted and the Shrimp au Gratin is thoroughly heated.

Shrimp Risotto

Makes 4 to 6 servings

1 onion, chopped
1 cup chopped green pepper
1 clove garlic, minced
¼ cup pure vegetable oil
1 cup uncooked rice
1 can (6 ounces) Hunt's Tomato Paste
2½ cups beef bouillon
½ teaspoon salt
¼ teaspoon basil
1 pound raw shrimp, shelled and deveined
1 package (10 ounces) frozen peas, thawed
1 can (4 ounces) sliced mushrooms, undrained
  Parsley

In a large skillet, cook onion, green pepper, and garlic in oil until tender. Add rice; cook and stir until lightly browned. Stir in Hunt's Tomato Paste, bouillon, salt, and basil; mix well. Cover tightly; simmer 30 to 35 minutes. Add shrimp, peas, mushrooms, and liquid to rice mixture; cover and cook 15 minutes longer. Garnish with parsley.

Charleston Shrimp

Makes 4 servings

6 tablespoons Planters® Peanut Oil
½ cup fine dry bread crumbs
½ cup finely chopped green pepper
½ cup finely chopped celery
¼ cup finely chopped onion
1 can (17 ounces) Italian plum tomatoes
2 tablespoons lemon juice
1 medium clove garlic, crushed
½ teaspoon salt
¼ teaspoon thyme leaves
¼ teaspoon marjoram leaves
1 pound medium shrimp, shelled and deveined

Heat 2 tablespoons Planters® Peanut Oil in a skillet over medium heat. Brown bread crumbs in oil, stirring constantly over heat until golden. Remove crumbs from pan; set aside.

Heat remaining Planters® Peanut Oil in skillet over medium heat. Add green pepper, celery, and onion; sauté until tender, about 5 minutes. Mix in tomatoes, lemon juice, garlic, salt, thyme, and marjoram. Bring to a boil; reduce heat and simmer for 15 minutes. Stir shrimp into tomato mixture; cover and simmer 10 minutes, or until shrimp are done.

Place mixture in serving dish and sprinkle with prepared bread crumbs. Serve immediately.

Shrimp de Jonghe

Makes 6 servings

¼ cup butter, melted
2 teaspoons Lawry's Garlic Salt
⅓ cup chopped parsley
¼ teaspoon paprika
¼ cup dry sherry
2 cups soft bread crumbs
1¼ pounds cooked shrimp (about 4 cups)

In small bowl, combine butter, Garlic Salt, parsley, paprika, and sherry; add bread crumbs and toss. In 12×8×2-inch baking dish, arrange shrimp and top with crumb mixture. Broil about 3 inches from heat source 3 to 5 minutes, or until crumbs are browned. **Note:** This recipe may be prepared and broiled in 6 coquille baking shells.

Shellfish Classified

There are 2 basic kinds of shellfish, mollusks and crustaceans. **Mollusks** have a soft body fully or partially enclosed in a univalve or bivalve shell. Abalone, conch, and perwinkle are univalve mollusks; clam, cockle, mussel, oyster, and scallop are bivalves. The second type, **crustaceans,** have elongated and segmented bodies, eyes mounted on stalks, claws, and softer, jointed shells. Lobster, crab, and shrimp are of this group.

Each kind of shellfish is different from every other kind, and it's these differences that make them such interesting, delicious menu items.

Abalone: Fresh, obtainable only near the coast—canned and frozen elsewhere; a kind of marine snail only the foot of which is eaten; tough, must be tenderized before cooking.

Clam: Among the kinds are hardshell, softshell, surf, butter, littleneck, geoduck, and pismo clams, all bivalves; they burrow deep in the sand, were difficult to gather until a special dredge was invented; can be eaten raw or cooked—who doesn't love a clambake?—but the geoduck (long-necked and not very pretty) is used only for chowder.

Cockle: To be found in salt water both here and in Europe; eaten raw or cooked, as with clams; they have never caught on in this country.

Conch: We see the beautiful spiral shell more often than the creature that inhabits it; lives in waters of the Caribbean and off the Florida coast; excellent flavor, but tough and must be tenderized before cooking.

Crab: Common types are king (very big), dungeness, stone, snow, and blue; crab is eaten cooked, either hot or cold; the meat is difficult to pick out in the smaller kinds, but worth the effort.

Crayfish: In looks and taste, like a lobster, but usually much smaller; there are both freshwater (small) and saltwater varieties, the latter often called spiny or rock lobster.

Lobster: The Maine or northern lobster is, to lobster lovers, the only true one—spiny lobsters, of which only the tail is edible (they have tiny claws) are found in warmer waters than the Maine variety; cook in shell.

Mussel: Only the saltwater variety is eaten; more often consumed by gourmets in restaurants than by the general public at home.

Oyster: Found in salt water along both the East and West coasts, classified as Eastern, Pacific, and olympia; Eastern are of various medium sizes; Pacific are very large; olympic are tiny, no larger than a thumbnail, and exquisitely flavored; oysters are "farmed" to keep them in ample supply.

Periwinkle: Found in both fresh and salt water here and in Europe; not popular here, but beloved in the British Isles.

Scallop: We eat the "eye," or large muscle of these; bay scallops are tiny and sweet, sea scallops larger; beware of unscrupulous fish dealers who sometimes stamp rounds of "sea scallops" out of less expensive flat fish.

Shrimp: Best-loved (or, at least, most-often-eaten) shellfish in this country, they come in many sizes; shrimp should be cooked in the shell, may be served hot or cold.

Vary home menus with shellfish—they are quick/easy to cook, delicious plain or in salads, casseroles, or sauced dishes.

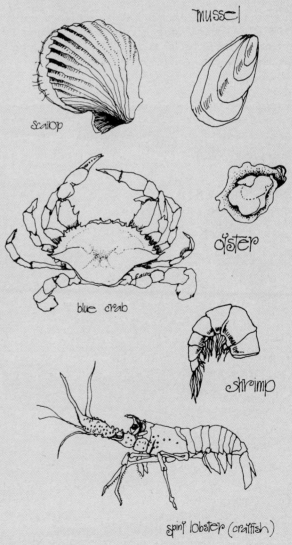

mussel

scallop

oyster

blue crab

shrimp

spiny lobster (crayfish)

Curried Shrimp Bake

Makes 8 to 9 servings

  ½ **pound bacon, cut in ½-inch pieces**
  ½ **cup chopped onion**
  ½ **cup chopped green pepper**
1½ **pounds cooked or canned shrimp**
  ½ **cup chopped peanuts**
  3 **cups cooked rice**
  1 **can (6 ounces) Hunt's Tomato Paste**
  1 **cup sherry**
  1 **can (13 ounces) evaporated milk**
  1 **tablespoon lime juice**
  2 **teaspoons curry powder**
  2 **teaspoons Worcestershire sauce**
  1 **teaspoon salt**

In a skillet, cook bacon until crisp; set aside. Cook onion and green pepper in bacon drippings until tender; drain fat. Thoroughly combine all remaining ingredients except bacon in a 9 × 13 × 2-inch baking dish; top with bacon. Bake at 350°F. for 45 minutes.

Shrimp Curry

Makes 2 to 3 servings

1 **tablespoon butter or margarine**
½ **cup chopped onion**
2 **teaspoons curry powder**
½ **teaspoon salt**
1 **tablespoon lemon juice**
1 **jar (10 ounces) Solo Apricot Sauce**
1 **tart apple, cored and chopped**
1 **cup cooked shrimp**
  Hot cooked rice

Melt butter in a large skillet and sauté onion until transparent. Add curry powder and cook until onion is tender but not browned. Add salt, lemon juice, apricot sauce, and chopped apple. Simmer 5 minutes. Add shrimp and heat. Serve over hot cooked rice.
Good idea: For accompanying condiments, provide bowls of chutney, flaked coconut, salted nuts, and chopped hard-cooked eggs.

Creamed Lobster in Patty Shells (page 108)

Shrimp and Vegetables

Makes 1 serving

½ **cup frozen cut green beans**
¾ **cup frozen cut corn**
¼ **pound large raw shrimp, peeled**
¾ **cup fresh snow peas**
1 **tablespoon margarine, diced**
1 **tablespoon water**
1 **tablespoon lemon juice**
Parsley flakes
Salt
Pepper

Preheat oven to 450°F. Place green beans, corn, and shrimp in a single layer on 12 × 18-inch sheet of Heavy Duty Reynolds Wrap aluminum foil. Top with snow peas, margarine, water, and lemon juice. Sprinkle with parsley, salt, and pepper to taste. Fold upper half of foil over food so top edge meets bottom edge. Seal edges together, making a tight ½-inch fold. Fold again. Allow space for heat circulation and expansion. Repeat to seal each side. Place foil packet on cookie sheet. Cook 16 minutes. To serve, cut "X" in top of foil packet; fold foil back.

Jumbo Shrimp with Roquefort

Makes 4 servings

20 **jumbo shrimp, cooked**
1 **ounce Roquefort cheese, crumbled**
2 **teaspoons butter**
3 **eggs, well beaten**
1 **cup milk**
1 **cup all-purpose flour**
1 **teaspoon salt**
Fat or oil
1 **cup tomato sauce**
Dash Tabasco pepper sauce

Peel and clean cooked shrimp. Partly split the back of each shrimp and stuff it with Roquefort and butter mixed together. Press to restore shape. Beat eggs, milk, flour, and salt until smooth. Dip shrimp into batter. Fry in deep fat preheated to 360°F for 2 to 3 minutes, or until golden brown. Drain on absorbent paper. Heat tomato sauce together with Tabasco sauce. Serve sauce over shrimp.

Shrimp Fra Diavolo

Makes 4 servings

     2 cloves garlic, minced
     1 small onion, sliced
     3 tablespoons butter or margarine
    ¾ pound fresh medium shrimp, peeled and
         deveined
     1 jar (15½ ounces) Ragú Homestyle Spaghetti
         Sauce
       Salt to taste
    ⅛ teaspoon cayenne
     3 to 4 drops Tabasco pepper sauce, or to taste
    ¾ package (16-ounce size) spaghetti, cooked and
         drained

In a large skillet, sauté garlic and onion in butter until onion is translucent. Add remaining ingredients except spaghetti; simmer 3 to 4 minutes, or until shrimp are pink. Spoon sauce mixture over spaghetti.

Boiled Lobsters

Makes 2 servings

     2 live lobsters, 1 pound each
     3 quarts boiling water
     3 tablespoons salt
       Melted butter

Plunge lobsters headfirst into boiling salted water. Cover and return to boiling point. Simmer for 20 minutes. Drain. Place lobster on its back. With a sharp knife, cut in half lengthwise. Remove the stomach, which is just back of the head, and the intestinal vein, which runs from the stomach to the tip of the tail. Do not discard the green liver and coral roe; they are delicious. Crack claws. Serve with melted butter. **Note:** For recipes requiring cooked lobster meat, cool lobsters and remove meat. Two live lobsters, 1 pound each, yield approximately ½ pound cooked lobster meat.

Lobster Newburg

Makes 4 servings

     4 frozen South African rock lobster tails, 4
         ounces each
     3 tablespoons butter
    ½ cup sherry
    ⅛ teaspoon paprika
    ⅛ teaspoon dry mustard
     1 can (10½ ounces) Campbell's Condensed Cream
         of Mushroom Soup
    ⅓ cup light cream
       Salt and pepper

Thaw lobster tails. With scissors, cut through thin under membrane. Open out and remove meat in 1 piece. Dice meat and sauté in hot butter until it turns white and opaque. Add sherry. Simmer gently until the liquid is reduced to half its original volume and the lobster is tender. Add paprika, mustard, soup, and cream. Simmer 5 minutes. Season to taste with salt and pepper.

Creamed Lobster in Patty Shells

Makes 6 servings

     6 frozen patty shells
     4 tablespoons butter or margarine
     1 cup chopped onion
     1 cup sliced mushrooms
     1 cup sliced celery
     1 cup warm light cream
     1 can (10¾ ounces) cream of tomato soup
     3 cups cooked lobster meat, cut in bite-size pieces
     1 tablespoon snipped parsley
     2 tablespoons brandy
     2 teaspoons lemon juice

Bake patty shells according to package directions. Keep warm. Melt 2 tablespoons butter in saucepan. Add onion and sauté until tender. Add 2 tablespoons butter, mushrooms, and celery to saucepan and continue to sauté until tender. Combine cream, tomato soup, and lobster and stir into saucepan. Heat until smooth. Stir in parsley, brandy, and lemon juice and heat through. Spoon lobster mixture into warm patty shells. Serve with remaining sauce.

Casco Bay Stuffed Lobster

Makes 4 servings

     4 lobsters
     2 cups Bell's Ready-Mixed Stuffing
     1 can (7½ ounces) minced clams
     1 tablespoon Slade's minced onion
     8 salted crackers, crumbled
    ¼ pound butter, melted
       Parsley, salt, and pepper to taste
    1¼ cups hot water
    ¼ cup sherry

Split 4 lobsters, remove lady and vein; pour half of melted butter on lobster. Mix together the stuffing, minced clams, onion, crumbled crackers, remainder of melted butter, parsley, salt, pepper, and hot water. Stuff the 4 lobsters and pour sherry over all. Bake at 500°F. for 30 minutes.

Lobster Thermidor

Makes 4 servings

 4 lobsters, about 1½ pounds each
 ½ cup butter
 1 teaspoon paprika
 2 tablespoons all-purpose flour
 ½ cup sherry
 1 can (10½ ounces) Campbell's Condensed Cream
   of Mushroom Soup
 2 egg yolks
1½ cups grated cheddar cheese

Drop lobsters into boiling salted water. Cook until lobster shells turn red, about 10 minutes. Drain and drench with cold water. Split lobsters lengthwise and remove tomalley (liver of the lobster) and lobster meat found in the claws, body, and tail. Dice meat. Melt butter in a skillet and add diced lobster and tomalley. Sprinkle with paprika and flour. Stir to blend. Stir in sherry. Mix mushroom soup and egg yolks, and stir into lobster mixture. Cook over low heat, stirring constantly, until sauce bubbles and thickens. Place lobster shells on a heatproof platter. Spoon lobster and sauce into shells. Sprinkle with grated cheese. Place under broiler; broil until cheese melts and becomes golden brown.

Lobster Cantonese

Makes 4 servings

 3 tablespoons cooking oil
 1 clove garlic, crushed
 ½ pound lean pork, coarsely ground
 ¼ cup soy sauce
 2 cups chicken broth
 1 teaspoon sugar
 2 lobsters, 1 pound each, cut into 2-inch pieces
 2 tablespoons cornstarch
 1 bunch scallions, cut into ½-inch chunks,
   including some green top
 1 egg, lightly beaten

Preheat Sunbeam Multi-Cooker Frypan to 340°F. Heat oil. Add garlic and pork and sauté until the pork loses its pink color. Stir in soy sauce, chicken broth, and sugar and bring to a boil. Add lobster. Cover, reduce heat to Simmer, and cook 10 minutes. Combine cornstarch and ¼ cup cold water in a small bowl to a smooth paste. Add to the lobster and stir until sauce is thickened and clear. Stir in scallions. Pour the lightly beaten egg over the lobster and cook, stirring, just until the egg is set. Serve immediately.

Timing Fish and Shellfish

Brevity may or may not be the soul of wit, but it is indubitably the essence of cooking fish of all kinds, no matter by what method.

Fillets: Of whatever fish, poached or broiled (broiling is wrong for all but thick fillets of fat fish), or breaded and pan- or deep-fried, fillets generally take between 9 and 12 minutes to cook. They are done when the flesh loses its translucency and flakes readily when gently poked with a fork. In the oven, cooked in liquid or butter-braised, the time may be as long as 17 or 18 minutes; test for doneness in the same way.

Whole fish: Baked on a rack in the oven, stuffed or not as you like, whole fish will bake in 30 to 50 minutes, unless you are cooking a monster—a whole salmon, say. Small whole "panfish"—sunnies and the like—should be done in about 10 minutes per side, sautéed in a skillet. Again, test all fish, however cooked, for doneness by flaking with a fork.

Big cuts of fish: One of the world's great treats is a large center cut of salmon, poached in court bouillon and served hot with lemon butter or Hollandaise, or cold with a cucumber-sour cream sauce. You'll need a deep kettle and an unusual kitchen tool, a ruler, as well as a piece of cheesecloth large enough to enclose the whole piece of fish with enough left over for a handle. Measure the fish at its thickest point; count on poaching the fish exactly 10 minutes for each inch. Bring the court bouillon to the boiling point. Tie the fish in the cheesecloth and lower it into the liquid, which should be deep enough to cover it completely. Turn down the heat and barely simmer until done. Take out and drain in the cheesecloth; remove carefully to a serving platter.

Fish steaks: These—swordfish, tuna, salmon, and the like—are most often broiled. A 1-inch-thick steak should be done in 10 to 12 minutes—do not turn. Test by flaking.

Shellfish: Again, be brief. Oysters need only be cooked until their edges curl, a matter of 3 to 4 minutes in their own liquor or in an oyster stew, or baked on a (filled) half shell. Clams take a little longer—their muscles are tougher. Shrimp can be simmered until they turn pink, 3 or 4 minutes, perhaps 5 if they are very large. A chicken lobster (1 pound) will cook whole in boiling water in 10 minutes, will broil—split—in about the same amount of time; for larger lobsters, add 4 minutes a pound. Abalone, sliced and pounded into submissive tenderness as abalone steaks, must be very briefly sautéed, or it will get tough all over again—3 or 4 minutes should do it. Bay scallops are at their best dipped in melted butter, rolled in dry bread crumbs, and sautéed no longer than 4 minutes; large scallops will take proportionately longer.

Linguine with Creamy Clam Sauce (page 116). Buitoni® Foods Corporation

Danish Lobster Tetrazzini

Makes 6 servings

2 cans (10½ ounces each) Campbell's Condensed Cream of Mushroom Soup
1 10¾-ounce can (⅔ cup) Campbell's Condensed Tomato Soup
3 cups cooked, shelled, and diced lobster
½ pound thin spaghetti
½ cup grated Parmesan cheese
½ cup grated sharp cheddar cheese
2 tablespoons dry bread crumbs

Combine and heat mushroom and tomato soups. Add lobster meat and cook for 5 minutes. Cook spaghetti in boiling water until firm but tender. Drain and rinse with boiling water. Pour spaghetti into a well-greased 2-quart casserole; spoon lobster mixture over spaghetti. Combine remaining ingredients and sprinkle over top of casserole. Bake in a preheated 375°F. oven for 15 minutes, or until browned on top. **Note:** This casserole may be prepared ahead of time and refrigerated—allow 25 to 30 minutes cooking time.

Lobster in Cream Sauce

Makes 2 to 3 servings

     1 lobster, about 2 pounds, cooked
     2 tablespoons butter
        Pepper and paprika
     1 tablespoon brandy
    ¼ cup sherry
     1 can (10½ ounces) Campbell's Condensed Cream
        of Mushroom Soup
    ¼ cup heavy cream
        Hot cooked rice (optional)

Remove meat from lobster and dice. Melt butter and sauté lobster. Sprinkle meat with a little pepper and paprika. Add brandy and warm slightly; set aflame. Stir in sherry. Simmer 5 minutes. Stir in mushroom soup and heavy cream. Simmer only until bubbly. Spoon, if desired, over rice.

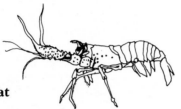

Party Crab Meat

Makes 6 servings

     3 tablespoons butter
     4 large mushrooms, sliced
     2 teaspoons finely chopped shallots
     2 tablespoons tomato paste
    1¼ cups heavy cream, divided
     1 pound lump crab meat, fresh, canned, or
        frozen, picked over but not broken up
        Salt and pepper
     2 egg yolks
     1 teaspoon snipped parsley
     1 teaspoon snipped chives
        Pinch tarragon
    ¼ cup brandy
        Hot cooked rice

Melt butter in Sunbeam Multi-Cooker Frypan at 280°F. Add mushrooms and cook about 5 minutes, stirring. Add shallots and cook until liquid from mushrooms has disappeared. Stir in tomato paste and blend thoroughly. Stir in 1 cup cream and cook, stirring constantly, until mixture begins to simmer and is well blended. Turn Frypan to Simmer. Add crab meat. Season to taste with salt and pepper. Stir gently and heat well. Beat together egg yolks and ¼ cup cream. Stir egg mixture slowly into crab meat. Add parsley, chives, and tarragon. Heat, stirring constantly, until mixture is hot. Do not boil. Stir in brandy. Serve immediately over hot cooked rice.

Barbecued Crab Meat

Makes 6 servings

    ¼ cup butter
    ½ teaspoon garlic powder
     1 cup chopped onion
    1½ cups chopped celery
     1 can (10½ ounces) Campbell's Condensed
        Chicken Broth
     1 soup can water
     1 cup canned tomatoes
     1 bay leaf
     2 tablespoons Worcestershire sauce
    ½ teaspoon pepper
     2 tablespoons soy sauce
     1 teaspoon chopped parsley
     1 tablespoon white vinegar
     1 pound (about 2 cups) lump crab meat

Melt butter; add garlic powder; sauté onion and celery until tender but not brown. In a saucepan, combine remaining ingredients except crab meat. Add onion-celery mixture. Cover and simmer for 1 hour, or until sauce is thick. Remove bay leaf and fold in crab meat gently. Simmer 10 minutes. Spoon over rice or a nest of fine egg noodles.

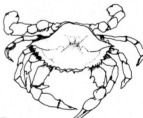

Crab Meat Bel Paese

Makes 4 servings

    ½ medium onion, chopped
     2 tablespoons butter
     6 mushrooms, thinly sliced
     1 pound lump crab meat, fresh or frozen
     1 can (10½ ounces) Campbell's Condensed Cream
        of Chicken Soup
    ⅓ cup white wine
     1 small avocado, peeled, pitted, and diced
    ½ cup grated provolone cheese
    ½ cup slivered almonds

In a saucepan, sauté onions in butter until tender. Add mushrooms and sauté until mushrooms are wilted. Stir in crab meat, cream of chicken soup, and white wine. Simmer 5 minutes, stirring occasionally. Fold in avocado. Pour mixture into a 1½-quart casserole. Sprinkle top with cheese and almonds. Bake in a preheated 375°F oven for 20 minutes, or until lightly browned and bubbly.

Crab Newburg Puff

Makes 4 servings

   6 slices day-old bread, trimmed and quartered
   1 cup grated mild cheddar cheese
   1 package (6 ounces) frozen Alaskan king crab
      meat
   4 eggs, beaten
   ¾ cup milk
   ¼ cup white wine
   ½ teaspoon salt
      Dash pepper

Preheat oven to 350°F. Grease an 8-inch square baking dish. Line bottom with half of bread squares. Dot with butter. Place cheese evenly over bread. Place crab pieces evenly over the cheese. Place remaining bread squares over crab. Combine eggs, milk, wine, salt, and pepper and beat well. Pour evenly over ingredients in baking dish. Bake for 20 minutes until golden brown and bubbly. Serve hot.

Scalloped Oysters

Makes 4 to 6 servings

   8 slices bread, toasted
   ¼ cup butter or margarine
   2 dozen oysters, shucked and drained
   ¼ cup oyster liquid
   1 thin slice onion
   2 tablespoons dry sherry
   2 tablespoons light cream
   1 teaspoon Worcestershire sauce
   ½ teaspoon salt
      Dash cayenne

Heat oven to 425°F. Spread toast slices with butter. Break 2 slices toast into blender container. Cover; blend at medium speed until coarsely crumbed. Empty onto waxed paper. Set aside. Repeat process with remaining toast slices. Sprinkle one-third of the crumbs into greased shallow 1½-quart casserole. Arrange half the oysters over crumbs. Put oyster liquid and remaining ingredients into blender container in order listed. Cover; blend at medium speed until onion is finely chopped. Pour half the mixture over oysters. Sprinkle with one-third of the crumbs. Repeat with remaining oysters, liquid mixture, and crumbs. Bake uncovered 30 minutes.

Clamming Around

Here are some common varieties of clams:

Chowder

Littleneck

Steamer   Cherrystone

To open a hard-shell clam, insert a clamshucker (if you don't own one, a blunt knife will do) near the hinge. Run the knife from end to end, then twist upward to pry off top shell.

Baked Clams with Mushrooms

Makes 3 or 4 servings

   1 can Doxsee Minced Clams
   2 tablespoons butter or margarine
   1 cup chopped mushrooms
   ¼ cup sliced pitted ripe olives
   ¼ cup chopped onions
   2 tablespoons chopped pimiento
   ¼ teaspoon salt
   ½ cup packaged dry bread crumbs.
   3 tablespoons butter or margarine, melted

Preheat oven to 400°F. Drain clams, reserving ¼ cup liquid. In medium saucepan, combine the clam liquid, 2 tablespoons butter, mushrooms, olives, onion, pimiento, and salt; mix well. Simmer uncovered 5 minutes. Add clams to mushroom mixture. Divide into 3 or 4 scallop shells or ramekin dishes. Top with a mixture of bread crumbs and melted butter. Bake 10 to 15 minutes, or until tops are browned.

Fried Clam Cakes

Makes 4 servings

- 1 **can Doxsee Minced Clams**
- 2 **eggs**
- ½ **cup dry bread crumbs**
- 1 **teaspoon lemon juice**
- 1 **teaspoon onion juice or powder**
- 1 **tablespoon parsley**
  - **Dash salt and pepper**
- 2 **tablespoons butter**
  - **Fat or oil**
  - **Rolls (optional)**
  - **Catsup (optional)**

Drain clams. Beat eggs; add Doxsee Minced Clams, crumbs, lemon juice, onion juice, or powder, parsley, salt, and pepper, and butter. Mix well. Shape in 4 flat cakes. Heat fat in a skillet. Add cakes. Fry until crisp and brown on both sides. Serve on rolls with catsup, if desired.

Clam Tetrazzini

Makes 6 servings

- 2 **tablespoons butter or margarine**
- 2 **tablespoons all-purpose flour**
- 1 **can (10½ ounces) condensed cream of mushroom soup, undiluted**
- ⅓ **cup milk**
- ¼ **cup sherry**
- 1 **cup grated sharp cheddar cheese**
- 2 **cans Doxsee Minced Clams, drained**
- 1 **package (8 ounces) spaghetti, cooked and drained**
- ½ **cup grated Parmesan cheese**

Preheat oven to 350°F. In large saucepan, melt butter; remove from heat. Stir in flour until smooth. Stir in soup, milk, and sherry. Bring mixture to boiling, stirring. Remove from heat; stir in cheddar cheese, clams, and spaghetti. Turn mixture into a shallow 1½-quart baking dish; sprinkle with Parmesan cheese. Bake uncovered 20 to 25 minutes, or until mixture is hot and bubbly.

Clams Capri

Makes 4 to 6 servings

- 2 **cloves garlic, minced**
- 1 **medium onion, chopped**
- 2 **tablespoons olive or vegetable oil**
- 3 **cans (6½ ounces each) minced clams**
- ¼ **cup chicken stock or dry white wine**
- 1 **bay leaf, crushed**
- ⅛ **teaspoon grated lemon peel**
- 3 **to 5 drops Tabasco pepper sauce**
- 1½ **tablespoons dry sherry (optional)**
- 1 **jar (32 ounces) Ragú Spaghetti Sauce**
- 1 **package (16 ounces) spaghetti, cooked and drained**
- 6 **scallions, chopped**
- 1 **to 2 tablespoons Gorgonzola or blue cheese, crumbled (optional)**

In a large skillet, sauté garlic and onion in oil until onion is translucent. Add clams with juice, chicken stock, bay leaf, lemon peel, and Tabasco sauce. Cook over high heat until most of the liquid evaporates; add sherry, keep warm, and set aside. In a saucepan, simmer sauce until heated through. Top spaghetti with sauce, clams, scallions, and cheese.

How to Store Fish and Shellfish

food	preparation	wrap/freeze	store/use
fish (whole, fillets, steaks)	prepare, cut up as for cooking; wash, leave wet	package individual pieces, then overwrap 1-meal amounts; whole fish can be frozen in water in tightly closed container	cook frozen or partially thawed; do not thaw completely; storage time, up to 6 months
shellfish (clams, shrimp, oysters, lobster)	rinse all; shrimp may be shelled or not as you prefer; shuck clams, oysters; cook lobster, remove meat from shell	freeze shrimp before wrapping, then pack in bags or containers; pack clams, oysters with their liquor, adding mixture of 1 teaspoon salt to 1 cup water to cover; pack lobster meat in airtight containers	thaw only enough to separate, prepare; storage time, 3 months

Oriental Hot Pot

Makes 4 servings

- ¾ pound cleaned raw shrimp, fresh or frozen
- 1 package (12 ounces) frozen scallops, thawed and cut into ¾-inch pieces
- 1½ pounds chicken breasts, skinned, boned, and cut across grain into bite-size slices (¼ inch thick)
- ¼ head cauliflower, separated into flowerets and sliced
- 4 medium carrots, cut diagonally into ⅛-inch slices
- ½ pound fresh mushrooms, thinly sliced
- 8 chicken bouillon cubes
- 3 cups hot cooked rice
  Lemon-Soy Sauce (recipe follows)
  Plum Sauce (recipe follows)

Divide seafood, chicken, and vegetables among serving trays or plates; arrange attractively. Garnish each with parsley, if desired; cover. Refrigerate until serving time. Measure bouillon and 2 quarts water into 12-inch skillet until about two-thirds full (add chicken bouillon and water as needed). Heat to simmering. Divide rice among 4 small bowls. Pass trays of seafood, chicken, and vegetables. Using chopsticks or fondue forks, guests place food in hot bouillon to cook until done—2 to 4 minutes. Serve with dipping sauces.

Lemon-Soy Sauce

Makes 1¼ cups

- ½ cup soy sauce
- ½ cup lemon juice
- ¼ cup sherry.

Combine ingredients and mix well.

Plum Sauce

Makes 1½ cups

- ½ cup chili sauce
- ½ cup plum jam
- ½ teaspoon red pepper sauce

Combine ingredients and mix well.

Q. *In restaurants, I am often served "drawn butter" with lobster. Can I make this at home?*
A. Easily. Drawn butter (also called "clarified butter" or "ghee"— an Indian term) can be made from sweet butter. Melt the desired amount in a saucepan; be careful not to stir or disturb it while it is melting. With a spatula, skim off the foam that appears on the top; what remains is "drawn butter." If you're especially particular, let the butter harden, then repeat.

Skewered Surf 'n' Turf (page 117). Photo courtesy of Thomas J. Lipton, Inc.

Linguine with Creamy Clam Sauce

Makes 2 servings

  2 tablespoons olive oil
  2 cloves garlic, minced
1½ cups whipping cream
  4 tablespoons butter
  2 cans (6½ ounces each) minced clams, drained
  2 tablespoons dried basil leaves
  ½ teaspoon salt
  ⅛ teaspoon cayenne
  ¼ cup chopped fresh parsley
  ¼ cup chopped watercress
  ¼ cup grated Parmesan cheese
  8 ounces Buitoni High Protein Linguine

In 3-quart saucepan, cook olive oil and garlic over medium heat, stirring occasionally, until garlic is lightly browned. Add cream, butter, and clams. Cook, stirring occasionally, until sauce is slightly reduced and thickened (12 to 15 minutes). Add remaining ingredients except Parmesan cheese and linguine; stir to blend. Meanwhile, cook pasta according to package directions. Stir in Parmesan cheese. Serve sauce over Buitoni Linguine.

Seafood au Gratin

Makes 4 servings

  ¾ pound scallops
  ¼ cup dry white wine
  3 tablespoons butter or margarine
  3 tablespoons all-purpose flour
  ⅛ teaspoon pepper
  ½ teaspoon salt
  1 cup milk
  ¼ pound process American cheese, grated
  1 cup cooked or canned lobster pieces
  1 can (3 ounces) sliced mushrooms, drained
  4 slices bread

Wash scallops. If large, cut into bite-sized pieces. Place in a small saucepan with ¼ cup water and white wine. Bring to a boil and cook 5 minutes. Drain, reserving liquid. Place all ingredients on a tray. Preheat Multi-Cooker Frypan to 260°F. Melt butter. Stir in flour, pepper, and salt. Slowly stir in milk and liquid from scallops. Cook, stirring constantly, until sauce is smooth and thickened. Add cheese and stir until cheese is melted. Add scallops, lobster, and mushrooms. Reduce heat to I of Simmer and heat thoroughly. Toast bread in Sunbeam Toaster. Cut into triangles. Serve hot seafood on toast.

Spanish Seafood Stew

Makes 6 to 8 servings

  1 lobster, about 1½ pounds, cooked just until red
  1 carrot, minced
  1 leek, minced
  2 celery stalks, minced
  1 small onion, chopped
  6 tablespoons butter
  1 teaspoon paprika
  1 cup white wine
  1 cup cognac
  1 can (10½ ounces) Campbell's Condensed Chicken with Rice Soup
  1 can (10½ ounces) Campbell's Beef Broth
  1 pound tomatoes, chopped
  ⅛ teaspoon almond extract
12 jumbo raw shrimp, shelled and deveined
12 red raw Spanish shrimp, shelled and deveined
12 littleneck clams, scrubbed
12 mussels, beards removed, scrubbed
  1 red snapper fillet, about ½ pound, cut into 1-inch cubes
  ⅓ cup olive oil
    Salt and pepper
    Chopped parsley
    Chopped tarragon
    White bread fried in olive oil

Remove head from lobster and grind or pound in a mortar until particles are very fine. Cut remaining lobster into slices. In a kettle combine lobster head, carrot, leek, celery, onion, and butter. Sauté until onion is golden. Add paprika, wine, and cognac. Set aflame. When flame dies, add chicken soup, beef broth, tomatoes, and almond extract. Simmer gently, stirring occasionally, until mixture is very thick, about 2 hours. Pour into a strainer and press out all liquid for sauce. In a large skillet, combine lobster slices, jumbo shrimp, Spanish shrimp, clams, mussels, red snapper, and olive oil. Sauté until fish is cooked and clams and mussels are open, about 10 minutes. Drain excess liquid and reserve ½ cup of this broth. Add lobster sauce and reserved broth (about 1½ cups of total liquid). Simmer for 10 minutes uncovered. Add salt and pepper to taste. When serving, place a variety of seafood on individual plates, and top with some of the sauce. Garnish each serving with chopped parsley and tarragon, and with quartered slices of white bread fried in olive oil.

Backyard Bonanza

The backyard is also a great place to enjoy the fresh, delicious taste of an array of shellfish.

Broiled Whole Lobster. Lobster is usually split before broiling, but this often results in dry lobster meat, tasteless and tough. Broil the lobster whole over coals, allowing about 15 to 20 minutes cooking time. Turn it to cook evenly. Split it after broiling, remove the intestines and stomach, and serve with plenty of melted butter and lemon quarters.

Broiled Split Lobster. You may split live lobsters and spread them lavishly with softened butter and sprinkle with salt, pepper, and paprika. Turn them flesh side down for about 3 minutes, then turn, spread on more softened butter, and continue grilling. The whole process should take from 15 to 20 minutes, depending on the size of the lobsters. Try fried bread crumbs, melted butter, and lemon juice, and crisp French-fried potatoes with broiled lobster.

Soy-Soaked Shrimp. Choose the very largest shrimps you can find. Split them through the back with sharp scissors and marinate them in equal quantities of soy sauce and vermouth for 2 hours. Remove from the marinade and broil for 3 to 4 minutes on the grill. Have a collection of sauces, a garlic and anchovy butter, a highly seasoned mayonnaise and a rich sherry-flavored tomato sauce. Peel the shrimp with your fingers; drop into your favorite sauce and eat.

Dill-Flavored Shrimp. Soak large split shrimp in white wine or dry vermouth to which you have added finely chopped garlic and fresh dill. After 2 hours, remove them from the marinade and broil 3 to 4 minutes. Serve the shrimp with dill-flavored mayonnaise and thinly sliced cucumbers marinated in olive oil, vinegar, salt, and pepper.

Charcoal-Baked Oysters. Arrange unopened oysters on the grill above a moderate charcoal fire. It will take anywhere from 6 to 8 minutes for the shells to open. Oysters must not overcook but they must heat through. Any type of restaurant oyster, especially the large ones from the New Jersey or Delaware coast or the extremely large Pacific oysters, is suitable for this particular treat. Each oyster may be served with melted butter, anchovy butter, tarragon butter, or with horseradish-flavored Hollandaise.

Broiled King Crab Legs. King crab legs may be purchased frozen in many parts of the country. The large legs should be slit in the soft part of the shell. They should be grilled with the split side up. Brush them lavishly with a mixture of melted butter, lemon or lime juice, and tarragon, and merely heat them through, for they are already cooked before they are frozen.

Shrimp Kebabs

Makes 6 servings

- 1 pound (or 18 pieces) medium shrimp, peeled and deveined
- 12 cherry tomatoes
- 12 fresh mushrooms, stems removed
- 1 bottle (16 ounces) Seven Seas Viva® Red Wine Vinegar & Oil dressing
- 2 cloves garlic, cut into thin slivers

Soak six 12-inch bamboo skewers in water briefly to prevent burning. Thread ingredients onto each skewer in following order: shrimp, tomato, mushroom, repeat, ending with a piece of shrimp. Lay kebabs in glass or enameled dish. Combine garlic and dressing; pour over kebabs. Refrigerate 2 to 4 hours, turning kebabs hourly in marinade. Broil or grill and serve hot.

Skewered Surf 'n' Turf

Makes about 8 servings

- 1 envelope Lipton® Onion or Beefy Onion Recipe Soup Mix
- ¼ cup lemon juice
- ¼ cup oil
- 1 can (8 ounces) pineapple chunks, in heavy syrup, drained (reserve ¼ cup syrup)
- 1 tablespoon soy sauce
- ½ pound shrimp, cleaned
- ½ pound boneless sirloin, cut into 1-inch cubes
- 16 cherry tomatoes
- 8 mushroom caps
- 1 green pepper, cut into chunks

In large shallow baking dish, combine Lipton Onion Recipe Soup Mix, lemon juice, oil, reserved syrup, and soy sauce; add shrimp and beef; cover and marinate in refrigerator, turning occasionally, at least 2 hours.

On skewers, alternately thread shrimp, beef, pineapple, tomatoes, mushrooms, and green pepper. Grill or broil, turning once and basting with remaining marinade.

Sandwich Specials

Fish and shellfish are perfect partners for wholesome fresh-baked bread. Next lunchtime, treat yourself and your family to a delicious assortment of sandwiches that range from good old tuna to turkey-shrimp pizza and oyster clubs.

Salmon-Artichoke Sandwiches
Makes 4 sandwiches
    1 can (7¾ ounces) salmon
    1 jar (about 6 ounces) marinated artichoke hearts
    2 teaspoons vinegar
    ½ teaspoon minced parsley
    ⅛ teaspoon pepper
    4 slices firm white, wheat, or rye bread
      Butter or margarine, softened
      Butter lettuce
    1 tomato, thinly sliced and halved

Drain salmon, reserving 2 teaspoons liquid; break into chunks. Drain artichoke hearts; reserve liquid. Combine reserved artichoke liquid, reserved salmon liquid, vinegar, parsley, and pepper. Spread bread with butter. Arrange lettuce, salmon, tomato, and artichokes on bread; drizzle with vinegar mixture.

Salmon Confetti Sandwiches
Makes 4 sandwiches
    1 can (7¾ ounces) salmon
    1 tablespoon minced green onion
    2 teaspoons lemon juice
    1 teaspoon minced parsley
    4 slices firm white, wheat, or rye bread
      Butter or margarine, softened
      Butter lettuce
    6 to 8 radishes, thinly sliced
    2 hard-cooked eggs, sliced
      Paprika

Drain salmon; break into chunks. Combine salmon, green onion, lemon juice, and parsley. Spread bread with butter. Arrange lettuce, salmon mixture, radishes, and egg slices on bread. Sprinkle egg with paprika.

Salmon-Avocado Sandwiches
Makes 4 sandwiches
    1 can (7¾ ounces) salmon
    4 slices firm white, wheat, or rye bread
      Butter or margarine, softened
    1 avocado, sliced
    1 small cucumber, thinly sliced
      Salt and pepper
      Lime Mayonnaise (recipe follows)

Drain salmon, reserving 2 teaspoons liquid for Lime Mayonnaise; break into chunks. Spread bread with butter. Arrange avocado, cucumber, and salmon on bread. Sprinkle with salt and pepper. Top with Lime Mayonnaise.

Lime Mayonnaise
Makes about ¼ cup
    ¼ cup mayonnaise
    2 teaspoons reserved salmon liquid
    1 teaspoon lime juice
    ¼ teaspoon grated lime peel

Combine mayonnaise, salmon liquid, lime juice, and grated peel and mix well.

Variation
Serve salmon, avocado, and cucumber in lettuce cup with Lime Mayonnaise and favorite bread on the side.

Salmon-Artichoke Sandwiches; Salmon Confetti Sandwiches; Salmon-Avocado Sandwiches. Alaska Seafood Marketing Institute

Tangy Salmon

Makes 4 sandwiches

⅔ cup flaked salmon
½ cup chopped cucumber
1 tablespoon chopped green onion tops
¼ teaspoon dill seed
¼ teaspoon salt
⅛ teaspoon pepper
  Few drops Tabasco pepper sauce
2 tablespoons sour cream
4 French rolls

Combine salmon, cucumber, green onion tops, dill seed, salt, pepper, Tabasco sauce, and sour cream. Let stand for at least 1 hour to blend flavors. Drain off any excess liquid that may seep from the cucumber. Split rolls; spread with salmon mixture.

Cheesy Kiwi Sandwich

Makes 4 sandwiches

4 slices whole wheat bread, toasted
6 ounces grated cheddar cheese
2 ripe Calavo kiwifruit, peeled and sliced
1 tablespoon mayonnaise
½ pound fresh frozen bay shrimp

Cover bread slices with grated cheddar cheese; broil until cheese begins to bubble. Remove from oven; top with kiwi slices in decorative overlapping manner in center of each sandwich. Combine mayonnaise and bay shrimp; spoon on top of kiwi slices. Serve immediately.

Dungeness Crab Cheddar

Makes 4 servings

1 pound shelled Dungeness crab meat, or 2 cans
    (7¾ ounces each) king crab meat, or 1 pound
    lump crab meat
¼ cup butter
½ cup white wine
4 English muffins, split and toasted
1 can (10¾ ounces) Campbell's Condensed
    Cheddar Cheese Soup
2 drops Tabasco pepper sauce
  Sprinkle cayenne
⅓ cup light cream
  Parsley
  Pitted black olives

Sauté crab meat in butter until hot. Add white wine and simmer 5 minutes. Place English muffins in a shallow pan. Spoon crab meat on muffins. Com-

bine remaining ingredients and heat until bubbly. Spoon sauce over crab meat. Place under broiler and broil until golden brown. Serve garnished with parsley and pitted black olives.

Crab Imperial

Makes 6 servings

1 can (6½ ounces) crab meat, flaked
½ cup finely chopped celery
½ teaspoon chopped green onion tops or chives
⅛ teaspoon garlic salt
2⅔ tablespoons sour cream
¾ teaspoon lemon juice
½ teaspoon horseradish
2 tablespoons soft butter
12 slices white bread
6 lettuce leaves
½ can (6½ ounces) tomato aspic
12 stuffed olives

Combine crab meat, celery, onion tops, garlic salt, sour cream, lemon juice, and horseradish. Spread ½ teaspoon butter over each bread slice. Place 6 bread slices on serving plates; top each with a lettuce leaf. Slice tomato aspic into 18 thin slices and arrange 3 slices on each lettuce leaf. Place ¼ cup crab meat mixture in center of aspic slices. Garnish with 2 stuffed olives. Cut remaining bread slices in half diagonally, and place 2 triangles on each serving plate, 1 on either side of the open-face sandwich.

Shrimp Salad Roll

Makes 6 sandwiches

¾ pound shrimp, cooked and cleaned
¼ cup chopped green pepper
½ cup shredded lettuce
1 teaspoon grated onion
¼ cup chopped celery
¼ cup chopped cucumber
¼ cup diced tomatoes
¼ cup mayonnaise or salad dressing
6 frankfurter rolls
2 tablespoons butter

Chop shrimp. Combine vegetables, mayonnaise, and shrimp. Mix thoroughly. Cut rolls almost through lengthwise. Spread with butter. Place about ½ cup salad on each roll.

Buy Now, Serve Later

Even if you don't live close to a good fresh-fish market, you can serve fish as often as you like. Canned **tuna** and **salmon** are familiar to everyone; they come in serve-one, serve two-or-three or family-size cans to be used in sandwiches, salads, casseroles, and a variety of other dishes. Be sure to choose the grade and the preparation suitable for the dish you have in mind: Tuna comes packed in oil or water, as a cut from a fillet to serve as is, or chunked or flaked for other dishes; salmon is available in whole pieces (which must have skin and bone removed before using), and in flat cans as whole steaks. **Sardines** are available in flat cans, either as whole fish or skinless and boneless, packed in oil or in a savory tomato or mustard sauce. Salty, flavorful **anchovies,** packed in oil, can be had as flat fillets or rolled around a caper to make a delicious edible garnish; they are also available packed in a variety of wine sauces. (If the anchovy flavor is a bit too strong for your taste, soak the little fish in milk for an hour or so, or rinse well under hot running water.) **Herring** comes most often in jars, pickled or in wine sauce or with sour cream and onion; in some places, notably Jewish and Scandinavian delicatessens, herring can still be found in bulk, in small kegs from which you can buy as little or as much as you wish. **Fish roe** —eggs, that is—can be found in both cans and jars. Gray-to-black, once in a great while golden, **caviar** is the roe of the sturgeon; this preserved real-thing product is slightly less expensive than the fresh variety, but still very expensive indeed. Less are the "mock" caviars, made from whitefish, cod, or other fish roes, salted, dyed, and flavored to resemble the real thing; they range in flavor from acceptable to awful. Not "mock" anything is **red caviar,** the roe of the salmon, handsome, strong-flavored—a love-it-or-hate-it delicacy. **Shad roe,** fresh for a very brief season, is available canned, in "pairs"—enough for 2 servings; find it in specialty food shops, expensive but not too expensive for those who find it one of life's great pleasures of the table. **Smoked fish** is available all year around in fish shops, specialty food stores, and delicatessens. Most familiar is peachy-pink smoked salmon. There are 2 varieties, the more familiar—and more readily available—"eastern" smoked salmon, to be thin-sliced, with nothing to interfere with its unctuous goodness except perhaps a squirt of lemon juice and a few capers. Nova Scotia is the best of the American smoked salmons; there are a number of lesser, but quite acceptable, kinds. Even better than Nova Scotia, some think, are the Irish and particularly the Scottish smoked salmons. (**Gravad lax,** the name sometimes shortened to gravlax, is often thought to be smoked salmon, but it is not. This fish, pickled in a salt-sugar-dill mixture that draws its juices, is a heavenly delicacy to those who enjoy fish. Somewhat similar is **ceviche,** a Latin American appetizer made of raw, white-fleshed fish, "cooked" by a marinade of lime or lemon juice.) Last—and most recently come to our tables—is western-style salmon, smoked in the Indian fashion over alder wood. It is thicker than the other smoked salmons, and quite different in both appearance and flavor. **Frozen fish** is available in wide variety—both kinds of fish and kinds of preparation. There are plain-frozen fillets and whole fish such as trout as well as whole frozen crab and crab legs in their shells; there are breaded fillets, coated with bread crumbs or with potato flakes, ready to cook or precooked, ready to heat and eat; there are fillets with various kinds of stuffings or sauces or both; there are fish sticks; there are shrimps, in or out of the shell, cooked or not; there are fish "bites," mouthfuls to serve as appetizers, to dip in your own sauces or those packed with the product; there are other appetizers, fish-stuffed, such as egg rolls and various kinds of dim sum. The fish in these products may be shrimp (very popular), or halibut, sole, perch, cod, whitefish, and a dozen others. Also available are whole dinners featuring fish, and entrées of fish accompanied by a vegetable and pasta or rice. Finally, there are **dried/salted fish** still available, although not as widely as they were before freezers were invented; they include lutefish, Scandinavian preserved and salted fish, usually cod; salt cod; and finnan haddie, which is salted-and-smoked haddock. All of these require preparation—soaking, cooking, often creaming—before they are served.

Sticks on a Bun

Makes 6 sandwiches

12 frozen fish sticks
¾ cup chili sauce
1 tablespoon lemon juice
1 tablespoon horseradish
½ teaspoon salt
6 rolls, toasted and buttered
6 slices (1 ounce each) cheese

Place frozen fish sticks in a single layer in a well-greased baking pan. Bake in a 400°F. oven for 15 to 20 minutes, or until heated through and crisp. Combine chili sauce, lemon juice, horseradish, and salt. Place 2 fish sticks on bottom half of a toasted buttered roll. Cover with a slice of cheese. Place under broiler until cheese melts. Top with approximately 2 tablespoons chili mixture and top half of roll.

Garden Tuna Sandwiches (page 125). Ralston Purina Company

Shrimp-Olive Swirls

Makes 16 sandwiches

¼ cup pimiento cream cheese
¼ teaspoon chili sauce
3 tablespoons finely chopped cooked shrimp
¼ teaspoon lemon juice
4 slices white bread
2 or 3 ripe olives

Combine pimiento cream cheese, chili sauce, shrimp, and lemon juice. With a 1½-inch cookie cutter, cut each slice of bread into 4 circles. Spread 1 teaspoon cheese mixture on each circle. Garnish top of each sandwich with slivers of ripe olives arranged in a swirl pattern.

Lobsternut Specials

Makes 6 sandwiches

½ pound lobster meat, cooked
¼ cup chopped walnuts
¼ cup chopped celery
1 tablespoon lemon juice
½ teaspoon salt
   Dash paprika
¼ cup mayonnaise or salad dressing
12 slices bread, buttered
   Lettuce

Chop lobster meat. Add the next 6 ingredients. Spread 6 slices of bread with lobster mixture; cover with lettuce and remaining 6 slices of bread.

Shrimp New Orleans

Makes 4 servings

12 slices white bread, toasted and buttered
24 butterfly or fantail shrimp, French-fried
⅓ cup Tartar Sauce (see index)
 2 cups shredded sharp cheddar cheese
12 green pepper rings, thinly sliced
    Tabasco pepper sauce
 4 tomatoes, quartered

On each of 4 slices of buttered toast, arrange 6 fried shrimp. Spread 4 more slices of toast with Tartar Sauce. Place on shrimp, sauce side down. On top of toast, sprinkle shredded cheese, then pepper rings; add 2 dashes of Tabasco sauce per sandwich. Place under broiler until cheese melts. When cheese is bubbling, top with third slice of buttered toast. Fasten with toothpicks; cut in 4 sections. Garnish with ripe tomato quarters between sections. Serve at once.

Good idea: Quick tartar sauce can be made by combining mayonnaise with India or sweet pickle relish in whatever proportions you like. Add a dash of horseradish for extra zest.

Q. *Must I remove the black vein on the bottom of shrimp before I cook them?*
A. The vein is not poisonous and has no taste; it is usually removed because the shrimp looks better without it.

Cheddar Shrimp Boats

Makes 4 servings

 1 can (4½ ounces) medium shrimp, rinsed and
    drained
1½ cups (6 ounces) shredded Land O Lakes
    Medium Natural Cheddar Cheese
 ½ cup (1 stalk) chopped celery
 1 cup salad dressing or mayonnaise
 1 teaspoon instant minced onion
 ¼ teaspoon dill weed
 2 tablespoons pickle relish, drained
 ¼ cup Land O Lakes Sweet Cream Butter,
    softened
 2 French rolls (4 × 6 inches), cut in half
    horizontally
 4 lettuce leaves

In 1-quart mixing bowl combine all salad ingredients; mix well (2 to 3 minutes). Cover; chill 2 to 3 hours. To assemble sandwiches, spread 1 tablespoon softened butter on each French roll half. Top with 1 lettuce leaf and ½ cup salad.

Crunchy Tuna Heroes (page 126). Ralston Purina Company

Turkey-Shrimp Pizza

Makes 6 servings

  1 can (8 ounces) refrigerated crescent dinner rolls
¾ cup chili sauce
  1 teaspoon *each* basil leaves and oregano leaves
½ teaspoon onion powder
¼ teaspoon garlic salt
¼ cup grated Land O Lakes Parmesan Cheese
  2 cups cubed (½ inch) Land O Lakes Turkey
  1 can (4½ ounces) medium shrimp, rinsed and
       drained
  6 rings (¼ inch) green pepper
  2 cup (8 ounces) shredded Land O Lakes Natural
       Mozzarella Cheese

Preheat oven to 350°F. Place crescent dough in 12-inch pizza pan; press over bottom and ¼ inch up sides to form crust. Add basil, oregano, onion powder, and garlic salt to chili sauce; blend well. Spread chili sauce mixture evenly over crust; sprinkle with Parmesan cheese. Layer turkey and shrimp evenly over crust; top with green pepper rings and cheese. Bake near center of 350°F. oven for 25 to 35 minutes or until crust is golden brown on edges. Cut in wedges and serve immediately.

Oyster Club Sandwiches

Makes 6 sandwiches

12 slices bacon
  1 pint oysters
½ cup all-purpose flour
½ teaspoon salt
⅛ teaspoon pepper
18 slices buttered toast
12 lettuce leaves
12 slices tomato
½ cup mayonnaise

Fry bacon and drain on absorbent paper. Drain oysters; roll in flour seasoned with salt and pepper. Brown on both sides in bacon fat, about 5 minutes. Drain on absorbent paper. Divide oysters and bacon over 6 slices toast. Top with 6 more slices toast. Arrange lettuce, tomatoes, mayonnaise on this layer; top with remaining 6 slices toast. Fasten with toothpicks. Cut diagonally.

Smoked Surprise

Makes 4 servings

  4 slices bread, buttered
      Scrambled egg
  8 pieces smoked eel
      Fresh watercress

On each piece of buttered bread place a strip of scrambled egg, with a piece of smoked eel on either side. Garnish with fresh watercress.

Halibut-Filled Rolls

Makes 6 servings

  2 cups flaked halibut
¾ cup grated cheese
½ cup mayonnaise or salad dressing
  2 tablespoons lemon juice
  2 teaspoons Worcestershire sauce
  1 teaspoon mustard
¾ teaspoon salt
      Dash pepper
  6 large buttered rolls

Combine all ingredients except rolls. Fill rolls with fish mixture. Place on a baking sheet and heat in a 350° F. oven for 15 minutes, or until heated through and cheese has melted.

Variation

Add ½ cup chopped celery and 1 teaspoon grated onion.

Husky Sardine Hoagies

Makes 6 sandwiches

  6 French bread buns
      Softened butter for spreading
12 thin slices caraway cheese
48 thin slices cucumber
  3 cans (3¾ ounces each) sardines

Cut buns in half horizontally. Spread thinly with butter. On each bottom half, arrange 2 slices caraway cheese, 8 cucumber slices, ½ can sardines. Top with remaining bun halves.
Note: These should be made when they are to be eaten. Their flavor is not enhanced if they have to wait around. If you want to do some advance preparation, put together everything except the sardines. Add these at the last minute.

Crisp-and-Creamy Sardines

Makes 12 sandwiches

  2 packages (3 ounces each) cream cheese
  2 cans (4 ounces each) Maine sardines in mustard
      sauce
  2 tablespoons mayonnaise
  1 teaspoon Worcestershire sauce
24 slices whole wheat bread
  1 small cucumber, scored and thinly sliced

Mash cream cheese and add sardines, mayonnaise, and Worcestershire sauce. Mix well. Spread on 12 slices of bread; top with thin slices of cucumber. Top with remaining bread.

Sardine Special
Makes 4 sandwiches
 1 can (4 ounces) Maine sardines
 1 package (3 ounces) cream cheese
 3 tablespoons mayonnaise
 2 tablespoons chopped radishes
 2 teaspoons minced onion
 1 teaspoon lemon juice
 ½ teaspoon grated horseradish
   Salt and pepper
 8 slices bread, buttered
 1 cucumber, scored and thinly sliced
   Lettuce

Drain sardines. Mash cream cheese and mayonnaise until soft. Add radishes, onion, lemon juice, horseradish, and salt and pepper to taste. Blend well. Spread cheese mixture on 4 slices of buttered bread. Arrange sliced cucumbers on cheese and top with sardines. Cover with lettuce and remaining bread slices.

Garden Tuna Sandwiches
Makes 4 sanwiches
 ¼ cup mayonnaise or salad dressing
 ¼ teaspoon salt
 ¼ teaspoon dill weed
   Dash ground pepper
 1 can (6½ ounces) Chicken of the Sea® Chunk
   light tuna, drained and flaked
 ¾ cup small curd cottage cheese
 ½ cup chopped cucumber
 ¼ cup grated carrot
 2 tablespoons snipped chives
 2 tablespoons snipped parsley
   Spinach leaves
 8 tomato slices
 4 small pita loaves, split, or onion rolls

Combine mayonnaise, salt, dill weed, and pepper. Mix in tuna, cottage cheese, cucumber, carrot, chives, and parsley. To fill pitas, layer spinach leaves and a tomato slice in each pocket; spoon in tuna mixture.

Tunacado Buns
Makes 6 servings
 1 can (6½ ounces) Chicken of the Sea® Chunk
   light tuna, drained and flaked
 1 avocado, peeled and diced
 ½ cup chopped tomato
 2 tablespoons chopped onion
 ¼ cup mayonnaise or salad dressing
   Salt and pepper to taste
 6 hamburger buns
   Cherry tomatoes (optional)
   Watercress (optional)

Combine tuna, avocado, tomato, onion, and mayonnaise. Season with salt and pepper. Fill buns with mixture. Garnish with cherry tomatoes and watercress, if desired.

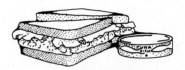

Accompaniments

Almost anything will cheer up an individual serving of salad or a sandwich—a handful of potato or corn chips or shoestring potatoes, a couple of olives, a pickle or two. But you can do better. Small vegetable shapes or small stuffed vegetables add appeal and good taste. A deviled egg is pretty, and adds substance to the meal. Marinated vegetables, such as asparagus or artichokes vinaigrette, mushrooms à la grecque, or wilted cucumbers make a fine addition to a salad or sandwich plate. Or sandwich halves of pitted cherries or walnuts with a half-and-half mixture of blue and cream cheese for a delectable garnish. Jellied relishes and herb-and-wine jellies make unusual and tasty garnishes, too.

As for a tossed green salad, there are literally dozens of additions that not only garnish it but improve it immeasurably. Among them are cubes or slivers of cheese, broken pretzel sticks, sliced raw mushrooms, sliced or shredded red or white radishes, coarsely crumbled corn or potato chips, crumbled crisp bacon, Chinese noodles, rings of sweet onion, nuts—plain, salted, or toasted—sliced water chestnuts, canned French-fried onion, hard-cooked egg slices, anchovies, bamboo shoots, and many more.

Whatever you serve, for the simplest of meals or the most elegant, garnish it attractively—and deliciously—to delight the eyes and the taste buds of family and guests.

Cheesy Kiwi Sandwich (page 121). Courtesy of Calavo

Crunchy Tuna Heroes

Makes 4 servings
 4 hero rolls, split
 ½ cup mayonnaise or salad dressing
 ½ to 1 teaspoon curry powder
 1 cup shredded carrots
 ⅓ cup chopped green onion
 ⅓ cup chopped peanuts
 1 can (6½ ounces) Chicken of the Sea® Chunk
    light tuna, drained and flaked
 1 tablespoon bottled oil-and-vinegar salad
    dressing

Hollow out bottom of each roll slightly with a fork. Combine mayonnaise and curry powder; spread on rolls. Spoon carrots, onions, and peanuts, alternately, across bottom half of each roll. Combine tuna and oil-and-vinegar dressing. Toss lightly to mix. Spoon on top of vegetables. Cover with tops of rolls.

Tuna Skyscraper

Makes 5 sandwiches
 1 can (9¼ ounces) tuna
 ¼ cup sour cream
 ¼ teaspoon Worcestershire sauce
 ¼ teaspoon oregano
 ⅛ teaspoon garlic salt
    Dash pepper
 1 package refrigerated biscuits
 ⅓ cup chili sauce
 5 slices large tomato
 5 slices Bermuda onion
 5 thick slices sharp cheddar cheese
    Watercress

Drain and flake tuna. Mix with sour cream, Worcestershire sauce, oregano, garlic salt, and pepper; shape into 5 patties. On buttered baking sheet, roll biscuits into ten 3-inch circles. Spread 5 biscuits with chili sauce; top with tuna patties, tomato slices, and onion slices. Bake 10 to 15 minutes in 450° F. oven. Remove from oven and top sandwiches with plain, baked biscuits, then cheese slices. Bake an additional 3 to 5 minutes or just until cheese melts. Garnish with watercress.

Tuna Hong Kong

Makes 6 sandwiches
 2 cans (6½ or 7 ounces each) tuna
 ½ cup chopped onion
 2 tablespoons tuna oil
 ½ cup chopped celery
 ½ cup chopped green pepper
 1 cup ketchup
 1 cup water
 2 tablespoons brown sugar
 2 tablespoons vinegar
 2 tablespoons Worcestershire sauce
 1 teaspoon prepared mustard
 ½ teaspoon salt
    Dash pepper
 6 hamburger rolls

Drain tuna, reserving oil. Break tuna into large pieces. Cook onion in oil until tender. Add remaining ingredients, except tuna and rolls. Simmer uncovered for 20 minutes, stirring occasionally. Add tuna and simmer 10 minutes or longer, stirring occasionally. Split rolls and toast. Place approximately ½ cup tuna mixture on bottom half of roll. Cover with top half of roll.

Index